P9-DJU-422

Daily Wisdom from God

365 Real-Life Stories That Will Give You Peace, Hope, and Joy

Publisher's Note

Daily Wisdom from God: 365 Real-Life Stories That Will Give You Peace, Hope, and Joy written by Vonette Bright © 2017 Bright Media Foundation. All rights reserved. Contains material from *My Heart in His Hands: Lead Me in the Way Everlasting* (Winter), *My Heart in His Hands: Renew a Steadfast Spirit Within Me* (Spring), *My Heart in His Hands: Set Me Free Indeed* (Summer), *My Heart in His Hands: I Delight Greatly in My Lord* (Autumn), written by Vonette Bright © Bright Media Foundation (previously published as © 2001 Vonette Zachary Bright). All rights reserved. Published and distributed by FC&A Publishing 103 Clover Green, Peachtree City, GA, 30269.

No part of this book may be reproduced, stored in a retrieval system, or transmitted in any form or by any means-electronic, mechanical, digital, photocopy, recording, or any other-except for brief quotations in printed reviews, without prior permission in writing.

Unless otherwise indicated, Scripture quotations are from the New International Version, © 1973, 1978, 1984 by the International Bible Society. Published by Zondervan Bible Publishers, Grand Rapids, Michigan.

Scripture quotations designated Amplified are from The Amplified Bible, © 1965 by Zondervan Publishing House, Grand Rapids, Michigan.

Scripture quotations designated TLB are from The Living Bible, © 1971 by Tyndale House Publishers, Wheaton, Illinois.

Scripture quotations designated The Message are from The Message: New Testament with Psalms and Proverbs, © 1995 by NavPress, Colorado Springs, Colorado.

Scripture quotations designated NKJ are from the New King James version, © 1979, 1980, 1982 by Thomas Nelson Inc., Publishers, Nashville, Tennessee.

Vonette Bright was cofounder of Campus Crusade for Christ, now CRU, along with her husband, Bill Bright. She also founded Women Today International and is best remembered for her work to establish the National Day of Prayer in the U.S. Vonette's son, Brad Bright, leads the Bright Media Foundation, established to extend the legacy of Bill and Vonette Bright.

For more information about how to grow in new life through Jesus Christ, and to receive a copy of The Gospel of John write:
FC&A Publishing, Dept. JC 99, 103 Clover Green, Peachtree City, GA 30269

ISBN 978-1-935574-63-7

Finding True Freedom

The Spirit of the Lord is on me,
because he has anointed me
to preach good news to the poor.
He has sent me to proclaim freedom
for the prisoners
and recovery of sight for the blind,
to release the oppressed,
to proclaim the year of the Lord's favor.

LUKE 4:18,19

The cry for freedom in the '70s encompassed everything from clothing to occupations. Unfortunately, some of the zeal to express freedom led to acts of rebellion.

True freedom, however, brings responsibility. Paul writes, "You, my brothers and sisters, were called to be free. But do not use your freedom to indulge the sinful nature; rather, serve one another in love" (Galatians 5:13). Knowing Christ, the source of our freedom, we are free to express our individuality, pursue satisfying career goals, and have meaningful relationships. We fulfill the command to "live as free people, but do not use your freedom as a cover-up for evil; live as servants of God" (1 Peter 2:16).

The desire for freedom within each individual is no surprise to any mother. Children learn to express their desire for freedom at quite a young age. Childish innocence can be dangerous, so the guiding hand of a mother protects a child from harm and injury.

A person who has accepted Jesus Christ as their Savior has a powerful Protector – the Holy Spirit who indwells him or her. He will guide your thought life and guard your heart from the evil one. But let us not think only of the ways freedom must be restrained. We need to accept the beautiful freedom we have in Christ and to live a life that demonstrates freedom of originality, creativity, and expression, and encourages others to find ways to enjoy the freedom that comes from knowing Christ.

Clear Conscience

Guilt, shame, and responsibility. That's what Julian began to feel. But it took him seventeen long years to get there.

In 1977, he committed a horrendous violent crime. He and an accomplice broke into a home in Southern California. Mary Stein, 73, was home at the time.

The two criminals beat her to death with a piece of wood. Remarkably, during the beating, Mary Stein called out to God, "Oh, Lord, I'm coming home."

Like a laser imprint, Mary's last words burned into Julian's mind, haunting him. A year after the murder, he placed his trust in Jesus Christ.

Soon, the guilt, the shame, and the sense of responsibility for killing Mary Stein began to set in. God began rebuilding this man's once-corrupted conscience. As Julian grew in his faith, God continued to establish a foundation of morals, values, and conscience.

The police did not actively consider him a suspect. But those feelings of guilt, shame, and responsibility didn't go away. They only intensified.

In God's timing – some seventeen years after the murder – Julian did what God and his conscience told him to do. He confessed his crime.

Today, he's serving a prison sentence for the murder. But the freedom in his heart cannot be confined.

Friend, that's what knowing God is all about. God paid the price for sin by giving His only Son. When you confess your sin to Him and place your trust in Him, He forgives you. Like Julian, your heart will be free from the bondage of sin.

It's never too late to turn to Christ – to confess your sin, to clear your conscience. You can do that right now. See "Beginning Your Journey of Joy" at the back of this book to learn how.

Remember, God loves you more than you know. He wants to give you life, eternal life.

HIS WORD

"He who conceals his sins does not prosper, but whoever confesses and renounces them finds mercy" (Proverbs 28:13).

MY PRAYER

Is there some sin from the past that is pricking your conscience? Whatever it is, confess it to God. He will forgive you, and He will lead you to make things right, however difficult. Then you will know true freedom.

MY STUDY

Joel 2:32; Romans 6:17,18

Becky's grandmother was larger than life to her children and grandchildren. They lovingly called her "Big Mama." She was the grand matriarch of the family.

Loved and adored by all, she was the glue that held the family together. Her unflinching faith in God gave great stability to a family torn by death and divorce.

Her first husband had died unexpectedly, leaving her with four children. She worked hard to keep food on the table. Later, she fell in love and married again. She and her second husband had four more children. Sadly, the marriage ended in divorce. She was left alone, but this time with a total of eight children.

Through it all, her abiding faith in God never wavered.

Big Mama had a big, well-worn Bible next to her favorite chair. It was so obvious she loved God. She depended on Him completely, and He always came through.

Big Mama lived with her eldest son and his wife. Like Big Mama, they trusted God and walked faithfully with Him.

Many years after Big Mama died, Becky visited her aunt. As she was leaving, she said to her aunt a bit offhandedly, "I'll see you here, there, or in the air."

"I hope so," her aunt responded.

Shocked, Becky said, "What do you mean you *hope* so?"

From the ensuing conversation, Becky discovered that neither her aunt nor Big Mama had complete confidence in their eternal destiny.

Becky was so sorry to learn that her grandmother was uncertain about whether she'd go to heaven when she died. She'd never enjoyed the peace and assurance God wanted her to have.

My friend, God says if you place your faith in Him, He gives you eternal life. There's no uncertainty in His promise.

When God makes a promise, He keeps it! He promises you freedom and a place in heaven. Trust Him.

HIS WORD

"To as many as did receive and welcome Him, He gave the authority (power, privilege, right) to become the children of God, that is, to those who believe in (adhere to, trust in, and rely on) His name" (John 1:12, Amplified).

MY PRAYER

Do you have any doubts about where you will go when you die? If you have accepted Christ as your Savior, the Bible says you are a child of God and will spend eternity in heaven. If you still have doubts, search God's Word for His promises or talk to your pastor.

MY STUDY

Psalm 16:9,10; Isaiah 60:3

Pour Out Your Heart

Kris was ten years old when she asked Jesus to be her Savior. To this day, she remembers that moment as if it were yesterday.

Kris had trusted Christ with her life, but her parents didn't teach the Bible in their home. Her family prayed at mealtimes and went to church on Sundays, but that was about all.

Eventually, no one in her family went to church but Kris. Even as a young teenager, Kris would go to church with friends or alone. Kris knew that she'd made a commitment to follow Christ, but she didn't know how to grow or how to ask someone to help her grow.

Doubt about her commitment to Jesus Christ crept into her heart and nagged her for about ten years. During that period of doubt, she asked Jesus to come into her heart every day! But she continued to go to church and Bible studies.

Finally, in her early twenties, Kris told a friend about her struggle. After a long discussion, the friend said, "Kris, you need to pour out your heart to God."

So Kris spent a long time alone talking with God. She told Him everything on her mind. She remembers only these words: "God, I'm tired of not knowing if You're in my life. If You're real, help me know with certainty." Nothing dramatic happened, but about two weeks later, Kris began to notice a few changes.

First, she hadn't questioned God about His presence in her life or hadn't asked Christ into her life since that day.

Also, when she read the Bible, it was making sense to her like never before. All of her doubt was gone!

Dear friend, maybe you feel like Kris did. Pour out your heart to God. Read His Word. And most importantly, trust Him.

HIS WORD
"Trust in him at all times, O people; pour out your hearts to him, for God is our refuge" (Psalm 62:8).

MY PRAYER
Right now, talk with God. Tell Him everything. Ask Him to help you know He's real and He's in your heart. He's a faithful God. I'm confident He'll do for you what He did for Kris. Ask Him today. Your life will never be the same.

MY PRAYER
Isaiah 12:2; 1 John 5:11–15

True Liberty

Several years ago, my friend Ney Bailey was traveling in a country where Christianity is strictly forbidden. For decades, its citizens have been under the thumb of a hostile, controlling government.

While touring the countryside, Ney saw a woman and asked, through an interpreter, if she could take her picture. To Ney's delight, the woman was pleased to have her photo taken by an American tourist. After the camera snapped, she thanked Ney by saying, "Go in peace."

Ney responded, "May the Lord's peace be upon you."

Later, the interpreter told Ney that the woman had been quite bold to say, "Go in peace." It's the greeting of a believer, and for her to reveal herself to a foreigner was quite risky.

Thousands of miles from home, in the middle of nowhere, standing in a cornfield in a country where it was unlawful to be a Christian, Ney met a sister in Christ. Although they could not communicate in each other's language, they recognized the Spirit in the other and made a powerful connection.

Ney captured this moment in a picture that has ministered to many of us. The woman's wrinkled and weatherworn face reveals a very hard life. Even so, her radiance glows. Though she lives in bondage, she is personally free.

In Galatians 5:1 we read, "It is for freedom that Christ has set us free. Stand firm, then, and do not let yourselves be burdened again by a yoke of slavery."

Where we place our faith determines our liberty. If we trust in ourselves, we are bound by our own limitations. If we trust in the government, we are bound by what it can provide. If we trust in any human institution, *we are bound to be disappointed!*

But when we place our faith in God through the person of Jesus Christ, we experience true liberty.

HIS WORD
"If the Son sets you free, you will be free indeed" (John 8:36).

MY PRAYER
"Lord Jesus, thank You for being a loving, faithful God. May I learn to depend more and more on You each day and not on the attractions of this world. You alone are worthy of my trust. In Your holy name, amen."

MY STUDY
Psalm 86:12,13; Isaiah 61:1

Do Not Be Afraid

Fear plagues many in our society today, stopping them dead in their tracks. But fear is nothing new.

The greatest story ever told, the Christmas story, contains several references to fear. Reread the accounts in Matthew 1–2 and Luke 1–2. Four times in the story, God speaks to His people and uses the same exact wording: "Do not be afraid."

He said it first to Zechariah, the priest who "was gripped with fear." Then He said it to Joseph, the fiancé of Mary. Next, to Mary, the one who would be the mother of our Lord. Finally, He said it to the shepherds on the hillside, "Do not be afraid."

So what did these people do with their fear? They did exactly what God wanted them to do:

- The priest completed his time of service.
- Joseph accepted Mary as his wife even though she was pregnant.
- Mary carried and gave birth to our Lord Jesus.
- The shepherds went to Bethlehem just as they'd been told.

That's the model. When you're afraid, do exactly what God has called you to do. As you obey, your fear will be replaced with peace and joy.

You can let worries and concerns frighten and enslave you, or you can choose, like those men and women in the Christmas story, to do what God wants you to do. Dear friend, what does He want you to do? *Trust Him!* Begin right there. Surrender your life to the lordship of Christ. Ask Him to fill you with His Holy Spirit. By faith, claim the strength you need to obey His Word.

Experience the freedom from fear that God wants you to have. God has not left us without a Resource. The Holy Spirit will help you overcome fear as you place your circumstances in His hands.

HIS WORD

"Seek first his kingdom and his righteousness, and all these things will be given to you as well. Therefore do not worry about tomorrow, for tomorrow will worry about itself. Each day has enough trouble of its own" (Matthew 6:33,34).

MY PRAYER

What are you afraid of today? What anxious thoughts consume you? There's no need to be afraid. You can surrender all your anxieties to God — this very moment. He can handle anything. Trust Him and you'll have peace.

MY STUDY

Jeremiah 7:23; Psalm 23:4

For most children, every day is filled with carefree adventure. But tragically for some, life is bound with pain, fear, and disappointment.

That's the way it was for Adam.

Mary first heard about him in her prayer group. It was there that Adam's schoolteacher prayed for him. His family life was so fractured and he was so distraught that he saw no future, no escape. At the tender age of eight years old, Adam told his teacher he wanted to die.

Deeply moved and concerned for this little boy, Mary began to pray in earnest for Adam, a little boy she didn't even know.

The next week, Mary was at church, rushing to get to choir rehearsal on time. As she rounded a corner, she and a little boy almost collided. He was also in a hurry and was quite upset. Mary noticed his tears and asked him his name. "Adam," he said.

Suddenly, Mary sensed this was the little boy she'd been praying for all week long. She said, "Where are you going, Adam?"

He admitted, "I'm running away because I want to die."

At that very moment, Adam was heading out of church to get some drugs he had stashed. He was on the way to ending his life.

Mary sat with Adam and held him, sharing the love of God with this distraught little boy. She told him that he was Jesus' little boy and could tell Him all of his secrets. Adam cried and cried.

As Mary prayed for little Adam, God's love penetrated his broken heart. And when the prayer was finished, Adam looked back at Mary with a new light in his eyes.

A chance meeting. A few moments of love. A hug. A welcome prayer. And a life is changed – from one of despair and disappointment into one of hope.

HIS WORD
"There is surely a future hope for you, and your hope will not be cut off" (Proverbs 23:18).

MY PRAYER
Dear friend, many around you do not have the hope that you and I do. Always be prepared to share with them the reason for your hope, to share what Christ has done in your life. Then pray for God to make you sensitive to opportunities to do so.

MY STUDY
Isaiah 40:30,31; Romans 15:13

Putting Your House in Order

Maria was only forty-five years old. It appeared that there was nothing the doctors could do. She had only two days to live and needed to get her house in order.

Maria went home and started doing the laundry. She was getting her house in order – right? But she soon realized that getting her house in order was about relationships, not laundry. Immediately, she thought about her stepfather.

This man had abused her as a child. She despised him and hated her mother for allowing the abuse to happen.

A few years earlier when her mother became very ill, she desperately needed care, and wanted to come live with Maria. In spite of her misgivings, Maria agreed.

Her mother, normally very reserved, reached out and took hold of Maria's hand. In that moment, Maria was convicted of her hatred for her mother. Christ melted her heart. They forgave each other, and her mother received Christ. Three days later Maria's mother slipped into a coma and died.

Now Maria was close to death herself. Maria had never released the bitterness she felt toward her stepfather and knew that it was time to let go of it and let God heal her heart. In prayer, she gave over to God all the hatred she harbored.

Through a series of miracles, one of which involved the surgical skill of a wonderful cardiologist, Maria made it through her life-threatening situation and is alive today to tell this account of God's healing. More important, she was able to be at her stepfather's side when he died, sharing the gospel with him in the final moments of his life.

Friend, don't allow your life to be destroyed by bitterness and hatred. Give it to God. He is able to heal your broken heart, and only He is able to put your house in order.

HIS WORD

"If your enemy is hungry, give him food to eat; if he is thirsty, give him water to drink" (Proverbs 25:21).

MY PRAYER

At times, we all have events in our lives that might cause us to become bitter. These events can enslave us, but God wants us to have freedom. That means we must forgive those who have hurt us. Is there someone you need to forgive? Do it today.

MY STUDY

1 Samuel 24:8–13; Luke 6:27–36

Lori's life was turned upside-down when she was a junior in college. A young man she thought was a friend needed a ride home. She obliged. He led her into his apartment and raped her four times throughout the night, then let her go in the morning.

When her boyfriend found out what happened, he left her. For months, the rapist taunted and degraded her. Even though Lori was a Christian and grew up in the church, she began to believe his lies. Many times she came close to taking her own life.

Nothing in Lori's upbringing prepared her for this. She was in a state of shock and was gripped by fear. Nighttime was unbearable. Every noise terrified her. She was desperately seeking anything that would bring security.

Finally, Lori shared her dilemma with two godly older women. They graciously led her to the Word of God and showed her how to combat her fear.

The more Lori read her Bible, the more help she found. She said, "In three days, I had no more fear and haven't had any fear since."

Lori's story is a graphic reminder of how important the Word of God is in our lives. It's not only important to read it, it's vital to memorize it. The beauty and wisdom of God's words give us quick access to His power and comfort.

I realize that I'm speaking to two kinds of people: those who are, at this moment, trying to recover from a personal disaster and those who will experience one in the future. Both of you can overcome the aftershocks of fear.

I encourage you to seek comfort in the Lord and gain strength from His Word. Commit meaningful verses to memory and rely on these verses to guide your life. You won't be disappointed! God's Word will never fail you.

HIS WORD

"When you pass through the waters, I will be with you; and when you pass through the rivers, they will not sweep over you. When you walk through the fire, you will not be burned; the flames will not set you ablaze" (Isaiah 43:2).

MY PRAYER

Memorizing God's Word is a valuable tool for combating the temptations that attack us everyday. Try this, my friend. Purpose in your heart to memorize one verse a week for at least the next month — perhaps the verses provided in this book. You'll be glad you did.

MY STUDY

Psalm 4:1; John 14:27

A New Lease on Life

For some, being diagnosed with cancer is a death sentence. For Edwina Perkins it meant a new lease on life.

A 31-year-old mother of two, Edwina never dreamed the lump she found in her breast could be cancer. Confident the biopsy would reveal nothing, Edwina made the 45-minute drive to her doctor alone.

Normally quite jovial, the doctor was somber. He faced Edwina and said those words every woman fears: "I'm sorry. It's cancer."

On the long drive home, Edwina was not alone. God was there. Edwina reviewed a mental checklist of things that were important to her and things that were not. She decided right then that it was time to get rid of her number one problem – anger.

All her life, Edwina had been an angry person, harboring hurt and resentment, letting anger simmer and stew. As a Christian, she knew this was wrong, but nothing seemed to help. She'd memorized the verses in Ephesians 4:26,27, which say: "Do not let the sun go down while you are still angry, and do not give the devil a foothold." She desperately wanted to let go of anger. She just didn't know how.

Now, returning home to share the bad news with her family, Edwina made a vow. "I will no longer allow anger to rule my life," she prayed. "I want it to be gone!"

Through surgery, chemotherapy, and radiation treatments, Edwina survived the fight with breast cancer. To this day, anger no longer characterizes her life.

Oh sure, she gets upset, but she doesn't allow herself to burn with those old feelings. She chooses to let things go so that anger won't rob her of one more day's joy.

That's what God wants for you. Friend, don't wait for a scrape with death to begin living the abundant life. Start living God's best right now!

HIS WORD
"Refrain from anger and turn from wrath; do not fret — it leads only to evil" (Psalm 37:8).

MY PRAYER
"Loving heavenly Father, please forgive me for those times when I hold on to my anger. Anger steals my joy. Help me to always be patient and quick to forgive — as You are patient and forgiving of me. In Jesus' holy name, amen."

MY STUDY
Ecclesiastes 7:9; James 1:19,20

Paid in Full

Corrie ten Boom, my personal mentor, spent many years in a concentration camp during World War II. While there, she was constantly degraded, but never more so than in the delousing shower.

Corrie felt she had – by grace – forgiven those cruel men who had robbed her of her dignity while guarding the shower stalls.

Years later, Corrie was speaking on forgiveness in a church in Munich. After the sermon, a man came toward her with his hand outstretched. Corrie's heart froze. Here was one of the very men who had stood outside the camp shower and leered at her and the others.

She thought, "I cannot forgive. I cannot forgive. Oh, God, forgive me. I cannot forgive." As Corrie gave her resentment to the Lord, she felt the forgiveness of God for *her* lack of forgiveness. Corrie's heart melted and she extended her hand to him.

A debt was owed to her, but she chose to release it. The sword of God's truth surgically removed this blemish on Corrie's heart.

Friend, just like Corrie, you too can release a debt owed to you and be set free.

First, acknowledge that you've been hurt. Be very specific about the injustice. Write it down.

Second, determine what that person owes you. What do you want from here? This is where a lot of people create false expectations, and it really helps to define what you want. Write that down.

Third, honestly consider the likelihood that you'll never get paid, that you'll never get what you want.

Then, finish by writing these words at the bottom: "Paid in full. Debt retired."

Let the debt go. Say, "I'm not going to require justice here. The debt that is owed me is gone. I've forgiven that, and I'm not going to take that debt back."

That's heart surgery! The process may hurt and take time, but it's definitely worth the effort. You will be free indeed.

HIS WORD

"Do not say, 'I'll do to him as he has done to me; I'll pay that man back for what he did'" (Proverbs 24:29).

MY PRAYER

"Lord Jesus, I owed a great debt. You came to earth, were beaten, bruised, and crucified; and on the third day, You arose. All this to pay for my debt. I am humbled beyond measure by this gracious gift. Help me to forgive those who owe me a debt. Thank You, my Savior, amen."

MY STUDY

Exodus 23:4–6; Colossians 3:13

Satisfaction

Cristi was dissatisfied with her singleness. Growing up, her family and church promoted the idea that she was made for a man. It seemed that marriage was the only road to happiness.

Her desire was to serve the Lord by being the best wife and mother possible. But Cristi's hopes were shattered after two serious relationships ended in disappointment.

Finally, she realized that for years most of her prayers had been about her desires for marriage. She had been seeking relationships rather than the Giver of relationships. Only God could love her unconditionally. Relationships come and go, but His love and fellowship remain constant.

So she completely gave her life over to God by praying, "Lord, if marriage isn't in Your plans for me, then I don't want to waste my life in the waiting room. Please show me what You would have me do."

The process of surrendering her desires was not easy. But as she concentrated on getting to know the Lord better and sought His purpose for her life, God began to work in her.

She left her career as a newspaper journalist and began writing for a Christian magazine where her newfound desire for ministry could be fulfilled.

Cristi developed intimate, lifelong friendships with her roommates. She invited her friends' children over for slumber parties. She met weekly with a high school sophomore for Bible study. She even planned activities for singles at her church.

My friend, if you ever struggle with dissatisfaction — whether single or married — rethink your situation. No man can ever perfectly fulfill your needs or help you live your life to the fullest. Only God can do that.

Pursue His unique purpose for your life and place your desires in His hands. Only then can you reach the potential He has in mind for you.

HIS WORD

"I will betroth you to me forever; I will betroth you in righteousness and justice, in love and compassion" (Hosea 2:19).

MY PRAYER

Friend, are you ever dissatisfied with your life? First, consider the source of your dissatisfaction. Is it God or man? If it's man, you are not pursuing God wholeheartedly. If it's God, He is trying to move you in a different direction. Whichever it is, listen to God's leading.

MY STUDY

1 Timothy 6:6; Proverbs 15:16

I remember vividly the day Bill and I helped our youngest son, Brad, pack his car to move to Washington, D.C. He was leaving home to launch his new career.

As we walked him out to the car, my mind wandered back to the many other times we'd said good-bye to Brad. Each time, I had to realize that my two sons have never belonged to us in the first place. They were entrusted to us by God, and the goal all along had been their independence. Now both our sons have children of their own and our nest is empty.

The good news is that the empty-nest syndrome doesn't have to be deadly. It can be the beginning of a richer, fuller life. Many couples find profound satisfaction during this period.

If you find yourself with an empty nest or if you're getting ready for this stage, let me offer four suggestions.

First, *let go*. As our children become mature adults, we must consciously give them back to God's care.

Second, *accept the change*. Nothing you do will bring them back. Instead, take advantage of a great opportunity. Both you and your husband have changed over the years. Enjoy the adventure of a greater intimacy and a creative partnership with each other.

Third, *adopt a positive attitude*. Self-pity and inflexibility only make a difficult transition harder. But a positive outlook opens our hearts and minds to the Lord's healing and helps to ease the pain.

Fourth, *walk into the future*. Use the empty nest as a stepping-stone toward living a purposeful life. Prayerfully decide with your husband which direction the Lord wants you to take, and use your extra time, energy, and money to make a difference.

Friend, there doesn't need to be emptiness in your home when God is there. It can be full of the joy and abundance only He can bring!

HIS WORD
*"Serve the LORD
with fear and rejoice
with trembling"
(Psalm 2:11).*

MY PRAYER
*"Oh Father, let me be sensitive to the leading of Your Spirit in making
choices that will honor You and contribute most to our marriage and
lifetime goals. I place my heart in Your hands. Amen."*

MY STUDY
Colossians 3:23,24; Isaiah 43:2

Let It Go

In his book *A View from the Zoo*, Gary Richmond, pastor and former zookeeper, described the day he received a telephone call from the head veterinarian. They needed to perform surgery on the eyelids of a king cobra.

This was a physically demanding procedure that required several men. It involved capturing the snake and holding it down on the table. For twenty-minutes, the doctor would perform the tedious surgery.

A team gathered in the operating room and, together, managed to bring the snake down. When uncoiled, the cobra was over six feet long.

Once they grabbed the snake, Gary was assigned to hold the snake by the back of the neck for the duration of the surgery. For the entire procedure, the fangs of the cobra discharged yellow venom – enough poison to kill hundreds of men.

When the surgery was finally completed, the doctor looked at Gary and said, "You need to know that the easy part is grabbing hold of the snake. The hard part is letting go."

Sin is like that cobra, isn't it? It's often much easier to grab hold of something very dangerous than it is to let it go.

In life there are many temptations. Something may appear harmless on the outside, but once you have it in your grip, it becomes a habit. Before long, you can't let go.

My friend, be sure you're not allowing anything to enter your life that you won't be able to let go – whether it's what you're reading or watching, something you're drinking or eating, or the friends with whom you are associating.

There's nothing the enemy would like more than finding something that will capture your attention and take your focus off the Lord. Give those issues to the Lord, and trust Him to give you the strength to resist. He wants to help you. And He will!

HIS WORD

"You, dear children, are from God and have overcome them, because the one who is in you is greater than the one who is in the world" (1 John 4:4).

MY PRAYER

Do you have anything in your life that has the potential to take your sights off the Lord — something no one knows about or that seems insignificant? Friend, be careful. Refocus your life on Christ. Take time in prayer now to turn the temptation over to Him and begin to rely on Him alone.

MY STUDY

Genesis 3:1–19; Proverbs 1:10–16

The late Dr. Louis Evans, a dear friend, told this story from his childhood experience.

As a young boy, he and some of his playmates found a dead bird. They decided it needed a decent burial, so they made a shoebox casket and dug a hole. Then they chose one of the friends to preach at the bird's funeral and another to sing. Ceremoniously, they dropped the makeshift casket into the earth.

They had so much fun that the next day they decided to dig up the box and have another funeral! This time someone else preached and someone else sang.

The next day they did it again with different roles for different friends.

Finally, Louis's father realized what they were doing and put a stop to it. He said, "Boys, leave that bird buried! When something is dead, you don't keep digging it up again!"

A simple, innocent story, but the lesson is profound, isn't it?

The Bible says, "If we confess our sins, he is faithful and just and will forgive us our sins and purify us from all unrighteousness" (1 John 1:9). When John wrote these words, he knew that even Christians continue to sin. But when you become aware of your sin, you need to confess it. You simply agree with God that you were wrong.

Then, you can *know* you're forgiven. Even your guilt and shame are removed. God never brings it up again.

Yet too many times forgiven Christians are tempted to dig up old stuff, to revisit issues that have already been resolved. They don't know that they've been forgiven.

When you don't know you're forgiven, the guilt will rob you of peace with God and prevent you from reaching out to others with the true message of God's love and forgiveness.

My friend, your sins are buried and forgotten – don't keep digging them up!

HIS WORD
"As far as the east is from the west, so far has he removed our transgression from us" (Psalm 103:12).

MY PRAYER
I encourage you to read the book of 1 John. When you do, pay attention to the number of times the word "know" is used in that book. This will help you to stop digging up the things that God wants to leave buried. Your sins are forever forgiven!

MY STUDY
Isaiah 43:25 Hebrews 10:22

The Healing Touch

Fifteen years ago when Peggy was pregnant, her husband insisted she have an abortion, and tragically, she obliged. The guilt and remorse that followed were far beyond Peggy's anticipation. She fell into deep depression, and her marriage fell apart.

When Peggy became a Christian, God began to work in her heart. She was employed as a computer operator during the week and served as the singles' director for her church on the weekends.

Peggy kept her secret locked up tight. She was afraid of rejection if she told the truth.

Eventually, she decided to let her friends and associates know about her past. She wanted to be honest and to help others avoid the same mistake.

Peggy saw God take the most horrible event in her life – the death of her baby – and replace it with an abundance of love for others. Today, Peggy invests her time reaching young children in the inner city. Through creative outreach programs, Peggy finds joy in bringing the good news to underprivileged families.

When Peggy trusted God, He forgave her. He also gave her a new purpose in life.

Maybe you're struggling with a hard issue like Peggy's. It may not be abortion, but perhaps something else is hindering you in your relationship with God.

Be encouraged, my friend. Seek His forgiveness, and see what He will do.

The tragedy of Peggy's past became the springboard for her present ministry. She's able to reach out to others. They respond to her heart of compassion because they know she understands. She's been right where they are.

Don't let the tragedy of your past mistakes keep you from experiencing the fullness He wants to give you in the present.

Open your heart to the Lord today. Let Him reach into your life with His healing touch. Then you will have what it takes to reach out to others.

HIS WORD

"Praise be to the God and Father of our Lord Jesus Christ, the Father of compassion and the God of all comfort, who comforts us in all our troubles, so that we can comfort those in any trouble with the comfort we ourselves have received from God" (2 Corinthians 1:3,4).

MY PRAYER

"God of all comfort, you know the pain in my heart. Please reach into my life today and heal the wounds of yesterday that keep me from living to the fullest. Show me how to use my past experiences to help others. Amen."

MY STUDY

Genesis 50:20; Psalm 40:1–3

A family was staying in a high-rise condo on the beach. As the mother walked into the living room, terror filled her heart. Her three-year-old son was perched precariously on the outside of the balcony's guardrail. Hands stretched behind him, he was hanging onto the railing looking down at the beach.

She was afraid if she startled him, he'd let go. So despite her panic, she remained calm.

She said softly to her son, "Honey, hold on for Mommy." Then she eased her way up to him. When she was close enough, she thrust out her hands and grabbed his arm – gripping him tightly with the loving force of a caring mother. She breathed a sigh of relief.

The little boy was now secure because one who loved him more than words could ever say had a *never-let-go* grip on him.

My friend, that's a graphic reminder of God's promise that He will never leave you, He'll never let you go. Consider the determination with which that loving mother held onto that adventurous son. That little guy had no idea how much danger he was in and from what he was being protected!

When you feel like you're dancing on the edge of life, don't worry. The One who loves you more than words can say knew you might feel that way sometimes. So He made it a point to say to you, "Never will I leave you; never will I forsake you" (Hebrews 13:5). He will keep a *never-let-go* grip on you.

There is great freedom in knowing God will never leave you. You can face anything! God is aware of everything in your life and He is with you.

Remember the old song, "He's got the whole world in His hands." Today, picture yourself resting securely in His hands, even if you're on the edge. He will never let you go.

HIS WORD
"The LORD himself goes before you and will be with you; he will never leave you nor forsake you. Do not be afraid; do not be discouraged" (Deuteronomy 31:8).

MY PRAYER
"Ever-present Father, thank You that no matter where I go or what happens to me, You are there — leading, guiding, and protecting. Your comforting, yet firm, grip on me is a constant source of security. May I always remember Your strength. In Jesus' mighty name, amen."

MY STUDY
Psalm 9:10; Hebrews 10:23

Single and Content

Some of the most important people in my life are single women. The woman who led me to faith in Christ many years ago was a woman who never married. She spent her entire life serving the Lord.

Several of my dearest friends are single. I love them deeply, and I respect and admire them. They're among the most dynamic people I know. They're single, and content.

The Bible contains many examples of women who weren't married. As far as we know, Mary and Martha were single adults, and dear friends of Jesus. They are models of women who opened their home, practiced hospitality, and reached out to care for the needs of others, including our dear Lord.

Sometimes I look at women I know who've never married and I wonder why. I so love being married it makes me want to find husbands for them!

But when I look at their lives and observe how God is using them, I'm impressed. When I consider the time and energy they're able to devote to the cause of Christ and to others, I'm grateful God has left them single, at least for now.

If you're single, God has a very special plan for you. God wants to use these years in your life in a most unique way.

Today, put your life in God's hands. Then watch how He opens doors. He's promised to meet *your* every need. Whether it's a practical need, an emotional need, or a financial one, He'll take care of you.

If you're lonely, tell Him. If you're afraid, tell Him. If you're confused, tell Him. As you depend on Him, your relationship with Him will grow. And *that* relationship is the only thing on this earth that can meet you at the point of your greatest need and deepest longing.

HIS WORD
"Delight yourself in the LORD and he will give you the desires of your heart" (Psalm 37:4).

MY PRAYER
Are you ever sad that you are not married? Don't despair, my friend. Instead pray, "Lord, I want to trust you with all my life, including my marital status. Please show me how to use my time for Your glory. I'm completely Yours. Amen."

MY STUDY
Isaiah 26:4; Philippians 4:19

Jackie was a student when she came to Christ. She had no understanding of Christianity, but she learned quickly and taught others.

From all appearances, she was solid in her faith and sure of what she believed, but deep in her heart that was not the case. She had put herself on a standard of performance that no one could achieve. She was torturing herself with thoughts of what she should be. *I ought to be better. I ought to do more. I'm not good enough. I'm a failure.*

With those destructive thought patterns, Jackie drove herself to succeed. When she was successful, she felt proud. When she failed, she condemned herself and felt as though God condemned her, too. As this negative spiral went on for years, she was quietly destroying herself.

Finally, she fell apart emotionally and cried out for help. She knew this couldn't be the Christian life – trying to be perfect and hating herself for failing.

She studied God's grace. She read, talked with her friends, and prayed. Eventually, she understood.

Today, Jackie is like a new person. Understanding the grace of God transformed her life. She is a marriage and family therapist who specializes in family abuse issues.

If God were the hard taskmaster Jackie feared, none of us could bear it. In our humanity, we could never live up to His perfect standard. So we have only two options: give up or hide. Jackie was one of the many who hid. She couldn't let anyone see her weakness. She had to pretend it wasn't there.

Once she realized that God is a God of grace, everything changed. God knows we're not perfect. We only need to receive His acceptance, forgiveness, and grace. He doesn't ask us to change ourselves or perform to some impossible standard, but just to trust Him and let Him change our lives.

HIS WORD
"Come to me, all you who are weary and burdened, and I will give you rest" (Matthew 11:28).

MY PRAYER
Can you relate to Jackie? Are you trying so hard to fix yourself, doing what you think you should, that you're about to explode? Remember God's grace today. Be honest with Him about where you are and what you need. Then rest. Let His grace transform your life.

MY STUDY
Exodus 33:14; Psalm 68:19

Believe the Truth

Karen placed her trust in Christ when she was a small child. But when she was eleven years old, her world dramatically changed. A relative abused her, a younger brother died, and her family made a major move. Confusion and pain became a part of her once-peaceful life.

She was popular in high school, but that wasn't enough. Looking for more approval and acceptance, she asked a guy friend if she needed to lose weight. "Just a few pounds would help," he answered. Her downward spiral into anorexia had begun.

She immediately set about losing five pounds. It didn't take her long. "It made me feel good," she said. She became even more popular.

She said, "I began to equate love with thinness. I became obsessed with perfection." Whenever Karen consumed calories, she exercised them off.

Her condition worsened. She eventually dropped from 155 pounds to just 82 pounds. She struggled for nine years, coming close to death twice.

One Sunday morning, she was alone in the hospital. She said, "I was face to face with myself." She began to write out a list of lies she'd come to believe. Then she contrasted them with the truth of God and His love, which she'd known deep in her heart for a long time.

She said, "I gave complete control of my life back to God. I asked forgiveness for my self-centeredness, and asked God to help me trust Him to handle my weight."

God answered her prayer. Through extensive therapy, medical help, and the prayers and love of her family and friends, she broke free of the vicious cycle. She gained a more balanced view of herself and a life-changing trust in God.

Friend, I don't know what your day-to-day struggles are. Today, choose to believe the truth of what God says about you. He loves you very deeply just as you are. Remember that always.

HIS WORD
"Then you will know the truth, and the truth will set you free" (John 8:32).

MY PRAYER
"Wonderful Savior, sometimes I forget that it doesn't matter to You how much I weigh or how I look. You love me because I am Your creation. I am precious to You. Help me to see myself through the eyes of truth — Your truth. Amen."

MY STUDY
Psalm 103:6; Hosea 14:9

Dark and dirty and housing almost seven thousand inmates, the 300-year-old Russian prison was a picture of despair.

Ward Coleman and a team of Americans were visiting the prison as part of Operation Carelift, an annual ministry outreach to the people of the former Soviet Union sponsored by the Josh McDowell Ministry.

As Ward approached cell number sixteen, a very small metal flap was unlocked by a guard. Immediately, a face appeared. "The face I saw stunned me," Ward said. Unexpectedly, it was the face of a calm and peaceful man – Victor.

Four years earlier, Victor was arrested, charged with a crime and imprisoned, but never convicted. Yet, he was a man at peace.

For a moment, Victor went to the back of his cell. When he returned to the small window, he handed Ward an amazingly intricate sculpture of Christ on the cross. He said, "Give this crucifix to Mr. McDowell. I've read his books. They've helped me so immensely in prison."

Victor explained he'd saved the morsels of bread served with his meals. From those, he molded an ornate cross and a figure of Jesus Christ. For color he used coffee and the vegetables on his plate.

Victor told Ward, "I'm happier now than I've ever been in my life. Before, I had a large apartment, money, and I knew influential people. But now, I have Jesus Christ."

In that moment, Ward thought, *Victor, I'd like to be there where you are, because I sense there's more freedom in there than out here.*

Victor experienced spiritual freedom through God and His Word. No matter what your circumstances, He promises to do the same for you. Today, you may feel trapped in a pit of despair or a sea of pain. You may be a prisoner of debt or addiction. No matter what it is, God knows. He's waiting to help.

HIS WORD
"We are hard pressed on every side, but not crushed; perplexed, but not in despair" (2 Corinthians 4:8).

MY PRAYER
Turn to the Book of Psalms. Dear friend, there's comfort there for whatever you're facing. As you read, listen to God's words of compassion and understanding. Meditate on His truth. It's food for your soul; it's the Bread of Life. And He will set you free.

MY STUDY
Numbers 6:24–26; Psalm 34:14

What Sin?

One day, two children got into big trouble! The older child, Kelly, was given scissors to cut flowers for the table. Her little brother went along to watch.

When the mother checked on the children, she found her son with the scissors and the daughter nowhere in sight. She was angry with Kelly and scared of what could've happened to the young boy with a pair of sharp scissors. When Kelly showed up, she made matters even worse by lying to her mother.

Later that night, after appropriate discipline and apologies, peace was restored to the household. Kelly asked her mother for forgiveness, and it was granted.

The next day, Kelly came to her mother and said, "I feel really bad, Mommy. I feel bad because I lied to you."

"What do you mean?" her mother said.

"Yesterday. When I lied to you. I feel bad."

"Honey, what lie? I've forgotten about that. I forgave you, remember? It's something in the past now."

What a graphic illustration for a little girl who's just learning about forgiveness. When you and I sin, the Bible instructs us to confess our sin. "Confess" means to agree with God that what we did was wrong. Then we ask for forgiveness. Not only does He forgive completely, He forgets it ever happened.

Corrie ten Boom used to say, "He puts our sin in the deepest ocean and then puts up a 'No Fishing' sign." I love that word picture.

Our human tendency is to remember when we've been wronged. God isn't like that. He forgets and doesn't bring it up again.

Many Christians carry guilt and shame in their hearts, making them feel defeated. Dear friend, it doesn't have to be that way. You are forgiven. When you understand that, you'll want desperately to share that good news with others. Understanding God's love and forgiveness in Christ is the greatest need of our time.

HIS WORD

"I will forgive their wickedness and will remember their sins no more" (Jeremiah 31:34).

MY PRAYER

Ask God to show you anything in your life that's not pleasing to Him. Write it on a sheet of paper. Now ask God to forgive you. Next, write the words of 1 John 1:9 across the page. Thank God for His forgiveness, then tear up the list. The next time you feel guilty about anything on that list, say, "Thank you, Lord. That's forgiven and forgotten. I don't have to worry."

MY STUDY

Psalm 32:1; Ephesians 1:7,8

A correspondent from The Voice of the Martyrs tells how religious cultures clashed in a Muslim country through a simple friendship.

Saleema, 17, was a Christian. Her schoolmate, Raheela, 18, was Muslim. They were friends at school. Saleema often invited Raheela to her home after school.

They talked about God, the God of the Bible. Saleema gave Raheela a Bible and taught her Christian songs. Then Raheela, without her parents' knowledge, would teach the songs to her younger sister.

When Raheela's parents learned about the Christian songs, the younger sister told them where Raheela was learning them.

Saleema invited Raheela to a church service. Raheela heard the gospel and placed her trust in Jesus that day. She grew in her faith, and God changed her life.

Raheela was very open about reading her Bible and praising God. When her family learned of her conversion to Christianity, they were furious. After she refused to accept marriage to a Muslim man, their anger grew, and she ran away.

Raheela's family accused the pastor, his family, and Saleema of kidnapping her. They were arrested, severely beaten, and tortured.

Tragically, Raheela was killed by her own family. Saleema and the pastor were charged with her murder. Through the help of a good lawyer, the charges were eventually reduced to "converting a Muslim."

Our only consolation is *knowing* Raheela is now truly free to worship the Lord Jesus Christ.

The Voice of the Martyrs boldly works to bring us the good news of Jesus Christ's work in countries where Christians are persecuted.

When one member of the Body of Christ suffers, we all suffer. It's my hope that we'll always pray for these dear brothers and sisters who cannot worship as they please.

HIS WORD

"Remember those in prison as if you were their fellow prisoners, and those who are mistreated as if you yourselves were suffering" (Hebrews 13:3).

MY PRAYER

Post Hebrews 13:3 on your refrigerator along with a small map of the world. Use these to remind you to pray for Christians in countries where people are not free to worship the true God. Also pray for continued religious freedom in America and look for ways to share our biblical heritage.

MY STUDY

Psalm 69; Isaiah 58:7

Do the Right Thing

Cindy was a calm and peaceful person. The story of her life, though, is anything but peaceful. She and her second husband lived in several countries, but ended up back in the States after he was diagnosed with a rare form of liver cancer. Before he died, they were fugitives from the law as well as from God.

He was involved in illegal businesses before he met Cindy. After meeting her, he used her good name and credit rating to begin yet another. She didn't know what he was doing, but she knew something wasn't right. The only thing that kept her with him was their young daughter whom he continually threatened to kidnap. So she stayed with him as they ran from justice.

During that time, God caught up with her. She prayed for a way out. When her husband became ill, she made up her mind to surrender. She knew she couldn't keep running, nor did she want to. She wanted to be with her daughter, not go to prison for years. She counted the cost. She knew by turning herself in she might have to face a prison term. But her love for her daughter and her deep desire to do the right thing compelled her.

So Cindy surrendered to authorities. After four days, the judge agreed to set bail for her. Many other miracles followed, and she's now confident that God is working His plan for her life and the life of her daughter.

She's still not completely free, but she's experienced freedom in Christ. Cindy sacrificed to do the right thing.

What is God asking of you? Be obedient to Him today. Sometimes obedience is hard. But God always enables us to make the right choice and follow through. He's promised to provide everything you need and more. Trust Him. He'll make a way.

HIS WORD

"But the man who looks intently into the perfect law that gives freedom, and continues to do this, not forgetting what he has heard, but doing it — he will be blessed in what he does" (James 1:25).

MY PRAYER

Is God asking you to do something that you find difficult? What is keeping you from obedience, my friend? Fear? Pride? God can take care of those things if you will trust Him. Try it. You will be amazed at the results.

MY STUDY

1 Samuel 15:22; Psalm 51:16,17

God wants us to be authentic, not fake. Even the world longs to see people who are real, honest, and consistent.

Being authentic means that we live out in practice what we profess to believe in principle. It means that we say what we mean and mean what we say. It means that we aren't afraid to be vulnerable by expressing the truth, even if we have made a mistake or wronged someone.

We often struggle with being authentic because we're afraid. We think people will perceive us as weak. No one wants to admit she's wrong or doesn't have all the answers. We think this shows weakness when it actually shows strength of character – God's character in you. In the Bible, Christ tells us, "My grace is sufficient for you, for my power is made perfect in weakness" (2 Corinthians 12:9). When we are vulnerable, God's strength is allowed to show in all its glory.

From experience, I can tell you that a person who admits her mistakes is much easier to trust than one who never admits wrong. It is also a command from God. James 5:16 says, "Confess your sins to each other and pray for each other so that you may be healed." Think of it this way. Confession rids the wound of the emotional and spiritual bacteria. Prayer is the agent through which the Holy Spirit heals the wound.

So when you are wrong, be quick to admit it. Don't let it fester into a wound that is difficult or impossible to heal. Instead, express your sorrow and repentance to those you've hurt. This will cleanse your soul of what's ailing it. Your humility is evidence of authenticity – and it honors God.

HIS WORD
"The LORD detests lying lips, but he delights in men who are truthful"
(Proverbs 12:22).

MY PRAYER
"God of truth, help me live what I profess. Don't let me proclaim one thing and live another. May people see You in me, in all of my activities. May Your Spirit have such control of me that people will be drawn to You and the life that only You can give. Amen."

MY STUDY
Numbers 5:6,7; James 5:16

God Is in Control

Carol was a self-proclaimed worrier. Even her ten-year-old daughter said her mother worried too much. That's when Carol found new perspective from a Bible story popularized in the movie *The Prince of Egypt*, which is about the life of Moses.

Jochebed, an Israelite and the mother of Moses, had plenty to worry about. When Pharaoh ordered all newborn Israelite boys killed, Jochebed hid her infant son for three months. She knew that she could not hide him forever if he was to have any kind of meaningful life. So she developed a plan and took a chance. Jochebed placed her son in a waterproof basket and sent him down the Nile River. He was rescued by Pharaoh's daughter.

In a miraculous turn, Jochebed was selected as the nurse for the child in Pharaoh's household. Eventually, the loving mother gave Moses to Pharaoh's daughter to be her son.

Jochebed did all she could for her son, then released him. She probably prayed all the while.

Carol learned how to deal with her worries from this ancient mother. Can you identify with Jochebed or Carol? We all go through times when worry seems to enslave us. But you can have victory over this anxiety. All you have to do is trust God – trust Him because He is all-knowing and all-powerful, and because He loves you. In Romans 8:28, we read, "In all things God works for the good of those who love him, who have been called according to his purpose." He promises to work for our good.

The next time you are worried, remember that God is in control and that He is looking out for you. Then make a conscious effort to stop worrying about things you can't control and start trusting the God who controls all things. You'll live a more peaceful life.

HIS WORD
"Cast all your anxiety on him because he cares for you"
(1 Peter 5:7).

MY PRAYER
The next time you find yourself overwhelmed with worry, try this. Make a list of your worries. Next, develop a plan to take action. Before you begin to work on the steps of your plan, surrender it all to God. We can't control the outcome, but we can take control of our emotions.

MY STUDY
Psalm 37:5–11; Matthew 6:25–34

Do you ever struggle with submitting your desires to God? Maybe you feel that you are giving up your freedom. Or perhaps you think that God will make you do something you won't like.

Truthfully, that's the age-old struggle of the Christian life. We often do the very thing we hate. The apostle Paul speaks of this in Romans 7:15: "I do not understand what I do. For what I want to do I do not do, but what I hate I do." As Christians, we know right from wrong, but as humans, we still have fleshly desires pulling at us. Tragically, sometimes they win.

This can be especially true when rearing children, running a home, and keeping a marriage together. Sometimes, the last thing you feel like doing is being obedient to God. But that is what God expects of us. In John 14:23, Jesus tells us, "If anyone loves me, he will obey my teaching." But how do we do that? By surrendering our will to God.

The beauty of God's design for our lives is that when we give up ourselves, we are free to receive all that God has planned for us. The Bible tells us, "Whoever loses his life for my sake will find it" (Matthew 10:39). Through surrender we receive life.

The life God has for us is always much better for us than what we can do on our own. God tells us the reason in Isaiah 55:8: "My thoughts are not your thoughts, neither are your ways my ways." We often don't understand how God works. However, through many experiences in my life, I've learned that His ways are always best.

Oh, friend, tell God about your hurts, heartaches, and desires. His heart of compassion is eager to comfort you and give you guidance. Then trust His direction completely. Our heavenly Father knows best!

HIS WORD
"I know, my God, that you test the heart and are pleased with integrity. All these things have I given willingly and with honest intent" (1 Chronicles 29:17).

MY PRAYER
"Holy Father, forgive my stubborn self-will. I know that You only want what is best for me. Help me daily to withstand the temptations that come my way so I may follow Your righteous plan instead. Give me the wisdom to discern Your perfect will. Amen."

MY STUDY
Psalm 119:1,2; 1 Thessalonians 4:7

Rewards of Obedience

A pastor and his wife were visiting their daughter at college. The parking lot at their hotel was full, so the manager told them to park in a space reserved for handicapped guests. Thinking it would be okay, the pastor did as he was directed.

Some time later as they were leaving, the pastor noticed an older gentleman watching him. The man's eyes met his with a disgusted look. Then the pastor noticed the man's wife in a wheelchair. The pastor felt horrible, but he learned a good lesson from this situation: Don't trust what others tell you if it is contrary to what God would want you to do.

Friend, the Bible is clear. In Acts 5:29, Peter tells us, "We must obey God rather than men." Even when we receive instruction from a person in authority, we must weigh that against God's instructions. Are they in conflict? If so, then we must choose to obey God. He has given us many guidelines in His Word.

One of the instructions God has given us that we can apply to this situation is in James 4:17: "Anyone, then, who knows the good he ought to do and doesn't do it, sins." Sins are not only things that we do, but also things that we should have done but didn't do.

Sometimes doing the right thing is hard. It may put us in conflict with others who are not following God and don't understand our actions. But He expects us to do what we know to be right, no matter what.

The rewards of obedience are many. It gives us greater intimacy with God, credibility with others, and freedom from guilt. Obedience provides us with a clear conscience; it helps others God has placed in our path; it keeps us focused on Him rather than ourselves; and above all, it brings honor and glory to God.

HIS WORD

"The wicked man earns deceptive wages, but he who sows righteousness reaps a sure reward" (Proverbs 11:18).

MY PRAYER

Think of a time when you had a conflict between an authority figure and God. How did you handle it? How would the principle you just learned have helped you? As you apply God's Word to your life, you will be blessed.

MY STUDY

Ruth 2:12; Luke 12:41–48

One year in the fall, a friend began her first semester of Bible school in Wisconsin. Winter soon invaded the land, and she was unprepared for the chill. Temperatures were lower than normal that year and her feet were always cold.

She prayed one morning for help in keeping warm. That very day, in her mailbox, she found a pair of warm socks.

God was the only one who heard her prayer. And He had moved someone to answer this physical need even before she asked.

This is a simple illustration that can be echoed *thousands* of times by those who trust God for their needs. Our heavenly Father knows our needs *before* we pray. Our job is simply to ask Him and trust Him to provide.

What's your greatest need right now? If you are a mom at home, it might be patience. If you are a professional, it might be wisdom, strength, courage. If you are in your later years, it might be for good health and a clear mind. It might be for all of these things.

But no matter now long or hard you think, you will never be able to come up with a need that God can't meet. I hope this is great news for you today.

The Bible tells us this in 1 John: "This is the confidence we have in approaching God: that if we ask anything according to his will, he hears us. And if we know that he hears us – whatever we ask — we know that we have what we asked of him" (5:14-15).

Do you trust God to do what He says He will do? It's so simple. If we believe God will do what He says, the Bible tells us He will meet our needs. So, go ahead. Place your trust in God and expect a great blessing from Him.

HIS WORD
"If you, then, though you are evil, know how to give good gifts to your children, how much more will your Father in heaven give good gifts to those who ask him!" (Matthew 7:11)

MY PRAYER
"Dear Father God, I am so grateful that You care about every need in my life, whether it's big or small. I know that when I come to You in prayer, You always do what You think is best. I trust Your will because I trust Your love for me. Thank You, Lord. Amen."

MY STUDY
Hebrews 4:14-16; Romans 8:26-27

He Cares for You

Leisha faced fear head-on. And she overcame it — with God's help. She's a working mom whose life has been far from "normal." As a child, Leisha was physically and sexually abused. As a teenager, she placed her faith in Christ. It wasn't long before her young faith was tested.

Leisha was attacked by a serial rapist. He was captured, and when his trial came around, she courageously faced her attacker on the witness stand — *twice*. He went to prison, but escaped — *twice*. And her worst nightmare came true: the rapist came after her again. Even though this was a terrifying experience for Leisha, she refused to let fear rule her life. Instead, she chose to trust God.

In the Scriptures, God says, "Do not fear, for I am with you ... I will strengthen you and help you" (Isaiah 41:10). This is a wonderfully comforting promise from God.

Are there times when you are afraid? Perhaps the things you fear aren't as life-threatening as what Leisha faced. But just the same, God's promise holds true.

Fear is based on our lack of knowledge of the future. We want to know what is going to happen to us, but there is no way that we can know. Only God knows the future. We can trust God with our future because He loves us and has our best interests at heart.

You can remind yourself of this fact with 1 Peter 5:7. It says, "Cast all your anxiety on him because he cares for you." This verse does not leave any care to our own efforts. God provides for us in everything.

Dear friend, the Lord has proven Himself faithful to Leisha, and He will for you too! Confess *your* fear to the Lord today. Trust Him to care for you and protect you.

HIS WORD
"The LORD is my light and my salvation — whom shall I fear?" (Psalm 27:1).

MY PRAYER
"All-powerful God, forgive me for being afraid. I know that You control everything and that not even a sparrow falls without Your notice. Help me to live each day wholly trusting in Your mighty power and wisdom. In Jesus' blessed name, amen."

MY STUDY
Nehemiah 4:14; 2 Timothy 1:7

One Monday morning, I awakened to news that a dear friend of mine had died. Although Ann had been quite ill, she had recovered and was so vibrant and active. I was not prepared for the news of her death. I was stunned and heartbroken.

By noon that same day, I received word of the death of one of my dearest friends — a woman I'd known and loved for more than forty years. Mrs. Atkinson was 103 years old. She'd lived a full and meaningful life, yet there is something profoundly sad about her death. I will never again hear her say, "Well, honey, I'm still here. God must have something for me to do."

Then later that week, I learned about the homegoing of a lifelong friend and classmate. She stood as my bridesmaid.

That unusual week has left me very thoughtful about the realities of life ... and death.

The day after my friend Ann died, her young granddaughter said, "Mommy, what do you think grandmother is having for breakfast with Jesus this morning?"

We all smiled. The little girl grasped a reality that some of us as adults can easily miss. She knew her grandmother was gone, but she was still alive, in heaven with Jesus. She was in the presence of her dear Savior, enjoying the place that He'd prepared for her. I know this because it's what the Bible teaches. It's real.

Three of my friends experienced the blessed hope of heaven. The Lord Jesus Christ had gloriously appeared to them, and they were ready to meet Him.

My question to you is this: Are you ready?

Life is very brief. Before we know it, our years on this earth will come to an end. The most important thing that we can do in this short period of time is to prepare for eternity — eternity with God.

HIS WORD
"When the perishable has been clothed with the imperishable, and the mortal with immortality, then the saying that is written will come true: 'Death has been swallowed up in victory'" (1 Corinthians 15:54).

MY PRAYER
If today were your last day to live, would you be ready? Do you know where you would spend eternity? My friend, you can know for certain. See "Beginning Your Journey of Joy" at the back of the book to learn how you can place your heart in His hands for eternity.

MY STUDY
Isaiah 25:8; Psalm 68:20

Your Choice

Everyone suffers in life at one time or another, but it's our response to the suffering that matters. It determines whether we'll be bitter or better.

The biblical story of Ruth shows that she had every reason to be bitter – her husband, brother-in-law, and father-in-law had all died. She didn't have children, and she had no way to support herself. She could have gone home to her family, but she loved her mother-in-law, Naomi, and was committed to her. She told Naomi, "Where you go I will go, and where you stay I will stay. Your people will be my people and your God my God" (Ruth 1:16).

Ruth and Naomi moved to Bethlehem. There Ruth was considered an alien, but she worked hard in the barley fields to provide for herself and Naomi. In God's providence, she met Boaz, married him, and had a son. That child was King David's grandfather.

Ruth could have become bitter. Instead, she chose to use the circumstances in which she found herself to demonstrate the biblical virtues of faithfulness and love. With peace in her heart, she went where God led her, and He proved faithful.

What tragedies or unexpected events have occurred in your life, recently or in the past? How have you responded to them? If you have become bitter, dear friend, it's never too late to turn a hurtful or stressful circumstance into an opportunity for growth. God has given us free-will, so it is our choice to allow bitterness to take root or to allow God to heal our hurts and guide our lives.

Bitterness is destructive. Today, choose to recognize God's hand in your life. He is watching over you, and He makes no mistakes. No matter how your circumstances look at the moment, God is with you. It's your choice. Trusting Him will make you feel better, not bitter.

HIS WORD
"Above all else, guard your heart, for it is the wellspring of life" (Proverbs 4:23).

MY PRAYER
"Lord Jesus, You know the bitterness I have in my heart. The wound is old and deep. I surrender it to You now, Lord. Please heal the pain so I may be free again to experience life as You want me to experience it. In Your name, amen."

MY STUDY
Ephesians 4:30–32; Isaiah 5:20

The Source of Wisdom

The fear of the Lord is the beginning of wisdom; all who follow his precepts have good understanding. To him belongs eternal praise.

PSALM 111:10

Never before in history has there been so much information available. It has been well said that "information is power, but only to those who know how to use it."

I am grateful for the marvelous grace of God in allowing me to meet so many knowledgeable and capable people. I never want to stop learning and filling my mind with information and ideas that will better equip me to share the gospel. As Bill and I have faced serious issues about his health and attempted to make wise decisions about treatment and medications, we have realized our total dependence on the wisdom that only God can give. There is great security in trusting God to illumine our minds and confirm His Word in our hearts.

Do you have any idea how many choices you made today? It would be impossible to accurately count. The many options available for everything from breakfast cereal to automobiles is staggering. It is easy to see why young people have such a difficult time choosing a career path.

When we seek God's wisdom and rest our heart securely in His hands, we have a solid foundation for our lives. We can rest in His promise: "If you want to know what God wants you to do, ask him, and he will gladly tell you, for he is always ready to give a bountiful supply of wisdom to all who ask him; he will not resent it" (James 1:5, TLB).

His Treasure

While on a speaking tour in Taiwan, we were given generous gifts by our hosts. My traveling partner was given a beautiful cloisonné vase.

Unfamiliar with the art of cloisonné, my friend had no appreciation for the treasure she had received. She had never witnessed the craftsmanship required to create her beautiful vase, never knew about the countless hours invested by many people who tediously designed, ground, sanded, and polished the vase.

She admitted the vase didn't quite complement her decor so she had tucked it safely in a closet!

Several weeks later, a catalog from an exclusive store arrived in her home. While browsing its pages, she found an exact replica of her vase – along with a hefty price tag. Immediately, the vase came out of hiding and into a prominent place in her living room. She has since absolutely fallen in love with this wonderful piece of artistry.

What changed? The value of the vase. When it was worthless in her eyes, she treated it as such. Once she discovered what people paid for such an item, she treated it with care and respect.

My friend's misunderstanding is not unlike misjudgments we make. But we can change. If we take a good, long look at the world and the people around us, we'll see them through the eyes of their Creator. Regardless of outward appearance, achievements, gifts, or abilities; regardless of where we've been or who we know, we are all His treasure. Therefore, we should treat each other with dignity and kindness.

Understanding this truth will also impact the way we see ourselves. When I'm discouraged over my own inadequacies and failures, when I consider areas of my life that aren't what I want them to be, I need to remember that my worth is not tied to those things. I am a treasure to the living God. So are you.

HIS WORD

"Rich and poor have this in common: The LORD is the Maker of them all" (Proverbs 22:2).

MY PRAYER

Do you have anyone in your life that you're treating like an unwanted vase? Maybe you're treating yourself that way. You're worth so much more! We all are. Remember, God paid a supreme price for you and for me. He values you!

MY STUDY

Job 34:18,19; Matthew 10:29–31

Mary and Martha

The Bible tells us that Martha welcomed Jesus into her home for dinner. But she was so busy with her preparations for the guests that she didn't have time to sit and listen to Him. However, Mary, her sister, did take the time to listen intently to the Lord. Martha was not happy about this, and the Lord told her, "Martha, Martha, you are worried and upset about many things, but only one thing is needed" (Luke 10:38–41).

Can you relate to the story of Martha? Suzanne can. She has a hard time sitting still, too. The need to constantly be doing something is ever-present in her life. After learning about Martha, Suzanne wanted to make a change. So she posted a note that said, "Be Mary, not Martha!"

Then she tried to be Mary. She tried to sit quietly and listen to God, but it was difficult. Soon her mind was racing to her "to do" list. Even though her will wanted to be like Martha, the rest of her was not ready for it.

Finally, Suzanne realized that Jesus never told Martha to *be* Mary. He told her not to worry about the unimportant things. When Jesus came to visit Mary and Martha, the important thing was not the food and preparations. The important thing was that the Lord Jesus was preaching the gospel.

That's a great lesson for us all: We must not focus on the cares of this world. There is a time for everything. There is a time for taking care of worldly concerns – cooking, cleaning, etc. But our focus is always to be on the Lord. When He wants to meet with us, we must shut out all distractions.

Remember, the Christian life is a *relationship* with God. He cares about you and wants to spend time with you! Will you give your attention to Him?

HIS WORD
"One thing I ask of the LORD, this is what I seek: that I may dwell in the house of the LORD all the days of my life, to gaze upon the beauty of the Lord and to seek him in his temple" (Psalm 27:4).

MY PRAYER
The next time you are worried or anxious, stop to consider if these things are really important. I can guarantee you that most, if not all, of them are not. Take some time to sit at Jesus' feet and listen. Your worries will quickly fade away.

MY STUDY
Hosea 10:12; 1 John 2:15–17

Good or Better

It's a temptation that confronts all of us. You know what you *should* do, but what you *want* to do is something entirely different.

Let me use a simple illustration to make a very serious point.

Let's say there's a world-class ice cream store near your home. Each time your car gets near that street, you have a little conversation with yourself that goes something like this:

"I think I'll stop and get some ice cream."

Another voice says, "You shouldn't have any. You don't need it."

"I love it; I really want some."

"You shouldn't have any. It's not good for you."

The voice saying you can't have any Praline Supreme makes you want it all the more. So you stop in and make your purchase.

As you leave the shop, you can still hear the voice saying, "You shouldn't be eating this." Something in you feels guilty, but you keep right on eating.

That's the illustration. Now, let's make the point.

Rather than choosing between a *want* and a *should*, let me suggest you start choosing, instead, between two wants.

Do I want to get some ice cream? Or do I want to be healthy?

Which do I want more? It's not a choice of feeling guilty versus good. It's a matter of choosing between good and better.

That kind of thinking gives you freedom! When you drive by the ice cream store, you can extend a little grace to yourself.

So often I speak to women who have put themselves beneath a huge load of guilt. They're overwhelmed by all the self-imposed "shoulds" in life.

Remember, it's God's grace that gives us the freedom to be obedient to His will. In John 8:36, Jesus said, "If the Son sets you free, you will be free indeed."

Isn't that what we really *want*?

HIS WORD

"I have set before you life and death, blessings and curses. Now choose life, so that you and your children may live and that you may love the LORD your God, listen to his voice, and hold fast to him. For the LORD is your life" (Deuteronomy 30:19,20).

MY PRAYER

Take time to think about how this applies to you. Are you bound by a strict set of artificial rules that you've made up yourself? Do they weigh you down and force you to react out of guilt more than a desire to make the best decision? Apply God's grace to these situations.

MY STUDY

Proverbs 4:25–27; Ephesians 6:7,8

At 43, Frank was diagnosed with an incurable form of cancer that spread from his legs to his lungs, spleen, and various parts of his body. Within days, Frank gave his life to Jesus – something his wife, Cathy, and his sons had prayed about for many years.

Until now, Frank had been a stern and stoic father. He taught his three boys to be strong and tough. Only manly handshakes were exchanged at bedtime. He was better at giving advice than he was at listening.

God worked miraculously in Frank's life at a FamilyLife Marriage Conference. He went home a changed man, husband, and dad.

Hugging and loving his sons became commonplace. He shared from his heart with the boys, cried with them, told them how proud he was of them, and how very much he loved them. He also became the listening, loving husband every wife dreams of.

His last four months were filled with laughter and good times with his family. Even though the cancer was overcoming his body, God gave him a good quality of life to the end.

Three weeks before Frank died, the boys' uncle encouraged them to write their dad a letter of love to ensure that nothing would go unsaid. Each boy read it to their dad and, together, son and father wept for the blessing they were to each other.

When Frank died, the boys were at his side. The family came to that moment with no regrets. They had the chance to prepare.

Many of us will not have that chance. We won't have advance warning when a loved one dies. Unfortunately, some of us will live the rest of our lives wishing we had a little more time – just one more chance.

Friend, you can't take back yesterday, and we aren't guaranteed tomorrow. Make the most of today! You won't regret you did!

HIS WORD

"Timothy has just now come to us from you and has brought good news about your faith and love. He has told us that you always have pleasant memories of us and that you long to see us, just as we also long to see you" (1 Thessalonians 3:6).

MY PRAYER

Don't wait to tell your parents, your spouse, or your children how much they mean to you. Don't wait until tomorrow to make memories. Take time today to plan meaningful times with those you love.

MY STUDY

2 Samuel 1:26; Proverbs 3:3,4

Fact, Faith, Feeling

Julia had earned a Bible degree from a Christian college, and she attended church faithfully. But something was missing.

Over coffee with a friend, Julia shared her problem: "I just don't *feel* like I'm a Christian anymore. I don't *feel* like reading the Bible. I know I should, but I just don't."

Her friend offered a simple illustration to try to help. She told her to picture a train with three cars. The engine represents *fact* – the truth of God and His Word. The coal car behind the engine represents *faith* – our trust in God and His Word. Finally, the caboose represents *feeling* – which is the result of our faith and obedience.

All three are important, but a train can run without its caboose. In the train of our spiritual life, our confidence must be in the only reliable engine – God and His Word. Feelings shouldn't pull us along. It's not that feelings don't exist, but we can't *depend* on our feelings to provide power for our lives.

Over the next two weeks, Julia started reading the Bible again and believing its truth. She prayed that the Holy Spirit would empower and direct her life. Julia's life began to take on a whole new meaning. She began rediscovering the truth about herself, about God, and about the world around her.

If you find yourself on a spiritual roller coaster, it's possible you're being pulled by the wrong engine! Turn to the Scripture and choose to rely on God's Word rather than your feelings.

Maybe you've been trying to live the Christian life on your own power and you, like Julia, *feel* defeated. Today, renew your commitment to God and quit relying on the caboose of feelings to power your train! Get into the habit of putting your faith in the facts, and the feelings will follow. It's simple, but life changing.

HIS WORD
"The LORD is good, a refuge in times of trouble. He cares for those who trust in him" (Nahum 1:7).

MY PRAYER
"Lord Jesus, forgive me for trying to live the Christian life on my own power. I want Your Spirit to empower and direct me. From this point on, I will trust in You and Your Word and not my feelings. In Your holy name, amen."

MY STUDY
Psalm 125:1; Ephesians 1:18,19

Relieving Stress

According to the Department of Health and Human Services, 43 percent of adults suffer adverse health effects from stress.

No wonder the newsstands are lined with magazines that include articles on managing stress! These emphasize that eating well, getting adequate rest, exercising regularly, and maintaining friendships are all essential to coping with stress.

King David recognized that the greatest stress buster is a loving relationship with a sovereign God. In Psalm 37, he gives us this advice: "Trust in the Lord ... Delight yourself in the Lord ... Commit your way to the Lord ... Be still before the Lord and wait patiently for him; do not fret ..." (vv. 3–7).

God understands our tendency to be worried and stressed about our lives. He extends His great compassion and mercy to us when we're burdened by life's demands. Philippians 4:6 says,

> Do not be anxious about anything, but in everything, by prayer and petition, with thanksgiving, present your requests to God. And the peace of God, which transcends all understanding, will guard your hearts and your minds in Christ Jesus.

Reading God's Word for even ten or fifteen minutes at the beginning of a busy day helps me put everything in the right perspective. I'm reminded of what's important to God – my character and my trust in Him – not what's important to me.

My mind will revert back to worry unless I am persistently praying. At the beginning of the day, I like to tell God about every activity and important relationship. As the day goes on, every time I start to be concerned about something, I cast my cares upon God.

Begin each day by reading His Word and by praying. God didn't intend for you to be ineffective due to worrying. He wants to use you, and He wants you to experience His peace as you walk closely with Him.

HIS WORD

"Therefore let everyone who is godly pray to you while you may be found; surely when the mighty waters rise, they will not reach him" (Psalm 32:6).

MY PRAYER

Set aside a time each day for you to connect with God through Bible study and prayer. Pick a quiet place where you won't be distracted or interrupted. Make it a priority in your life. It will relieve stress, keep you close to your heavenly Father, and set you free.

MY STUDY

Jonah 2:1–6; Matthew 11:28–30

Focus on Him

When my young friend Kara became engaged, she was thrilled with the prospect of marrying the man she loves. Kara read numerous wedding planners, grilled her married friends for ideas, and used every spare moment thinking about how to make her wedding day special.

Instead of being satisfied as her plans fell into place, she felt more and more empty and unfulfilled. *What happened?* she thought. *Where have I gone wrong? I thought this was supposed to be a fulfilling experience.*

It finally dawned on her that during this time of transition, she had lost sight of God. Caught up in the details of planning the big day and focusing solely on her new life with her mate, Kara had taken her eyes off Jesus.

My friend, God can use transition times in our lives to teach us how much we need Him. As our earthly props are removed, we find ourselves spiritually lacking.

It's an uncomfortable place to be. It's frustrating, confusing, and lonely to be at the end of ourselves. But that's exactly where we need to be to get back on track with God.

When Kara realized that her preoccupation with wedding plans had caused her to lose sight of God, she knew something had to change. She confessed to God that she'd gone her own way, not pursuing Him as her first priority.

Let me ask you: Have your props been knocked out from under you? Have you taken your eyes off the Lord? Well, there's hope! You can tell God exactly where you are – the stresses you face, the challenges to make it through the day. You can confess anything that might be keeping you from a close relationship with Him.

Satan would love nothing more than to distract you! He would have total victory if He could get you to take your eyes off Jesus. Don't let him.

HIS WORD

"To love [God] with all your heart, with all your understanding and with all your strength, and to love your neighbor as yourself is more important than all burnt offerings and sacrifices" (Mark 12:33).

MY PRAYER

"Heavenly Father, I confess my lack of love for You. You are the only One who can fill the emptiness and instill my life with meaning and purpose. While I am doing good things, keep me focused on You alone. In my life, Lord, be glorified. In Jesus' name I pray. Amen."

MY STUDY

Proverbs 19:21; Deuteronomy 6:5

Eternal Investment

What is most important in your life? Have you ever seriously thought about this question? For many the answer would be power, position, satisfaction, or happiness.

I love what Corrie ten Boom, a survivor of the holocaust, once said about the elusive "treasures" of this world: "The more firmly I hold on to something, the more it hurts when God has to pry my fingers away from it!"

Jesus put it best when He asked this probing question in Matthew 16:26, "What good will it be for a man if he gains the whole world, yet forfeits his soul?"

Yes, we all have to earn a living. We must provide for our families. But the greatest investment we can make is not on Wall Street. It's in the life of another. It's in loving, teaching, and caring for your children, your spouse, your parents. It's in reaching out to your friends, neighbors, and colleagues with the love of Jesus. It's putting their concerns above the financial investments or possessions we own.

Sometimes that's by directly sharing the gospel message. Sometimes it's by listening to a broken heart, praying together, providing a meal or an hour of baby-sitting. Other times it's by going for an ice cream cone during a moment of discouragement, or giving a comforting hug.

Those are the attitudes and actions that will develop character, godliness, love, compassion, and joy in your life. Those are the characteristics that Christ modeled throughout His life on earth and the only factors that matter in light of eternity. The rest will fade away.

Dear friend, where is your treasure? On what do you have a tight-fisted grip? What is most important in your life? Once you know the answer to that question, the real work of living the Christian life, day to day, can begin.

HIS WORD

"[The LORD] will be the sure foundation for your times, a rich store of salvation and wisdom and knowledge; the fear of the Lord is the key to this treasure" (Isaiah 33:6).

MY PRAYER

"Lord Jesus, forgive me for not making You the most important person in my life. Show me how I need to re-prioritize my life. I want You to be first above everything, and reflect that in my attitudes and actions. In Your matchless name, amen."

MY STUDY

Proverbs 15:6; 1 Peter 1:17–19

Infinite Security

Many people never think they will end up in a homeless shelter. Edmond was one such person. After the construction company where he had worked folded, Edmond worked part-time at a grocery store while his wife, Shirley, cleaned houses. Even so, they soon started falling behind on house payments.

Then one night, faulty wiring started a fire in their house. Two days later, their furniture was stolen.

In the months that followed, Shirley and their six daughters stayed with relatives while Edmond tried to fix the house. The damage was beyond repair, and the six children were too much for Shirley's mother. Swallowing his pride, Edmond agreed to try the shelter, but only for a few weeks.

Feeling ashamed, Edmond withdrew. The only prayer he could mutter was, "Lord, get me out of here." Edmond felt that all eyes were on him wherever he went, as if he wore a scarlet "H" for "homeless."

Eventually, Edmond found a job with a landscaping company, but it was a long time before they were freed from their financial woes and could leave the shelter.

One night, Edmond opened his Bible and realized he hadn't been praying for help – only for an escape. Clutching his Bible, he prayed, "I am here, God. And so are you. Please help me."

Edmond's shame began to dissolve. God's presence made the shelter a home. He needed to make himself available to God *no matter where he and his family lived.*

Though they now have a home of their own, they learned some invaluable lessons. Above all, they realized that the eternal is far more significant and secure than the temporal.

My friend, the temporal things of this world will all pass away. Place your faith in the infinite security of eternal things – God's things. He will never let you down.

HIS WORD

"Now we know that if the earthly tent we live in is destroyed, we have a building from God, an eternal house in heaven, not built by human hands" (2 Corinthians 5:1).

MY PRAYER

Are you feeling hopeless today? Maybe your soul is restless or circumstances have left you questioning if God is really there. Friend, wherever you might be today, He is our shelter, our refuge. Rest in the promise of God's presence, knowing your heart is in His hands.

MY STUDY

Psalm 23:6; Deuteronomy 33:27

Your Gift to the World

Bob, at 42, was a husband, father, and pastor. Not too long ago, he was golfing with two doctors, both ten years his senior. He asked them this question: "What would you tell a guy like me about the next ten years – the years between 42 and 52?"

The doctors discussed this thoughtful question. They found agreement on two main points. First, you should recognize it's unlikely you will make a great contribution to the world at large. Second, realize that the best legacy you will leave is in the lives of your children.

Friend, I believe all of us can see the wisdom in these words. Only a handful of people will truly impact the entire world, but there is more to the story. We have access to the One who *has* impacted the entire world – Jesus Christ. And each of us has our own "world" of influence – people with whom we have contact day to day. Through Christ's power we can have a positive effect on their lives.

If you are a parent, you know that the most important lives you will affect are those of your children. In Psalm 127, we're encouraged to build godly homes. Then we're reminded that children are a gift and blessing from God. Verse 3 tells us, "Sons are a heritage from the Lord, children a reward from him." We need to cherish the blessing of children. We are responsible for modeling Christ in their lives so that they may come to know Him personally and follow His will for their lives.

Dear friend, tenderly care for your children. Invest your time and energy in them. Teach them the Word of God. The most effective way to do this is to model Christ through your life in your day-to-day activities. Your children will be your greatest contribution to the world!

HIS WORD
"If any of you lacks wisdom, he should ask God, who gives generously to all without finding fault, and it will be given to him"
(James 1:5).

MY PRAYER
"Father, give me a wise heart as I consider my personal goals and ambitions along with the responsibilities, challenges, and rewards of rearing children. Help me to realize that childrearing requires only about one-third of my life, then I have two-thirds of my life to devote to personal pursuits. In Your merciful name, amen."

MY STUDY
Deuteronomy 32:46,47; Psalm 34:11

Slowing Down

By nature, we are impatient. We rush through life, working hard to accomplish a goal, to move forward, to better our position.

I'm reminded of that every time I land at an airport. I can hardly wait to unbuckle my seat belt. I hurry out of my seat only to stand and wait uncomfortably in the aisle for another five minutes until the door is opened.

We're always in a hurry to get ahead! But I'm convinced that much of the joy in life is found not in finishing or in getting ahead, but in the process of living and growing.

The late Erma Bombeck did so much to make us laugh, to help us see things from another perspective, and to help us realize that life, at times, cannot be taken too seriously.

I remember something she wrote long ago:

> If I had my life to live over again, I would have waxed less and listened more.
>
> Instead of wishing away nine months of pregnancy and complaining about the shadows over my feet, I'd have cherished every minute of it and realized the wonderment growing inside me would be my only chance in life to assist God in a miracle.
>
> I would have cried and laughed less while watching television ... and more while watching life
> ... There would have been more I love yous ... more I'm sorry ... more I'm listening.
>
> But mostly, given another shot at life, I would seize every minute of it ... and never give that minute back until there was nothing left of it.

Life only passes once. We cannot fix the past. We can find forgiveness, certainly, but we cannot change history.

Dear friend, let's live every moment doing good under God's power. You'll have a more joyful life.

HIS WORD

"You have made known to me the path of life; you will fill me with joy in your presence, with eternal pleasures at your right hand" (Psalm 16:11).

MY PRAYER

Are you constantly in a hurry? Friend, slow down. Take time to enjoy the process of living and growing in your faith. "Lord, remind me to take time to see the beauty of Your creation and to take time to love those who are dear to me."

MY STUDY

Ecclesiastes 3:1–8; Romans 14:17,18

Issues of the Heart

The late pastor Ray Stedman told the story of how he worked his way through seminary as a mortuary attendant on the night shift.

Dr. Stedman discovered that the undertakers had special connections with clothing manufacturers. Since they bought large quantities, they were able to buy dark blue funeral suits rather inexpensively.

Just beginning his preaching career, Dr. Stedman needed a new suit. So he asked the owners of the mortuary if he could buy a suit from them for himself. They agreed, and he was fitted for one. He soared with enthusiasm. He thought he'd gotten a real bargain!

Well, the next Sunday morning he put on his new suit. He brushed down the pleat of the pants, then the sleeves of the coat. He looked proudly into the mirror.

When he picked up his wallet and keys, his pride quickly turned to dismay. He searched in vain for a place to put them. This wonderful, handsome new suit had *no pockets*! The suit was made for a dead man, a man who didn't need pockets!

That's pretty funny, but it's true. I once heard someone say, "I never saw a hearse pulling a U-Haul."

Even though we know that things are temporary, our lives are consumed at times with accumulating them. Our attention gets focused on some possession we want to acquire. Aren't there times you find yourself thinking, *I have to have that purse, those draperies, that food processor, that dress?* Those *things* seem so important, more important than they are.

Friend, things don't last forever, and in the long run, they don't satisfy. Issues of the heart are what really matter.

Are you investing your time, energy, and money in what will last forever? You are when you read God's Word, enjoy fellowship with Christian friends, or reach out to nonbelievers. You are when you serve. These are eternal investments. What lasts for eternity is what's in the heart, not the pocket.

HIS WORD

"Seek first his kingdom and his righteousness, and all these things will be given to you as well" (Matthew 6:33).

MY PRAYER

"Heavenly Father, please forgive me for placing my pursuit of possessions before my pursuit of You. I want You alone to be the focus of my life. I want to invest myself completely in Your will, to serve You. In Jesus' righteous name, amen."

MY STUDY

Psalm 86:11; Jeremiah 24:7

The Elevator

When stepping into an elevator, I'm always amazed at how silent things become. Aren't you?

You step into that little cubicle with several people, and when the door glides shut, there's a synchronized code of silence. Everyone turns to face the doors and looks up to watch the lighted numbers change.

No one moves! No one seems to breathe. It's a rare moment when someone shares a genuine greeting and exchange inside an elevator.

This experience is a snapshot of American life. The closer we get to one another, the more silent many people become. The more heated and controversial the issues, the more discrete Christians become – not wanting to draw any personal attention.

This concerns me. Nothing will kill the impact of Christian influence more than apathy and silence!

Dr. Philip Zimbardo, a professor of psychology, wrote an article for *Psychology Today* called "The Age of Indifference." He said this: "I know of no more potent killer than isolation. There is no more destructive influence on physical and mental health than the isolation of you from me and of us from them ... The devil's strategy for our times is to trivialize human existence in a number of ways: by isolating us from one another while creating the delusion that the reasons are time pressures, work demands, or anxieties."

My friend, I wonder if you've begun to buy into the lie. Have you become isolated in your perspective on social concerns, whether they are local or national? Have you grown dependent on others to express your viewpoints?

Please know how critical it is for you to remain engaged, involved, and outspoken in your Christian views! Those who do not believe in your values are vocal and are influencing others to their way of thinking. Freedoms are meaningless unless we exercise them.

Be a light to a dark world.

HIS WORD

"When the righteous thrive, the people rejoice; when the wicked rule, the people groan" (Proverbs 29:2).

MY PRAYER

Are you informed about current events that affect you and your fellow citizens? You can become involved in social issues through various organizations, share your views with your government representatives, and fast and pray with other concerned Christians.

MY STUDY

Isaiah 33:5,6; Acts 17:26–28

How we spend our time says so much about us. It says, *This is where my heart is. This is what's important to me.*

In her mid-twenties, Sarah Dunn Clarke spent many hours on an "elaborate" decoration for her house. When it was finished, this question penetrated her heart: *What are you doing to decorate your heavenly home?* That question changed the course of her life.

She began to understand the sacred value of time and how she was spending God's precious time on things that wouldn't last. He began to show Sarah it was the *souls* of men and women that were important.

A few years later, Sarah moved to Chicago. One day while preparing for yet another social event, she said "no." Instead, she put on casual clothes and began visiting poor and needy families.

She wrote this: "In ministering to their needs I found such real soul satisfaction – such a consciousness of God's approval – that I was at once convinced my mission in life had been revealed."

That was in the mid-1800s, Civil War days. Times were desperate. Sarah and a few others founded a mission Sunday school, a little haven where children could be children. She lovingly taught them about Jesus Christ and His love.

In her late thirties, Sarah married a businessman in real estate. He didn't share her passion to reach the poor and needy. But some years later, God changed his heart. He and Sarah began the Pacific Garden Mission, which continues to reach the homeless and poor.

Ask yourself, *Where am I spending my time? Is it counting for eternity?* Then, ask God to make your time count for Him.

Like George and Sarah Clarke, you can make a difference in people's lives. A difference that leads others to Him and gives you "real soul satisfaction."

HIS WORD

"Command them to do good, to be rich in good deeds, and to be generous and willing to share. In this way they will lay up treasure for themselves as a firm foundation for the coming age, so that they may take hold of the life that is truly life" (1 Timothy 6:18,19).

MY PRAYER

Do you want "real soul satisfaction"? Make this commitment: "Compassionate Father, I am willing to spend my life doing Your will and making a difference in people's lives. I choose the souls of men over the pleasures of this world. In Jesus' name, amen."

MY STUDY

1 Samuel 12:24; Proverbs 27:1

Life to the Full

While waiting for a friend at a bookstore café, Julie faced three temptations. She browsed through the mugs on sale, thinking that a special, new mug would give her a happy, full experience of drinking coffee. But she realized coffee and mugs don't meet her needs. God does.

Next, she saw many secular books and magazines. Reading them would bring her up to date with this ever-changing culture. That would make her more effective in sharing the gospel message with others.

Well, she recognized that wasn't at all true. She didn't need all that information. Besides, she'd always be tempted to read them instead of her Bible.

Julie made this observation: "God gives us what we need in order to influence the people He's placed in our lives. If I don't stay in the Word of God, which is my spiritual food, I will have nothing of lasting substance to offer."

The third temptation came as she watched a young couple in love. A successful relationship might make her happy. That, too, was a lie. She knew that only a relationship with Christ would bring lasting love and fulfillment.

This is the point: There's absolutely nothing wrong with any of these things. What's wrong is that the world tells us we *need* all of these things to have a satisfying and fulfilling life. That is not true.

Jesus said, "I have come that they may have life, and have it to the full" (John 10:10).

He is our example. When He faced forty days of temptation by Satan, Jesus chose not to sin, but rather to quote Scripture. Don't believe the lies that the world tells you. Friend, knowing Jesus, praying, and memorizing Scripture are your best weapons against temptation and the only way to have true fulfillment.

HIS WORD

"Submit yourselves, then, to God. Resist the devil, and he will flee from you. Come near to God and he will come near to you" (James 4:7,8).

MY PRAYER

Begin memorizing the truths of God's Word today. When you're tempted, go to God immediately. Quote the verses you have memorized (a good one is 1 Corinthians 10:13). If possible, leave the situation that is tempting you. Call a friend. Talk and pray with her until the temptation passes.

MY STUDY

Genesis 3:1–3; Psalm 119:151,152

My friend Luci Swindoll tells the story of learning to tithe. "Tithe" sounds like an old-fashioned word. The Bible talks about bringing our "tithes and offerings" to contribute to the work of God. A tithe is defined as a tenth of one's income.

Luci grew up in a Christian home. Her parents were faithful to tithe their income. When Luci became an adult, she struggled with tithing. She was always generous and wanted to give to the cause of Christ, but she was nervous about committing a full tenth of her income. As a single, independent adult, she was solely responsible for herself. She didn't want to take any chances.

As she got older, she wondered if she was doing the right thing – giving only occasionally when she had extra money or giving only a limited amount. One day she asked her brother, Chuck, what he thought she should do.

Chuck Swindoll said to her, "Oh, Sis, by all means, you should always tithe."

"I'm afraid I'll run out of money," she responded.

"No, Sis," Chuck said, "you'll never run out ... Don't give just ten percent, either. Give more."

"How about eleven?"

"That's great!"

That was many years ago. Luci took Chuck at his word that she'd never run out. Since then she's given an increasing percentage to the work of Christ and other charitable causes. She *delights* in doing this. Not only that, she's never been more financially secure.

God has given us the incomparable privilege of being involved in bringing His love and forgiveness to the entire world. God could certainly come up with other ways to finance the work of His kingdom, but He wants to involve you and me.

If you've never been involved, take it from Luci Swindoll, Chuck, or me. Take it from God Himself. When you tithe, God will bless you.

HIS WORD

"'Bring the whole tithe into the storehouse, that there may be food in my house. Test me in this,' says the LORD Almighty, 'and see if I will not throw open the floodgates of heaven and pour out so much blessing that you will not have room enough for it'" (Malachi 3:10).

MY PRAYER

My friend, do you tithe? It's not about the money; it's about putting God first in every area of your life and trusting that He will provide for your needs. He will prove faithful. Test Him.

MY STUDY

Proverbs 3:9,10; 2 Corinthians 9:6–9

Simplify

Matt and Rhonda had a "typical" middle-class family – nice home and lifestyle, two cars, two children, and two incomes, which meant two parents working full-time.

But life was moving too quickly for them. Their schedule was keeping them from being with their children. Rhonda remembers making every effort to be there for them, but she was struggling to keep it all together. As this family grew in their Christian faith, one idea began to stir in each of their hearts: their family should be a higher priority than a comfortable lifestyle.

In the spring of 1996, Rhonda told Matt she believed God wanted her to be home – immediately. Matt struggled over Rhonda's decision to leave her successful occupational therapy practice. Her job provided sixty-one percent of their income. "We bought into the lie that a family can't make it without two incomes," Matt says.

As Matt left to attend a golf tournament, God worked on his heart. Matt sensed God assuring him that if he trusted Him with this matter, He'd provide. So Matt told Rhonda it was okay to leave her job. He said that with God's help, they were going to make it on one income.

The decisions they made were difficult, but Matt and Rhonda couldn't be happier. They now encourage others to follow God's plan. They have lived on both sides of the fence, and there's no question that they are where God wants them.

Oh dear friend, I'm so encouraged by their willingness to make lifestyle changes to simplify their lives. I'm even more encouraged that they listened to what God was telling them and obeyed.

What's right for one family is not necessarily right for another, but what's important is letting God set your priorities. Let Him provide the plan and the pattern for you. Ask Him and He'll show you. You can be sure of that!

HIS WORD
"Better one handful with tranquillity than two handfuls with toil and chasing after the wind"
(Ecclesiastes 4:6).

MY PRAYER
"All-knowing heavenly Father, forgive me for setting my own agenda. I want You alone to guide the priorities of my life. Give me wisdom to discern Your will in all I do. In Your Son's precious name, Amen."

MY STUDY
Psalm 119:73; 1 Thessalonians 4:11,12

Welcome Back

As a child, Dwayne placed his trust in Christ. "As I grew older, if anyone had asked me, I would've proclaimed that I loved the Lord, and that He was the most important person in my life," Dwayne said.

But something happened to Dwayne that happens to many Christians. It subtly robs Christians of their joy and a vibrant walk with God.

Dwayne said, "Over the years, in very subtle ways, other people and things had become more important to me than my relationship with Jesus Christ. Christianity has always been a part of me, but not *all* of me."

Dwayne gradually put school, women, career, money, and other activities ahead of God. As he did, his relationship with God suffered.

Later, a restless gnawing on his conscience developed. Dwayne tried to keep God in his family by taking them to church and leading them in prayers. But he was doing little more than just going through the motions.

A friend told Dwayne that he was living what some call a "carnal" life. In other words, Dwayne had placed his trust in Christ, but he wasn't living like it. He was living his life his way, not as God would have him live it. Dwayne began to get the picture.

Driving home after that conversation, Dwayne stopped his car, bowed his head, confessed his sin, and asked God to forgive him. Then He invited Christ, in the power of the Holy Spirit, to resume control of his life. God answered, and Dwayne became a changed man.

Friend, many of us wander away from God. One step at a time, we walk away. But God said in His Word that He will *never* leave us. He waits patiently and quietly for us to return. When we do, He forgives us and lovingly welcomes us back.

HIS WORD
"I the LORD do not change ... Return to me, and I will return to you" (Malachi 3:6,7).

MY PRAYER
"Dear Father, I need You. I acknowledge that I've been directing my own life. As a result, I've sinned against You. Thank You for forgiving my sin. I now invite You to direct my life. Fill me with Your Holy Spirit. Help me to walk in His power. As an expression of my faith, I thank You. In Jesus' name, amen."

MY STUDY
Psalm 80:3; 1 Peter 2:25

Let Them Go

A missionary had a great and immediate need for a large sum of money. The letter expressing the need was read aloud at a luncheon for Christian women. The president of the organization asked the guest speaker to lead in prayer, asking God to provide the funds.

To her surprise, the speaker said, "No, I won't pray for God to meet the needs of this missionary. But I'll tell you what I will do. I'll give every dime of cash I have in my pockets and place it on the table. I'm asking each of you to do the same. If we don't have four thousand dollars, then I'll pray for God to meet their needs ... I challenge you to give what you have now. No credit cards, no checks."

Then he took all of his cash out of his wallet and pockets, and placed it on the table. Though a bit reluctant, three hundred luncheon guests followed suit. Wallets and purses were opened and emptied. When the cash was counted, it was well above four thousand dollars.

Then the speaker said, "You see, we didn't need to pray that God would provide the resources. They were already there. *We just had to let them go.*"

Isn't that true? Many times we hear about the needs of missionaries or families in our churches and neighborhoods. We say we'll pray for God to provide. But what we really need to do is ask God to help us let go of our own wallets, our own resources.

When three hundred people gave what they had, it was more than enough to cover the great need. That's the way God works.

The next time you hear of a need, consider your resources and how you can help. Ask God to help you know what to do. Then do it. You'll be a blessing to others and glorify God.

HIS WORD
"Just as you excel in everything — in faith, in speech, in knowledge, in complete earnestness and in your love for us — see that you also excel in this grace of giving" (2 Corinthians 8:7).

MY PRAYER
"Great Provider God, You have blessed my life abundantly, materially, and spiritually. I know that it isn't the amount that is important, but the heart of the giver that matters to you. Help me to give willingly and cheerfully. In Your Son's holy name, amen."

MY STUDY
Proverbs 11:24,25; Jeremiah 22:16

Nancy heard the tour guide say, "On Tuesday morning we're going to the leper colony." Fear gripped her heart. *No way!* she thought. She'd signed up for a short-term mission trip to West Africa, but nowhere on the schedule had she read "leper colony." She was terrified.

As the team was preparing to leave for the leper colony, she felt a little embarrassed, even silly, for not going. But she also felt safer, more secure, and less afraid by staying put. Then the missionary said he didn't know if these lepers had ever heard the gospel.

Suddenly, Paul's words in Acts 20:24 gripped her heart: "I consider my life worth nothing to me, if only I may finish the race and complete the task the Lord Jesus has given me – the task of testifying to the gospel of God's grace."

In that instant, God showed Nancy that there is something greater than her own personal safety. If she held her life dear to herself, she would never finish the course and the ministry God had for her. That ministry, she believed, was to declare the gospel of the grace of God. Suddenly she felt compelled to join the group.

That morning, through an interpreter, she shared the gospel with a small group of lepers. God met with them in a special way and almost all received Christ. Nancy was thrilled to participate in what God was doing. And to think, she almost missed out on that joyous occasion because she was afraid!

Since that mission trip, Nancy has faced fear and insecurity, but she's held God's hand and kept going, reaping great rewards and joy. She's experienced the power of God's grace. She says, "When life comes down to the bottom line, I want mine to have counted for all eternity."

Dear friend, you can make your race count for eternity.

HIS WORD

"This is what the Lord has commanded us: 'I have made you a light for the Gentiles, that you may bring salvation to the ends of the earth'" (Acts 13:47).

MY PRAYER

Oh dear friend, don't be content with your own salvation. Be willing to take the gospel message to others. Start by praying for one person you can talk with about Christ. Read through an evangelistic booklet with them. Help them understand how to put their faith in Jesus Christ. Sharing Him with others will change your life. And their eternity.

MY STUDY

Psalm 97:11,12; Isaiah 51:4–6

As the Deer

In Psalm 42, it says, "As the deer pants for streams of water, so my soul pants for you, O God. My soul thirsts for God, for the living God" (vv. 1,2).

The psalmist, inspired by God, compares himself to a beautiful and swift deer, which can sprint through the forest. But deer tire quickly and need to be refreshed with water throughout the day. He didn't compare himself with a camel, which is slow and walks through the desert for days without water.

We take time during the day to *physically* refresh our bodies with food and water, with exercise and sleep. But we need spiritual refreshing as well. Because God has fashioned us to be like deer, we need to have this time of renewal, not only daily, but many times throughout the day.

What seems to be depleting your spiritual resources? You want to be an attentive, ever-present parent. You want to be a loving, supportive wife. You want to be a faithful, efficient employee. You want to be a loyal, caring friend. There are so many areas that demand your time and energy. It is very easy to suddenly find yourself exhausted – physically, emotionally, and spiritually.

How do we get refreshed spiritually? By talking with God and reading His Word. The Bible gives us a simple, yet life-changing direction in 1 Thessalonians 5:17: "Pray continually." This verse instructs us to keep an open line of communication with God. God gives us wisdom to deal with each situation we encounter throughout the day. He guides us with His Spirit.

Spending time in God's Word is also important. Deuteronomy 8:3 tells us, "Man does not live on bread alone but on every word that comes from the mouth of the Lord." The Bible is God's unchanging Word to His creation. It gives us spiritual nourishment to feed our hungry soul.

Seek God daily. He'll refresh you as nothing else can.

HIS WORD

"Jesus declared, 'I am the bread of life. He who comes to me will never go hungry, and he who believes in me will never be thirsty'" (John 6:35).

MY PRAYER

Take time out of your busy schedule to be alone with God. Let those around you know how important and necessary this time is. Do all that you can to always keep your day's most important appointment. God will give you the energy you need to face the day.

MY STUDY

Psalm 63:1; Isaiah 26:8

True Value

I once heard a story of two pranksters who played a trick on a store manager. They decided to switch the price tags on various items displayed on the shelves.

After hours, they lurked down each of the aisles. Before long, mink coats carried tags of $5 and cotton blouses were $3,500. Tuxedos were $2.50 and men's neckties were $900.

After the store opened the next morning, it wasn't long before customers filled the check-out lines. Predictably, the manager found no humor in this prank and hurried to make things right.

This incident illustrates a reality in life. It's easy for us to devalue those things that are of tremendous worth while squandering our time, energy, and money on things that are of relatively little value.

We overlook the treasure of those people we hold dear and invest instead in bigger cars, better technology, and more possessions.

Let me ask you: Has someone played a trick on you? Are you allowing the price tags to be switched on the very things you hold most dear? What are you trading for these valuables today?

What about those things you can live without, possessions that come and go, that rust and wear out? Are they treated like they are your real treasures? Don't be deceived. We all fall into this trap and need to be reminded to put first things first.

Do you know what will help you more than anything else to keep your priorities in order? Nothing will keep you on track any more than a consistent walk with God – filled daily with His Spirit.

Viewing the world through Spirit-filled eyes will allow you to know the true value of the things around you. Then you won't be fooled when you are tempted to switch the price tags.

HIS WORD

"Wisdom is more precious than rubies, and nothing you desire can compare with her" (Proverbs 8:11).

MY PRAYER

Dear friend, stop, look around you, and listen. What would you miss the most if it were taken from you? Make a list of those things you would define as valuable. Are the things of eternity high on your list? Regularly review this list to remind yourself of what's truly important.

MY STUDY

Ecclesiastes 2:26; 1 Peter 2:4–6

Treasures in Heaven

The cold Chicago Sunday began as it always had for the Mokry family. Ace and Marj went to church, then prepared for a relaxing afternoon with their family. After lunch, they enjoyed a lazy afternoon, sitting in front of the warm hearth, occasionally stoking the fire.

Then someone thought they smelled smoke. Ace headed for the garage, thinking he ought to at least check out the concern. When he opened the door, a huge fireball surged over his head. Billows of thick smoke were sucked into the house.

Everyone needed to get out – fast! Within seconds, flames engulfed the house, turning their afternoon of delight into an inferno of disaster.

The fire engines quickly arrived, but it was too late. From the front lawn, Ace and Marj watched a lifetime of dreams and memories be destroyed.

Dear friend, it may not be a fire on a quiet Sunday afternoon or the loss of your earthly possessions. But every family will confront times of difficulty, times when flames of destruction will come through the back door – a complete surprise.

God never promises life will be without difficulty. That's why it's essential to be grounded in His Word and in touch with what's most important to Him. Only then can we know the kind of peace the Mokrys felt when the fire struck their home. Their earthly treasures were gone, but they had an overwhelming sense that what mattered most to them could not be destroyed. Their treasure is in heaven.

The Mokry family had built their lives on the trustworthiness of God and His Word. Nothing in this world could take that away. Not only did they survive, but God and His Word gave them peace.

God can do the same thing for you. What family crisis are you facing right now? Keep your eyes focused on God.

HIS WORD

"The earth is the LORD's, and everything in it, the world, and all who live in it" (Psalm 24:1).

MY PRAYER

Perhaps you will encounter disease, financial disaster, or an enemy threatening the welfare of your family. Make it a practice to talk about the goodness of God to your family and recount specific ways you have experienced His guidance and protection. Encourage your family to openly express their awareness of God's trustworthiness. Recognizing Him in the little things prepares us to see Him when major struggles occur.

MY STUDY Isaiah 45:6,7; Philippians 4:11–13

Have you ever had something happen in your life that put everything in perspective for you? Judy did. Here is her story.

It was a busy, yet exciting time. Judy was preparing for a relaxing vacation on a cruise ship. As she checked off her long "to do" list, the phone rang. Her husband and two sons had been in a terrible car accident.

Her boys were going to be alright, but her husband had been very seriously hurt. He suffered twenty-two broken bones, and for a while the doctors weren't sure he would live. Thankfully, he did survive and in time recovered fully.

Since the accident, Judy has often thought about how simple she used to think her life was. Now, she was discovering simplicity had new meaning. When life had suddenly become a question of survival, few things seemed truly important. All the peripheral issues that she was concerned about from day to day became insignificant.

So what did Judy discover was *truly* important to her? Four things: the Lord, His Word, His people, and the precious time she had with her family. Everything else fell way down on the list.

In Matthew 22:37–39, Jesus tells us what He considers to be truly important: "Love the Lord your God with all your heart and with all your soul and with all your mind ... Love your neighbor as yourself." Loving God first and then loving others are the two greatest commandments that He gave us. These are simple commands that, if followed, will have a profound impact on your life and the world around you.

Friend, what's important to you? Does your lifestyle reflect this perspective? Don't wait for something catastrophic to happen to start living the way God wants you to live. Don't be burdened with the cares of this world, but be set free because of the great love God has shown you for all eternity. Start right now.

HIS WORD

"Whom have I in heaven but you? And earth has nothing I desire besides you" (Psalm 73:25).

MY PRAYER

"Heavenly Father, the one true God, thank You for Your unconditional love for me; for Your Word given for my benefit; for Your people who inspire and support me; and for the family You have given me to love and care for. In Jesus' wonderful name, amen."

MY STUDY

Deuteronomy 30:6; 1 Corinthians 8:6

Sacrifice

Diagnosed with breast cancer, Jane declined chemotherapy to treat it. It would have harmed her unborn child. She also declined a doctor's suggestion of abortion.

Baby Jessica was born healthy. But two years later, Jane tragically lost her battle with cancer. She left behind her husband, Todd, and two dear children.

Todd wrote, "Scripture says 'greater love has no one than this, that he lay down his life for his friends.' And Jane courageously showed us that type of love by giving up her life for our daughter — a sacrificial act of obedience to God and His Word, done with joy, peace, and contentment."

What a sad, but incredibly special story! Jane is a perfect example of the kind of love Jesus often spoke of — unconditional, sacrificial love. Jesus demonstrated His love for us when He suffered and died on the cross for our sin.

Oh, friend, we may never have to die for another. But God does call us to daily give up our lives, our selfish desires — willingly, obediently, even joyfully. In Luke 9:23, Jesus tells us, "If anyone would come after me, he must deny himself and take up his cross daily and follow me."

Sometimes denying ourselves means not taking the easy way out. Let's look at Jane's example again. If she were thinking only of herself, she would have had the chemotherapy or the abortion. Her life could have gone on for many more years. But Jane knew that God did not want her to do those things because the resulting death would have been against His law. Instead, she placed her trust in Him. Even though she didn't know how things were going to turn out, she followed Him. Today, her daughter is alive with a loving family. And Jane is with Jesus for all eternity.

Are you willing to take up your cross daily and follow Him *wherever He leads?*

HIS WORD

"Whoever wants to save his life will lose it, but whoever loses his life for me will save it" (Luke 9:24).

MY PRAYER

Many times throughout our lifetime, we are faced with difficult decisions. But we have a guidebook and a Counselor to help us. When we follow God's commands, we will always come out better. Next time you have a big decision, seek instruction through His Word and prayer.

MY STUDY

Proverbs 7:1–3; Isaiah 25:8

We women often spend a lot of time on our appearance. There's nothing inherently wrong with that or with wanting to represent God well. Appearances do make a difference! But the beauty that God cares more about is on the inside.

Besides the many general principles in the Bible that can be applied to both men and women, Proverbs 31 speaks specifically to us women. It describes the kind of woman we should all strive to be:

> She is worth far more than rubies. Her husband has full confidence in her ... She sets about her work vigorously ... She opens her arms to the poor ... is clothed with strength and dignity ... speaks with wisdom, and faithful instruction is on her tongue. She watches over the affairs of her household.

Wow! That's quite a list — and there's more to it. Don't be discouraged, friend. God doesn't expect you to fulfill perfectly every single item on that list. It is meant to be a goal to which all women can strive. If you rely on God for guidance in your daily decisions, you will find that many of these items will become less difficult.

Proverbs 31 ends like this: "Charm is deceptive, and beauty is fleeting; but a woman who fears the Lord is to be praised ... Let her works bring her praise" (v. 31). External appearances don't tell the whole truth about someone, and they will fade with time. The qualities that will be praised by God and people are those that come from an intimate, daily walk with Him. Through the Holy Spirit, God will produce in us what we read in Proverbs 31.

Friend, cultivate your relationship with God. Spend time reading His Word and talking with Him. Under His power, seek to exhibit the characteristics of a "Proverbs 31" woman — wisdom, compassion, dignity, and reliability. Then when your outer beauty fades, it won't matter — to you or anyone else.

HIS WORD

"Who is wise and understanding among you? Let him show it by his good life, by deeds done in the humility that comes from wisdom" (James 3:13).

MY PRAYER

Read all of Proverbs 31. Think in practical terms about how these qualities can fit into your life. How can you cultivate them to become more like the Proverbs 31 woman? Remember, this is not something you achieve under your own power but through God's power.

MY STUDY

Job 28:28; Psalm 111:10

Priorities

If you had seven days left to live, what would you do with them? Ramona was asked this question, and it forced her to reevaluate her life. She asked herself: What would I do first? *Straighten out my finances? Organize my desk and photo albums? Or make the most of time with friends and loved ones?*

None of us knows the time at which we will leave this earth. God alone has power over life and death. Even so, it is useful to keep our mortality in focus. Thinking about how short life really is forces us to think about our true priorities.

Contemplating this question, Ramona concluded what her true priorities are. The first was her relationship with Christ. As with close human relationships, it is important to work at maintaining our intimacy with Christ. We maintain closeness through conversation (prayer) and understanding (studying the Bible).

Next, Ramona discovered that serving others was very important. Even though Jesus was God, He demonstrated servanthood when He washed the disciples' feet. They were stunned by this supreme act of humility. In John 13:15 Jesus puts His act in perspective for them. He says, "I have set you an example that you should do as I have done for you." When we serve others we are doing as Jesus would want us to do.

Last, Ramona realized the great value of setting aside times for refreshing. She said, "It's so easy to get caught up in day-to-day duties and miss the joy and true meaning of life."

When we slow down to reconnect with God, we are better able to see the beauty around us. We are better able to hear the still small voice inside us, which is the Holy Spirit guiding and directing.

Friend, you can reset your priorities today. What is truly important to you? Think about it.

HIS WORD
"Teach us to number our days aright, that we may gain a heart of wisdom" (Psalm 90:12).

MY PRAYER
"Father, am I spending my time to the greatest advantage? Show me what's most important to You. I ask Your guidance to help me rearrange my schedule today to reflect Your will and my true priorities. Remind me to do this every day, to live a life sold out to You, a life that will bring the greatest satisfaction, peace, and joy."

MY STUDY
Ecclesiastes 8:5,6; Romans 13:11–14

Thomas Traore is a pastor in West Africa. A passion for evangelism was born in Pastor Traore at *Amsterdam '86*, an international conference sponsored by the Billy Graham Evangelistic Association. What he learned changed his heart, then his church.

Pastor Traore said, "My church has made evangelism its highest priority. When a new Christian joins the church, the first thing we try to teach him is that he is an evangelist, too; that he too should go out and witness and lead people to God."

Becoming a Christian changes your life – for all eternity. What more loving thing could you do for a fellow human being than to introduce that person to the Source of true life?

Not only is it the loving thing do to, God expects us to do it – He commands us to do it. It is called the Great Commission. In Matthew 28:18,19, Jesus said, "All authority in heaven and on earth has been given to me. Therefore go and make disciples of all nations, baptizing them in the name of the Father and of the Son and of the Holy Spirit." So Jesus, as the ultimate authority, has given us a directive.

As we go about our daily lives, we are to keep constantly in our minds the fact that many around us are not yet disciples (followers) of Christ, and will spend eternity away from God. This should motivate us to seek out ways to share the gospel with those we encounter. Don't be intimidated; just share what Christ has done for you and how they can share in this eternal life.

Today, make a list of friends and neighbors who need to know God. Then make it a priority to tell them about God's redeeming love. You can use the information in the back of this book to assist you. You too can help change the world!

HIS WORD
"I will extol the LORD at all times; his praise will always be on my lips"
(Psalm 34:1).

MY PRAYER
"Lord Jesus, my Savior, thank You for Your gift of salvation. I want to help others come to know You. Help me to be sensitive to Your leading, that I may be bold and courageous as I tell them of Your love. In Your holy name, amen."

MY STUDY
1 Chronicles 16:23–25; 2 Peter 3:8,9

Caring for Others

He who refreshes others will himself be refreshed.

PROVERBS 11:25

Being alone is more than a physical reality. A recent study, in which 66 percent of respondents said they were lonely, concluded that this is one of the greatest changes in women's lives from years past. With over half of adult women working outside the home and living in heavily populated urban areas, loneliness seems impossible.

Unlike our mothers who often lived their entire lives in the same town with relatives, we are very mobile. But this mobility leaves us little opportunity to develop relationships that nurture our emotional and spiritual needs.

Every believer has the Holy Spirit as a source of comfort and strength, and complete satisfaction can be found only in a relationship with Jesus. But we also need relationships with others.

Think about your relationships in three categories:

- *Casual:* Acquaintances – You meet these people in social settings on an irregular basis. These are people with whom you can share your faith.
- *Close:* Friends – You see these people on a regular basis, and have the privilege of forming close, personal friendships.
- *Covenant:* Family – Your family members are precious gifts from God and deserve your commitment to their development. Spend time with them and guard them from ungodly influences. Remember: you choose your friends, God chose your family.

The Contract

When Bill and I were newly married, we left our home state of Oklahoma for California. Only a few short weeks after unpacking, we entertained in our new home. Bill had met a businessman who didn't know Christ and invited him and his wife to dinner.

I had much to learn about what God expected for hospitality. The only dishes I had to complete four settings were green glass "oatmeal china." I was elated that my dinner was scheduled on St. Patrick's Day. How appropriate that we had green "china."

We spent the evening sharing our faith with the businessman and his wife. At that time, Bill and I were very inexperienced in how to lead a person to Christ, but the couple was responsive to what we said. I began to understand how to use what we had to bring honor and glory to Christ, and this began an exciting lifelong journey of ministry with Him.

The Lord was preparing our hearts for our second year of marriage, when Bill suggested that we sign a contract with God, totally surrendering our lives to Him. Bill had signed hundreds of contracts as a businessman, so an agreement between the Lord and us seemed reasonable to him.

That contract has formed the basis of our lives and ministry. We surrendered our lives completely and irrevocably to the Lord and to each other. Sharing our faith immediately became a lifestyle.

God is gracious! He places no value on our possessions. He doesn't pressure us to perform, or require us to be sophisticated. Instead, He sees our hearts and understands our needs. Through the power of His Holy Spirit, He uses us where we live to help heal the hurts and broken spirits of those who need His love. Relying on His strength and wisdom, I learned confidence in life sharing.

Have you given everything you are and have to God? That's the greatest decision you can make as a believer. It will set your life on a course far different and more glorious than you ever dreamed.

HIS WORD

"Here is a trustworthy saying: If we died with him, we shall also live with him; if we endure, we shall also reign with him"
(2 Timothy 2:11, 12).

MY PRAYER

Our lives are more than a chronology of events. Turn your life over to God's complete control. Reaffirm your decision daily as you walk with Him.

MY STUDY

Exodus 32:29; Psalm 16:7,8

Soul Mates

Few of us would argue that women tend to be more relational than men. But for busy women these days, sometimes valuable time with friends gets squeezed out.

Do you have a *soul mate*? Is there someone in your life with whom you can share your deepest feelings, fears, and frustrations?

I have heard this description of a best friend. Maybe you'll identify with this:

"There's very little we can't say to each other. Our relationship is based on a sense of trust and years of maturing together. We share the good and the bad. We play together and pray together. And in emotional emergencies, we're there for each other."

Do you have a friend like that?

The Bible contains many examples of this kind of friendship: Elizabeth and Mary, Ruth and Naomi, David and Jonathan. Each of these pairs not only acted as confidantes, but also as spiritual guides and supporters.

I think friendship with other women is more necessary today than ever before. But it can also be more difficult.

In this journey of life, we're called to a variety of responsibilities. For some, this entails being the wife of a husband, the mother of children, or the keeper of a home. For others, it is a call to singleness, a life spent in service to God and to others. To make an impact for Christ, we must work together.

Someone has said that to have friends you have to make yourself friendly. I encourage you to take the next step toward developing a close relationship with at least one other woman.

As with any worthwhile effort, building deep friendships takes an investment of time and a sacrifice of personal desires. The foundation should be spiritual to give an eternal perspective. And the relationship should involve lighthearted fun. A true friend nurtures your soul, as you nurture theirs.

HIS WORD

"Two are better than one, because they have a good return for their work. If one falls down, his friend can help him up"
(Ecclesiastes 4:9,10).

MY PRAYER

Seek to become acquainted with someone you would like to get to know better. Develop a relationship that includes prayer and Bible study and times just to catch up and share what's in your heart. Schedule regular visits with your friends. God often uses the platform of friendship to foster spiritual growth and maturity.

MY STUDY

Proverbs 27:10; Romans 16:3,4

A friend of mine has six children, including two high schoolers, living at home. At times she has felt overwhelmed, as if her parenting responsibilities were about to crash in around her.

In the middle of this difficult and busy time, some younger mothers approached her, asking if she would meet with them once a month. They wanted encouragement and advice about parenting. My friend thought, *Why would they want to come to meet with me, after all the mistakes I've made? What do I have to offer them?*

However, she knew what Titus 2 says about older, godly women influencing younger women, because as a young mother she had been mentored by an older woman. Young women need mentoring and encouragement from more mature women who have walked the same path, even if they too have stumbled a few times along the way.

You may have to do a little prayerful searching for a mentor. Ask God to help you spot someone who's just ahead of your season in life and can counsel you from her experience. Your church family is the best place to start. The main point is to find someone who has established a track record of walking with God.

Take the initiative to ask if you can phone her or meet her for coffee or lunch. Tell her you'll bring the questions – all she needs to do is listen and share with you. Assure her she doesn't even need to know all the answers; all you need is her time and perspective.

If someone happens to ask *you* to take on the role of mentor, don't resist the opportunity. Wives and mothers don't need help from a Superwoman – they need a friend who has walked some distance in their shoes. I'll always be grateful for those women who helped me in my early years as a wife and mother.

HIS WORD

"Apply your heart to instruction and your ears to words of knowledge"
(Proverbs 32:12).

MY PRAYER

Mentoring doesn't have to be a formal meeting or arrangement. It can be a lifestyle situation. It's as simple as spending time with someone you're committed to praying for and encouraging. Keep your eyes open to these rewarding opportunities.

MY STUDY

Ecclesiastes 12:9,10; Titus 2:3–5

Our Advocate

Guilty as charged!" Only Lois and Steve can fully identify with the shock of hearing those words in a court of law. Lois and Steve are Christians, and quite active in their local church. Through a very strange and complex sequence of events, Steve was falsely accused and convicted of murder. He was sentenced to forty years in a maximum-security prison.

We can only imagine the devastation that must have struck their family — not only Lois and their three young children, but the extended family as well.

Lois would not be shaken. Never doubting his innocence for a moment, she stood by her husband throughout the entire ordeal. With three precious children and her whole life ahead, Lois could have left Steve to start over, but she chose to honor the vows of her marriage.

She persisted in her fight to convince authorities that Steve was not guilty as charged. Finally, in a subsequent court case, the truth was exposed. The investigating officers had fabricated their evidence to obtain a quick conviction.

Steve was immediately released from prison to resume his life — after three-and-a-half years behind bars. Today, Steve says that Lois was his life support while he endured the nightmare.

In much the same way, every one of us has been given a life sentence. But, unlike Steve, we are guilty. The charge, of course, is sin. The sentence is an eternity in hell, separated from God and our loved ones.

When the gavel of divine justice slams down in God's courtroom, and the word "guilty" defines our status, that's when Jesus steps forward as our Advocate. He paid the penalty for our sin by dying on our behalf.

It is my hope and prayer today that you will acknowledge His love for you. Although you have been found guilty of sin, He stands by your side, waiting for you to respond to His love and forgiveness.

HIS WORD

"Be imitators of God, therefore, as dearly loved children and live a life of love, just as Christ loved us and gave himself up for us as a fragrant offering and sacrifice to God" (Ephesians 5:1,2).

MY PRAYER

Guilty as charged! Those three words impacted Steve and Lois forever. But in God's courtroom, another word applies: forgiven! If you've never experienced God's complete forgiveness, turn to the back of this book and find out how.

MY STUDY

Nehemiah 9:26,27; Psalm 51:1,2

We've all seen them. Leaning against buildings, waiting by the curb, dressed provocatively – some pitifully young. We often respond with judgment. Or sarcasm. Or even disdain.

Remember when Jesus encountered the prostitute in Simon's home (Luke 7:36–50)? Simon was a prominent Pharisee in the first century.

It was customary for dinner guests to recline around a low table, propped up on their elbows to eat the meal. In this setting, they would often discuss politics and religion. Uninvited neighbors were free to come and listen to the discussions without partaking of the meal.

While the others in the room listened to the conversation, the sinful woman was on a different mission. She had heard about Jesus, and she came to bring him an expensive gift – precious perfume in an alabaster jar.

The Bible tells us that she approached the table behind Jesus, clutching the gift in her hands. She began to weep, and her tears splashed on Jesus' feet. Spontaneously showing her reverence and affection, she attempted to dry His feet with her hair. She kissed His feet, in an act of love and respect, and poured the precious perfume on them.

Can you picture the response? The room became very quiet. Simon was disgusted. The guests were shocked because they knew this woman's reputation. But when Simon grew indignant, Jesus rebuked him.

Jesus responded to the woman's expression of love by saying, "Your sins are forgiven. Your faith has saved you; go in peace."

The woman had given Jesus love. Jesus had given her peace. To Him, she was His priceless creation, made in God's image.

Dear friend, the next time you are in the presence of someone you find unlovely, remember the behavior that Jesus modeled for you.

HIS WORD
"This is my prayer: that your love may abound more and more in knowledge and depth of insight" (Philippians 1:9).

MY PRAYER
"Loving Lord Jesus, Your beautiful example of love and forgiveness is one I want to follow in my life. I want Your indwelling Spirit to guide me daily so I may speak Your love to hurting hearts. In Your precious name, amen."

MY STUDY
Ruth 2:8–13; Psalm 133:1–3

Somebody's Hero

Cartoon heroes are easy to spot. They have flashy costumes, muscles of steel, and booming voices to make their presence known.

Real-life heroes are a bit different. They look like you and me. They get tired, even sick at times. They probably don't recognize themselves as heroes. In fact, it may never even occur to them.

Millions of men, women, and children lost their lives during the holocaust. Throughout this ugly era of world history, many heroes valiantly attempted to rescue the men and women under persecution.

As a young woman, Stephanie hid thirteen Jews in her tiny apartment attic for two years. Her family knew nothing of this, and had she been discovered, it would have cost Stephanie her life.

We all know the heroic acts of Corrie ten Boom who spent years in a concentration camp after she was caught protecting the lives of others.

Who has marked your life in a significant way? Who is your hero?

I immediately think of my mother, Margaret Zachary, a model of stability, commitment, and faith. I also thank God for Henrietta Mears, who inspired both Bill and me to be involved in full-time Christian work.

Have you stopped to realize that you could be someone's hero? Someone in your sphere of influence takes his or her cues from your example. Are you living up to that expectation?

You may never need to risk your life to hide someone in your attic, but you can be sure there are those who look to you as a model of character, integrity, Christian conviction, and faith.

Nothing will make a greater impact on America and the world than women who are sold out to Jesus Christ – leading holy lives of faith, walking daily in the power of the Holy Spirit, and sharing their faith. They are the true heroes of our generation.

HIS WORD

"He has given us this command: Whoever loves God must also love his brother" (1 John 4:21).

MY PRAYER

You may not feel like a hero today, my dear friend, but take another look at that toddler around your knees. Some of the greatest men and women in leadership in this generation pay honor to their mothers as heroes in their lives. You have an important role in your children's lives, as well as in the lives of those around you.

MY STUDY

Proverbs 17:17; Job 29:15,16

A Melting Pot

Every day, men and women leave their native land to live in the United States. They come in pursuit of the American dream.

This migration brings a world of opportunity to our doorstep.

Still, there are sensitive cultural and economic implications when minorities flood a society. Since God has allowed this wide breadth of cultures to join our own, we have the wonderful opportunity of welcoming many of them as brothers and sisters in Christ. We can expose others to biblical truth and share our Christian heritage as never before.

The vast array of cultures in the U.S. also means we find the influence of world religions right next door – Muslims, Hindus, and Buddhists, just to name a few.

I'm afraid that many Christians withdraw from these people. Instead of accepting their cultural influences as a wonderful opportunity, some American believers choose to be isolated, rather than visionary; intolerant, rather than loving.

Wouldn't it be much better if immigrants discovered what made our country so great? Newcomers should be enlightened about our rich Christian heritage and those who founded this nation on biblical principles.

Think about your own neighborhood, your own town. Have you seen the influx of different races and religions? Do their lifestyles irritate you or are you extending God's love to them?

How about going to the home of those new neighbors and welcoming them to the community? Let them know you're glad they're on your street. Build a relationship with them that creates an atmosphere of trust and respect.

Don't hesitate to ask them questions about their cultural traditions. Become a student of their heritage. When you take the time, you will find that right next door is a world of opportunity – opportunity to share the gospel.

HIS WORD

"You will receive power when the Holy Spirit comes on you; and you will be my witnesses in Jerusalem, and in all Judea and Samaria, and to the ends of the earth" (Acts 1:8).

MY PRAYER

Pray for opportunities to share your faith and ask God to give you a spirit of understanding. He will help you know what to say and when to say it. Immigrants you befriend may ask you questions, wanting to know more about your faith. You can tell them about Jesus and what He's done for you.

MY STUDY

Leviticus 19:34; Psalm 146:9

People on the Move

The United States is the most mobile society in the world. No other nation moves from home to home, city to city, or state to state as frequently as we do.

If you live in a neighborhood with a lot of turnover, it may not be unusual for you to see a new family move in and then realize that you didn't take the time to get acquainted with the family that moved out!

After that happened to some friends of ours, they determined not to let it happen again. So when the house across the street had a "Sold" sign on it, they began preparing and praying for their new neighbors. On move-in day, they immediately crossed the street and introduced themselves and their children.

For the next week, they offered to help the newcomers get situated in their new home, providing whatever they could to make it easier — tools, ice, even meals. They gave input about the nearest hardware store, the best grocery store, and the local schools.

Then they introduced the two young children to playmates in the neighborhood.

Finally, they planned a weekend block party for all the neighbors in the cul-de-sac, a time for everyone to get acquainted. The invitation included a map of all the homes on the street with the names of the people who lived in each house.

The barbecue and block party brought all the friends and neighbors together. It provided a wonderful starting point for relationships that continue.

The journey of a lasting friendship starts with one step — a step toward your neighbor's door. This may seem like a small step, but it is much more than that! Dear friend, don't miss out on an opportunity to shine the light of Christ in your neighborhood.

HIS WORD
"Do not withhold good from those who deserve it, when it is in your power to act. Do not say to your neighbor, 'Come back later; I'll give it tomorrow' — when you now have it with you" (Proverbs 3:27,28).

MY PRAYER
"Oh, Father, I confess sometimes it's easier to keep to myself than to break the ice and make new friends. But I cannot keep the message of hope to myself! Lord, show me how to reach out to my neighbors, letting them know that I care and that You care about them."

MY STUDY
Deuteronomy 10:17–19; 1 John 4:7–12

I've never known anyone who lives what they believe like you do." Dianne's supervisor said those words to her on her last day on the job. That led Dianne to reflect on the lessons God taught her at work.

She learned to pray. As a new Christian, she felt inadequate to share her faith. So she prayed for her coworkers daily as she drove to work. She always asked God to give her the opportunity to share about Him.

She also began to speak openly about church activities and Bible studies, and to bring a Christian perspective to office conversations, especially those involving major news stories or local tragedies.

She allowed others to glimpse her life before Christ. When appropriate, she'd tell a story from her former life so others could see God's changing power.

Seeing coworkers through Jesus' eyes was an invaluable lesson. When tempted to avoid someone who irritated her, she made an effort to view that person as someone Jesus loves.

Finally, she learned to not be surprised by rejection. Dianne didn't let those who rejected her message keep her from gently sharing Christ with others who might be more responsive.

On her last day at work, Dianne gave each coworker a book or CD that would point them to Christ. She included a personal note telling them about God's love. She was determined to leave something in their hands that contained the gospel.

In their closing conversation, Dianne's supervisor asked how she became a Christian. For the first time, Dianne gave her full testimony to her supervisor.

Dear friend, what a beautiful example Dianne is of a Christian devoted to living a life for the glory of God and His kingdom. Perhaps you too can use in your life the lessons Dianne has learned.

HIS WORD
"You are my witnesses,'
declares the LORD,
'and my servants whom
I have chosen!'"
(Isaiah 43:10).

MY PRAYER
God will give you opportunities to share. Just ask Him. Pray for the courage to speak up, and pray for each of your coworkers. You don't have to know everything about their lives or how they will respond. God uses willing hearts. He'll use you if you let Him!

MY STUDY
Proverbs 31:26; Matthew 25:34–40

Unconditional Love

I'd like to share with you one of the most heartwarming love stories I've ever heard.

Dr. Ed Wheat, a popular Christian psychologist, wrote this touching account in his book *Love Life for Every Married Couple*.

A man loved his wife tenderly and steadfastly for fifteen years without any reciprocal love on her part. There could be no response because she had developed a brain disease.

At the onset of the disease, she was a pretty, vivacious lady of sixty who looked at least ten years younger. Initially, she experienced intermittent times of confusion. As the disease progressed, she gradually lost all her mental faculties and did not recognize her husband.

For the first five years, he took care of her at home by himself. During that time, he often took her for visits. Although she had no idea where she was, she looked her prettiest, and he proudly displayed her as his wife.

He never made an apology for her; he never indicated that there was anything wrong with what she said.

The time came when the doctors said she had to go into a nursing home for intensive care. She lived in the home for ten years – and he was with her daily, never in any way embarrassed that she was so far out of touch.

This was unconditional love, not in theory, but in practice!

Dr. Wheat concludes the story with this statement: "I can speak of this case with intimate knowledge, for these people were my own wonderful parents."

Are you trying to change someone to make him or her more lovable? The solution lies not in changing your loved one, but in changing the way you love! You must learn to love by Christ's example – unconditionally.

HIS WORD

"My command is this: Love each other as I have loved you. Greater love has no one than this, that he lay down his life for his friends" (John 15:12,13).

MY PRAYER

Become a reflection of God's love in your home, at your work, in your neighborhood, and in your community. When you choose to love unconditionally, you will become a model of God's love to a dying world.

MY STUDY

Proverbs 9:9; Isaiah 63:7

It wasn't a huge argument, just silly, angry words. But it hurt. Her husband's last remark before he left for work prompted something ugly inside her to retaliate, insult for insult. She couldn't erase the incident or her anger from her mind.

Later, her son sat on the kitchen floor, writing on something. The sound of the soft scratching floated in the air: *Scribble. Scribble … swish*. Sue stepped around him, busy with dinner and nursing her grudge. She found her attention focusing on the peculiar pattern of sound her son made: *Scribble. Scribble … swish*. Finally, Sue paused and looked down at him.

Her son's hand clutched a stubby piece of chalk as he scribbled on a slate. Then in one quick movement, he swished the eraser across it. The scribble marks disappeared.

Sue discovered a hidden lesson. Husbands and wives are human. They have moments of failure, scribbling on one another's lives, leaving dark, ugly words – ones that mar and wound. The work of forgiveness makes the scribble vanish, erases the wrong, and remembers it no more.

"Lord," Sue prayed right then, "I've been so wrong to cling to this small, scribbled slate of wrong done to me. With Your help, I erase it now, wiping away every mark placed there. It's forgiven." *Swish*. The sound of forgiveness seemed to echo in her heart. And it was done without a moment to spare. Just home from work, Sue's husband breezed through the door. His look was more uncertain than angry. "About this morning," he began, looking at the floor and then at her. "I'm sor ..."

"Oh, I'm sorry too!" she exclaimed without hesitation. As they embraced in the kitchen, all was silent except for a faint and magical swish somewhere in the room.

HIS WORD

"Bear with each other and forgive whatever grievances you may have against one another. Forgive as the Lord forgave you. And over all these virtues put on love, which binds them all together in perfect unity" (Colossians 3:13,14).

MY PRAYER

Forgiveness is not optional, no matter how large or small the offense. Christ has forgiven us, so we must also forgive others. Using your Bible concordance, look up all the references on forgiveness. God has the power to forgive. His power is there for you. By His Spirit, you can forgive others.

MY STUDY Genesis 45:1–15; Proverbs 27:9

Why Am I Still Lonely?

A friend of mine was going through a rough time after moving to a new place. She expected it to take a while to make some new friends — but not *two years!*

Surrounded by people every day at work, she still felt lonely and isolated.

I was proud of my friend for asking painfully honest questions. She wondered, *If God is such a great companion, why do I still feel so lonely?* I'm glad to say that her honesty led to a discovery.

At first, she concluded it was a spiritual problem. So she began to spend more time with God in prayer. Finally, she realized it was people — God's people — she needed.

As Christians, we really do need each other! Consider Adam. Isn't it interesting that Adam had it all — including a perfect relationship with God — and still, he had a need for companionship? God provided Eve, his helper.

God made each of us with a need to connect — a need to have a relationship, first with Him and then with other people.

Christ is all-sufficient and meets all of our needs in many different ways. One of His favorite tools is another believer — someone to distribute love and grace.

You may live in the most populated area in the country, surrounded by people. Yet there's an emptiness in your life.

Don't immediately assume that there's something wrong in your relationship with God. He created you to need people in your life.

Let me encourage you to take the initiative. Be a friend. Connect with another person. Even if you're not feeling friendly right now, someone around you is. Take time to ask that person questions. Your interest will not only help your friend, but will also alleviate your loneliness.

The scriptural principal works!

HIS WORD
"Be devoted to one another in brotherly love. Honor one another above yourselves" (Romans 12:10).

MY PRAYER
Learn how to love. Loving others, as an expression of your faith, is often the greatest cure for feeling lonely. First, seek out new people to get to know. Then, start talking to them; find out about their lives; and tell them about yours. Before you know it, you will have a new connection.

MY STUDY
1 Samuel 18:1–4; Proverbs 10:12

Are You Listening?

Some call *listening* the work of genuine love.

Have you ever thought about how others perceive your ability to listen? You may be listening to every word, but if the person speaking doesn't know you are listening, they may feel ignored or even rejected.

A friend tells about a little boy in her Sunday school who held onto her leg and chattered away while she was trying to greet parents and students at the classroom door. Finally, in total exasperation, he raised his voice and said, "Teacher, you are not listening to me!"

The teacher stooped down to him and said, "Yes, I am listening."

The little boy responded, "Not with your eyes."

Someone observed that God created us with two ears and one mouth so we should listen twice as much as we talk. Maybe we should also remember that we have two eyes. Those eyes making contact with someone can establish the fact that we are indeed listening.

Listening involves more than just hearing the words spoken. Think about listening to a hymn or praise song. Really hearing the lyrics impacts our emotions and evokes an attitude of worship. In the same way, really listening to someone communicates respect. We signal that we are taking in everything they are saying and are giving them our undivided attention.

The following items show the importance of listening:

- The Bible says listening to God and wise counselors shows true wisdom.
- Surveys show children who listen well do better in school.
- Listening enhances relationships and increases success.
- The Book of Proverbs is full of admonitions to "listen," "hearken," "hear," "attend," and "give ear to."

Be a good listener. It takes work but shows genuine love and true biblical wisdom.

HIS WORD

"Let the wise listen and add to their learning, and let the discerning get guidance" (Proverbs 1:5).

MY PRAYER

Ask God to help you be a good listener. You can practice listening. First, stop what you're doing. Second, focus your undivided attention by looking the other person in the eyes. Third, ask a question to clarify. Fourth, rephrase what you've heard. That shows you've listened.

MY STUDY

Ecclesiastes 9:16; Mark 9:7,8

'Til Death Do Us Part

One of my favorite women in the Bible is Ruth. She was an incredible lady and a committed friend. The main character in the Book of Ruth is Naomi. Naomi, her husband, and her two sons moved to another country to escape a severe famine. Over the next ten years, Naomi's two sons married foreign women, Orpah and Ruth.

All was going well until tragedy struck. Naomi's husband died, as well as their two sons.

As a widow with no one to support her, Naomi decided to return to her hometown. She didn't expect her two daughters-in-law to go with her. They would be foreigners, and she could promise them only a life of poverty and prejudice.

That's when Ruth made her incredible statement:

> Don't urge me to leave you or to turn back from you. Where you go I will go, and where you stay I will stay. Your people will be my people and your God my God. Where you die I will die, and there I will be buried. May the Lord deal with me, be it ever so severely, if anything but death separates you and me (Ruth 1:16,17).

What a friend! Consider five very quick lessons about the benefits of committed relationships.

First, committed friends enable us to give and receive love.

Second, committed relationships foster a secure identity. Ruth and Naomi enjoyed a sense of belonging to each other.

Third, committed relationships provide physical protection and material needs.

Fourth, committed relationships have the potential of providing the deepest fulfillment of which we're capable. This happens when each person wants to do what is best for the other.

Committed relationships help us grasp God's commitment to us.

HIS WORD
"A friend loves at all times, and a brother is born for adversity" (Proverbs 17:17).

MY PRAYER
"Loving heavenly Father, thank You for Your unconditional love, even with all of my imperfections. Help me to show Your love to those around me. Help me to be a good friend to those closest to me. I want to be a walking example of Your infinite love to the world. Amen."

MY STUDY
Malachi 3:16; Acts 2:46,47

When Barry and Nancy married, they weren't believers. But Nancy's coworkers were, and they lived a beautiful Christian example before her and answered her many questions. Then one day Nancy simply prayed, "Jesus save me."

That prayer changed her life and launched Nancy into a new adventure. Unfortunately, the excitement of the spiritual adventure for Nancy caused her marriage to suffer. For the first year, she lived out a daily campaign to push her faith on Barry. She preached and left open Bibles around the house.

Nancy's behavior was destroying her marriage. Barry wanted his "old" wife back.

A Christian coworker gave Nancy a book about prayer. That book opened Nancy's eyes to what her responsibility was toward her husband. She simply had to trust God to reach Barry's heart. She read and reread the book, putting into practice what she learned. She prayed for Barry, loved him, and was available to discuss spiritual matters. She was careful to let Barry initiate the questions and did not try to go beyond his interest level. Nancy accepted the fact that only the Holy Spirit could convict Barry and bring him to a point of accepting Christ. Her responsibility was to live a godly life and love Barry as her husband.

After twenty-one years, she's still loving Barry and praying he'll someday trust Christ.

It's so difficult to understand how a mate could resist the desire to accept Christ as Savior when an example of His love and grace is being lived out in the home every day. I certainly don't know how to explain it. But I do know that many, many times an unbeliever accepts Christ as a result of the influence of his spouse. No matter what the situation, trusting God is the only option. He alone can change a heart.

HIS WORD
"Be strong in the Lord and in his mighty power" (Ephesians 6:10).

MY PRAYER
Are there people close to you who don't know Christ? Perhaps a spouse, a parent, a brother or sister, or maybe a friend. The best thing you can do for them is to love them with the love Christ has given you, pray for them, and be ready — when the time comes — to share Christ with them.

MY STUDY
Proverbs 18:10; Isaiah 8:17

Living Your Christian Faith

Melissa was judgmental, constantly belittling Suzy's faith. Melissa and Suzy had been neighbors for years, and their children spent a lot of time playing together. The children frequently would repeat a comment that Melissa had made about Suzy's beliefs. Suzy's heart would ache. The children didn't understand the deep meaning of what was going on, and Melissa's children were nice friends.

Many nights Suzy would pray, "God, bring someone else to minister to her!" But the Lord always responded that He could help her love Melissa. She knew that if they had a major philosophical disagreement or an open debate about religion, it would have made things worse.

Suzy knew that she must live a consistent and faithful life before Melissa. When the family drove off for church on Sunday, Suzy would always wave or shout out the window, "Have a nice day."

Suzy realized that if she couldn't win Melissa, at least she could share her faith with the children. Melissa did allow her children to go to Vacation Bible School with Suzy's children, and they had a great time. One of them accepted Christ as Savior and began attending church regularly.

When a "For Sale" sign went up in Melissa's yard, Suzy was surprised. The house sold quickly, and Suzy offered to help Melissa pack. As they packed things for the movers, Suzy picked up an old family Bible. Melissa explained that it had belonged to her grandmother. Suzy told Melissa that no matter where she lived, if she ever wanted to talk about spiritual things, Suzy would be available.

Melissa's reply was encouraging: "Suzy, I've watched you, and you really live your Christian faith. I'm beginning to think more about it."

A life led in obedience to Christ is the best witness you can give of Christ's love.

HIS WORD

"You yourselves are our letter, written on our hearts, known and read by everybody" (2 Corinthians 3:2).

MY PRAYER

"Dear Father, sometimes a daily witness is more difficult than just telling someone what it means to be a Christian. Please, dear Father, let my life reflect the love of Jesus enough to penetrate the heart of even a difficult person. I ask Your help to keep my attitudes what they should be to honor You. In Jesus' holy name, amen."

MY STUDY

2 Chronicles 31:20,21; Psalm 34:11,12

Beyond Appearances

The first time I received a letter from Linda, she asked for my suggestions on helping high school students improve the moral fiber of their community. She was a teacher who worked closely with teenagers. After that, Linda wrote regularly to tell me about her work and the exciting opportunities she had to see many students come to know Christ.

I heard from Linda for three years, then learned she had volunteered to care for the children during a Campus Crusade Staff Training. I eagerly anticipated meeting her. After talking with Linda and arranging a time for us to meet, a friend said, "Linda doesn't think you'll like her after you see her." I realized from her comment that Linda had a physical handicap or deformity.

Later that week we were introduced. As she talked, she anchored her elbow in one hand to hold her chin steady as she tried to speak coherently. It was a joyful experience for both of us as we talked briefly. As she turned to leave, I recognized the spastic condition of her frail body. Seldom have I been more moved than I was after meeting Linda.

What gave this woman the purpose and radiance she obviously experienced? What motivated her to strive for fulfillment and accomplishment? I knew that Linda would answer those questions without hesitation: Jesus Christ had given her real life.

Can Jesus really affect the way in which Linda and others live their daily lives? Should there be any noticeable difference between the person who believes in Christ and the one who doesn't?

The Bible indicates that knowing Christ is the most exciting adventure the human mind can comprehend. This adventure is waiting for those who love our Lord. Open your heart and your life to this adventure. You'll never be sorry.

HIS WORD

"The fruit of the Spirit is love, joy, peace, patience, kindness, goodness, faithfulness, gentleness and self-control. Against such things there is no law" (Galatians 5:22,23).

MY PRAYER

The Christian lifestyle is not one of legalistic do's and don'ts, but one that is positive, attractive, and joyful. How do you represent Christianity? Be different from the world. Yield to Christ to let His love shine through you no matter what your circumstances may be.

MY STUDY

Deuteronomy 26:16; Psalm 15:1–5

Tender Hearts

Jay sat on the floor of a bookstore with his four-year-old daughter, Samantha. She snuggled in his lap while he read her a Sesame Street book. Jay loved to read to Samantha. When she saw a word she recognized, she was quick to help him read the story.

Teachable moments come spontaneously with children, and Jay always tried to capture those moments to impart a biblical truth.

Jay's animated reading style attracted the attention of a nearby six-year-old who couldn't resist plopping down in front of Jay and Samantha to listen in.

As Jay moved his head back and forth to imitate the Sesame Street character, he asked Samantha, "Who made Big Bird?"

"God," his daughter confidently answered.

"Who?" their new six-year-old friend asked. She was genuinely puzzled. It was as though she'd never heard such a question before. Samantha did a great "four-year-old" explanation of God's work in creation. The wide-eyed listener seemed a bit dismayed that a four-year-old knew something she didn't. As Jay watched the girls interacting, he realized how precious those teachable moments were. At home that evening, Jay talked to his wife about having a structured time when the neighborhood children could come to their home for storytime.

It was a great idea, and from that day in the bookstore, they've used a weekly storytime to share Christian love with the neighborhood children. It has proved to be a great time to insert biblical concepts that have opened many questions by the children as well as their parents.

Make sure your heart is tender toward children. Take time for them and teach them about God's love. This is the most priceless gift you can give them.

HIS WORD

"Come, my children, listen to me; I will teach you the fear of the Lord" (Psalm 34:11).

MY PRAYER

If you have the opportunity to be with young children, please do not assume that concepts about God and His character are too deep for their understanding. Children can embrace concepts about God that lay a foundation for all their future understanding. Share biblical truths as God gives you opportunity.

MY STUDY

Deuteronomy 4:9,10; Ephesians 6:4

The story of Jill and Rob is one that is played out many times. It is difficult to identify when or where the problem started, but for this Christian couple the reality came when they moved from a small town to a big city. Perhaps the stress of moving magnified their problems, but suddenly their marriage was in crisis. Jill felt lonely. Rob felt unfulfilled. By any counselor's standards, the red flags were flying.

Life in a new city was defined by loneliness and isolation for Jill. The one person who could provide comfort was the very one she withdrew from. Jill loved Rob, but any attempt to express her love failed.

Jill was faithful in her Bible reading and had found God's Word to provide comfort and direction many times in the past. However, now when she read her Bible, there was something different. One cloudy morning as she sat curled up in her chair, she read the passage in 1 Peter 3. Wow, there it was!

What Jill hadn't realized was that a seed of resentment had begun to grow in her heart from the time they decided to move. She had allowed that seed to flourish and grow. Now it was keeping her from expressing love and support to her husband. Everyday, Jill sincerely prayed for her own life and for her husband's. Soon a freedom came for her to express her love to Rob.

At first Rob didn't pick up on the change in Jill's attitude. But within six months, Jill noticed a marked difference in their relationship. He began to initiate expressions of love for Jill and finally restored the joy of his salvation.

Rob and Jill now share a fresh excitement about their faith, and Jill has the joy of hearing Rob publicly acknowledge the part she played in helping them rediscover their love for each other and their love for Jesus Christ.

HIS WORD

"However, each one of you also must love his wife as he loves himself, and the wife must respect her husband" (Ephesians 5:33).

MY PRAYER

Remember, friends, actions speak louder than words. Jill applied the truth of God's Word to her heart and demonstrated her love to her husband. Do you have "warning signs" of impending trouble in your marriage? God will help you, but first you must acknowledge your need. Please do that today.

MY STUDY

Psalm 31:21–24; Jeremiah 32:40,41

Friends Through the Fire

Friendships are forged in the good times and the bad. That's what Catherine learned when her friend, Edwina, was diagnosed with breast cancer.

Before the discovery, these two women were casual friends. It was the crisis, however, that brought them close together.

After the doctor delivered the bad news, Catherine decided to check on Edwina every day, just to see how she was doing. Sometimes they'd talk for a few minutes; other times, for half an hour. Sometimes they'd laugh. Sometimes they'd cry. A true friendship was born.

Catherine was there when Edwina needed help caring for her children. Often, when returning from the doctor, they'd sit and talk. And cry. They went through lots of boxes of tissues during those months of treatment.

Catherine became a make-do hairdresser, trimming Edwina's hair when chemotherapy took its toll. She was an encourager, helping Edwina plan for the future. And she was a comic, making Edwina laugh when the weight of circumstances became too great. More than anything, Catherine just listened when Edwina needed to talk.

What a wonderful example of friendship. I think it's the kind of friendship mentioned in Proverbs 18:24: "There is a friend who sticks closer than a brother." In the good times and the bad.

You may know someone who's going through a difficult time right now. Would you be that Proverbs kind of friend to that person? Can you reach out like Catherine did? I'm afraid sometimes our good intentions fail for lack of action. We think great thoughts but don't follow through with them. We intend to provide comfort but get too busy. We hear about a friend's trial but fail to pray with her.

Put your faith into action today.

HIS WORD

"Therefore encourage one another and build each other up, just as in fact you are doing" (1 Thessalonians 5:11).

MY PRAYER

Don't allow feelings of inadequacy to stop you. Edwina didn't need people to say anything. She needed someone to listen and to care. Perhaps you know someone who has just lost a mate or a child. Or maybe a friend of yours is going through a divorce. Ask God to show you how to reach out to those who are hurting.

MY STUDY

1 Samuel 23:16–18; Psalm 37:3

After fifty-two years of marriage, I have a greater appreciation for my dear husband than ever before. He's a wonderful person – loving, kind, wise, faithful. I respect and trust him completely.

Yet, like everyone else I know, we have occasional conflicts. Those moments are usually inspired by a petty, little issue. We have one story we've told so many times that our Crusade staff call it the "Knife Story."

The kitchen is usually my domain, but Bill had been complaining about the dullness of our kitchen knives. One night to my dismay, Bill came home with a large, very expensive set of new knives. He thought I'd be happy! He bragged about their virtues: they'd never need sharpening and could cut through anything, including steel.

I strongly objected. They were black in an ugly brown box, and I could just imagine how awful they'd look on my pretty white counter.

My solution was to buy a knife sharpener for our old expensive knives. After we each defended our purchases, things grew very quiet between us.

Finally, we realized what was happening. We were harboring resentment toward each other over a very minor thing.

Too many misunderstandings start with ridiculous things like this. There's only one solution: have enough courage to say, "I'm so sorry. I was wrong. Please forgive me. I love you." You must be willing to resolve the little conflicts.

Bill and I are careful to keep Christ in control of our lives. We pray together when we wake up and just before we fall asleep. Nothing has brought more harmony in our marriage than prayer.

You'll never guess what happened to those knives. In the end, I gave them to Bill as a gift. And he gave me the knife sharpener! Both are great reminders that we value each other much more than conflict and cutlery combined!

HIS WORD
"Wives, in the same way be submissive to your husbands ..."
(1 Peter 3:1).

MY PRAYER
If you're married, let me encourage you to make a commitment to pursue peace every day. And pray together. When our eyes are focused on God, the little irritations resume their perspective — insignificant.

MY STUDY
Genesis 2:24; Psalm 25:9

True Friends

The five Warner brothers amassed a fortune through their family business. They've made some of the most successful films in the history of Hollywood. When the last surviving brother cashed out of his Warner Brothers stock, it was worth $640 million.

A curious reporter posed this question of Jack Warner: "Jack, after all you've accomplished in the business, you must have a lot of friends. How many friends do you have?" Jack Warner, one of the wealthiest men in America at that time, gave the reporter this sad response, "I don't have one."

Not a single friend! How tragic to have achieved such financial success, yet have no one to call your friend. Think about what you're doing to develop good friendships. Are you pursuing friendships with others and making real efforts to *be* a good friend?

Let me offer some thoughts for you to consider.

Being a good friend takes time. Both scheduled and spontaneous times are essential to friendship.

A good friend is forgiving. When mistakes are made, the words, "I'm sorry," need to come easily. I've heard it said this way: "True friends don't rub it in ... but they choose to rub it out."

A good friend can keep a secret. Friends must have absolute confidence that their discussions never leave the room. Nothing will drive a wedge any quicker than betrayal of this trust.

A true friend is honest. Don't allow yourself to gloss over problem areas. If you spot a flaw, first pray about it and seek God's direction about saying something. In Proverbs 27:5,6 we read, "Better is open rebuke than hidden love. Wounds from a friend can be trusted."

Finally ... *Good friends never quit.* When life becomes intense, a true friend hangs in there. Hold onto them even tighter than you would your greatest earthly treasure. True friends are precious gifts from God. Hold them close to your heart.

HIS WORD

"A man of many companions may come to ruin, but there is a friend who sticks closer than a brother" (Proverbs 18:24).

MY PRAYER

Author and scholar C. S. Lewis said, *"Is there any pleasure on earth as great as a circle of Christian friends by a fire?"* Treasure your friends. Let them know how you feel. And pray for them daily.

MY STUDY

Daniel 12:3; Philippians 2:19–23

Read the words of Jesus from John 15:15: "I no longer call you servants, because a servant does not know his master's business. Instead, I have called you friends, for everything that I learned from my Father I have made known to you."

As Christians, our mission is to share the friendship we have with Jesus with those who don't know Him personally, and then help them grow in their new faith.

I began at an early age to see how rewarding a life of sharing can be. When I was growing up, Mother and Dad loved to invite friends to our home. Some of my earliest recollections are of Mother teaching me to pass out napkins, to wait to be served last, and to pay attention to details that make guests feel comfortable and appreciated.

In those days, the population of Coweta, Oklahoma, was only 1,500, but we enjoyed an amazing number of formal events. Several professional couples had moved to the community, and it was important to them to preserve some of the culture they brought with them.

As a child, I observed afternoon teas and candlelight dinners. As a teenager, I enjoyed formal parties and looked forward to the ice cream socials and watermelon feeds held by churches and various groups in the summer. I was so impressed with these events that I thought, *It'll be so much fun to go to these parties when I'm grown up*.

Home and hospitality were so important to me that I chose to major in home economics in college. I didn't know at the time how God would use the things I was learning.

Of course, God knew all about me and about the plans He had for my life. None of my desires were a surprise to Him!

After many years of ministry, I'm even more excited about how sharing our lives through hospitality can influence people. It is a tool to help open their hearts.

HIS WORD
"Offer hospitality to one another without grumbling. Each one should use whatever gift he has received to serve others, faithfully administering God's grace in its various forms" (1 Peter 4:9,10).

MY PRAYER
As Christians, we have the privilege of extending hospitality to those who may not even recognize their need for God. It could be coffee and cookies at home or sharing a muffin with a coworker. But look for opportunities, then graciously do them.

MY STUDY
2 Kings 4:8–17; Proverbs 11:25

Always Learning

You would never have guessed that Brenda was a battered wife. She lived in a beautiful neighborhood, and her family was in church every Sunday. But as she gradually withdrew, no one in the church noticed.

No one, that is, except Eva.

Eva, an older woman, was concerned. She didn't believe it when Brenda's husband said that she had emotional problems. Eva's suspicions grew when he insisted that no one should visit her.

Eva and Brenda gradually developed a relationship. Finally, Brenda admitted the truth. She'd been too embarrassed to tell her other friends, but Eva's love and compassion broke through.

Eva became a spiritual mentor to Brenda. Over time, restoration and healing were brought into that troubled home.

A Bible story about two women gives us a further example of how a friendship can provide strength. Mary was unmarried and pregnant. She was filled with emotions – excited to be expecting, but embarrassed about her status. When she traveled to see her cousin, she was not sure what the reaction would be to her circumstances.

Her cousin was delighted to see her and invited her to stay for an extended visit. They were together for the next three months, sharing a critical time in any woman's life – the expectancy of a first child.

I'm speaking, of course, about Mary, the mother of Jesus, and Elizabeth, the mother of John the Baptist. God used Elizabeth to confirm His promise to Mary and affirm Mary's faith and character.

Every woman can benefit from the wisdom of another woman. Prayerfully consider the women you know and identify someone you respect and admire. Cultivate a relationship that would allow you to feel confident in seeking advice or sharing your struggles. God can use another woman to provide help and hope at any age.

HIS WORD

"My soul will boast in the Lord; let the afflicted hear and rejoice. Glorify the Lord with me; let us exalt his name together" (Psalm 34:2,3).

MY PRAYER

"Heavenly Father, thank You for giving us friendships that allow us to love and support each other. Help me to seek mentors and to be a mentor to others so we may grow in Your love and grace. In Jesus' holy name, amen."

MY STUDY

Ruth 3:1–5; Acts 11:25,26

Frances Green was eighty-three years old and lived alone in San Francisco. She had very little, but gave one dollar a year to support the Republican National Committee.

One day, she received an elegant invitation to come to the White House to meet President Reagan. Friends helped her save enough to make the trip. What Frances didn't notice, however, was the RSVP note inside her envelope, the one that required a substantial contribution in order to be included.

When she arrived at the White House gate, this dear elderly lady was turned away by the guard. Her name didn't appear on his official list. She was devastated.

Behind her in line was a kind man who overheard her conversation with the guard. He could tell what had happened, so he asked her to meet him at nine o'clock the next morning at the White House. She agreed.

When Frances arrived the following morning, this gentleman had arranged for a wonderful White House tour. He personally guided her and talked about the many wonderful rooms and historical items.

When Frances and her escort arrived at the Oval Office, high-ranking generals were coming and going. Then President Reagan spotted Frances outside the door.

He got up from his desk and said, "Ah, Frances! Those computers, they fouled up again! If I'd known you were coming, I would have come out there to get you myself!"

He invited Frances to join him in the Oval Office. There they chatted about California, her family, and how she was doing.

The President knew this woman had nothing to give. But he knew he had something to give Frances. He gave her compassion and kindness.

A little kindness can make the difference in someone's life. And it is so easy to share!

HIS WORD
"Therefore, as God's chosen people, holy and dearly loved, clothe yourselves with compassion, kindness, humility, gentleness and patience" (Colossians 3:12).

MY PRAYER
In our high-tech and demanding culture, we're often rushing to and from events, never taking time to stop and consider those around us who have profound needs. Let's learn a lesson from one of our nation's great patriots. Take time to share the love of Jesus with those who are waiting at the gate, perhaps without a ticket to enter in.

MY STUDY *Genesis 50:15–21; Jeremiah 9:24*

A Gentle Answer

When I first began to read and study the Bible, I considered it great literature. And it is. I found it a fascinating historical record, but the Bible is so much more. By studying God's Holy Word, I've come to appreciate it for the wonderful ways it speaks to every dimension of life.

In each aspect of my life – every decision, every relationship, every problem – the Bible has something to say. It instructs me on what to do and how to have healthy attitudes. That's why I read the Bible every day. I consult it constantly. When I do, I understand God's way. So does my friend Sallie.

Recently, Sallie moved into a new home. Several large limbs from a neighbor's tree hung over Sallie's back fence. They needed to be trimmed.

Sallie consulted a tree surgeon. She approached her neighbors to explain the situation. The woman of the household gave Sallie a verbal agreement to do whatever was necessary.

The workmen came and began to cut the limbs. The neighbor's husband was the only one home that day, and apparently his wife hadn't told him about the tree-trimming.

He was furious. The workers referred him, of course, to Sallie.

Can you imagine Sallie's surprise when her irate neighbor appeared at her front door?

In the midst of this frightening encounter, God brought to her mind His Word. God reminded her of Proverbs 15:1. It says, "A gentle answer turns away wrath, but a harsh word stirs up anger."

She said, "Oh, I am so sorry. There must be some misunderstanding ... I need a neighbor a lot worse than I need the tree work done."

The answer helped to calm the situation, and together they found a solution. The neighbor apologized and a relationship began to develop that day. Truly, a gentle answer can work miracles!

HIS WORD

"Let your gentleness be evident to all. The Lord is near" (Philippians 4:5).

MY PRAYER

As you grow in your understanding of how to apply God's Word, your life will be changed. Read your Bible daily, asking God for wisdom to apply it to your life. Then you will begin to observe some exciting changes in your life and heart.

MY STUDY

Proverbs 14:29; Isaiah 40:11

There's nothing like a mature, wise friend to give us counsel and direction. As a seasoned veteran with a depth of experience, a mature friend can share wisdom unavailable elsewhere.

I heard about a church in Southern California where older couples attend the Sunday school classes of younger people. These couples don't teach the class; they simply attend all the events and become acquainted with everyone who comes. By their presence, they provide an example, a model to follow. The more mature adults often counsel their younger friends, or pray for them, as the need arises.

Sometimes it's a joyful experience – celebrating a promotion or the birth of a baby. Other times, mentoring younger couples requires tremendous strength and sensitivity – helping husbands and wives resolve conflict, showing how to handle problems with in-laws, or dealing with tragedy in their lives.

What a wonderful way to strengthen the body of Christ!

So many young people enter marriage without a model. Often, their parents are divorced. It's so helpful to have someone at church who's advising them, taking them under their wing, praying for them – mentoring them.

It doesn't require a special program, or need to fit in the context of a Sunday school class. You might reach out to someone in your neighborhood. Regardless of your age, you have talents and gifts to contribute to the family of God – especially to someone younger.

To mentor others, we must be real with them, sharing our joys and sorrows. We must give of our time and our wealth of experience.

Of this I am absolutely sure: as you minister to others, your life will be enriched! For as you serve one another, you are a reflection of God's love.

HIS WORD
"I thought, 'Age should speak; advanced years should teach wisdom.' But it is the spirit in a man, the breath of the Almighty, that gives him understanding. It is not only the old who are wise, not only the aged who understand what is right" (Job 32:7–9).

MY PRAYER
Look for ways to reach out to younger and older women who need you. Establish relationships. Let them know you're praying for them. Invite them to visit in your home. Talk openly about your relationship with God, and find ways to encourage and support them.

MY STUDY *Proverbs 31:20; Romans 16:1,2*

Loving Your Neighbor

James Bryan Smith tells this story in his wonderful book, *Embracing the Love of God.*

At first, the call was a bit mysterious. Though the voice sounded familiar, it had been a long time since James had heard it.

It was Marge, a neighbor from years earlier. Marge still lived in the home behind the house where James grew up, but *his* family had long since moved.

Marge asked about his mother. "I was trying to reach your mother. Where does she live now?"

James gave her his mother's telephone number. Then Marge explained why she was asking. Her oldest son had recently died of complications related to the AIDS virus. "I just need to talk to your mom," Marge said. "She's always so accepting. No matter what happens, I know I can always call her and she will stand by me. I love your mom so much."

How we all need someone in our lives like James's mother. And we all need to *be* that kind of neighbor in the lives of others.

James's mother was a neighbor others could call on. She had a listening ear and a compassionate heart. Even when separated by distance and time, a neighbor in need remembered her gentle manner.

In 2 Corinthians 1:4, the apostle Paul writes, "[God] comforts us in all our trouble, so that we can comfort those in any trouble with the comfort we ourselves have received from God."

Have you cultivated the kind of attitude that allows others to feel they can confide in you in their times of need? Do you emanate a spirit of acceptance or of criticism? Comfort others as God has comforted you, then give Him all the glory.

HIS WORD
"The second [greatest commandment] is this: 'Love your neighbor as yourself'" (Mark 12:31).

MY PRAYER
Are you the neighbor someone could come to for compassion, understanding, and comfort? Today, open your door — the door to your home and the door to your heart. Reach out with God's love. Embrace and comfort your neighbors with your attention, concern, and His Words of truth.

MY STUDY
Leviticus 19:18; Proverbs 22:2

A Daughter of the Heart

Donna and Kimberly met at a church committee meeting. They immediately liked each other. Kim was young, single, and just getting started. Donna was married and well-established. At the end of their conversation, Kim told Donna to call her if there was any way she could help her.

Donna Otto tells this story in her book *Between Women of God*.

A few weeks after meeting Kim, Donna got really busy with a big project. She was so involved, she didn't have time to run needed errands. Then she remembered Kim and her offer to help. So she called her.

Donna asked Kim if she could run those errands. Kim hesitated, then explained, "I'd love to, but I don't have a car."

Donna offered her the use of a car. Kim explained she actually had a car, but couldn't afford the insurance. She said, "I'm disciplining myself to ride the bus as a way to get my finances in order."

Donna and her husband, David, had been discussing what to do with their home. With their daughter away at college, it seemed too large and empty. They'd prayed for someone they could take into their home. Kim might be the answer to those prayers.

"Well," Donna said, "if you came to live with us for thirty days, you would have the money for the car insurance and you could help me a few hours a week in return."

Kim not only moved into Donna and David's home, she moved into their hearts. She didn't stay for just a month, she stayed for two years. Donna says Kim became a "daughter of her heart."

They worked together, prayed together, laughed together, and had a few spats together. By the time she moved into her own apartment, she was debt-free and had a savings account.

That, my friend, is a wonderful picture of the art of mentoring.

HIS WORD

"If anyone has material possessions and sees his brother in need but has no pity on him, how can the love of God be in him? Dear children, let us not love with words or tongue but with actions and in truth" (1 John 3;17,18).

MY PRAYER

"Heavenly Father, open my eyes to see creative ways to reach out to someone. I want to invest my life in others. You have been so generous with me and I am so thankful for Your guidance. Please make me a blessing! Amen."

MY STUDY

Isaiah 32:8; Psalm 41:1–3

Words To Save a Marriage

All relationships have a measure of misunderstanding, hurt, and pain. And in this fallen world, there's certainly no such thing as a perfect marriage. Disagreeing on occasion doesn't mean you don't love each other.

Bill and I have been married fifty-two years. Because longevity in a relationship has become quite rare in this culture, I'm often asked to identify our secret.

We've decided any marriage will survive if the partners will memorize and use just twelve words. You could probably guess what they are:

> "I love you."
> "I am sorry."
> "I was wrong."
> "Please forgive me."

Sometimes uttering those twelve simple words can be tough to do in the heat of emotional battle. But in a healthy marriage, practicing forgiveness must come easy.

A friend teases me about the time she heard me talking to my husband on the phone. She says she knew we were having a disagreement because she first heard me call him "Honey," then "Bill," and then "Bill Bright."

As my terms intensified, so did the tone of my voice! When that happens, I pray, "Lord, give me the power to love Bill like you love him. Don't let me get stuck in these momentary feelings of frustration with him."

Then I'm able to swallow hard and speak those simple words.

I must admit the few times when my husband has hurt my feelings, I've been tempted to hurt him back. When he said something offensive, I wanted to respond in the same tone.

I know that's a silly and immature attitude. It doesn't accomplish anything. But with God's help, we can be sensitive to our mate and love him as God expects us to.

HIS WORD

"If you are offering your gift at the altar and there remember that your brother has something against you, leave your gift there in front of the altar. First go and be reconciled to your brother; then come and offer your gift" (Matthew 5:23,24).

MY PRAYER

When we determine that divorce is not an option, it's only by God's power that we can work through our differences and truly understand each other. In a loving way, we can communicate and resolve whatever conflict comes our way.

MY STUDY

Proverbs 3:3; Job 22:29

Twenty-year-old John Bisagno was engaged to be married, finishing college, and going into the ministry. His future father-in-law, Dr. Paul Beck, shared a bit of advice with John to prepare him for the challenges he'd surely face.

A minister for many years, Dr. Beck had observed many young people going into vocational service for God. His simple yet profound words were, "John, stay true to Jesus! Make sure you keep your heart close to Jesus every day."

Dr. Beck found that just one in ten people who began full-time service for the Lord at age twenty-one had stayed on track until age sixty-five. Discouragement, moral failure, financial pressures, and other issues robbed them of the joy of ministry.

Shocked and incredulous, John went home and wrote in his Bible the names of twenty-four men who were his peers. Christians, walking with God, they all shared a common desire to be used by God and were trained in ministry.

John served as pastor of the First Baptist Church of Houston for many years. He stayed true to Jesus. Sadly, from time to time, he's had to turn to that page in his Bible and mark out another name. After thirty-three years, only three of those twenty-four men had stayed true to Jesus.

Author and speaker Steve Farrar told John's story in his book *Finishing Strong*. Steve wrote these words, "In the Christian life, it's not how you start that matters. It's how you finish."

Finishing strong, dear friend, means staying true to Jesus. It applies to us all. No matter who you are or what your occupation, staying true to Jesus all your life is what matters most. It means walking with Him moment by moment, every day. You do that by spending time with Him – reading His Word and talking to Him in prayer.

Stay true to Jesus. He always stays true to you. He sets you free and enables you to finish strong.

HIS WORD

"When he arrived and saw the evidence of the grace of God, he was glad and encouraged them all to remain true to the Lord with all their hearts" (Acts 11:23).

MY PRAYER

Maybe today, you've already lost your way. Perhaps you're discouraged, or you've failed morally. You feel stuck. Dear friend, tell God right now about those defeats. Talk to Him. Entrust your heart into His hands. It's never to late to find forgiveness and start your healing!

MY STUDY

Jeremiah 23:24; Psalm 64:10

A Fresh Start

Brothers, I do not consider myself yet to have taken hold of it. But one thing I do: Forgetting what is behind and straining toward what is ahead, I press on toward the goal to win the prize for which God has called me heavenward in Christ Jesus.

PHILIPPIANS 3:13,14

Did you know that you have a gift at your door every morning? The gift of a new day is to be treasured and used to bring glory and honor to the giver of the gift, the Lord God Almighty.

Each day brings challenges and trials that can overwhelm us and keep us from seeing the real possibilities available to us. Unfortunately, many of us carry the burdens of yesterday into our present, day after day. Jesus came to give us a life that is free of the burden of sin and filled with hope for the opportunities of a new life in Him.

Enjoying the freshness of each new day is up to you. During the times when you can't understand what God is doing, you may need to remind yourself daily of your choice to accept God's grace and receive the gift of His forgiveness.

A whispered prayer is the guarantee of a fresh start. With prayer, the beauty of life will come into clear view.

So Great a Debt

Some eighty years ago, Czar Nicholas reigned in Russia. Late in the evenings, he'd put on a disguise and slip out into the streets of his beloved homeland. While walking among the commoners under his rule, he'd check on their living conditions. He'd listen to their concerns and to what was said about him.

As he passed the gate of a military base late one night, he found the guard sound asleep. He noticed a gun and some official financial books.

As Czar Nicholas looked closer, he realized the guard had been embezzling money from the army. Underneath the loaded gun was a note – apparently a suicide note. It read: "To my horror. I decline. So great a debt. Who can pay it?"

That night, the soldier had been overcome with guilt about what he had done. He saw no way out of his wrongdoing except suicide.

As the soldier woke up and reached for his gun, his eyes were drawn to the note. There was something else written next to his question: "Who can pay it?" He looked closer. It read: "I, Czar Nicholas, have paid it."

Oh, dear friend, that's what God did through the death of His Son, Jesus Christ. He paid the price for our sins, canceled our debt, wiped the slate clean. He gave us forgiveness. It's as if He wrote the words "I, the Most Holy God, the Father of Jesus Christ, have paid it."

All you have to do to experience forgiveness is to repent and confess your sin. Then receive God's provision for it by placing your faith in Christ.

If you've never done so, invite Jesus Christ to come and live in your heart. Simply pray to ask Him to come in, and He will. A simple explanation of how to receive Christ through prayer is given in "Beginning Your Journey of Joy" at the back of this book.

HIS WORD

"If you confess with your mouth, 'Jesus is Lord,' and believe in your heart that God raised him from the dead, you will be saved" (Romans 10:9).

MY PRAYER

"Merciful Lord, I praise Your name and thank You that You have paid the debt for my sin. Even though I deserve death, You have given me life. Even though I deserve the pain that You suffered, You have given me peace. Many thanks, my Lord. Amen."

MY STUDY

Psalm 51:1,2; Micah 7:18,19

Walk in Newness of Life

As a single Christian in her early thirties, Kelley looked forward to the day when she would meet the right man. In the meantime, she tried to be faithful to God in every area. Kelley wanted nothing more than to please God.

Then unexpectedly, an old friend popped back into her life. They had dated for a while in college. Now ten years later, he was back and wanted to rekindle the flame.

Kelley was torn. She had loved him very much. But he wasn't walking with God and had no desire to change.

On one hand, Kelley shouldn't compromise her standards for marriage. She was waiting for a man who loved God. On the other hand, she thought, "It couldn't hurt to see him now and then, could it?" So they saw each other for dinner and enjoyed a nice conversation.

Before long she had slipped back into the relationship – and not just casually. She found herself doing the things she'd promised herself she'd never do.

Unfortunately, Kelley's situation is all too common. We all get carried away with our feelings. Our guard is dropped. Lines are crossed. Sin is committed.

Kelley knew that she had a choice: either continue in a relationship that was not pleasing to God or get back on track with what she knew to be right.

The Bible says in 1 John 1:9, "If we confess our sins, he is faithful and just and will forgive us our sins and purify us from all unrighteousness."

Confession and true repentance involve turning away from our sins and walking in newness of life. Kelley decided to end the relationship, as hard as that was. Now, she is resting in the assurance that her sins are forgiven.

HIS WORD

"Blessed is he whose transgressions are forgiven, whose sins are covered" (Psalm 32:1).

MY PRAYER

Is there an area in your life that you know is not pleasing to God? Confess it from your heart and receive God's forgiveness. Now, complete your repentance by turning from the sin. It might be difficult, but God will richly bless your obedience.

MY STUDY

1 John 1:8–10; Isaiah 55:6,7

Dr. Henrietta Mears, a tremendous influence in my life, told the story about a brilliant young man who was preparing to become a brain surgeon. He questioned Miss Mears about surrendering his life to God. He was convinced that becoming a Christian would mean the destruction of his personality, that he'd be altered in some strange way, and that he'd lose control of his own mind. He feared becoming a mere puppet in God's hands.

So Miss Mears asked him to watch as she turned on a lamp. One moment it was dark, then she turned on the switch. She explained, "The lamp surrendered itself to the electric current and light has filled the room. The lamp didn't destroy its personality when it surrendered to the current. On the contrary — the very thing happened for which the lamp was created: it gave light."

The same would apply to other appliances — toasters, coffeepots, washing machines, vacuums. No electrical appliance is of any use until it's plugged into a source of power.

The young man got the point. He said, "If I surrender myself to God, I'll become plugged into His power. God will illuminate my mind and fingers to make them more skillful."

That's exactly right.

People are often afraid God will step into their fireplace and put out the fire, or He'll take their violin and break all the strings. That's false! He's eager to turn your hearth into a raging fire, and He'll make beautiful music on the strings of that violin. He wants to give you a life filled with the joy of knowing with confidence that you're connected to the only Source of real power.

God has a plan for your life. It isn't for you to lose your identity or your fun. He has a wonderful plan to ensure you'll become all He created you to be.

HIS WORD

"'For I know the plans I have for you,' declares the LORD, 'plans to prosper you and not to harm you, plans to give you hope and a future'" (Jeremiah 29:11).

MY PRAYER

"Omnipotent God, I am amazed that You have given me access to Your mighty strength. I am only a weak human vessel, but I accept the power of Your Holy Spirit who dwells in me. Help me to die to myself daily and let You work through me. Amen."

MY STUDY

Philippians 1:9; Psalm 106:8

To Be Wanted

My mother didn't want me!" the woman said. That's how Pamella's tumultuous life began. In time, drugs became her single focus to cover her pain. And selling herself was the way she got them.

But God did not give up on Pamella. When she was a child, her father's second wife took her to church. Although she heard about the God who loved her, Pamella was lost in her own painful world.

Her life plummeted. She stole liquor as a youngster, and the alcohol led to sex. As a teenager, Pamella had her first child. Eventually, she was taken in by a pimp in New York City. Pamella said, "He showed me the lights of Manhattan. And whatever he said, I did." And when she didn't, he beat her. He gave her drugs. Soon, she was prostituting for drugs. She had a second child; both children were taken in by relatives.

A crack cocaine charge landed Pamella in prison. While serving her sentence, she worked with the chaplain. "Every night, I'd write out fifty Scriptures and pass them out to other inmates," she said.

When released from prison, she was penniless and hopeless. For five years, she survived among other homeless people in the Port Authority, the city's bus terminal.

Her last dose of crack had absolutely no effect. She decided then that she'd either live or die. Crying out to God, she said, "Lord, if You'll just give me my life back ..." And as is God's way, He heard the desperate cry of His dear child. He lovingly rescued Pamella and dramatically changed her life.

"I needed a chance and God gave me a chance," she said.

It wasn't easy for her to be freed from the bondage of alcohol, drugs, and sexual promiscuity, but God *never* let her go. He wanted her as His child — even when her mother didn't.

HIS WORD

"The LORD your God is with you, he is mighty to save. He will take great delight in you, he will quiet you with his love, he will rejoice over you with singing" (Zephaniah 3:17).

MY PRAYER

"Righteous Father God, I thank you that You loved me enough to send Your Son to die for me. Thank You that You love me even when it seems no one else does. Help me to always remember how valuable I am to You. Amen."

MY STUDY

Titus 3:5,6; Psalm 27:10

In 1979, Rusty Welborn was arrested and convicted of murder. At twenty-three years of age, he waited on death row. There he sat in a dirty, roach-infested cell.

Then he met Bob McAlister, the deputy chief of staff to South Carolina's governor. Bob was a very busy man, but one who wanted to reach out to inmates, particularly those on death row. He found Rusty.

Rusty was pitiful, unresponsive, and convinced no one cared. But that didn't stop Bob. He kept going to that filthy cell, reaching out to Rusty with the love of Christ. Bob continually reminded him that – even on death row – he could experience God's forgiveness. He kept praying for and with him.

In time, Rusty began to respond, at first tentatively and unsurely. Then one day, Rusty broke down and began to cry. That day, Rusty Welborn, a murderer, came to know Christ personally.

Bob began to see dramatic changes in him. Rusty cleaned up his cell, and he cleaned up himself!

Rusty was "amazed and thrilled" at the love of God. To receive it freely was overwhelming and life-changing.

The day Rusty was to be executed, he told Bob, "You know, the only thing I ever wanted was a home. Now I'm going to get one." He knew he'd be entering heaven for all eternity.

That night, Bob read the Bible to him. Thinking Rusty had fallen asleep, he placed a blanket over him and kissed Rusty on the forehead. Later, as Rusty was walking to his death, he said, "What a shame that a man's gotta wait till his last night alive to be kissed and tucked in for the very first time."

Dear friend, the Lord Jesus Christ changes lives: my life, Rusty's life, your life. He also gives us unconditional love and support, things Rusty waited his entire life to receive.

HIS WORD

"I will give them an undivided heart and put a new spirit in them; I will remove from them their heart of stone and give them a heart of flesh" (Ezekiel 11:19).

MY PRAYER

Is there someone you know who hasn't yet experienced the life-transforming touch of Jesus Christ? Pray for those individuals and reach out to them today. Share what Jesus has done in your life. Show them how they can receive Christ using the info in "Beginning Your Journey of Joy" in the back of this book.

MY STUDY

2 Peter 3:13,14; Psalm 84:2–4

New Life

Jane's early life was so dark, so abusive. Memories were stuffed below the surface of her mind where she hoped they would never appear again. But they did — nearly thirty years later.

Sexual abuse. Physical abuse. Verbal abuse. Immorality. Alcohol. These characterized Jane's childhood home life. Sin was so commonplace that she had no sense of normalcy. Before she was old enough to enter kindergarten, her innocence was stolen by her own parents and a next-door neighbor.

Jane fought back with a vengeance by becoming a model child and student. She earned straight A's and did all she could to fit into the social mainstream. No one knew that her home life was so ugly.

Then, during her high-school years, Jane suffered another violation. She was date-raped — an act no one talked about back then. Like all of her other problems, she stuffed this tragedy deep into her private world.

Jane finally came to her breaking point, blaming herself for the dark side of her life. She began drinking and using drugs. It wasn't until she lay in a hospital recovering from a drug overdose that Jane recalled what someone had told her at age fifteen: that God loved her and Jesus had given His life for her.

Jane sought out more information and ultimately gave her life to Christ, leading to an exciting period of recovery. Today her life is healthy and joyous.

Jane's life was filled with horrific circumstances and events. She had no hope. But we serve a compassionate God. He can take our sorrows, wipe them away, and give us new life through His Son. It's never too late to turn it all over to Him — the hurts, the sins, everything!

HIS WORD

"Show the wonder of your great love, you who save by your right hand those who take refuge in you from their foes" (Psalm 17:7).

MY PRAYER

Do you have something in your life, perhaps a pain from your past, that you still haven't turned over to God? Reflect today on this pain and give it to God in prayer. Allow Him, the Wonderful Counselor, to heal you completely. Your life will never be the same.

MY STUDY

Revelation 21:3,4; Exodus 3:7–10

L eonardo da Vinci's masterpiece, *The Last Supper*, has captivated millions of viewers for hundreds of years. This fifteenth-century Italian skillfully captured the facial expressions of Jesus and His disciples. There's an interesting story behind those faces. You may have heard the account, but it's worth repeating.

Just as da Vinci was about to start working on *The Last Supper*, he had a bitter quarrel with a fellow painter. Leonardo was so angry and resentful that he decided to paint the face of the hated artist onto the face of Judas – the disciple who betrayed Christ. This face was one of the first he completed.

Later, when he tried to paint the face of Jesus, he lost all inspiration. No matter how hard he tried, he couldn't make any progress.

Leonardo finally realized that his mental block and loss of creativity was caused by his unresolved resentment toward his fellow artist. So he forgave the other painter, then proceeded to repaint the face of Judas so that he no longer looked like his enemy.

When he went back to work on the face of Jesus, he was inspired again. And the success of that depiction has been recognized through the centuries.

Leonardo da Vinci experienced both the bondage of anger and the freedom of resolving it. By letting go of his resentment, the destructive power of his anger was broken.

That's really what it means to forgive someone.

My friend, let me urge you to bring your emotions to God. Tell Him about the situation.

As you put into words whatever is causing your resentment, explain to God exactly how you feel. Confessing your anger opens the door for Him to heal your wounds, and enables you to exchange anger for love.

HIS WORD
"Get rid of all bitterness, rage and anger, brawling and slander, along with every form of malice. Be kind and compassionate to one another, forgiving each other, just as in Christ God forgave you" (Ephesians 4:31,32).

MY PRAYER
Think about someone you resent. Ask God to forgive you for harboring this bitterness in your heart. Next, go to the person and ask for forgiveness. Then, let the resentment go. Move forward and remember the hurt no longer.

MY STUDY
Proverbs 25:21,22; Exodus 23:4,5

Transforming Grace

Her name is Vicki. She knows God's transforming grace firsthand. Though she had asked Jesus to be her Savior when she was young, Vicki wandered away from the truth during her college years.

It was at college that Vicki befriended an artistic group of friends. They were aspiring actors and actresses, many of whom led alternative lifestyles.

In this setting, Vicki became involved in immoral relationships and began to experiment with drugs. She hid these habits from her parents, and even tried to hide them from God.

A few years after graduating from college, Vicki was contacted by a Christian friend. She challenged Vicki to take a good look at her life and her relationship with God.

Vicki knew she had strayed from the truth and she really wanted to change. So, with the help of her friend, Vicki turned back to God.

It was a long road to recovery, but slowly and surely, Vicki allowed God to remove her bad habits. Before long, she began to use her skills for God's glory.

During the summer, she took part in a missions project – working among Navajo Indians. With her background in theatrics, Vicki helped to stage skits and plays portraying the love of Christ to junior high school students. Her creative talents were put to use, and she took delight in watching young people respond.

What a turnaround from a life of depravity! God is transforming Vicki before our very eyes.

Philippians 1:6 says, "Being confident of this, that he who began a good work in you will carry it on to completion until the day of Christ Jesus."

Just as in Vicki's life, God will be faithful in transforming your life into one that will bring glory and honor to Him.

HIS WORD

"We, who with unveiled faces all reflect the Lord's glory, are being transformed into his likeness with ever-increasing glory, which comes from the Lord, who is the Spirit" (2 Corinthians 3:18).

MY PRAYER

"Lord Jesus, thank You for Your infinite love and boundless grace. Thank You for loving me when I am unlovable. Thank You for continuing to mold me and shape me into Your likeness. In Your precious name I pray, amen."

MY STUDY

Deuteronomy 7:6–9; Psalm 145:13,14

In the Book of Genesis, God said of marriage, "A man will leave his father and mother and be united to his wife, and they will become one flesh" (2:24).

Becoming one is not something that will happen in the first week of marriage or even in the first year of marriage. Becoming one is a lifetime adventure. It's a process, and it's full of both delight and difficulty!

Marriage is delightful because you and the one you love are now setting out on a brand new course. You're heading in the same direction, down the same path, sharing each other's dreams and desires.

On the other hand, becoming one is difficult because you and the one you love must master the art of cooperation and interdependence. At times, you both must learn to give up your own ambitions to achieve something together.

The love that you and your spouse share today can grow and become an even deeper romance and a richer experience, but only as you become one. You are not two people coming together to cheer each other on as you pursue separate goals. You are two people coming together to create a formidable team of one.

Your personality *and his*, your gifts *and his*, your interests *and his*, your desires *and his*, your goals *and his* all come together to shape a glorious picture of love. The Bible says it's the same kind of love that Christ has for His bride, the Church!

Dear friend, God will take you beyond your wildest expectations in the love He gives you for each other. All He requires is that you walk with Him and trust Him as the two of you become one. No matter how long you've been married, it's never too late to start again, to become the unique team God wants you to be.

HIS WORD

"In the Lord, however, woman is not independent of man, nor is man independent of woman. For as woman came from man, so also man is born of woman. But everything comes from God" (1 Corinthians 11:11,12).

MY PRAYER

Thank God for your husband. Go to your husband today and tell him how much you appreciate him. If you haven't already done so, set up a time each day when you can have a devotional time together studying God's Word and praying.

MY STUDY

Mark 10:6–9; Proverbs 18:22

Guilt Free

I find that too many Christians are caught in the vicious trap of sin and guilt, sin and guilt. They know God has forgiven them, but they still keep coming back to guilt and defeat, time after time.

My friend Dr. Jack Hayford gives a wonderful illustration of this cycle.

One day Pastor Jack was meeting with a young man. Bob had been deeply troubled about sin. He couldn't get victory over a recurring sin in his life. He felt like a failure as over and over he'd given in to temptation. But on this particular day he had good news to report to Dr. Hayford.

Bob said he had sinned and went, yet again, to God in prayer. While praying, the Holy Spirit taught him a profound and liberating truth. "Lord," he began praying, "I don't even feel like I deserve to come to You about this. I've failed in this way so many times. And I did it again today."

As Bob finished that prayer, he sensed the Holy Spirit whispering these words to his heart, "Did what again?"

Did you catch that? The Holy Spirit spoke to Bob's heart of confession and humility, and asked, "Did *what* again?"

God seemed to say to Bob, "I don't remember." It was only in that moment Bob finally understood complete forgiveness.

In Psalm 103:12, King David tells us, "As far as the east is from the west, so far has he removed our transgressions from us."

That's a distance that can't be measured. It's so far that we can't even imagine it! If God doesn't remember it, then why should we dwell on it? We need to let go of the guilt and experience God's forgiveness. Then we will experience real peace.

HIS WORD
"Then I acknowledged my sin to you, and did not cover up my iniquity … and you forgave the guilt of my sin"
(Psalm 32:5).

MY PRAYER
"Dear loving Lord Jesus, help me to let go of the past. You have removed my sins from Your memory. Help me to do the same so I may live in the peace of Your infinite forgiveness. Thank You for Your grace and mercy. Amen."

MY STUDY
Hebrews 8:12; Isaiah 1:18

Imagine giving your ten-year-old son away, having him smuggled to another country.

That's exactly what happened to little Lukas. In 1976, his Albanian parents were in despair over the repressive rule of their government. Albania was fiercely communist at the time.

Albania was also fiercely atheistic. The government did not allow any sign of God or symbol of Christianity within its borders.

So that year the parents of Lukas had him smuggled to America, hoping that he'd have a better life. They took a chance, not knowing if they would ever see him again.

Lukas came to live with his relatives in Des Moines, Iowa. Four years later, he heard the gospel and trusted Christ. He began to pray every day that his parents would also receive Christ.

Imagine the excitement when he returned to Albania in 1996 after communism had crumbled. He found that someone had already brought his parents the Good News, and they'd trusted Jesus Christ as their Savior the year before his arrival. God had answered his prayers!

A team from Campus Crusade for Christ had been in this family's village. They brought the *JESUS* film, a dramatic presentation that clearly tells the story of God's love. And they stayed in the area to provide follow-up and discipleship training.

That God would bring this family together physically as well as spiritually is nothing short of a miracle. Lukas received Christ in the United States. His parents received Christ sixteen years later and half a world away, and now they will be united for eternity.

HIS WORD
"They replied, 'Believe in the Lord Jesus, and you will be saved — you and your household'" (Acts 16:31,32).

MY PRAYER
Do you have family members who don't know Christ? Pray for them daily. Look for opportunities to share with them about the difference Jesus has made in your life. Let them see Christ in you through your kindness toward them. Love them righteously but unconditionally.

MY STUDY
Exodus 20:12; Proverbs 23:24

A New Creation

He was a preacher's kid, but in two years he earned twenty-two notches on the knife he all too often brandished. That's one notch for every time he used the knife to hurt someone.

Tom had been a model child who learned to behave as expected. In high school he was a superior student — president of the student body, the lead in school plays, member of the baseball team, and so on. But on the inside, rebellion was brewing.

One night he was walking down the street in Harlem when some guys jokingly asked him if he wanted to become a Harlem Lord, a gang member. Without much thought, he said, "Yes."

Tom spent several weeks causing havoc — fighting others, breaking into stores, and stealing. Then he decided to challenge the leader to a fight. Tom won, and he became gang leader for the next two years.

Amazingly, he managed to keep it a secret from his parents. He stayed active in church and school activities.

One night as Tom sat planning an attack strategy for a huge fight among several gangs, a man on the radio began talking about God. Tom didn't want to listen, but neither did he want to get up to change the station. Soon the program captured his attention. At the end of the message, Tom confessed his sin, placing his trust in Jesus Christ. His life was changed.

Though difficult, a few days later Tom showed true courage. He told 129 knife-wielding gang members about his new faith in God. In the days that followed, many of them and others from rival gangs trusted Christ. Tom later became a distinguished evangelist.

No matter what your life has been like, when you become a follower of Christ, you are made a new creation to the glory of God.

HIS WORD

"Therefore, if anyone is in Christ, he is a new creation; the old has gone, the new has come!" (2 Corinthians 5:17).

MY PRAYER

What difference has Christ made in your life? Has He changed your attitude, actions, and how you treat others? Can you tell someone your experiences to help them know Christ personally? Practice doing that and it will make a difference in someone's life.

MY STUDY

Isaiah 64:6–8; Psalm 1:1–3

During the Vietnam War, a 19-year-old soldier was critically injured when a grenade exploded nearby. He lost both legs and both eyes.

For seven hours, Dr. Swan worked hard to save his life. To the surprise of many, the soldier survived.

Noting the soldier's condition, other doctors ridiculed Dr. Swan. They chided, "He'd have been better off dead." Those harsh words haunted Dr. Swan for twenty years. Eventually he decided to find out whether his life-saving efforts had been a mistake. After a two-year search, he finally located the soldier, now a thirty-nine-year-old man.

Quite relieved, Dr. Swan was reunited with a veteran who had a strong faith in God. He had a loving family, two daughters, and a good job. Above all, this once wounded soldier had a reason for living and a spirit full of joy!

Like the soldier, many of us have been wounded in different ways – physically, emotionally, even spiritually. We live in a fallen world. People hurt us and we hurt others, continuing the cycle. But these hurts cannot defeat us when we place our lives in God's care. When we are feeling dejected, His arms are around us.

My friend, have you been hurt? Will you let God and His Word heal your broken heart and stitch up your wounds? God's Word is full of promises and comfort. To receive God's healing, start by memorizing the verses that speak to your need. Meditate on them. Then give God all that concerns you. In return, He will give you a life worth living.

It takes time to heal. But God can, and will, put you back on your feet. He can, and will, turn your sorrow into joy!

HIS WORD
"The LORD is close to the brokenhearted and saves those who are crushed in spirit" (Psalm 34:18).

MY PRAYER
"Heavenly Father, You know all of my wounds and pain. I give them to You right now and ask for Your healing. Thank You for being the God of all comfort that I may come to You with everything and receive Your peace. In Your wonderful, matchless name I pray, amen."

MY STUDY
Isaiah 61:1–3; 1 Peter 4:12–16

Head to Toe

Becky was sweet and lovely. She carried a healthy confidence in herself and a genuine love for others. One day, a friend asked Becky why she had such a good self-image.

Becky explained that it came from her mother. Her mother would hold her in her arms and, starting with her toes, say: "I love your little toes. I love your little feet. I love your little ankles. I love your little legs. I love your little thighs." And so on.

Proceeding all the way up her little body, her mother named the various parts, saying: "I love your little neck ... chin ... mouth ... nose ... eyes ... ears ... face ... hair ..."

Then she'd continue, "I love you when you're good. I love you when you're bad. I love you when you're clean. I love you when you're dirty."

There was no doubt in this child's mind that she was loved. Her mother loved everything about her, and frequently told her so.

This little ritual meant so much to Becky. Even when she was twelve, she still climbed into her mother's lap and asked to hear these very same words.

Well, friend, that's how God loves you. He loves everything about you. He created you and knows every detail about you. He loves you when you're good; He loves you when you're not. His love never changes, no matter what. He loves you just the way you are – not like the way you wish you were. He loves you unconditionally.

He invites you to come to Him so He can demonstrate to you His love, grace, and mercy. Remember, you're loved by Him from the top of your head to the tip of your toes.

HIS WORD
"Before I formed you in the womb I knew you, before you were born I set you apart; I appointed you as a prophet to the nations" *(Jeremiah 1:5).*

MY PRAYER
Tell God how thankful you are that He loves you unconditionally. How can you express to those close to you that you love them unconditionally? Start by telling them. Then demonstrate a more patient and loving attitude with them as you depend on the Holy Spirit's power. It will have a wonderful effect on them.

MY STUDY
Matthew 10:29–31; Psalm 145:15,16

Randy had talked with God, his wife, his sons, and others about moving to the inner city for a few years. A year prior to their move, Tina and Randy wondered whether they were really called to this work. They reasoned that their personalities and backgrounds didn't fit the profile of what a person would need to succeed there.

Randy's an uptown kind of guy who has advanced degrees and likes opera. He could stand for an hour in front of just one painting, a strange phenomenon even among suburbanites. He wondered, "Can I learn to value, serve, befriend, and love the poorest people in the city?"

God helped the Whites see that He was bigger than all of their concerns. Their effectiveness was up to Him. As it turned out, their new neighborhood needed people with their qualities. And they have been surprised by their capacity for adapting when necessary!

In 1 Corinthians 9:22, the apostle Paul talks about intentionally becoming weak. Randy realized he could learn to talk with people with minimal education, learn to wear denims instead of slacks, learn to appreciate mariachi music, and maybe learn to eat Vietnamese food without crying.

If he tried to minister from the outside and then went home to his comfortable, insulated environment, would he really earn the credibility it would take to proclaim the gospel with authority to the inner city? He was convinced that becoming weak, as Paul said, meant living in the city and having his flower boxes stolen, seeing a car fire-bombed in the alley, experiencing gunfire on New Year's Eve, and hassling with the city to get the streetlights back on.

Reaching others for Christ may require you to go somewhere new, start over, or even become weak. Friend, don't be afraid to follow God's leading to a new and exciting adventure in life.

HIS WORD
"Be strong and take heart, all you who hope in the LORD" (Psalm 31:24).

MY PRAYER
Is God calling you to a different ministry at your church or even to a new city or job? Don't be afraid. Ask God for His peace and strength. He promises to answer your prayer in a far greater way than you could imagine.

MY STUDY
1 Corinthians 9:20–22; Isaiah 41:10

Flesh for Stone

"I am Olga. I am a communist! And will be until I die. I am an atheist! And will be until I die."

Those were the words of a 55-year-old Russian schoolteacher. Staunchly, she stood to introduce herself to her discussion group.

This was the first day of a four-day teachers' conference in Moscow, a conference about a biblically-based morals and ethics curriculum led by Americans and other Westerners. Without judgment, they demonstrated the love and acceptance of Jesus Christ to the conferees.

On day three, Olga once again stood in her discussion group. She said, "Today, I publicly denounce atheism and publicly embrace Jesus Christ as my Savior and Lord." Her heart had melted.

Nancy, one of the Americans leading the conference, said, "In one week, Olga's countenance had changed so much we didn't recognize her. It was a new Olga!"

At a party later in her home, Olga stood and again renounced communism and atheism and professed her new allegiance to Jesus Christ.

Then she revealed something remarkable. She thanked God for her two grown children who lived in Siberia, hundreds of miles from Moscow. Years earlier, they'd placed their faith in Jesus Christ. For ten years they prayed that their mother would come to Christ. Faithfully, the God of love and mercy answered their continued prayers.

Olga has grown tremendously in her faith. She prays with other Christian teachers, uses the Bible as she teaches morals and ethics, and helps more than one hundred students in a semiweekly after-school Bible study.

Pray for the Olgas in your life. Love them with God's love – with mercy, tenderness, and acceptance.

Oh, friend, reach out to your neighbors and colleagues. Spend time with them. Share His Word. Demonstrate His love. Like Olga, their hardened hearts will melt right into the hands of the Savior, Jesus Christ.

HIS WORD
"I will give you a new heart and put a new spirit in you; I will remove from you your heart of stone and give you a heart of flesh" (Ezekiel 36:26).

MY PRAYER
Think about your neighbors and colleagues. Do they know Christ as Savior? If not, how can you help introduce them to Him? How about inviting them to a musical at your church or a Bible study? Or maybe you could ask them at an appropriate time, "If you were to die today, are you sure you would go to heaven?"

MY STUDY
2 Peter 3:9; Psalm 86:5

A Child Shall Lead Them

In her book *A Window to Heaven*, Dr. Diane Komp tells the story of Ann and the impact her young son had on her life.

When Ann married, she gave up her nominal Christian belief, which seemed irrelevant to her new life. Although this couple was economically privileged, the romance faded early and she soon considered her marriage a disaster. But the lifestyle had its rewards, and she adored her children, especially her youngest son, T. J.

Ann never sent her children to Sunday school, and the name of God was never mentioned in their house. But one day T. J. said, "Mama, I love you more than anything in the world, except God. I love Him a little bit more!"

Stunned, she pondered, "Why would he speak of God?" Even more mysterious was why he should love a God whose name he'd never heard from her.

Two days later he followed along while his sister was horseback riding. T. J. crossed a snow-covered creek and broke through the ice. He died immediately.

The first words out of Ann's mouth when she heard the news were, "I hate you, God!" Even as she spit out the words, she felt herself held in loving arms. As her world shattered around her, she remembered that T. J. had bought her a Christmas gift that week at the Secret Santa shop at school and kept trying to give it to her. Each time he tried, she laughed and told him to put it away until Christmas. He did. After he died, she opened it. It was a beautiful necklace with a cross.

"From the mouths of babes." What an influence that little five-year-old boy had. His whole family changed. His mother experienced the true love of God in her grief. His father became a Christian. Slowly, their materialism faded away, their marriage was healed, and they became new creatures in Christ.

HIS WORD
"... and a little child will lead them" (Isaiah 11:6).

MY PRAYER
Have you ever had a tragedy in your life? How did God turn something devastating into something good? Do you know someone going through a tragedy right now? Perhaps you could go and pray with that person. Share the pain and share God's love.

MY STUDY
Luke 10:21; Psalm 8:2

True Faith

When Becky Tirabassi surrendered her life to Christ twenty-two years ago, she changed almost instantly. She had been a self-described "morally loose, beer-drinking, bar-hopping 21-year-old." Kevin, the man she was living with and hoped to marry, was astounded that she wanted to move out, and expressed genuine concern for her emotional stability.

She begged Kevin to consider the claims of Christ for himself. She struggled emotionally with the potential loss of one tangible love to hold onto the love of God, whom she couldn't see. Every night she cried herself to sleep, but finally realized that she had to give up on Kevin.

When she moved from California to her hometown in Ohio to develop her new relationship with God, Kevin stayed behind. They drifted apart. They eventually married other people and lost track of each other.

While visiting California recently, she was surprised to run into Kevin outside a store. Becky immediately recognized her old boyfriend and tried to get his attention. At first he didn't recognize her, but when he did, he stood stunned in the middle of the street.

Most significant to Becky about that meeting was not the reminder that she'd lost Kevin all those years ago, but that she'd gained an intimate, eternal relationship with God. Faith in God had completed her and given purpose and meaning to her once addicted, lost life. Becky has written ten books, runs her own company, been happily married to the same man for eighteen years, and reared a son.

As she says, "The transforming power of faith hinges on a relationship with the living, loving God." True faith should, will, and does change our lives and how we live. Dear friend, step out in faith and completely trust Him today. He'll do for you what He did for Becky, and me, and millions of others.

HIS WORD
"Come near to God and he will come near to you. Wash your hands, you sinners, and purify your hearts, you double-minded" (James 4:8).

MY PRAYER
Have you ever had to say good-bye to something or someone because it wasn't pleasing to God? How has God blessed you for your faithfulness and obedience? Ask God for His guidance that you may continually be in His will.

MY STUDY
Psalm 103:1–5; Isaiah 48:17

Their fathers were ministers. They were students at a private Christian college. They were in love. And they were sexually involved.

"In the arms of this man, I thought I'd found love," Sydna said. As they pursued their relationship, the unexpected happened. Sydna became pregnant at nineteen years of age.

"After I walked through the [clinic] doors and they told me I was pregnant, I was faced with a choice. Here I was — a boyfriend who was unsupportive, who said he'd leave me, walk away; a mother who'd been through a traumatic divorce, who I know would've been shamed; ... and a baby I was carrying that I loved. Faced with these odds, stacked in this corner, I chose the one option I thought would erase my mistake. But it erased nothing."

As she walked up the steps to the abortion clinic, she sensed the Holy Spirit saying, "Don't do this." But she went on. Sydna asked the abortion counselor, "Will this affect me psychologically?"

"Oh, no," said the counselor, "It will make your problem go away; it will make your life easier."

Sydna will be the first to tell you that it was a lie. The abortion did affect her for many years, emotionally and physically. In a Bible study for women who've been through abortions, Sydna dealt with the issues in her life, discovering the assurance of God's forgiveness and learning to forgive herself.

Today, Sydna manages the Crisis Pregnancy Center Ministry of Focus on the Family. It provides resources for more than three thousand crisis pregnancy centers across the country.

Sydna encourages women to remember that there's no sin God won't forgive. However, you may need help forgiving yourself. God, through His people, will compassionately and lovingly help you deal with it.

Friend, *that's* a God of love and mercy. Turn to Him today.

HIS WORD
"I, even I, am He who blots out your transgressions, for My own sake, and remembers your sins no more" (Isaiah 43:25).

MY PRAYER
Have you, or has someone you know, ever experienced abortion? If you have asked for forgiveness, then you are forgiven. If you are still having trouble dealing with it, seek out a good Bible-based support group. They can lovingly minister to you without condemnation. You can have peace.

MY STUDY
Psalm 85:2; Lamentations 3:22

True Hope

Sue was struggling. She and her ex-husband were trying to reconcile their troubled marriage. Then one day, Sue met Robert and Mary.

One evening, the two couples talked for hours. Sue was so encouraged by this discussion that she asked Robert and Mary if they could help her and her ex-husband in their reconciliation.

Robert and Mary agreed to try. But the more they learned about this couple's background, the more difficult the task seemed. Robert told them they simply had no hope without God!

Robert looked at the most basic need in this couple's life – their need for Christ. He shared with them the message of God's love and forgiveness. Realizing their deep sin, the struggling couple placed their trust in Christ. There they found true hope.

Today this couple is reconciled. They have put the past behind them and together are continuing to grow in the truth of God's love and forgiveness.

Friend, are you struggling? Is your marriage in trouble? Are your children rebelling? Have you lost your joy? Turn to God. As Robert said, there is "no hope without God." How true that is! Whatever circumstance you are facing, God is your only hope. Don't turn to Him when you have exhausted all other avenues of help – turn to Him first.

In the psalms, we read that only God can give us rest from our struggles and solid support in our distress. "Find rest, O my soul, in God alone; my hope comes from him. He alone is my rock and my salvation; he is my fortress, I will not be shaken" (62:5). What firmer foundation could we have than placing our trust in the God of the universe, who is the same yesterday, today, and forever?

HIS WORD

"But now, Lord, what do I look for? My hope is in you" (Psalm 39:7).

MY PRAYER

Have you ever felt hopeless about a circumstance or life in general? Reflect back on that time. What gave you comfort? Perhaps that time is now. If so, ask God for His comfort and read His Word. The verses below are a good place to start.

MY STUDY

Romans 5:1–5; Jeremiah 17:7,8

Cristi packed her belongings and headed west. She was a single journalist obeying God's call to join our staff. On her U-Haul truck were her great-grandmother's wedding band, her grandfather's oak secretary, and a prized oak china cabinet she had scrimped and saved to buy. There were also photo albums, electronics, and personal items – everything she needed to set up housekeeping.

Unfortunately, the truck was stolen from the parking lot her first night in California. She moved through the first few days in shock.

Three days later, the truck was discovered in the Mojave desert a couple of hours away. But her photo albums, her bed, and some odds and ends were all that was left.

As she visited the home of some staff women a few months later, the women wanted to encourage her. They told how God had provided for them to buy a home and each item inside the home. It was quite an impressive tour. The home was beautifully furnished with antiques, and the stories of *how* God had provided for them were overwhelming. In fact, at the end of the evening, Cristi thought to herself, "Yes, God can do that for you, but He will never do that for me."

She believed that God was *able* to do it; she just did not believe that He loved her and was *willing*. But four years later, as a newlywed, she sat in her apartment sharing with a friend how God provided for each item in her home.

Today, her home is full of antiques. She and her husband are still ministering for Christ. As guests come into her home, she tells how God provided their furnishings, giving God the glory for what He's done.

Dear friend, God loves you and wants to provide in tangible ways. Trust Him.

HIS WORD

"Now to Him who is able to do immeasurably more than all we ask or imagine according to his power that is at work within us, to him be glory" (Ephesians 3:20,21).

MY PRAYER

"Father, the Great Provider, thank You for all that You have given me. I am constantly amazed at how much You care for my every need. Help me to continually trust You and not be concerned about the provisions of life. In Your omnipotent name I pray, amen."

MY STUDY

Psalm 34:10; Isaiah 26:3,4

Into the Depths

All of us have sins of the past, things for which we have difficulty forgiving ourselves, let alone forgetting about. Do you hold on to sins of your past? If so, why don't you let them go? God has. The prophet Micah writes about God: "You will tread our sins underfoot and hurl all our iniquities into the depths of the sea" (7:19).

Jerry Bridges, in his book *Transforming Grace*, writes about this vivid picture of God's deliberate forgiveness. He relates the picture to his own days in the Navy.

As a naval officer, he dragged grappling hooks across the bottom of the sea, looking for lost equipment. After searching all day, he realized the equipment was lost forever in the unfathomable depths of the ocean. Can you imagine losing something in such a vast place? It would be irretrievable. The same applies to our sins.

Our sins don't accidentally fall overboard. But, as Jerry says, God intentionally *hurls* "them into the depths of the sea to be lost forever, never to be recovered, never to be held against us." All because God has fully dealt with them through the death, burial, and resurrection of His Son, Jesus Christ.

If something in your head tells you that your sins can't be forgiven, don't believe it. It is a lie from the evil one, put there to keep you from having peace and joy in your Christian walk. Instead, believe the Word of God. If Christ is your Savior and you've accepted His salvation, your sins are at the bottom of the sea, exactly where God put them.

Confess your sins today and receive His forgiveness. Then, forgive yourself. His peace awaits you.

HIS WORD

"God made him who had no sin to be sin for us, so that in him we might become the righteousness of God" (2 Corinthians 5:21).

MY PRAYER

"Dear Lord, our Righteousness, I am amazed that You would provide salvation for a person so undeserving. That You would forgive my sins is incredible. That You would put my sins so far away from You and remember them no more is unfathomable. Thank You, Lord Jesus. Amen."

MY STUDY

Isaiah 25:9; Psalm 68:20

Many of us look for love and approval in all the wrong places. We look for our identity and value in how others see us instead of how God sees us.

Pam lived in a Southern town. She was known for her deep friendships. She had a wonderful ministry, felt valued by others, and was influential for Christ. She had a secure life.

Then she moved away from this place of comfort. Although Pam didn't change, her environment did. Suddenly, in this new place, she no longer had the same influence or ministry. It seemed that even her questions sometimes offended people.

Throughout all this transition, Pam held fast to God and His promises. She turned to the Bible to remind herself who she was in God's sight.

In Deuteronomy 33:12, God says, "Let the beloved of the LORD rest secure in him, for he shields him all day long, and the one the LORD loves rests between his shoulders."

We are all susceptible to insecurities. We want approval and acceptance from those around us. When we don't get it, we sometimes lose our security about ourselves and our place in the world. Then we try harder to meet others' expectations of us. But the truth is, my friend, the only opinion that matters is that of the One who created us. We are the "beloved of the LORD." Can you imagine that? We have a position of importance to God Almighty!

Rest securely in the marvelous truth of His Word. Take it to heart and remind yourself of it every day. You are beloved of God and wonderfully made in His image.

HIS WORD

"You are a people holy to the LORD your God. The LORD your God has chosen you out of all the peoples on the face of the earth to be his people, his treasured possession" (Deuteronomy 7:6).

MY PRAYER

Do you have trouble remembering how valuable you are to God? Maybe this will help you. Take some index cards and, as you read the Bible, copy down the verses that speak of God's love for you. Carry the cards with you or put them in prominent places. Read them over and over again.

MY STUDY

John 3:16; Psalm 34:15

Trust and Obey

L ife is full of challenges. Sometimes the choice is a simple one, yet difficult to make: obey or disobey? The dilemma facing Melanie is one that we all face at various times in our lives.

For two years Tim and Melanie had discussed a job change that meant relocating. Although Tim sensed God's calling to go, Melanie's heart wanted to stay. Finally, she agreed to go. She didn't want to fail to obey God.

The Lord says in the Gospel of John, "If you love me, you will obey what I command" (14:15). She loved God and desired to follow His will.

Even though she had agreed to the move, the reality of the decision hit Melanie when the time came to sell their house. She burst into tears and refused to sign the contract. The thought of leaving the security of her home, friends, neighbors, and church was more than she could bear. Even though she knew that she should be obedient, the fear of change was overwhelming.

Proverbs tell us, "Whoever listens to me will live in safety and be at ease, without fear of harm" (1:33). When we listen to God and obey His leading, His peace will be with us. There is no need to fear. This was a truth that needed to sink into Melanie's heart. It did. Finally, she chose obedience. Placing her trust in God, she signed the contract. And can you guess what happened to Tim and Melanie? God blessed their move.

Friend, is there some area where you are struggling with obedience to God – a relationship, a job, a stronghold, a gift you aren't using? Take it to Him in prayer. Be sensitive to His leading. Then obey and trust that God will bless your obedience!

HIS WORD

"Teach me to do your will, for you are my God; may your good Spirit lead me on level ground"
(Psalm 143:10).

MY PRAYER

Think about an area of your life where you feel resistant to God's leading. Are you afraid? Worried? Insecure? Read Philippians 4:13. Ask God to forgive you. Then ask Him for courage. Now, you can take the necessary steps to obey God's will.

MY STUDY
Matthew 25:20–23; Exodus 24:7

A spiritual dry spell was a bit unusual for Carol. Even though she was a Bible teacher and had frequent exposure to the Scriptures, her prayers felt like they went nowhere.

She did everything she knew to do, but she just couldn't reconnect with God. Nothing helped. Singing, praying, and reading Scripture still left her empty.

Finally, in desperation, she cried out to God. There were no words, but it seemed the Spirit within was interceding for her. This was a new experience for her and a turning point in this valley of her spiritual walk. She knew that God was there.

Romans 8:26 tells us just that: "The Spirit helps us in our weakness. We do not know what we ought to pray, but the Spirit himself intercedes for us with groans that words cannot express."

Are there times when you feel the need to pray, to receive a fresh Word, infilling, or touch from God, but you don't have the words to adequately express your need? Don't fret, my friend. Instead, cry out to God. He will hear you call His name, and the Spirit will intercede for you, expressing what you cannot.

Stay in God's Word every day. The Scriptures hold answers to any and every circumstance of life and all of the emotions that go with it. Hebrews 4:12 says, "The word of God is living and active." It speaks to your needs today, just as it has to innumerable people for thousands of years.

If you are going through a dry spell like Carol did, don't give up. Keep reading the Word. Keep praying. Ask God how He would have you pray. God will meet you! He will be your turning point.

HIS WORD

"Whoever drinks the water I give him will never thirst. Indeed, the water I give him will become in him a spring of water welling up to eternal life" (John 4:14).

MY PRAYER

"Dear loving heavenly Father, reveal to me why I lost the joy I had when I first knew You. I know that it was not just a feeling, but help me to reconnect with You so I may know Your presence, moment by moment. In Your precious name, amen."

MY STUDY

Deuteronomy 8:11–14; Psalm 42:1–5

It Is Not I

St. Augustine's influence on Christianity has been immense. His works on theology have been foundational for centuries and his autobiographical *Confessions* is a classic. Perhaps his influence is all the more powerful when you consider the struggles he had in his life.

Augustine lived in fourth-century North Africa. Early in his life, he was a hot-blooded rebel who was a womanizer and a cult member. He truly lived the low life.

Even after he placed his trust in Christ, his old life continued to chase him. Occasionally, he was faced with the temptation to return to his old ways.

One day he saw an attractive female acquaintance. She invitingly called out to him, but Augustine kept walking. She kept pursuing, calling out, "Augustine! It is I! It is I!"

"Yes, I know," he replied. "But it is *not* I."

Oh, dear friend, God changes lives! Augustine became a great Christian philosopher.

Remember what the Bible says happens when you place your trust in Christ: "Therefore, if anyone is in Christ, he is a new creation; the old has gone, the new has come!" (2 Corinthians 5:17). We are new creations, no longer slaves to what we used to do. We are "dead to sin." Although we may feel the temptation to give in to these old sins, their power over us is gone.

What is more, God has provided a way to escape the temptation of sin. "God is faithful; he will not let you be tempted beyond what you can bear. But when you are tempted, he will also provide a way out so that you can stand up under it" (1 Corinthians 10:13).

So, when you are tempted, call out to God. He *will* help you!

HIS WORD
"Because he himself suffered when he was tempted, he is able to help those who are being tempted" (Hebrews 2:18).

MY PRAYER
Where is your greatest temptation? Is it coveting, lust, anger, gossip, or something else? What do you do to withstand temptation? Do you pray for strength, remove yourself from the situation, or get angry with yourself and feel defeated? Ask God for help. He will provide it.

MY STUDY
Romans 6:11–14; Psalm 119:11

Put Down Roots

Have you ever enjoyed that wonderful sweet camellia smell on a warm summer morning? Ahhh, that's what Mary Lou longed for! And to be warmed by Southern sunshine.

You see, God transplanted Mary Lou from the Southern U.S. to the Pacific Northwest over ten years ago. But in Oregon, the sun doesn't shine as much and camellias are hard to find! Mary Lou was homesick.

Through those years, Mary Lou refused to bury her roots. Her constant prayer was "How much longer, Lord?" She saw this as a temporary assignment until God took her back to where she longed to be.

Then one day Mary Lou saw a missions film that struck a chord in her heart. She sensed the Lord asking her, "Will you go *anywhere* for me?"

She realized her home was where the Lord led her. She decided to be content, no matter where He sent her – even Oregon!

Have you ever moved to a new place? It's tough. You have to find new friends, a new doctor, a new mechanic, a new hair stylist. That's on top of learning your way around town and adjusting to a new work environment. It can be very scary, and if you aren't careful, you will look back so fondly at the situation you came from that you won't be able to fully appreciate your new circumstance.

God said, "Never will I leave you; never will I forsake you" (Hebrews 13:5). No matter where you are, God is always with you. So don't fret, my friend. Learn to be content with where the Lord has planted you. Don't be afraid to let the roots grow. And breathe the sweet fragrance of His sovereign plan for you.

HIS WORD

"The man who trusts in the LORD … will be like a tree planted by the water that sends out its roots by the stream. It does not fear when heat comes; its leaves are always green. It has no worries in a year of drought and never fails to bear fruit" (Jeremiah 17:7,8).

MY PRAYER

Are you content? Why not? Do you believe God placed you where you are? Pay close attention to your environment. You'll find blessings all around. Praise God for them and for His constant presence. Repeat this as needed.

MY STUDY

Isaiah 54:10; Proverbs 18:24

Shadow of the Almighty

For two days, Houng Taing and his wife, Samoeun, had been walking. Now they were on the brink of death. They desperately needed water.

When Samoeun could go no further, she begged to stop. She cried out, "I must drink water, or I think I will die now!"

They began to pray. They were only a half day from reaching freedom. They couldn't give up.

Houng prayed, "Lord Jesus, if You want us to die here, we are ready. But if You want us to live and serve You, then please show us where there is water to drink so we can go on."

Minutes later, they discovered God's provision — a hidden pool of rainwater. They rejoiced in praise to God. He renewed their strength. And late that night, they slipped across the border into Thailand, to freedom.

It was 1979, and the Taings were forced to escape their Cambodian homeland. Four years earlier, communists had taken over.

Houng and Samoeun were "guilty" of three offenses for which the communist regime was executing Cambodians. They were well-educated, had traveled abroad, and were Christians.

After the communists came to power, the Taings were in constant danger. Time and again, they turned to God in prayer. He provided, giving them shelter and protecting them. It was an extraordinarily difficult and miserable time. Death continually lurked in the shadows, but the Taings kept the faith and always trusted God.

If you have ever been in danger, did you cry out to God? Scripture gives us an emergency "911 number" to call when we are in trouble. It is Psalm 91:1, "He who dwells in the shelter of the Most High will rest in the shadow of the Almighty." We are secure in God's shadow. In what safer place could we be?

HIS WORD

"The eyes of the LORD range throughout the earth to strengthen those whose hearts are fully committed to him"
(2 Chronicles 16:9).

MY PRAYER

"Our Father, Great Provider, You provide shelter for me and my family. You give us food to eat and water to drink. You clothe us and put shoes on our feet. For all of this and much more, I thank You. May Your name be praised forever. Amen."

MY STUDY
Psalm 91:1–16; Revelation 12:10–12

S he was dearly loved by her husband. But she lived in constant fear that he'd leave her for someone else, that his love for her would die.

The fear became paralyzing, controlling. It plagued her by day and jolted her awake at night. All the while, her husband was true to her. In fact, his devotion consistently deepened. He was a wonderful provider, an encouraging counterpart, a faithful friend, and a devoted father to their seven children.

The fear was a result of the fact that her husband had been married before, as a very young man, and had left his first wife.

Later, though, he placed his faith in Christ and God changed his life dramatically. He became a brand new person inside. When he remarried, it was for keeps. He loved God, and he loved his wife. He wanted nothing more than to be true to her. And he was.

After years of struggle with no relief, the woman received counsel from my husband. We'd been friends with this couple for years, but that conversation calmed her fears and changed her life.

First, Bill asked her to be honest with God, to tell God about her troubles and what she was feeling. Then, she must admit to God that she wasn't trusting Him. The Bible says to trust Him with *everything*. When you don't trust Him, it's a lack of faith. The Bible calls that sin.

Once she admitted her sin, she asked God to forgive her. He did. Then she thanked Him for His forgiveness and asked Him to fill her with His Holy Spirit.

As she trusted God, she was able to trust her husband. Eventually the fear subsided, and they enjoyed many years together in fruitful ministry.

My dear friend, whether you struggle with fear, doubt, or something else, learning to trust God and walk by faith is the key to life.

HIS WORD

"Trust in the LORD with all your heart and lean not on your own understanding; in all your ways acknowledge him and he will make your paths straight"
(Proverbs 3:5,6).

MY PRAYER

Reflect on your fears. Do they keep you from being all God wants you to be? Take each fear and write it down. Then search the Scriptures. There are 365 "fear nots" in the Bible — one for each day. Place a few beside each fear. Recite them. Soon you will experience victory over them.

MY STUDY
Philippians 4:6,7; Psalm 32:8–10

Truth, Grace, and Time

My friend Bill became a Christian when he was a student at the University of Michigan. During the early months of his Christian experience, Bill says he felt caught between two worlds. He was a smoker and carried a pack of cigarettes in his pocket. Eventually he had a desire to quit smoking, but that took a while.

Someone had given him a small pocket Bible about the size of a pack of cigarettes. When he was with his buddies at the fraternity house, he put the cigarette pack in his shirt pocket and the Bible in his hip pocket. When he was with his Christian friends, he reversed the two. One day he forgot to make the switch and found himself sheepishly explaining to his fraternity brothers why he carried a copy of the Bible!

Bill did not feel the freedom to be himself. He'd somehow gotten the message that Christians would be critical of him because he smoked.

Jesus demonstrated care and concern for people. He didn't label them. He knew that people need the truth. But they also need grace and time. Being like Christ means loving and caring for others, accepting them, and giving them time to change.

We can choose not to be judgmental of what others do, an attitude Jesus condemned in the Pharisees. We can choose to love those who struggle with things that we do not. We can choose to accept someone whose lifestyle differs from ours. We need to fight our tendency to do anything other than this. It's through our love that others will understand the acceptance of Jesus.

People like Bill need to know they are accepted by Christ and that they're accepted by us right where they are. God is the one who creates change in the lives of others. He changed our lives. He can change anyone. It only takes His truth, His grace, and time.

HIS WORD
"Accept one another, then, just as Christ accepted you, in order to bring praise to God" (Romans 15:7).

MY PRAYER
We don't accept sin, but we love people. Think of someone you have a hard time accepting. Now read 1 Corinthians 13:4–7. Go through each attribute of love and evaluate how it would help you accept this person. Look for opportunities to demonstrate this love. Review this practice frequently.

MY STUDY
Proverbs 17:9; Leviticus 19:18

Nurturing

Therefore, as God's chosen people, holy and dearly loved, clothe yourselves with compassion, kindness, humility, gentleness and patience. Bear with each other and forgive whatever grievances you may have against one another. Forgive as the Lord forgave you. And over all these virtues put on love, which binds them all together in perfect unity.

COLOSSIANS 3:12-14

The desire to nurture that God has placed within the heart of women should not be limited to the realm of children. A woman's capacity to nurture is deep and extensive. For example, studies have shown that one of the greatest attributes in female business executives is that of nurturing. Creating an environment where people can develop and lending an understanding ear and helping hand can make all the difference for co-workers or employees.

Nurturing is a process that takes time and commitment. When we fill our hearts and minds with the Word of God and His Spirit controls our lives, the impact of our nurturing can bring life-changing results.

When you have the joy of leading someone to Christ, how wonderful it is if you can also nurture or disciple your new friend as she grows in her Christian walk! You will share her excitement as she discovers the goodness of God.

Thank God for giving you the desire and ability to influence the lives of your family members, co-workers, neighbors, and friends.

In Christ Alone

When you work outside the home, achievements are measurable. You have reviews, raises, and accolades. But when you're a stay-at-home mom, sometimes your best work goes entirely unnoticed – let alone valued.

Maybe you're home with children right now, and you're missing the tangible rewards of the workplace. Perhaps you'll identify with Dee Dee, Lori, and Holly. Each of these ladies gave up her position in the work force to be a full-time mom. The transition wasn't easy.

When Dee Dee gave up an influential ministry to women, she immediately felt a sense of loss. Sure, it was wonderful to experience the joys of her first-born. But all the travel, speaking engagements, and influence came to a screeching halt when little Jeremy came along.

Lori enjoyed managing a corporate office – tackling complex accounting issues, planning marketing strategies, and motivating her staff. Her family's dual income was nearly cut in half when she decided her children needed her complete attention.

Holly managed the test kitchen for a very large food company. She invented recipes millions of people would use. You can imagine the adjustment she made in moving from the industrial kitchen to a small residential kitchen where today she tries to find something little Mark and Steven will agree to eat.

Maybe you have a similar story. It's essential for every mom to find her identity, not in her children or in her achievements, or her husband, or any other facet of life. They're all important. But it's critically important our identity comes only from Christ, who made us, loves us, and holds the key to our self-esteem.

Your work is not your life. Your home is not your life, even your children are not your life. *Christ* is your life.

Whether you're at work, at home, or managing both worlds, remember, dear friend, that your identity is found in Christ alone. Then whatever you're doing is rewarding.

HIS WORD
"For to me, to live is Christ and to die is gain" (Philippians 1:21).

MY PRAYER
Do you ever question your decisions in life? Have you ever lost sight of your identity? Next time you do, stop, pick up the Bible, and read all the wonderful words that God wrote just for you. You are beloved of God.

MY STUDY
Exodus 15:2; Psalm 73:25,26

Blessed Are the Meek

The Bible is filled with paradoxes, profound truths wrapped up in contrasting statements. Today, we're looking at one of the Beatitudes from the Sermon on the Mount found in Matthew 5:

> Blessed are the meek, for they will inherit the earth. (v. 5)

Well, what does it mean to be meek? It sounds pretty passive, almost wimpy.

Far from it!

One of the finest testimonies of contemporary meekness is from the late Corrie ten Boom. In her classic book, *The Hiding Place*, she told the amazing story about surviving World War II and the Nazi concentration camps.

At one point, she and her sister Betsy obtained a small bottle of vitamins. Since they and the other prisoners were severely malnourished, the vitamins held the key to life. In the camp, vitamins were far more valuable than gold.

Corrie's natural instinct was to hide the bottle from the others. But Betsy gently corrected her sister, saying, "If we are to be like Jesus, we should share what we have with the least of these."

So every day, Corrie opened the little bottle and dispensed the precious vitamins to the other women in their bunkhouse. Every day she worried that they would soon run out. Miraculously, the tiny bottle kept the whole bunkhouse supplied for several months!

Betsy taught Corrie and the other women in the bunkhouse the biblical principle that "meek" love is the kind that honors others enough to give away what we value most.

How about you? Do you live a life of meekness? Are you gentle in spirit?

Ask God today to help you develop this character in your life. It has rich and wonderful rewards.

HIS WORD

"Do nothing out of selfish ambition or vain conceit, but in humility consider others better than yourselves" (Philippians 2:3).

MY PRAYER

Reflect on your life. Do you put others' needs before your own? Do you exhibit a gentle, generous spirit? Ask God to conform you to His likeness, to create a gentle spirit within you. Thank Him for His goodness.

MY STUDY

Psalm 25:8–10; Isaiah 53:7

Spilt Milk

Young Richard was at that awkward stage when a boy's voice changes. His face hadn't quite caught up with the growth of his nose, and he was clumsy. When he walked through the house, things broke!

One day while reaching into the fridge, he knocked over a pitcher of milk. It shattered on the floor. His pent-up frustration finally got the best of him, and he screamed, "I hate myself!"

His mother quickly wiped up the mess, wrapped her arms around him, and said, "I don't care how many pitchers of milk you spill – I love you. Everyone goes through this stage, and you *will* grow out of it, too!"

There's a lesson here for all of us. God doesn't demand perfection. He doesn't love us for how we look, what we do, or how we serve Him. He loves us as a mother loves a son or daughter – whether that person is young or old in the faith.

God doesn't stand over us with His hands on His hips, yelling. No, God will gladly clean up the mess, awaiting us with open arms.

When you accepted Christ by faith, you entered into a relationship with God that is based on His unconditional love. That means you can't do anything too terrible for Him to forgive. No mess is too big for Him to clean up.

My friend, don't get caught in the trap of trying to please God through perfection. You'll end up a very frustrated, defeated Christian.

The Christian life is not about keeping laws and trying to be a good person. No, the Christian life is recognizing your need for a Savior. You desperately need God's undying love and forgiveness.

Striving for perfection? Give yourself a break. Place all your confidence in Jesus, and in Him alone. That's the kind of woman who pleases God, and that's the kind of woman God uses.

HIS WORD

"I pray that you, being rooted and established in love, may have power, together with all the saints, to grasp how wide and long and high and deep is the love of Christ, and to know this love that surpasses knowledge" (Ephesians 3:17–19).

MY PRAYER

"All-sufficient, loving heavenly Father, thank You for Your grace. Thank You that You love me even though I am desperately imperfect. Help me to trust only in You and not in my own abilities. Make me into the woman that You want me to be. Amen."

MY STUDY

Jeremiah 31:3; Psalm 146:5–10

Jealousy, nit-picking, infighting, selfish agendas — we'd like to think these problems don't occur among Christians, but we all know better! We have a lot of Kingdom work to do, but we'll crumble from within and be totally ineffective if we don't learn how to put others before ourselves.

With that in mind, I'd like to offer some practical advice on encouragement, all beginning with the letter "C": compliment, confidence, and compassion.

To *compliment* a friend means to tell her what you appreciate about her. It's taking note of ways she's making progress. Not idle flattery or back-patting, but admiration founded on solid evidence. "You're great in front of an audience, Sally. People really identify with what you say." Or, "You handled that sticky situation so well, Fran! I'm learning how to lead just from watching you!"

Express *confidence* in your friends. This is especially important when someone has made a mistake.

Peter denied Christ three times. It might have been all over — the friendship, trust, everything, but immediately after the resurrection, Jesus told Peter He still loved him and trusted him. In fact, Jesus gave Peter the enormous responsibility of caring for the rest of His followers.

Lastly, we can show *compassion*. When friends are going through hard times, they may feel unlovable. For these moments, we need to be especially supportive, to listen a lot. Instead of offering advice, we need to share in her pain, talk about our own failures, identify with her. This lets your friend know that she is not alone.

God could have selected any tool He wanted to change the world, but He chose people. We cannot function effectively unless we're working together in harmony in the home, in the office, in the church, and in our neighborhood. Let's develop the habit of encouragement. Let's stand back and be amazed at what God can do.

HIS WORD

"Do not let any unwholesome talk come out of your mouths, but only what is helpful for building others up according to their needs, that it may benefit those who listen" (Ephesians 4:29).

MY PRAYER

Practice the art of encouragement. Observe your friends or co-workers, and look for opportunities to compliment, express confidence, and show compassion. If you do at least one of these each day, you will be amazed at the marvelous work simple kindness can do in a person's life.

MY STUDY

Proverbs 16:23,24; Ecclesiastes 4:9,10

Prayer Warriors

A friend of mine is a popular Bible teacher. He describes the moment he realized the impact his mother had on his life and on the lives of his brother and sister.

One day he found a well-worn card above her kitchen sink. On it was a verse from Proverbs 18:

> A man's gift makes room for him,
> and brings him before great men. (v. 16)

She explained that she put it there because she'd claimed the verse for all three of her children long ago. For years, she asked the Lord to use the giftedness of her children to declare His glory.

That was many years ago. Since then, his brother, Orville, has become a respected preacher and evangelist in Latin America. His sister, Luci, is a popular Christian author and speaker. And the writer of the story? Chuck Swindoll is one of the best-known and most-beloved Christian leaders in America.

That's the power of prayer! A mother's prayer. Chuck loves his mother for faithfully holding him, Orville, and Luci before the Lord in prayer throughout their lives.

Let's earn our children's respect for years to come. Let's pray for them. Nothing will have a greater impact on their lives.

The wonderful thing about prayer is that any mother can be a prayer warrior. Chuck Swindoll's mother was a homemaker who posted notes to herself around the house as reminders to pray. But if you work outside of your home, you can put prayer reminders and verses in your car or on your desk at work.

You can also pray with other mothers. All across the country, mothers are gathering in small groups for one hour each week to pray. There's real strength and encouragement to be found when you can share your concerns with other moms and leave your worries in the hands of an all-loving, all-powerful God.

HIS WORD
"Again, I tell you that if two of you on earth agree about anything you ask for, it will be done for you by my Father in heaven" (Matthew 18:19).

MY PRAYER
Do you pray for your children, grandchildren, nieces, or nephews? How often? If you don't already have a prayer journal, start one. Keep track of the needs of these young people, pray faithfully for them, then rejoice as you write down each answer to prayer.

MY STUDY
Psalm 145:18,19; 1 Chronicles 16:8–11

Whenever I see young families, I am reminded of how hard it is to be young, how quickly time passes, and how important it is for our children to be nurtured – physically *and* emotionally.

Jesus demonstrated love and kindness to small children. He cared deeply about young people and gave them His undivided attention.

Are you a mother who is feeling a bit weary? The responsibilities of motherhood are relentless. The work can be frustrating. Yet there's no greater priority in life than the children whom God has entrusted to you. If you feel overwhelmed, anxious, or even angry by that burden, don't be afraid to get help. Those emotions are not unusual, and someone who understands can help you know what to do. Talk to a friend, a pastor, someone you trust. We all need help with something.

Perhaps you don't have children. Maybe you think children are not your responsibility. Let me challenge that thought. As a follower of Christ, there's no room to ignore little ones. The extent of your relationships with children will vary, but be sure to seize opportunities to demonstrate kindness when you can. There are thousands of ways to make young people feel important and special. You can take a walk with a child, buy something that her school is selling, read something she's written, or listen to her reading aloud.

When you're kind to children, you're like Christ. You may even be preparing the way for a child to come to Him.

These children represent our future. Don't forget, as the chorus says, "Jesus loves the little children. All the children of the world."

HIS WORD
"Jesus said, 'Let the little children come to me, and do not hinder them, for the kingdom of heaven belongs to such as these'" (Matthew 19:14).

MY PRAYER
Whether you have children or not, seek out opportunities to demonstrate God's love. Take an interest in the children in your neighborhood, volunteer to help in Sunday school, or ask the local school if they need help once or twice a week. Children need many positive influences. You could be one.

MY STUDY
Psalm 127:3; Proverbs 22:6

An Open Ear

Have you ever thought about the power of listening? Let me tell you the story of Jan and Tom Schuler.

Coming back from a vacation in Florida, the Schuler's van was involved in an accident with a semitrailer. Their daughter, Vanessa, was thrown from the vehicle and landed on her head. Little Vanessa was in a coma for three days. Two months shy of her sixth birthday, she died.

It was through a neighbor that Mark and Debbie learned of this tragedy. They'd never met Jan and Tom, but they could not get them off their minds.

So Mark found the couple's telephone number and called Tom. They agreed to meet. The next week, Debbie and Jan got together as well.

In the midst of the Schuler's grieving, a deep and lasting friendship was formed. Debbie spent time with Jan, crying with her, listening, and looking at Scripture. Debbie helped Jan – who was already a Christian – to focus on God and His character as she grieved the loss of her daughter.

In the meantime, Mark gave Tom materials about God and the Christian life. Tom had never placed his faith and trust in Christ as his Savior. Until Vanessa died, Tom thought he could handle anything. Now he felt powerless.

Mark continued to meet with Tom, listening and answering his questions about God. Within six months, Tom accepted Christ as his Savior.

The Schulers later told Mark and Debbie that they were the only ones who were willing to sit and talk. Sure, people brought meals and gave them hugs. But these new friends were the only ones who took time to go beyond the condolences. They were the only ones who listened as they struggled with deep questions about their daughter.

Make yourself available to hurting people. All it takes is an open ear and a sensitive heart. It will make all the difference!

HIS WORD

"Carry each other's burdens, and in this way you will fulfill the law of Christ" (Galatians 6:2).

MY PRAYER

Are you a good listener to those in need? Is this an area where you could improve? Ask God to give you a sensitive heart, one that hears the emotions behind the words. The words of hurting people will take on a whole new meaning.

MY STUDY

Proverbs 17:17; Job 2:11–13

Reaching Out

I'm sure you know someone who's hurting, physically or emotionally. Sharon had cancer, and was told by doctors that she couldn't be cured apart from a miracle. Through her experience, she learned a lot about how to be a good friend to someone in pain.

First, take time to personally visit your hurting friend. Phone calls are great, but a knock on the door is better. If she's sick, be sure to telephone before you visit. Keep your visit to fifteen or twenty minutes unless she insists you stay longer.

Second, look your friend in the eyes. And remember to smile! A smile eases tension and makes your friend feel comfortable and loved.

When your friend is giving an update on how things are going, listen carefully and give encouragement when you can. Don't gasp and say, "Oh, Sharon! Oh, dear!" Sometimes that tends to discourage people and make them think, "You know, I'm really worse off than I thought I was!"

Don't just say, "Let me know if there's anything I can do." Instead, be pro-active. Look around at what needs doing. And do it! Mow the lawn. Take out the garbage. Cook a meal. Clean the house. Baby-sit the children. Practical help lightens the burden.

When a friend is struggling, be sure to express your sadness. You don't need to have all the answers to her problems. She just needs to know you care.

Lastly, pray with your friend. Sometimes when people are hurting, they don't have the strength to pray for themselves. It can be a great comfort to hear someone else petitioning God on their behalf.

My friend, reach out in love to those who hurt. Not only will you comfort that person, you will know you're pleasing God. Nothing is more biblical or more Christlike than helping those in need.

HIS WORD

"Let us consider how we may spur one another on toward love and good deeds … Let us encourage one another" (Hebrews 10:24,25).

MY PRAYER

Do you know someone who has a serious illness or is going through a hard time? What can you do to help and encourage this person? Resolve to show this person in a real and practical way that God cares and that you care. Your kindness will touch them.

MY STUDY

Job 29:24; Psalm 72:12–14

Pray, Pray, Pray

Dr. Billy Kim of Suwon, Korea, the pastor of a ten-thousand-member Baptist church, tells this story.

Americans were on one side of the ridge, North Korean communists on the other. This was war! Bullets zipped, zoomed, and ricocheted from both zones. Many lives were lost as the ammunition often struck their targets.

This night on Heartbreak Ridge, so named by an American war correspondent, the battle was especially intense.

A bloodcurdling scream pierced the air. Fifty yards from the Americans' foxhole, in enemy territory, a young soldier was hit. In desperation, he cried out for help. Though several soldiers wanted to get to him, none dared leave the protection of the foxhole.

As time marched on, one soldier kept checking his watch. At the stroke of nine, without a word, he bravely crawled on his belly out to his wounded buddy. He grabbed him and quickly dragged him back to safety.

Later, the sergeant approached the brave soldier and asked, "Why did you wait until nine o'clock?"

The young man replied, "Sarge, when I left home my mother promised that she'd pray for me every morning at nine o'clock. I knew I'd be safe from the enemy if I went at nine o'clock."

This brave young man knew he could count on the prayers of his faithful mother. She promised to pray. He felt protected at the very moment that he knew she was asking God to keep him safe.

Do you have a child who hasn't trusted Jesus Christ, who is lost and wandering aimlessly, or who is in a dangerous circumstance?

Don't give up, my friend. God is a God who answers our prayers! Do you pray regularly for your children? Do they know you pray for them?

Today, make a commitment to pray for your children often, regularly, and without ceasing. When it counts the most, they will remember.

HIS WORD

"Pray in the Spirit on all occasions with all kinds of prayers and requests. With this in mind, be alert and always keep on praying for all the saints" (Ephesians 6:18).

MY PRAYER

Set aside a regular time of prayer for your children. Then be sure to tell them that you consistently pray for them. Even if they don't now, one day they will be grateful for your faithful prayers.

MY STUDY

Psalm 5:1–3; Deuteronomy 7:9

Nancy's two little boys were terrified by sirens. Whenever they heard an ambulance or fire truck, their faces filled with fear.

One day, a screaming siren caused Nancy to pull over to the side of the road. She glanced back at the boys. They were mortified. That's when she got an idea.

She said, "Whenever we hear a siren, let's stop and thank God that someone in need is getting help. We can pretend that the siren is God calling us to pray."

The boys seemed to like the idea, so Nancy said a quick and simple prayer. For years that simple prayer has taken fear from the boys' faces.

One day she and her three-year-old, Tommy, were shopping for groceries. As they stood in the checkout line, an ambulance with flashing lights and a wailing siren pulled into the parking lot. Nancy felt a tug on her jeans.

Tommy looked up at her, "Mom! Remember?" Nancy was reluctant to pray in public. Then she thought, "Will my boys later say, 'Do you *really* believe in God, Mom? Is everything that you've told us a game? Or is it real?'"

So, she stopped for a quick prayer. In that short, simple prayer, Nancy knew she and Tommy were meeting with God right there in the checkout line of the supermarket. It was not only a statement of consistency to her child, it was also a very genuine encounter with God.

What kind of example are you to your children? Do they know you to be a woman of consistency? A woman of prayer? Teach children the appropriateness of silent prayer, but don't disappoint their expectations.

The example they see from you will influence them the rest of their lives. And nothing will have a greater influence on the world than children who love and revere God. May He richly bless you, my friend, as you invest yourself in the rearing of those precious little children.

HIS WORD
"In everything set them an example by doing what is good. In your teaching show integrity" (Titus 2:7).

MY PRAYER
"Loving heavenly Father, thank You for the opportunity You've given me to influence these children. Help me to live a life of consistency and integrity each day so You may be glorified in their lives. Use me to show them Your ways. In Jesus' name, amen."

MY STUDY
Psalm 26:1–3; Malachi 2:5,6

Nail Clippers and Love

In his book *Letters to a Young Doctor*, Dr. Richard Selzer tells of spending his Wednesday afternoons in the local library for a time of refreshing.

While there, he noticed a number of regulars, mostly elderly people. Dr. Selzer knew them only by their clothes. He named them accordingly: Old Stovepipe, Mrs. Fringes, Galoshes, and Neckerchief.

One day he held the door open for Neckerchief, a stiff-walking man in his eighties. Shuffling by, Neckerchief pointed down to his knees and said, "The hinges is rusty." A wonderful friendship began.

One particular Wednesday, Dr. Selzer saw pain written all over Neckerchief's face. He asked him, "Is it the hinges?"

"Nope," Neckerchief replied. "It's the toes." He explained that his toenails had gotten too long because he couldn't reach to cut them.

Dr. Selzer left immediately to get his heavy-duty medical clippers.

When he got back, he took Neckerchief to the men's room. He stooped down and took off Neckerchief's shoes and socks. He took each toe and trimmed the nail, surprisingly thick and long. It took an hour to do each foot!

Dr. Selzer did Old Stovepipe's toes the next week, Mrs. Fringes' the next. He never again went to the library without those nail clippers.

What a wonderful picture of the kind of caring attention Jesus gives, which He demonstrated by washing feet!

Think of one simple, practical thing you can do for someone else. There are so many things you and I can do to show the love of Jesus to another. Do that one thing today.

Many people share faith in actions but not in words. Some share with words but show little concern by their actions. Look for ways to do both.

As you demonstrate your faith by love and service, the words you use to share your faith will be more valid.

HIS WORD

"Greater love has no one than this, that he lay down his life for his friends" (John 15:13).

MY PRAYER

Pray that God will make you more sensitive to others' needs and observant of the little things that need to be done for someone. Take the initiative and take action. Be a humble servant, as Jesus was.

MY STUDY

Psalm 41:1; Nehemiah 13:14

Dr. H. C. Morrison, a well-known minister, was walking down a busy street when he was stopped by a stranger. A man reached out and gave him a five-dollar bill.

"Thank you," the pastor said with a smile. He resumed his walk.

A few minutes later, he met a poor widow. He was aware she needed money, so he passed the five dollars along to her.

As Dr. Morrison went his way, he met another stranger. This person also gave him a five-dollar bill.

Soon Dr. Morrison came upon another person who also appeared needy. He said he felt strongly impressed that he should give the money to this person. This time, he decided to keep it.

Two times that day, strangers gave him unsolicited money. The first time he gave it away. The second time he kept it. No more five-dollar bills came his way that day.

He began to ponder the gifts and his response. He finally concluded, "I believe God would have continued the chain of money coming to me as I walked along if I had passed it on!"

We don't know what might have been. However, his story does illustrate a wonderful point: As he was being blessed, he became a blessing to someone else.

Giving to others doesn't necessarily mean giving money. There are thousands of things you can do to be an encouragement:

- Jot a note to your neighbor.
- Pick up a good book for a friend who's ill.
- Buy a bag of groceries for a single mom in your church.
- Call the visitors in your Sunday school class just to say hi.

The list is endless.

The next time you look in your wallet and see a five-dollar bill, think of Dr. Morrison. Let it remind you to be a blessing to someone today. It will honor God.

HIS WORD

"In everything I did, I showed you that by this kind of hard work we must help the weak, remembering the words the Lord Jesus himself said: 'It is more blessed to give than to receive'" (Acts 20:35).

MY PRAYER

Reflect on the last time someone gave you a gift of time, money, or effort. How did you feel after receiving the gift? Blessed? Did it make you want to give also? God set it up that way. Seek out ways to give of yourself and continue the cycle of blessing.

MY STUDY

Proverbs 3:27,28; Isaiah 58:10,11

A Mother's Love

In a dramatic display of courage, a cat raced into a burning building to rescue her kittens, darting in and out of the burning building five times. After rescuing her kittens, she moved them, one by one, across the street – a safe distance from the fire.

With her eyes blistered shut and her paws burned, she touched each one of her offspring with her nose, making sure she'd rescued them all.

The *New York Times* article said this: "It shows with all creatures, animals or people, there's no way of measuring a mother's love."

My friend, mothers are treasures. Their love is measureless. There is no end to what a mother will do for her children. Every mother I know would run into a burning building to save her child.

I've said many times, there's no greater call than that of a mother. I can think of no other occupation with greater responsibility or greater reward.

Every day is not a burning-building kind of day, but a dedicated mother comes to the rescue in thousands of other heroic ways. She changes endless numbers of diapers, gently kisses away the pain of hundreds of stubbed toes and scraped knees. She sacrifices lots of sleep for curfews, school projects, and children who are ill.

Your attitude toward motherhood makes a difference. Remember there are compensations at every age. Don't miss the joy of any one age. Sometimes these routine tasks may seem mundane, unrewarding, and even annoying, but they beautifully demonstrate sacrificial love – loving the way God loves.

That love is pervasive. It's all encompassing. It overrides any discomfort. It's a love that allows her to nurture and care for the child all her life, the kind of unselfish love that would drive her to run into a burning building and save her child.

Your measureless and sacrificial love will give your children more than life itself and will mark them forever, rescuing them from all kinds of situations, influencing families with God's love for generations to come.

HIS WORD

"A new command I give you: Love one another. As I have loved you, so you must love one another" (John 13:34).

MY PRAYER

"Lord Jesus, I love because You first loved me. Thank You for the infinite love You have given me for my family. May I always hold them dear and give tirelessly to them. And may they see You in my every breath. Amen."

MY STUDY

Ruth 1:14–18; Proverbs 31:27

Not long after graduating from college, I became a Christian. I met a dear woman, Dr. Henrietta Mears.

As the Christian education director at my church, Miss Mears took me under her wing. I wanted to know more about God, what He'd done for me, how I could please Him, and how He could change my life.

She was eager and thrilled with the opportunity to entrust to me all she knew about God. She taught me from God's Word, answered my questions, helped me through tough times, encouraged me, and prayed for me. She helped me grow.

Since then, God has given me the privilege of teaching others and helping them grow. I pass on to them what Miss Mears taught me. And often I hear how they're passing on to others what I've taught them.

"Discipleship" is the word used to define that kind of relationship, where one person is helping another grow in faith and become spiritually mature.

Are you in a relationship today where you're teaching what you've learned about God to someone else? Jesus is our example. He modeled discipleship when He taught His twelve disciples how to live the Christian life and then how to teach others.

All you have to do is trust God to use you. You can start today. You don't have to know everything about God before you start. Just begin today talking with your neighbor or a friend from church about the things you know of God.

Invest your life and your love for the Lord in someone else. You'll grow and learn together.

I've seen young students do it. I've seen moms do it. I've seen professional women do it. I've seen grandmothers do it.

It's all a matter of having a willing heart. And like my friend Dr. Mears, you'll touch lives all over the world.

HIS WORD
"Pay attention and listen to the sayings of the wise; apply your heart to what I teach" (Proverbs 22:17).

MY PRAYER
Do you know someone newer to the faith than you are? Have you considered discipling this person? Most people would welcome someone taking an active interest in their spiritual life. Ask this person if she would like to study the Bible or pray with you. You will both be blessed.

MY STUDY
John 21:15–17; Psalm 78:1–8

Sound Investment

Judy was thirty-four, single, and baby-sitting four children for some friends who were out of town for the weekend. When Judy arrived at their home, there was a seven-page note waiting for her.

It read something like this:

> Two children will arrive home at 2:30 and need a snack. They need to practice piano before one of them goes to soccer practice at 4:00.
>
> A neighbor will pick her up for soccer, and she will be home at 6:00. The third child will get home from her field trip at 5:30. She needs to clean her room.
>
> The first child needs to do her chores and homework. When the second child returns from soccer, order pizza from a specific pizza place with only certain toppings. They can eat, and then pack their lunches for the next day before you pick up child four at band practice at 9 p.m. Be sure to stop and get him a hamburger on the way home.

Judy was exhausted just *reading* the instructions, much less making it happen! Judy remembered her own mother sewing badges on her Girl Scout sash, getting her to school on time for band practice, washing her track clothes and basketball uniforms daily, driving, cooking, and then, of course, attending every event.

This is a tribute to Judy's mother and thousands like her. Thank you for all you've done to create well-rounded, happy children and for modeling Christlike servanthood.

If you're in the middle of childrearing, let me assure you it's worthwhile. At times, I'm sure, you really wonder. I did!

The time you invest in your child's life right now will reap rich rewards in the years to come. Hang in there!

God says of mothers in Proverbs 31:28, "Her children rise up and bless her. Her husband also." Today, I rise up and call you blessed. Someday your children will, too. I know, I'm there. I have two grown sons, two daughters-in-love, and four precious grandchildren. I have no regrets.

HIS WORD
"Trust in the Lord and do good … Commit your way to the Lord" (Psalm 37:3,5).

MY PRAYER
"All-knowing Father God, I am in awe of Your mighty wisdom. Thank You for the blessed institution of families. Thank You for mothers. Help me each and every day to be the mother You want me to be. Amen."

MY STUDY
Proverbs 29:15; 1 Timothy 5:8

Look Around

It was on a flight just days after the horrible plane crash in the Everglades that killed hundreds. As the flight attendants began serving a snack, a darling little eight-year-old girl preceded them. At each row, she stopped to ask every passenger, "Would you like some chips? Would you like somethin' to drink?"

A passenger asked her what kind of juice she had. She responded, "I 'on't know." Obviously, she was new at her job!

The attendant later explained, "When she got on board in Atlanta, she was terrified. She's never flown before, and she kept talking about what happened last week in the Everglades.

"She was breathless and her speech was halting. She asked us if we'd heard about the crash. So, we decided to get her involved in helping us.

"And now, she's as happy as can be. It's as if she's forgotten all about her fear."

Being a little hostess was the best thing in the world for her.

It's a wonderful illustration of the biblical principle "It is more blessed to give than to receive." The person who gives to others focuses her attention outside herself. She's usually happier than the person who doesn't give.

Do you ever feel caught up in your own life? Living in a world of self-centeredness where *your* feelings, fears, and agendas are the most important things?

God is big enough and caring enough to meet your needs. He focuses His attention on you, so you don't have to. This frees you to lovingly reach out to others. Your attitude sweetens and time stretches. You are encouraged because God has used you.

Today, are you thinking more about yourself than others? Look around. Focus your eyes on Jesus. Ask Him to give you the strength to give to someone else. Then do it! You will receive what you could never provide for yourself — peace of mind and joy.

HIS WORD

"Learn to do right! Seek justice, encourage the oppressed. Defend the cause of the fatherless, plead the case of the widow" (Isaiah 1:17).

MY PRAYER

"Heavenly Father, forgive me for my selfishness, for focusing on myself so much. Help me redirect my focus and reach out in service to others. Open my eyes and show me their needs so that I may show them Your love. Fill me with peace and joy. Amen."

MY STUDY

Matthew 25:34–36; Psalm 29:11

Love's Embrace

A little girl in England was very ill. After the doctor examined the child, he said that there was little hope she'd survive.

Like any parent, the mother tried to comfort her dying child. She quietly began talking to her precious daughter, preparing her for life beyond death's door.

"Darling," she said, "do you know you will soon hear the music of heaven? You will hear a sweeter song than you have ever heard on earth. You are very fond of music. Won't it be sweet?"

The little girl turned her head away, saying, "Oh, Momma, I am so tired and so sick that I think it would make me worse to hear all that music."

The mother then reminded her she'd soon see Jesus. "You will see the streets of heaven all paved with gold."

"Oh, Momma," the child cried out. "I am so tired I think it would make me worse to see all those beautiful things!"

Compassionately, the mother reached out to her child and gathered her up in her arms, holding her close to her heart. The little girl then whispered, "Oh, Momma, this is what I want. If Jesus will only take me in His arms and let me rest!"

Oh, dear friend, I've often longed for the arms of Jesus to wrap me up, hold me tight, and let me rest! I'm sure you've felt that way yourself. Life is sometimes very difficult. We get "so tired and so sick" that we can't even enjoy the lovely things in life. But Jesus is real. He wants to hold you in His loving arms of comfort.

If you're feeling sick, tired, lonely, or discouraged, look at God's Word. Trust what He says. Let Him comfort you with His gentle Words of grace. Like the strong and caring arms of that loving mother, His arms will wrap you up and give you rest.

HIS WORD
"Cast all your anxiety on him because he cares for you" (1 Peter 5:7).

MY PRAYER
Do you regularly feel God's loving embrace? Have you opened your heart to Him and shown Him all the hidden pain deep inside? My friend, He can make it better. Don't be afraid to let Him in. He will comfort you as no one else can. I promise.

MY STUDY
Exodus 14:13,14; Psalm 23

As a freshman in high school, Billy wanted desperately to play football. He practiced with the team every day. And every day Coach Mitchell would try to find a spot for Billy.

But Billy was short, overweight, and slow. He didn't look like a football player, and he couldn't run like one. His teammates nicknamed him "Turtle."

Billy's insightful dad talked with Coach Mitchell. He told the coach it was important to draw out the best in every player, to help them develop to their fullest potential.

Billy's dad also told the coach that he recognized Billy didn't look like a football player. But he tried to envision what his son would look like in a few years when he was a senior after Billy grew and developed with good guidance and coaching.

Then he asked, "Coach, can you see Billy with an all-American jersey covering his broad shoulders and narrow waist?"

That conversation changed Coach Mitchell. He said, "I learned to see people as they might be, not as they were or are ... to see people's strengths rather than focus on their weaknesses."

In the following four years, Coach Mitchell spent extra time with Billy. All the while, he pictured him with that all-American football jersey. And you know what? By the time Billy was a senior, he'd become a star football player and an all-American!

Who's the Billy in your life? You're convinced, right now, that they'll never trust God and never amount to much.

Begin praying regularly for that person. Ask God to help you picture her as she might be when she trusts Him.

Then reach out to her and draw out her best. You'll help her develop to her fullest potential, and you'll *demonstrate* the love of Christ. As you show His love to others, He'll reveal Himself to you and to them. You'll both become all He wants you to be.

HIS WORD

"Now faith is being sure of what we hope for and certain of what we do not see" (Hebrews 11:1).

MY PRAYER

Think of the Billy in your life. Then pray: "Lord Jesus, You created [name]. You have a plan for [name's] life. Help me to see this person as You do. And may I be a positive influence on [name's] development. Amen." Now allow God to use you.

MY STUDY

Job 8:5–7; Psalm 40:5

Make an Eternal Difference

My good friend Doris was diagnosed with cancer. The doctors gave her a good prognosis if she had aggressive treatment. Her friends prayed. Through it all, she maintained a sense of joy and peace.

The chemotherapy worked, but the celebration was short-lived. The cancer returned, this time much worse. The doctors gave no hope for Doris.

Soon Doris could no longer stay alone. Someone needed to be with her at all times. A mutual friend, Shirley, suggested her mother stay with Doris. Shirley described her mother as "cranky." And cranky she was. Her life seemed to be a series of complaints.

Doris agreed to hire Shirley's mother. What a contrast! Here was Doris, dying of cancer, maintaining a spirit of joy and trust in the Lord. And here was Shirley's mother, a picture of discontentment.

Doris began to talk to her about the Lord. She told her of His greatness, His love, His kindness, and grace. Eventually, Doris led her to faith in Christ. The joy that grew in that household was amazing. The woman's life changed dramatically.

Incredibly, during the few months she lived with Doris, she too was diagnosed with cancer. There was no treatment and no hope. Doris said, "Stay with me. We'll take care of each other." And they did.

Doris and her friend spent this time talking about life in Jesus Christ. Together they experienced the joy of the Lord, even in a desperate time of their lives.

Both women died within a month of each other. God used Doris even in her last days. God gave Doris the compassion that made an eternal difference in the life of our friend's mother.

My dear friend, God can use you. He can give you the compassion to make a difference in the life of someone else. Godly compassion will have a profound impact on your life too.

HIS WORD

"Just as the sufferings of Christ flow over into our lives, so also through Christ our comfort overflows" (2 Corinthians 1:5).

MY PRAYER

Do you know how to lead someone to a personal relationship with Christ? It's a wonderful experience. See "Beginning Your Journey of Joy" at the back of this book or use another evangelistic piece. Read through it, keep it with you, and share with those who are open. The Holy Spirit will do the rest.

MY STUDY

Psalm 73:23–26; Ecclesiastes 4:9–11

Hold My Hand

Jim was two years old and his family lived in a small apartment. His little bed was right next to his parents' bed. Frequently, his father would be awakened in the night by a little voice calling out, "Daddy? Daddy? Daddy?"

Quietly, his daddy would ask, "What Jimmy?"

"Hold my hand!" the toddler gently demanded.

His daddy would reach out in the darkness. He'd find the sweet little hand and swallow it up in his own, holding it with tender reassurance. Once safely in the grip of his big, strong daddy, Jim's arm went limp, and he began breathing deeply. Instantly, he fell soundly back to sleep.

Many years later, Jim wrote, "You see, I only wanted to know that he was there. Until the day he died, I continued to reach for him – for his assurance, for his guidance – but mostly just to know that he was there."

Jim went on to explain that when he became a father, he wanted to be like his dad. He said, "I wanted to be there for my children, a strong, warm and loving presence in their lives."

Who is little Jimmy? He is renowned child psychologist Dr. James Dobson, founder and president of Focus on the Family, a man whom God has used greatly to teach us about being loving, godly parents.

Friend, how do you love your children – with kindness, with gentleness, with fair discipline? Do you love them by showing interest in them, their joys and heartaches, their accomplishments and defeats? That's how God loves you!

That's how He wants you to love your children. Their greatest need is to be loved. Simply loved. Nothing else will ever give them greater security.

Tonight, take your child's hand in yours. Grip it with the reassuring love that only a parent can give. They'll remember it for a lifetime!

HIS WORD
"Above all else, guard your heart, for it is the wellspring of life" (Proverbs 4:23).

MY PRAYER
Do your children know how much you love them? Do they know that you are interested in them and their lives? Take time each day to show your love by asking them how they are. Then listen for the answer. Be a "warm and loving presence" in their lives.

MY STUDY
Galatians 5:22,23; Exodus 32:31,32

The Only Thing I Own

One day while taking a test, little Rachel began daydreaming. Lost in her thoughts, her eyes roamed the classroom. She accidentally peeked at her neighbor's paper.

Rachel didn't intend to cheat, but it was too late – she decided to use her neighbor's answer as her own.

Later in the day, her secret began to gnaw at her conscience. Guilt set in. Very timidly, yet honestly, Rachel confessed – she told the teacher what she'd done.

Her teacher was shocked. No one in her class had ever admitted to cheating in her class. Rachel explained what she'd learned from her dad. Character, she said, is the only thing she owns. Cheating would have taken that away. It would've changed her personality, and she didn't want that to happen.

Rachel's dad, who teaches social ethics at a university, explained how he taught his daughter character. He identified two essentials: communication and leading by example.

He said, "First and foremost, parents should talk to their children about character. Sit down with them and ask, 'Who do you want to become as a person?'

"You're not asking about what kind of job they'd like to have, but what kind of character qualities they want. Ask them what they're doing each day to help them become that kind of person."

His second response was to lead by example. Our children see everything we do. They know whether we're telling the truth or bluffing. No matter how much talking we might do, nothing replaces practicing what we preach.

Be honest with your children. Answer their questions truthfully. Then be quick to *catch* your children telling the truth and praise them for doing so. Don't just wait to catch them in a lie.

Children will make mistakes and blunders. But children of character will seek forgiveness – and in so doing, they'll stand out in the world as different.

HIS WORD
"Blessed are those who hunger and thirst for righteousness, for they will be filled" (Matthew 5:6).

MY PRAYER
Reflect on your life as a parent. Do you live what you teach to your children? Do they see you living a life of integrity before God? None of us are perfect. Pray and ask God to help you in those problem areas. He will.

MY STUDY
Proverbs 3:1; Deuteronomy 4:9–14

Marilyn and her husband were rearing children, but they were also caring for an elderly parent. Eventually, they needed to place his mother in a convalescent home.

Marilyn said, "This was wrenching. Hardly a day went by without visiting her out of a sense of love coupled with guilt. Seldom did I look at the residents to the right or to the left, fearing what I saw and heard. It depressed me, and it exhausted me physically, emotionally, and spiritually."

While Marilyn was visiting the nursing home, God began working it all together for good. One day Marilyn, an artist, noticed her sketchbook in the car, and sensed God prompting her to take it in with her. She began drawing a portrait of her mother-in-law.

Marilyn said, "Through art, God opened my eyes, turning my fear of the residents into love."

Marilyn's visits became longer and she began interacting with other residents. She even began drawing their portraits. All the while, she was talking, laughing, and even crying with them. For some, she was their only visitor. She had opportunities to share her faith in Jesus Christ, and some accepted.

She said, "Drawing their portraits gave me an entry into their lives, and relationships began to blossom. God brought blessings to me through circumstances I would never have chosen. He gave me love for the sick, hurting, disabled, and dying, and gave me a ministry within my unique circumstances."

Marilyn is an example of God's work. He knew her circumstances. He gave her a heart for the elderly. And He worked everything together for good, for Marilyn and for many, many others.

Friend, God has a plan for your life. It involves taking His love, mercy, and Word to others.

That's ministry: Making a difference for Christ in the lives of others *right where you are!*

HIS WORD
"Each one should use whatever gift he has received to serve others, faithfully administering God's grace in its various forms" (1 Peter 4:10).

MY PRAYER
Are you in a tough circumstance right now? Ministry often comes from painful situations that God sees us through. Ask God to show you the bright side. And ask Him to show you how this situation can be turned for His glory. Get ready! God will use you.

MY STUDY
Proverbs 3:3,4; Joshua 6:25

The Powerful

Several years ago while in England, Carolyn's husband had a brain tumor and was hospitalized for six months. There, Carolyn met Sophie, a tiny woman from Ghana who served tea at the hospital. Carolyn asked her if she knew Jesus, but the answer became obvious – yes!

Carolyn, an experienced discipler, suddenly found herself in the "student" role. Sophie taught her so much during those difficult days.

One day when Carolyn thought her husband would die, Sophie told her, "You go in and hold his hand and say, 'You belong to God.'" When the crisis passed, Sophie said, "He's better now. Didn't I tell you? Now every morning when you come in, I want you to greet the other patients and show in your face what God has done for you."

Carolyn said that at the hospital the doctors were thought to be the people with "power." But not to Sophie. She knew better. She said to Carolyn, "I pray for every patient. God heals the people."

Carolyn had always seen herself as one who could step into someone's life and help – be the wise one, the healer, the teacher. But as she observed Sophie, Carolyn changed her mind. Little Sophie, with her prayers, kind words, and cups of "hot, strong, sweet tea," was the really powerful person on the scene. She's the one who was like Jesus, bringing hope, love, and grace.

"Seeing Sophie, who did her part faithfully with joy and confidence in God, I began to pray God would make me more like her."

When we walk with God, we have the power to be used by God in another's life – no matter what our position. Let's all learn from Sophie. Pray for those around you. Bring words of hope when others are discouraged. Let the power of God be seen in you like it was in a sweet little tea lady from Ghana.

HIS WORD
"We have this treasure in jars of clay to show that this all-surpassing power is from God and not from us" (2 Corinthians 4:7).

MY PRAYER
"Almighty God, Your awesome power is beyond measure. That You would allow me the privilege of tapping into that power is unfathomable. Through Your great love, may I be a blessing to others and a source of encouragement in their time of need. Amen."

MY STUDY
Jeremiah 32:27; Psalm 136

B arbara has six children whom she loves dearly. Like most moms, there are some tough days when she doesn't feel as patient as she'd like or everything seems to go wrong. We've all been there.

Barbara was involved in a moms' prayer group at her children's school. The moms prayed for spiritual depth in their children.

But something happened every time Barbara began praying. She said, "The Lord always brought me back to myself. I couldn't pray for spiritual awakening in our children's lives without feeling like it was an incomplete prayer – I needed spiritual renewal, too."

On the inside, Barbara was struggling with feelings of anger toward her children. She said, "I was diligent in rectifying my mistakes when I made them – for example, if I yelled at the children, or if I disciplined them out of anger, I would ask their forgiveness."

But God wanted to help her deal with the attitudes of her heart behind the anger. It was difficult, she said. She had to face the reality of her own selfishness and her desperate need for God.

As she began working through the issues, she sensed God wanted her to talk with her children about them. So one evening, the family gathered in the living room. Barbara and her husband told the children of how God had been working in their lives.

Then Barbara confessed her sinful attitudes and asked the children to forgive her. Though stunned, one by one, each child expressed their forgiveness. Today, Barbara enjoys a deeper relationship with each child. The spiritual renewal has begun in her heart and in the rest of the family.

This may seem a bit unusual, but God used the renewing of Barbara's heart to draw them all closer to each other and to Himself. She set an example of confession and forgiveness. It's a lesson they'll not likely forget.

HIS WORD

"Confess your sins to each other and pray for each other so that you may be healed" (James 5:16).

MY PRAYER

Do you find yourself easily upset or irritated by things your children do? Ask God for forgiveness. Then go to your children to confess your sin and seek their forgiveness. Now live a life of peace and joy, a child of God because He is renewing your heart.

MY STUDY

Genesis 50:19–21; Psalm 34:22

"Will You Hug Me at Home?"

Susan overslept. Now she would have to move like lightning. It was going to be a busy day, like so many others.

It began with getting haircuts for the children. Afterward, she took them to their grandmother's house. Then Susan dashed to a meeting, raced through the mall, and picked up a fast-food lunch.

It was still early afternoon when everyone piled back into the van. On the way home, her two-year-old daughter Emily asked, "Mama, will you hug me at home?"

Susan said "Yes" to Emily's poignant question, but once at home, Susan forgot. The household chores needed to be done, and they kept her busy. Soon little Emily, fussy and cranky, became inconsolable. She was tired and needed comfort from her mom. Susan became impatient. She let her frustrations take over. In this moment, she had missed the opportunity to meet her child's need.

In 1 Corinthians 13:4,5, the Bible lays out a good model for how we are to love: "Love is patient, love is kind ... It is not easily angered, it keeps no record of wrongs." What a clear presentation of how we should treat those around us, especially our children.

My friend, I know it is hard to be a mom. We have all had those moments where everything is overwhelming – all the appointments, responsibilities, and different roles we have to play. But the most important role of a mother is to fill your children with your tender love. Slow down and take the time to hug and hold them. It exhibits God's love. This love builds security in your children. This, in turn, may even pre-empt some of those difficult moments – after all, a secure child is a happy child.

HIS WORD
"Sons are a heritage from the LORD, children a reward from him" (Psalm 127:3).

MY PRAYER
How often do you hug your children and tell them that you love them? Children need to be reminded in tangible ways that they are loved. Make it a point each and every day to reassure your children of their place in your heart.

MY STUDY
1 John 4:12; Exodus 2:1–10

It was a simple childhood incident, but it left an indelible mark on Karen's heart.

One evening, the family hurriedly piled into the car to go to a party. Her mom gently said to her dad, "What a busy day! I feel like I haven't seen you in a week!" Then she suggested they look into each other's eyes for a minute.

At the next light, Karen's parents held hands and gazed briefly into each other's eyes. Mom said, "Hi." Dad warmly responded.

Then the light changed, and the race was back on. It may seem an insignificant event. But to those parents and their children, it was an important reconnection in a hectic world.

Do your children really know how much you care for your husband? Do they see you being kind to each other and showing affection for one another? One of the best gifts you can give your children is the knowledge that their parents love each other and are committed to each other. It models for them what God intended love to be.

Perhaps you are a single mother or widow. You can demonstrate God's love through the way you treat your friends, family, or strangers. Real life is full of frustrations, challenges, and disappointments – and our relationships with each other are no exception. Life is not perfect, but love is.

One way we love is through connecting, heart to heart, with other people. It is not enough to listen with our ears – we need to listen with our hearts as well. Proverbs 27:19 says, "As water reflects a face, so a man's heart reflects the man." When we see a person's heart, we truly see them.

Dear friend, take time today to reconnect with those you love. Gaze into their eyes. See their hearts – and their love.

HIS WORD
"Now that you have purified yourselves by obeying the truth so that you have sincere love for your brothers, love one another deeply, from the heart" (1 Peter 1:22).

MY PRAYER
Reflect on the people you hold most dear. Take time today or this week to call, write, e-mail, or have lunch with one of these people. Go through your list. Make connecting a lifestyle. It will make for more meaningful relationships.

MY STUDY
Exodus 33:11; Psalm 25:14

A Rewarding Experience

Ron and Judy have retired. But not from spiritually influencing their grandchildren.

Every summer, they host a weeklong Kuzins Kamp for their grandchildren – no parents allowed! The children must be at least four years old and toilet-trained.

"One of the main objectives is to have a positive influence on our grandchildren," says Grampa Ron. "We want to reinforce the biblical truths they hear from their parents."

Character building and good manners are emphasized during Kamp. The children say they learn about loving one another and others. And in fun ways, they learn about sharing, kindness, and even obedience. God said in Deuteronomy 4:9, "Teach [My laws] to your children *and* to their children after them."

God does miraculous works not only to benefit the people at the moment, but also so that the glory of these works can be passed on from generation to generation. Exodus 10:1,2 says that God performed "miraculous signs ... that you may tell your children and grandchildren ... and that you may know that I am the Lord."

Perhaps you are a grandparent. Do you realize the important role that you play in the lives of your precious grandchildren? They respect you and look to you for guidance. Don't let this influential time in their lives pass you by – and it will go very quickly. Teach them about God's laws, but also about God's grace. Tell them of the miracles, big and not so big, that God has done in your life. In addition to telling them, show them with your actions how He lives in you today.

There's nothing like a grandparent! Spend time with your grandchildren. It's a rewarding life investment to them and to you!

HIS WORD
"Bring [your children] up in the training and instruction of the Lord" (Ephesians 6:5).

MY PRAYER
How often do you see your grandchildren? Do you take an active interest in them and their lives? Have you told them the story of what God has done for you? Take time to connect with your grandchildren in a real and meaningful way.

MY STUDY
Psalm 128:1–4; Exodus 13:8–10

Tricia felt helpless. She and Dan were exhausted, and they were only into the third month of graduate school. Family time with their two toddlers seemed to be a thing of the past.

Then one Sunday their pastor delivered a message that would change their course entirely. He urged his congregation to lay aside everyday tasks once a week for a day of rest. Use the time for spiritual growth, he suggested, for family activities, for restoration, for reading, and for spiritual refreshment.

Dan and Tricia fully understood their freedom in Christ and were in no way bound to keep this observance. On the other hand, they were tired. Very tired. And they were convinced that God was trying to get their attention.

In biblical times, keeping the Sabbath was meant to be a delight, not a duty. Keeping it brought great rewards, rejuvenation, and joy!

They thought it would be difficult, but Dan and Tricia decided to make Sunday special. Here's what they did.

First, they began to plan ahead. Tricia found that taking some time Saturday evening to do the ironing and prepare the next day's dinner prevented Sunday morning chaos.

Second, they set aside time to focus on the Lord. Before going to church, they created a worshipful atmosphere by playing praise music on their stereo. After church, and after a leisurely meal, they enjoyed reading Christian books.

Third, they took time for each other. Sunday afternoons were often spent on a date. Dan and Tricia looked forward to an undistracted, unhurried time together.

Friend, if you've not done so already, ask the Lord for wisdom in how to spend your Sunday. Consider how your family might make that day a very special time. If making such a commitment is scary to you, just give it a try. Take time to rest in the Lord!

HIS WORD

"This is the day the Lord has made; let us rejoice and be glad in it" (Psalm 118:24).

MY PRAYER

Reflect on your Sunday activities. Do you take time to enjoy your family and rest in the Lord? Make it a priority to plan ahead each week so that you can slow down. Then enjoy a peaceful, yet meaningful, time of worship and restoration every week.

MY STUDY

Genesis 2:2,3; Matthew 11:28–30

Love the Unlovable

David worked at a coffeehouse. Someone asked him to share the gospel with a young man sitting in the corner. David was happy to do so.

The young man's clothes hung like rags on his skinny frame. He was lapping up his tea like an animal. And he smelled awful.

But David sat next to him, and they began to talk.

David learned that the young man had grown up on the streets as an orphan and was only recently released from jail. He was quite hostile. David prayed silently, "Lord, I really want to love this man, but I don't have it in me. Please help me."

Suddenly, the man began to cry. David wondered where the belligerence had gone. Finally the young man said, "I want to pray with you so I can become a Christian." So they prayed together.

Then David pulled off his own thick, warm sweater, folded it, and presented it as a gift, saying, "I'm giving this to you in the name of Jesus. I want you to know that God loves you, and so do I."

The young man beamed. Then he pulled off *his* tattered sweater and gave it to David, motioning for him to put it on. David prayed again – asking God to help him show love and acceptance by slipping on the young man's dirty, smelly sweater.

With that selfless act, David finally saw the young man as God had seen him all along. God had seen beneath his repulsive appearance to his deep hunger for the love of Jesus Christ. Like everyone who accepts Christ, he had been immediately transformed on the inside. He still had an odor. But inside, he'd become a new creation.

Love by faith those who may seem unlovable. Like the man with the smelly sweater, people are waiting to be warmed with God's love and forgiveness.

HIS WORD
"I tell you the truth, whatever you did for one of the least of these brothers of mine, you did for me"
(Matthew 25:40).

MY PRAYER
"Loving heavenly Father, You created each person on this planet. Help me to see them as You see them. Give me a tender heart for the lost and lonely. May I never pass up an opportunity to minister in Your Name. Amen."

MY STUDY
Psalm 91:14–16; Isaiah 41:17–20

What Is Her Name?

Early in nursing school, Arlene's professor gave a quiz. She breezed through the questions with ease until she read the last one. It read, "What's the name of the woman who cleans the school?"

Surely this question is some kind of joke, she thought. Another student asked the professor if this question would count.

"Absolutely," the professor answered. "In your careers, you'll meet many people. All are significant. They deserve your attention and care."

Arlene learned the cleaning lady's name: Dorothy. And she's remembered that lesson ever since.

Friend, God says in Genesis that *all* people are created in His image: "God created man in his own image, in the image of God he created him; male and female he created them" (Genesis 1:27). God cared enough about what He was creating that He made us in His own image. How marvelous!

If God cares so much about each person He uniquely created in His image, shouldn't we do the same? Everyone is special, no matter what they look like, how they dress, or what they do for a living. Every day we encounter people in service positions, often very low-paying, thankless jobs. They work behind the scenes to make your life easier, cleaner, and more comfortable.

Show patience and compassion to the wait staff and sales people you encounter. Speak a kind word to the cleaning person at your school, church, office, or hotel. Let them know how valuable they are. Show them the dignity God gave to them. Through your kindness, they will see Christ in you. This will plant the seeds that may lead to their own personal relationship with Him. And, my dear friend, it will make you more like Christ.

HIS WORD

"As God's chosen people, holy and dearly loved, clothe yourselves with compassion, kindness, humility, gentleness and patience" (Colossians 3:12).

MY PRAYER

How many people in service positions do you encounter each day? Probably quite a few. In your brief encounters, make it a point to connect with people. Call them by name. Look them in the eyes. As you treat them with the dignity they deserve, they will see Jesus in you.

MY STUDY

1 Samuel 12:22; Psalm 139:13–16

Let Your "Yes" Be "Yes"

Cynthia will never forget a special time with her father when she was twelve years old. They'd planned it for months! *Finally*, the big day had arrived. Their night on the town was to include Chinatown, a movie, cable cars, and hot fudge sundaes.

So she traveled with her dad on a business trip to San Francisco. After his meetings, her dad returned to the hotel. But with him was an influential client, who invited them to dinner.

Cynthia held her breath. Would her father choose the client over her? Would all their plans be ruined? Cynthia sighed with relief when her father politely declined. He explained he'd planned a special evening with his daughter. Cynthia loved her dad for keeping his promise!

Her dad understood the importance of keeping his word, especially to his daughter. In Matthew 5:33 we're told, "Do not break your oath ... Simply let your 'Yes' be 'Yes,' and your 'No,' 'No.'" It's as simple as that.

Keeping your word is one of the most obvious indicators of the kind of character you have. It is particularly important to your children. Not only do they observe how you keep your word with others, but they also have good memories. And they trust you. When you don't keep your promises to them, they will remember, and your failure will chip away at their implicit trust.

Dear friend, I know sometimes it is difficult, but to the best of your ability, keep your promises to your children. By doing so, you are demonstrating to them that at least one of the two adults they count on most in the world is worthy of their trust. It will give them a security that is invaluable. That kind of atmosphere will help them grow and you will develop a closer relationship with them. And in you, it will build an honorable character!

HIS WORD
"Sons are a heritage from the LORD, children a reward from him" (Psalm 127:3).

MY PRAYER
"Father of all truth, thank You for keeping all of Your promises. It is an example I want to follow in my own life, with those around me. May I always keep my promises, especially to my children. In Jesus' name, amen."

MY STUDY
Deuteronomy 6:6–8; Mark 10:14

The Godly Woman

*Wives, submit to your husbands, as is fitting in the Lord.
Husbands, love your wives and do not be harsh with them.
Children, obey your parents in everything, for this pleases
the Lord.*

COLOSSIANS 3:18-20

Countless volumes have been written to help men and women understand the differences between them. Some of the differences are so obvious we smile, while some are much subtler. Our attitudes and actions reflect our basic beliefs about the roles and responsibilities that God has outlined in His Word.

We should understand two important concepts from Colossians 3: voluntary submission and sacrificial love. What a difference these can make in our attitudes toward each other as husband and wife.

If we truly honor each other as individuals and demonstrate respect, most challenges in relationships can be eliminated. When we accept the guidelines in God's Word for the pattern of our lives, we will find fulfillment and satisfaction. The need to compete with men will be replaced with the desire to complement the men in our lives.

Jesus saw people as individuals, not as male and female. He spoke to the Samaritan woman at her point of need. He used words of acceptance and kindness, which opened her heart to God's love. She in turn brought everyone she knew — male and female — to Jesus. Her testimony led many others to believe in Him.

God's forgiveness touches the hearts of men and women and allows us to function in harmony with each other to bring honor and glory to Him.

That's Power!

What kind of influence are you on the man in your life? One day the mayor of a city was walking down the street with his wife when they came upon a building under construction. A voice from several stories up called out to the mayor's wife, "Hi, Penny."

They stopped to chat with the construction worker, who they discovered was an old high-school flame of the mayor's wife.

As the couple continued walking down the street, the mayor commented to his wife, "You see, if you had married *him*, today you'd be a construction worker's wife."

Without hesitation Penny replied, "If I had married *him*, he would be the mayor of this city!"

Whether you're married to a mayor or a construction worker or you're single, God has uniquely equipped you to influence your world for Him.

Many women fail to see the opportunities all around them. They give in to their husband's identity — feeling, mistakenly, this is God's design for women. Instead, husbands and wives should help each other achieve their goals. It's okay to be ambitious for yourself and your husband. A woman can inspire her husband to great heights.

Recently, I heard a man say he wants his wife to be recognized as her own person, not just as his wife. I can appreciate that because Bill said that to me on our honeymoon. He has always encouraged me to fulfill my potential as a human being and, more importantly, as a child of God.

Being a helpmate to my husband is my first priority, and I find joy in that role. I haven't given up my sense of self and adopted Bill's life as my own.

I fully share Bill's achievements because I've had a part in all that he's done. I helped him just as he has helped me to achieve more than I thought possible.

I urge you to understand and appreciate the significant role God has given you. You can be a positive influence.

HIS WORD

"The Lord God said, 'It is not good for the man to be alone. I will make a helper suitable for him'" (Genesis 2:18).

MY PRAYER

God has given women the power to help change the world. For thousands of years, women have changed the course of history by influencing others. Identify specific ways you can be a positive influence in the lives of people you know.

MY STUDY

Proverbs 31; Matthew 5:13–16

Read again the familiar and beautiful words on the subject of love, written by the apostle Paul in 1 Corinthians 13:4–7:

> Love is patient, love is kind. It does not envy, it does not boast, it is not proud. It is not rude, it is not self-seeking, it is not easily angered, it keeps no record of wrongs. Love does not delight in evil, but rejoices with the truth. It always protects, always trusts, always hopes, always perseveres.

What a standard! Jesus Christ, through the power of the Holy Spirit, can give us the ability to live like that *every* moment of *every* day. That's true regardless of our circumstances, our personality, the pain we've endured, or how we were raised.

A friend of mine speaks freely about how much she hated her father. He was a well-respected attorney, but at home he was a tyrant. His rage made it difficult to trust him. He drank heavily every day. When he was in a drunken stupor, my friend would walk by him and feel absolute hatred toward him.

Then she became a Christian. For a few years, she continued to hate her dad. The distance between them grew and grew. Finally one day while reading her Bible, she came across this passage in 1 Corinthians. She was grieved to the point of tears when she compared the hate in her heart to the biblical definition of love.

God never said people would be lovable. But God's love is absolutely unconditional – no strings attached.

By faith, my friend began to ask the Lord to give her this kind of love for her dad. God answered that prayer. Within a very short time, her attitude toward her father started to change.

She began to think of creative ways to express her love for her dad. When she did, to her amazement, he'd respond. Eventually, their relationship improved dramatically.

By the time her dad died, he'd become a Christian.

HIS WORD

"Hatred stirs up dissension, but love covers over all wrongs" (Proverbs 10:12).

MY PRAYER

Who are you thinking about right now? Someone unlovable in your life? Do the words of 1 Corinthians 13 sound a bit far-fetched for your situation? Ask God to give you His love for that person, and accept His love by faith. Through His power, no one is unlovable. It's time to start praying.

MY STUDY

Leviticus 19:18; Luke 6:27–36

Husbands Need Respect

Rob and Deborah planned their camping trip, and left on time with their twins. Everything went fine until late afternoon. Rob couldn't quite remember the exit to take off the freeway. "Where's the map, honey?" Deborah asked when she noticed the concerned look on his face. Rob had left it at home. "I'll recognize it when I see it," he said, driving on.

At 9 p.m., it was dark. The twins were asleep. Deborah noticed Rob looked miserable. She gently massaged his neck. "It's okay, honey. Let's get a motel room."

The next morning, Rob had no defensive walls to take down. Deborah had chosen to honor him, despite his mistake. Without prompting, he asked for directions, and they arrived at the campsite in time for lunch.

Most husbands agree on the importance of one thing they want from their wives: respect. Honor means esteeming the position and importance of a person even if his actions are not always honorable. Honor is a choice that is not always easy. Elevating another above ourselves feels unnatural. It involves at least two elements: deference and preference.

Deference expresses courtesy, respect, and humility. It implies a courteous yielding of one's own judgment or opinion to that of another. Deference is putting another person first.

Another way to honor our husbands is to show preference for them. Even if you have children to care for, make your husband a priority in your life. It will keep your relationship strong and close.

To honor is to make a choice that is often difficult. Deference and preference don't come easily. I'm not suggesting your husband is always right or that you become a doormat. That's not the point. It honors God to respect your husband. But when we understand honoring as a sign of character, not of compromise, we make a powerful statement to our husbands and to the world.

HIS WORD
"Be devoted to one another in brotherly love. Honor one another above yourselves"
(Romans 12:10).

MY PRAYER
Ask God to show you ways you can honor your husband, even when he doesn't deserve it. Whatever your unique situation, God can show you what to do. When you do it, you will be honored — by God Himself.

MY STUDY
Proverbs 22:4; Psalm 45:11

Mickey Mantle began playing baseball for the New York Yankees at age twenty. "When I came to the Yankees," Mickey said, "I'd hardly ever had a drink. My father wouldn't have stood for me getting drunk. But the following spring, Dad died of Hodgkin's disease. I was devastated, and that's when I started drinking. I guess alcohol helped me escape the pain of losing him."

Mickey's father played an important role in his life. He did everything he could to help Mickey become an outstanding baseball player.

Despite Mickey's growing problem with alcohol, his career soared. He won many awards and his name became synonymous with baseball. He retired in 1969, but his drinking continued. By the early 1990s, Mickey's body began showing the effects. His liver was failing. Finally, he asked for help.

Mickey went to the Betty Ford Center and made an important breakthrough. "I told the counselor I drank because of depression that came from feeling I'd never fulfilled my father's dreams. I had to write my father a letter and tell him how I felt about him. It only took me ten minutes, and I cried the whole time. I said I missed him, and I wish he could've lived to see that I did a lot better after my rookie season. I told him I had four boys. He died before my first son was born. And I told him I loved him. I would have been better off if I could have told him a long time ago."

Mickey, who died in 1995, was sober the last two years of his life. At his funeral, former teammate Bobby Richardson told about a recent conversation he had had with Mickey. Bobby told Mickey Jesus loved him and would forgive his sin. Mickey placed his faith in Christ, saying, "I am trusting Christ's death for me to take me to heaven."

Although Mickey made peace with his past in therapy, think how meaningful it would have been if his father had heard him say the words. "I love you" are wonderful words to hear.

HIS WORD

"Dear friends, let us love one another, for love comes from God. Everyone who loves has been born of God" (1 John 4:7).

MY PRAYER

Have you told your father lately that you love him? Do you tell your family members what they mean to you? Don't hold back from saying, "I love you." Don't let it become a point of regret when it is too late to tell them in person.

MY STUDY

Hebrews 13:1; James 2:8

The Argument

As Keith and his wife finished breakfast and got the children off to school, he could feel the tension mounting. He had offended his wife. They circled each other warily. Then she began talking. Her words were righteous and were born from her need for the truth and a well-deserved apology from her husband.

Her husband had honed the art of winning an argument at any cost, especially when he was wrong. So Keith's mind clicked into action as his wife began to recite the details of his error in this matter. He prepared himself for his defense. But at that moment, God did something surprising. Keith was suddenly dumbstruck. No words spilled forth. He sat silently as she finished her speech. Then he watched her fall silent. She steadied herself for the verbal assault that he had well trained her to expect.

But this time, to the astonishment of both of them, the verbal assault did not come. Instead of Keith's argumentative tone, five words tumbled out of his mouth: "I'm sorry. I was wrong."

In that instant, he was transformed. Actually, they both were. He was no longer the picture of reason and control, driving his wife to distraction. She was no longer the competitor. Her countenance changed. The frown that seemed so firmly implanted on her beautiful face melted away. It was replaced first by confusion, and then by a look that silently communicated a flood of emotion. Her smile shouted from the rooftops: "You are the most wonderful man to me, for you love me more than your logic, your process, and your need to win."

God desires that we humble ourselves first before Him, and then in love toward one another. What a wonderful example Keith provided for people who love the Lord and each other and who are willing to humble themselves out of love for each other.

HIS WORD

"This is what the high and lofty One says — he who lives forever, whose name is holy: 'I live in a high and holy place, but also with him who is contrite and lowly in spirit, to revive the spirit of the lowly and to revive the heart of the contrite'" (Isaiah 57:15).

MY PRAYER

Do you have a need to be right or in control that keeps you from saying, "I'm sorry. I was wrong"? Is there someone you've wronged to whom you need to say those powerful words? Pray about it, then do it. Be sure to add the three gracious words, "I love you."

MY STUDY

Proverbs 8:13; 1 Peter 5:5,6

Amal was just seventeen years old when her father died. His death left a big hole in her heart.

Although she was reared in a Middle Eastern country in a family with an Orthodox background, Amal knew nothing about putting her faith in Christ.

The enormous pain of her father's death caused Amal to reflect on this long-neglected faith and consider God in a new way. When she heard about some American missionary meetings to be held, she wanted to go. It was there that she learned about God's forgiveness and how to have a personal relationship with Him.

The Bible tells us in several places of God's commitment to always be with us. In Hebrews 13:5, He says, "Never will I leave you; never will I forsake you." This message was very powerful and meaningful to Amal. God is the only one we can count on to always be dependable.

Another meaningful discovery for Amal was that God is a "father to the fatherless" (Psalm 68:5).

Amal said, "I needed a father who wouldn't leave and wouldn't die." Right there in one of those meetings, Amal knelt to pray and place her faith in Christ.

"After I prayed the prayer asking God to be my father," she said, "nothing changed externally; but internally, I knew." What she knew was that she now had a Father who would always be there for her.

As she grew in her faith, God filled the emptiness in her heart. When Amal married, she and her husband became missionaries in their own country so they could share with others how they could come to personally know the Almighty Father. Because she was secure in her Father's love, she could pass His love on to others.

HIS WORD
"A father to the fatherless, a defender of widows, is God in his holy dwelling" (Psalm 68:5).

MY PRAYER
Dear friend, what's missing in your life? Is there an emptiness in your heart? God is the answer. He will fill the void. He will make the difference. And He will never, never abandon you. He promises!

MY STUDY
Hebrews 13:5–8; Isaiah 63:16

Father Worth Knowing

When Dan's study door was closed, no one was to disturb him. But one day his son Steve barged in and sat down. Dan asked him what he wanted. His son said, "Nothing. I just want to be with you."

Later, Dan reflected on this incident and compared it to our relationship with God. "How often do we do that with God? So many of us barge into His presence and share with Him our shopping list for prayer requests, and then get up and leave. We fail to sit and just enjoy Him. We fail to become fascinated with Him, to adore Him, to admire Him."

Oh, friend, that's so true. Our loving heavenly Father wants us to enjoy being in His presence. Of course, we have the privilege of taking our needs and desires to Him, but we should also spend time just thanking Him for who He is.

One way to bring perspective to spending time with God is to make a list of all the things you want to talk with Him about. Prioritize your list based on the eternal significance. For example, if you are praying for a family member's salvation, make that a top priority. When you think about your list with eternity in mind, it quickly clarifies your true priorities.

When you have prayed through your list, stop and take some time to enjoy being with God – with no lists, no complaints – just *be* together. Your heavenly Father wants to spend time with you just as much as an earthly father wants to spend time with his children. The intimacy you will have with God will be priceless. And the perspective you gain in your life will be eternal.

HIS WORD

"Enter his gates with thanksgiving and his courts with praise; give thanks to him and praise his name. For the LORD is good and his love endures forever; his faithfulness continues through all generations" (Psalm 100:4,5).

MY PRAYER

"Loving heavenly Father, thank You for the awesome privilege of allowing me to just be with You — to learn who You are, to feel Your comforting presence, to know Your infinite love. Thank You for Your Word, which you have given for my benefit and blessings. In Your holy name, amen."

MY STUDY

Revelation 3:20; 2 Corinthians 1:3

Louise lives in Holland. Her daughter, Karen, attended college in Italy where she met a young American man who was a Christian. He invited her to a Bible study. In their long discussions about God, he told her of God's love and forgiveness. Soon Karen placed her trust in Christ.

Louise didn't understand the change in her daughter and was afraid she was getting involved in a cult. Karen, despite her mother's misgivings, continued to share her newfound faith with her family. One by one, each family member came to trust in the Lord. Louise's heart was very hard, but eventually she too came to Christ. Louise said of herself, "I was the last to come. I had the hardest heart."

I love that story. A young man far from home shared his faith; then a whole family, in yet another country, trusted Christ.

It is impossible to describe the joy that comes when you are the person God allows to be the instrument to lead someone to a saving knowledge of His Son, Jesus.

Karen's mother expressed fear about her daughter's newfound faith. That is not an unusual response to the zeal and exuberance of a new believer. But as Karen grew in her faith and lived out a Christlike example to her family, the change was evident.

The Bible tells us in 1 Peter 3:15, "Always be prepared to give an answer to everyone who asks you to give the reason for the hope that you have. But do this with gentleness and respect." The young man in this story lived this out and Karen's trust in Christ was the fruit. Karen lived this out and her entire family became believers. What greater reward could there be for a faithful witness than to see your family members come to Christ?

Enthusiasm is contagious, and an authentic changed life gives evidence of the Holy Spirit's power to meet the needs of anyone who will trust and obey Him.

Who can resist a contagious witness?

HIS WORD
"You will receive power when the Holy Spirit comes on you; and you will be my witnesses in Jerusalem, and in all Judea and Samaria, and to the ends of the earth" (Acts 1:8).

MY PRAYER
Friend, make a difference in your world — share your faith enthusiastically with those around you, wherever you are. Be sensitive to the Holy Spirit's leading. And be ready to give the reason for your faith.

MY STUDY
1 Chronicles 16:8,9; Psalm 9:11

Choose Commitment

Young couples spend much time and much more money planning the perfect wedding day. They stand before family and friends and exchange vows made to God and each other. After enjoying the ceremony, they face the reality of marriage.

One newlywed recently said: "Although I was filled with joy during my wedding, from the moment I stepped out of the church, my disillusionment with married life started. The thought was planted that we'd probably get a divorce."

This was an ominous beginning, but by God's grace, after two years her marriage improved. At a marriage conference, God led her to reject divorce as an option. She *chose to commit* to her husband and their marriage for life. Acting on that commitment influenced daily decisions on how she would react to every situation involving her marriage. Once the commitment was made, her options were limited to solutions that would keep her marriage strong and healthy.

God feels so strongly against divorce that He says, "I hate divorce" (Malachi 2:16). Those are clear words from our Creator. But God doesn't just leave us on our own in our marriage. We can come to Him with any problem or struggle.

Asking God for the strength and wisdom to keep your commitment is the best way I know to ensure a life-long marriage. Choosing to eliminate the possibility of divorce gives you confidence to work through any disagreement no matter how deep your differences might be.

Friend, marriage requires commitment. If yours is in trouble, ask for help. Talk to a pastor or church counselor, or attend a marriage seminar such as Family Life. Don't consider divorce an option. Matthew 19:6 states, "What God has joined together, let man not separate." God will help you.

HIS WORD

"For this reason a man will leave his father and mother and be united to his wife, and they will become one flesh" (Genesis 2:24).

MY PRAYER

Perhaps you have been divorced or know someone who has. God is forgiving. But part of repentance is starting fresh. Make a commitment to your marriage, and make Christ the center of it. Encourage others in theirs. Marriage is for life, and God will help it be a good one.

MY STUDY

Proverbs 2:6–15; Ephesians 5:22–33

Everyone loves words of appreciation, even the most modest people. Becky's dad was about to have his seventieth birthday. There were no special plans. It was well known in the family that he didn't like a fuss.

But Becky was determined to honor him in a special way. So she wrote, and rewrote, a four-page tribute to her father.

Not wanting to make her dad feel uncomfortable, Becky decided to have dinner at home. Maybe the privacy of home would be less uncomfortable for her dad than a restaurant. She prepared all her dad's favorite foods.

The evening arrived and the guests took their places at the table. Turning to her dad, she read her tribute. While Becky read the letter, her dad's eyes were fixed on her face. When she looked up at the conclusion of the letter, she saw glimmers of tears in his eyes. The hug was the real thanks, and she knew she had given him the right gift.

The apostle Paul regularly expressed his gratitude to and for the people he was addressing in his letters. "I thank my God every time I remember you" (Philippians 1:3). "We ought always to thank God for you, brothers, and rightly so" (1 Thessalonians 1:3). What an encouragement it must have been to receive those words!

Are you thankful for your father, even though he's not perfect? Have you told God what he means to you? Even if you have thanked God for him, it would be a wonderful gift if you expressed to him the great esteem in which you hold him.

Just like Becky's father, even the most humble and modest people appreciate kind words and gratitude from time to time. Whether it's your father or your mother, make it a point to express your sincere gratitude.

HIS WORD
"Honor your father and your mother, so that you may live long in the land the Lord your God is giving you" (Exodus 20:12).

MY PRAYER
Friend, God says in His Word, honor your father. Fathers need to hear their children's appreciation — even the shyest and toughest of men. Think about your dad. Then write a tribute to him, telling him specifically the things you appreciate. It will honor him and please your heavenly Father.

MY STUDY
Romans 16:1–3; Psalm 106:1,2

God Loves You

We talk often about God's love, but how do we *know* that God loves us? What gives us the confidence? Is it a feeling? Is it based on favorable circumstances? Is it wishful thinking? Is there any way to know for sure?

I once heard Brennan Manning tell this story. One winter, he lived in a cave in the mountains of the Zaragosa Desert in Spain. For seven months he saw no one, never heard the sound of a human voice. Each Sunday morning, someone from the village below dropped off supplies at a designated spot.

Within the cave, a stone partition divided the chapel on the right from the living quarters on the left. A stone slab covered with potato sacks served as a bed. The other furniture was a rugged granite desk, a wooden chair, a Sterno stove, and a kerosene lamp. On the wall of the chapel hung a three-foot crucifix. He awoke each morning at 2:00 and went into the chapel for an hour.

One night during what began as a long and lonely hour of prayer, he sensed Jesus Christ saying to him, "For love of you I left My Father's side. I came to you who ran from Me, fled from Me, who did not want to hear My name. For love of you I was covered with spit, punched, beaten, and affixed to the wood of the cross."

Brennan realized no man has ever loved him and no one ever could love him as Jesus does. He went out of the cave and shouted into the darkness, "Jesus, are You crazy? Are You out of Your mind to have loved me so much?"

God's love is neither sentimental nor some elusive dream. It is an objective reality, revealed to you and me in His Word and through the action He took on the cross when He died for our sin.

God loves you, my dear friend. Never doubt that.

HIS WORD
"For God so loved the world that he gave his one and only Son, that whoever believes in him shall not perish but have eternal life" (John 3:16).

MY PRAYER
"Father in heaven, I confess there are times when I doubt Your love for me. Then I remember the cross. Only Your deep, tender, abiding love could have sent Your Son to a horrible death so I might live eternally. Thank You, Father, for Your infinite mercy and love. Amen."

MY STUDY
Psalm 52:8,9; Exodus 15:13

Loving Dad

A dear friend heard a message about God's love taken from 1 Corinthians 13. She believed the truth in the message and sincerely wanted to demonstrate God's love. Then the truth blindsided her.

God's love is the same for *everyone*, and that didn't exclude her dad. God's love toward her dad was equally kind and patient, and it didn't take into account wrongs suffered.

My friend thought, "If God loves my father just the way he is, who am I not to love him also?"

Right then, my friend decided to love her dad just the way he was. She knew she needed God's help so she prayed daily for God's kind of love for her dad.

As God provided the strength, she took steps to restore their broken relationship. Though her dad never changed much, she did. The realization came to her one day that the miracle of God's love for us is most beautifully expressed when we give that love to others.

Have you ever had trouble loving someone because they did not reciprocate your love, or didn't do it in a way you wanted or expected? Jesus tells us in Mark 12:31 that the second greatest commandment is to "love your neighbor as yourself." So, loving others is a command from God Himself. It is not dependent on whether a person loves us in return.

Too often we place requirements and restrictions on our love. After all, it is easy to love someone who loves us. My friend, it is possible to express God's love to individuals without their response, and the only change we see may be what happens in our own hearts. But God will be pleased with our obedience.

If you have a difficult father (or other relative), love him the way he is, as God sees him. Your change in attitude will heal your hurting heart.

HIS WORD
"Dear children, let us not love with words or tongue but with actions and in truth" (1 John 3:18).

MY PRAYER
Consider God's great love. Then consider His commandment to love others. Ask God to help you love that difficult-to-love person in your life. He will help you. It's His way.

MY STUDY
1 John 4:7–12; 1 Thessalonians 3:12

Return to Romance

A woman I greatly admire, Edith Schaeffer, has written a book called *A Celebration of Marriage*. During her almost forty-nine-year marriage to Francis, she learned the importance of giving him three gifts: honor, creativity, and understanding.

Based on her principles, here are a few suggestions to help you rekindle the romance and renew the passion in your marriage.

First, respect and *honor* your husband:

- Learn to say, "I'm sorry. Please forgive me." And mean it!
- Let your spouse overhear you complimenting him to someone else.
- Praise his successes.

Another factor that makes a marriage thrive is *creativity*. Try some of these ideas:

- Serve his favorite meal in the way he enjoys it most. Does he love breakfast in bed? A candlelight dinner? A picnic at the park?
- Take time to do with him or for him something he really loves, even if you'd rather be doing something else.

The third factor is *understanding*. This simply means listening. James advises, "Everyone should be quick to listen, slow to speak and slow to become angry" (1:19).

Here are some ways to become a good listener:

- Make time to sit down and be available when he has something on his mind.
- Let him talk about things *he* wants to talk about.
- Learn to ask good questions. Let him know he is your absolute priority.
- Pray for him and *with* him.

Give your spouse the gifts that God has given you. He doesn't wait for you to love Him. He loved you first. The more you understand His love, the more you'll love Him and others. Why not start with your husband?

HIS WORD

"Let each man of you [without exception] love his wife as … his very own self; and let the wife see that she respects and reverences her husband [that she notices him, regards him, honors him, prefers him, venerates, and esteems him; and that she defers to him, praises him, and loves and admires him exceedingly]" (Ephesians 5:33, Amplified).

MY PRAYER

"Lord God, thank You for the gift of my precious husband, and for the role he plays in our family. Help me to be a loving wife who is sensitive to his needs. In Your wonderful name, amen."

MY STUDY

Song of Solomon 6:3; 1 Corinthians 13:4–7

The Daddy Moment

Does your family have special traditions that are simple, yet meaningful? The "Daddy moment" has become one such tradition in Vicki's family. It is a great idea for any family in these busy times.

Here's how it came about. Vicki's husband, the daddy of her children, seemed a bit neglected. Even if he hadn't noticed it, Vicki felt she had been too busy to pay him the attention he deserved.

Then she thought of having a "be-nice-to-daddy" moment. When this idea first came to her, she talked to the children about it, and they were excited to participate.

So one day when daddy walked in from work, things changed! Vicki spontaneously initiated a "be-nice-to-Daddy" moment. Their children, then ages 6 and 4, joined in enthusiastically.

They dropped their toys and activities, giggled and squealed, and ran to meet daddy. It was a simple celebration – foot rubs, shoulder rubs, a cool drink, and the newspaper. What a blessing it was to receive such heartfelt pampering! Daddy felt loved and respected.

The children, now teenagers, still enjoy expressing little acts of kindness to their father. Family mealtimes frequently are punctuated by laughs about some silly "Daddy moment" that didn't go quite as planned.

My friend, that is what families are for. You should not only share the tough times together, but also the good times, the fun times, the times that you will talk about and laugh about for years to come. Families are also a place to build each other up and make one another feel special. Vicki and the kids did that for her husband.

Special days are set aside to celebrate moms and dads, but the greatest joy a Christian family can share is the day-to-day blessing of living as a family who respects and appreciates each other.

HIS WORD

"Therefore encourage one another and build each other up, just as in fact you are doing" (1 Thessalonians 5:11).

MY PRAYER

Dads with young children may feel neglected not just by their wife, but by the entire family. Family and school activities create a hectic pace. Be sure to take time to make your husband feel special, not just as a daddy and head of the house, but as a person.

MY STUDY

Psalm 126:2; Romans 14:19

A Command with a Promise

I always take a promise seriously. That's especially true when it comes from God.

Did you know that the biblical commandment to honor your parents is the first command that comes with a promise? In Deuteronomy 5:16, God says,

> Honor your father and your mother ... so that you may live long
> and that it may go well with you.

I remember a kind man who got up early every Sunday morning to make pancakes for the family – so that mother could sleep in. That man was my father. Later after church, we took long afternoon walks together, we'd go to a swinging bridge, and I caught crawdads in the stream while my father fished.

With children of my own, I can only now fully appreciate how he sacrificed for his family. Dad worked hard to provide for us, but he always took time to play and make us feel special.

He wasn't perfect, but respecting Dad has always come naturally to me. Honoring him was not a chore.

I realize that this may not be your story. Perhaps your father was not a strong, loving, family man. But whether your relationship was wonderful or painful, the command is to honor him.

How do you show honor to your father? Let me offer a few practical ideas.

Tell him what you appreciate about him. Be specific. If he was a good provider, tell him so. If he's been faithful to your mother, tell him how important that is to you. Bring up favorite memories from growing up. Thank him for everything he did right. And tell him you love him.

Even if you have a difficult relationship with your father, you can still obey God's command to honor him. In your case, honoring him may start with forgiving him. Ask God to replace your bitterness and anger with compassion.

HIS WORD

"Listen to your father, who gave you life, and do not despise your mother when she is old" (Proverbs 23:22).

MY PRAYER

Honoring your father is a two-way blessing. It is a blessing to the parent who receives thanks for what he did right. And it's a blessing to the grown child who can grow old with nothing left unsaid. Honor your father today.

MY STUDY

Exodus 20:12; Matthew 15:3–9

Have you heard anyone recently share their excitement as they talked about their grandchildren? Or have you listened to a young man who has just discovered the woman he wants to marry? These people are so full of the joy in their relationships that they couldn't possibly keep quiet about it.

So our relationship with God can overflow as we share with others our hearts full of joy, love, and gratitude concerning what God has done for us.

As a new believer, I wanted to tell others about Christ, but I was afraid I couldn't do it well because I wasn't familiar with Scripture. I knew we were commanded in Scripture to share our faith; I just didn't know the rest of the story.

Then I read 1 John 1:3: "We proclaim to you what we have seen and heard, so that you also may have fellowship with us. And our fellowship is with the Father and with his Son, Jesus Christ." From that verse, I realized that all I had to do was share what I had "seen and heard" — what God had revealed to me to that point in my life. As I did, I found many people were looking for the answers I had found. Even though I didn't know a lot about the Bible, people were interested in what had happened to me.

Not everyone with whom you share your faith will respond positively. Only God can bring results. I have learned that whatever reasons may prevent a person from responding, my responsibility is clear: I simply must share Christ in the power of the Holy Spirit and leave the results to God. When I am obedient to Him, I experience overflowing joy.

HIS WORD

"You did not choose me, but I chose you and appointed you to go and bear fruit — fruit that will last. Then the Father will give you whatever you ask in my name" (John 15:16).

MY PRAYER

As you actively seek to develop an intimate relationship with Jesus Christ, your life will naturally overflow with the joy of His presence and the truth of His Word. Share what you have seen and heard with all who will listen so that others might trust Christ too.

MY STUDY

Psalm 66:16; Joel 3:13,14

No Regrets

In many homes across America, Father's Day is a happy time of expressing love. For others, though, it's a time of loneliness, even anger and disappointment.

You may have grown up in a happy home like I did, so obeying this command comes easy. But for many, honoring their father is a stretch. It's an act of obedience, because their memories aren't all good. In fact, some of them are downright painful.

Let me tell you about Dodie, a woman in her late twenties. When she was very young, her dad left her mother. Throughout her childhood, she was deeply angry and hurt.

During those impressionable years of innocence, he wasn't there to tuck her in or to sit her on his knee. During the scary and volatile teenage years, again he wasn't home to answer questions or to meet her friends. And when she began making decisions of her own, he wasn't there to give her counsel and affirmation.

For most of her life, her memory of "Dad" was that he was *gone*, and she resented him for it.

As an adult, Dodie decided to obey the command to honor her father, knowing that, as she does this, God will honor her. She deliberately reached out to him in love and forgiveness. Dodie chose to focus on what he did *right*, instead of what he did *wrong*.

When she treats him with respect, she hopes that he'll taste God's love and forgiveness and decide to give his life to Christ. That is called *honoring by faith*.

So, when God gave the command to honor your parents, do you think He knew about *your* father? Of course He did! He is giving you an opportunity to display His compassion in a difficult relationship.

HIS WORD
"Finally, all of you, live in harmony with one another; be sympathetic, love as brothers, be compassionate and humble" (1 Peter 3:8).

MY PRAYER
When you prepare for Father's Day, let me urge you to obey God and honor your father by faith. You'll be so glad you did! Dodie and her father have a brand new healing friendship that's emerged from the ashes. It doesn't make the past right, but it sure makes the future a lot brighter.

MY STUDY
Matthew 5:44; Psalm 27:10

Ney Bailey stood on the edge of the swimming pool. She was barely three feet tall and scared to death of deep water. But her father stood in the pool, coaxing her to jump in.

He said, "Jump in, Ney! I'll catch you."

Finally, Ney jumped. Her head went under and she came up sputtering and thrashing. Her father wasn't there. He had moved back in the water, hoping she would swim to him.

Ney began to cry. "Daddy, you moved! You said you wouldn't!" Her father laughed and said, "Ney, you've gotten upset over nothing. You know I wouldn't let anything happen to you!"

That innocent experience had a *devastating* effect on Ney's tender young mind. She had trusted her father completely, and he had let her down.

Over the years her lack of trust evolved into anger. By the time she entered college, there was a deep rift between the two.

While away at school, Ney gave her life to Christ. Early in her walk with the Lord, she learned that faith is not a feeling. Faith is being willing to take God at His word. Faith means believing God and choosing to be obedient, regardless of emotions.

Ney knew the description of love in 1 Corinthians 13. "Love is patient, love is kind, love is not provoked." She realized that if God loved her father in this way, she must do that, too.

Ney decided to take God at His word and to love her father without regard for his performance.

The next weekend, Ney approached her father about all the bitterness she had held and asked for his forgiveness. Without reservation, he forgave her. From that time on, he was warmer and kinder than ever before.

A few years later, Ney's father died. She was so glad to be free of regrets about their relationship.

HIS WORD

"If you forgive men when they sin against you, your heavenly Father will also forgive you. But if you do not forgive men their sins, your Father will not forgive your sins" (Matthew 6:14,15).

MY PRAYER

Are you nursing some old wounds? Maybe a member of the family has hurt you. Don't you think it's time you put those hard feelings to rest? Give them to the Lord. Then trust God to remove all of the turmoil and anger. As you act in obedience to Him, He surely will.

MY STUDY

Proverbs 10:12; 1 Peter 3:9

To Dad With Love

While in college, Cindy became a Christian. The closer she got to God, the more she wanted a closer relationship with her dad. Cindy knew it would only happen if she took the initiative.

Don was the kind of dad who had difficulty showing emotion. He worked long hours and, when at home, he didn't want to be disturbed. Cindy felt estranged from her father.

Cindy often made it a point to hug her dad. At the end of phone conversations, she'd always say, "I love you, Dad." The closest he ever got to reciprocating was "Me too."

Then it came time to move across the country to begin a new job. When she loaded up her car and waved good-bye to her family, Cindy didn't yet know the significance of this farewell.

A few weeks later, a fleeting thought popped into her mind. She should send her father a card. For most people, sending a card was no big deal. For Cindy, that wasn't the case. The only time she'd ever sent her father a card was on his birthday. But she knew she had to do this.

So she found a silly card and wrote a short note:

> Hi Dad! Things are going well here. Just wanted to let you know I was thinking about you.
>
> I love you, Cindy

It didn't take much effort. It almost seemed insignificant. But not to Cindy's father. He was bowled over. For weeks, the card was almost all he talked about.

By her father's reaction, Cindy knew that fleeting thought was a prompting from God. It gave her the opportunity to very clearly let her father know how much she loved him.

One month after sending the card, Cindy's father died unexpectedly. Her farewell before leaving home was the last time she saw her dad. Yet she knew she'd left no words unspoken.

HIS WORD

"Be imitators of God, therefore, as dearly loved children and live a life of love, just as Christ loved us and gave himself up for us as a fragrant offering and sacrifice to God" (Ephesians 5:1,2).

MY PRAYER

Friend, think about your relationships. Is there something you've left unsaid? Don't wait until it's too late. Do you need to write a letter or make a phone call? Maybe a visit would be appropriate. Let your loved ones know what they mean to you. If you do, you'll live with no regrets.

MY STUDY

Romans 13:7; Proverbs 3:27

In his book *Point Man*, Steve Farrar tells the fascinating story of George McCluskey.

When George McCluskey married and started a family, he made another commitment as well. He decided to invest one hour each day in prayer. His supreme desire was for his children to follow Christ.

He prayed as they grew up, married, and had their own children. George then began praying for his grandchildren, too. In later years, he included his great-grandchildren in those faithful prayers. Every day, from eleven to noon, he prayed for all three generations.

George first saw his two daughters commit their lives to Christ. Each one married a man who went into the ministry.

Between the two couples, they had five children – four girls and one boy. Each one of his granddaughters married preachers, and his grandson became a pastor.

The first two children of the next generation – George's great-grandchildren – were boys. When those two young men graduated from high school, they went to the same college and were roommates.

During their sophomore year, one boy decided to go into the ministry. The other didn't. Instead, he had a growing interest in psychology.

Eventually, the young man earned a doctorate. After that, he began writing books on parenting, which almost immediately became best-sellers. Then he started a radio program. That program is now heard every day on hundreds of stations around the world.

If you haven't already guessed, the man is ... Dr. James Dobson of Focus on the Family!

God graciously honored the consistent prayers of James Dobson's faithful great-grandfather! And God will do the same for you and me. Pray for your family regularly. It will affect them for generations to come.

HIS WORD

"If you believe, you will receive whatever you ask for in prayer" (Matthew 21:22).

MY PRAYER

"Loving heavenly Father, that You hear my prayers and have compassion on me and my family is truly a source of peace and joy for me. Thank You for being a compassionate, merciful God whose love is everlasting. In Your mighty name, amen."

MY STUDY
Psalm 145:18; Luke 11:9

"Love One Another Deeply"

Rachel grew up in what she thought was a pretty normal home: a mom, a dad, a sister, a couple of brothers. A normal house on a normal street.

However, Rachel's parents argued privately. Year by year, there were more arguments on the other side of the house. They got louder and longer.

Rachel's dad was developing an alcohol addiction. He was a great guy when he was sober. But the minute he took a drink, even in private, his personality changed. He wasn't violent, just different. After a few drinks, he'd become obnoxious. Then he slept. Rachel *hated* his drinking. And like the arguments, his drinking was private.

By the time Rachel went off to college, things were really bad. Her dad was drinking a lot more and her parents' relationship had all but dissolved.

Rachel, who had trusted Jesus Christ as a youngster, was learning to walk with God. Now, God became her source of strength and comfort.

Soon after she came home from college, Rachel's dad learned he needed an operation. Through this difficult time, God was working in her heart.

Rachel stood at her dad's bedside in the hospital. She looked at him and silently prayed, "Lord, let me love Dad just the way he is, even if he drinks the rest of his life."

Rachel knew that God loved her just as she was. And she knew she needed to show her dad the same kind of love, so he would see Jesus in her.

God answered Rachel's prayer. She has loved her dad, no matter what, ever since. Yes, there were difficult times, but her love made them easier.

Today, her dad is sober. That wonderful personality she loves in her dad is back. And they share a good relationship.

HIS WORD

"Now that you have purified yourselves by obeying the truth so that you have a sincere love for your brothers, love one another deeply, from the heart" (1 Peter 1:22).

MY PRAYER

We all have someone in our life who is difficult to love. Dear friend, who is that person in your life? Ask God to give you a sincere love for him or her as only He can do. He will love through you if you will let Him.

MY STUDY

Song of Songs 8:6; Ecclesiastes 7:9

You Never Know

It was Father's Day in a very busy, but quaint, French restaurant where Roger and Lori were enjoying their meal together. They were stealing a few quiet moments alone without their four small children.

At the table next to theirs, a harried father sat at a long table with his *five* little children. They were beautifully dressed. His serene wife sat at the other end.

Roger and Lori looked at each other and whispered, "Wow! They have five children! And they've brought them to a French bistro with linen tablecloths for Father's Day! That's brave!"

Throughout the meal, the children were up and down for various reasons, as children often are. At one time or another, each of the children spent a few moments on Dad's lap as he attempted to navigate a few bites of his own meal around their squiggly bodies.

It didn't seem like a relaxing Father's Day for this gentleman. The mother – who had an infant snuggled on her shoulder the entire time – seemed unaffected. She smiled her way through the whole experience.

Roger wondered how the father had managed all this. He must be independently wealthy, maybe a doctor. They looked like one big happy, busy family.

When their meal was done, Roger and Lori complimented the mother on such a beautiful family.

That's when they discovered the real story. It wasn't a husband and wife at the table. The woman at the table owned the restaurant, and the infant on her shoulder was her only child. She and her husband were treating this dear man and his four children to a fine meal at their restaurant because his wife was her dearest and best friend. Only a few weeks before, her best friend had been struck and killed by a car while crossing a busy intersection. The father's caring friends didn't want this precious family to go through Father's Day without lots of company and love.

Dear friend, that is what it means to love your neighbor as yourself.

HIS WORD
"We who are strong ought to bear with the failings of the weak and not please ourselves. Each of us should please his neighbor for his good, to build him up" (Romans 15:1,2).

MY PRAYER
We must treat friends, neighbors, and strangers with compassion, asking God to help us know how to reach out to others with love and understanding. Only God knows the heart. Yet He's chosen us to be His instrument. Only He can give us wisdom and courage to reach out with grace.

MY STUDY
Psalm 86:15; Lamentations 3:22,23

Talk About God

L isa, the wife of a U.S. senator, attended a Bible study every week. But she made it clear that her perfect attendance represented her curiosity, not her belief.

One day after the study, Sallie, who led the group, stopped to talk with Lisa. Sallie asked, "Lisa, what do you think about what you've been learning from the Bible?"

Lisa was quick to reply. She said, "Sallie, do you want to be my *friend* or just convert me?"

In her soft, gentle manner, Sallie told Lisa, "More than anything else in life, I want you to know Jesus. But if you never believe, Lisa, I'll still love you."

Every week Lisa would go home and tell her husband, the senator, all about the things she'd discovered in the Bible. Her husband did not know Jesus Christ either, but was curious.

The senator, like many of his colleagues, had gone to Washington with high hopes. But in time, he grew frustrated with the bureaucracy and became discouraged. He began looking for answers that weren't in Washington. He sensed they were in what his wife told him each week after her Bible study.

Then one day, Lisa called Sallie. She said, "Sallie, I think my husband wants to know God." So Sallie asked an associate to meet with the senator and to share the gospel with him.

One morning a few days later, Lisa reported that her husband had tossed and turned all night. He got up and went downstairs. "I think he beat me to it," she said. "I think he did what you've been wanting me to do." The senator had knelt alone in the night and trusted Jesus Christ.

He started a Bible study in his senate office and spoke openly of his faith.

God's Word is far-reaching – to places we never expected. Talk openly about your faith because you never know who's listening.

HIS WORD

"My word that goes out from my mouth ... will not return to me empty, but will accomplish what I desire and achieve the purpose for which I sent it" (Isaiah 55:11).

MY PRAYER

You don't need a special gift to be God's messenger! When you talk about God, others become interested. God will lead the way. He wants to use you to achieve His purposes. Talk about Him and His Word. He'll make the truth known.

MY STUDY

Matthew 28:18–20; Psalm 40:9,10

No Substitute

A fter a fun day fishing with a friend and her father, an eight-year-old demanded of her mother, "I want a dad." For the next few minutes, she and her six-year-old sister begged their mom to marry and give them a dad. They even began listing eligible men.

"The conversation pierced my heart like an arrow," wrote their mother, Sandy, a reporter for the *Los Angeles Times*. She continued, "I thought I'd built a nice life, a complete life, my girls and I, in the years since their father died. I thought I'd stepped ably into his shoes, filling the roles he'd played in their lives."

Sandy earns a comfortable income, providing well for her three daughters. She taught them to roller skate and ride bikes, and she takes them on hiking and camping trips. She even learned to play basketball so she could coach her oldest daughter's team.

But all she does to fill those empty shoes hasn't been enough to fill the empty spot in those three hearts. The girls want, and need, a daddy. He was the big guy who let them ride on his broad shoulders and snooze with him in front of the TV.

In one quick moment he was gone, and their lives changed forever. Sandy wrote, "The children have been shortchanged, their childhoods diminished by the loss of something that, for all my posturing, I can never replace."

Children need their daddy. There is *no* substitute. I don't know why God allowed these three girls to lose their daddy. It's all dreadfully tragic.

Many men and women today are thinking of getting a divorce and leaving their children. I can't imagine how painful that must be for little ones. You made a commitment in your marriage vows. God says those are not to be easily broken. Friend, God is a God of love, mercy, and grace. It grieves His heart to see broken relationships.

We can find hope in God, His Word, and His Spirit. Turn to Him today.

HIS WORD
"Commit to the Lord whatever you do, and your plans will succeed" (Proverbs 16:3).

MY PRAYER
Turn to God and let Him heal your marriage, for the sake of your children and yourself. If your marriage is in trouble, I urge you to get help.

MY STUDY
Psalm 71:1; Proverbs 16:9

It Takes More Than Love

"Adoration" is the word Claire uses to describe her dad's love for her mother. And "total commitment" is how she describes her mother's love for her dad. Theirs is a great love, a love that's endured more than sixty years. Claire also had another model of love in the marriage of her husband's parents.

Following that legacy of love should have been easy, or so Claire thought. When Claire married, she assumed she'd have a similar marriage, strong and loving.

Children need deep, abiding love and godly commitment between their parents. But it isn't automatically passed on, and it wasn't passed on to Claire.

She loved her husband, and he loved her. But, friend, love, in and of itself, isn't enough to make a marriage work. She said, "My husband and I had to build our own relationship one day at a time."

The models of their parents' relationships gave them an example to follow. But Claire and her husband were individuals with many differences, likes and dislikes, hopes and dreams. They had to grow together. They had to develop their unique relationship, their own bond of love.

So they worked at their marriage, and they discovered one essential ingredient that made all the difference.

Claire describes it like this: "It was not until we began to go together, in faith, to God's Word for its guidelines and promises that our marriage really began to get a firm footing. That Word provided the solid rock we needed to build on."

Friend, it's never too late to turn to God. If you've never made Him a part of your marriage, start now. Your love for God and for each other will grow in ways you never imagined. He will help you build together on His foundation of love.

HIS WORD

"Everyone who hears these words of mine and puts them into practice is like a wise man who has built his house on the rock. The rain came down, the streams rose, and the winds blew and beat against that house; yet it did not fall, because it had its foundation on the rock" (Matthew 7:24,25).

MY PRAYER

Tonight after the children are in bed, read Ephesians with your spouse. It's a wonderful place to begin to build a solid foundation for a stronger marriage. Remember, it takes more than love.

MY STUDY

Psalm 127:1; Isaiah 51:1

I t had been twenty years since Travita Kenoly had renewed her commitment to Christ. Though she'd placed her faith in Christ some years earlier, she wasn't walking with God.

One day she chose to return to her faith, surrendering once again to Christ. When she did, she began praying for God to change her and her husband, Ron.

Travita said, "As I saw changes in my life, I could pray for Ron." She asked a group of Christian friends to pray as well. They reassured her that God would answer their prayers. "However long it takes, Ron will come back to faith," they said.

God answered the prayers of those faithful women. Just a few months later, Ron returned to the faith in Christ that he too had once walked away from.

As the Kenolys began growing in their renewed faith, they began praying for their three sons. They wanted their lives to make a difference for Christ. "We tried to live an exemplary, godly life," Ron said.

Suddenly, their oldest son, Tony, who was sixteen, ran away from home. They were heartbroken. "It brought us to our knees, weeping, and wailing, and hurting," said Ron.

Tony was gone three years. Although they saw him occasionally, they never knew where he lived.

Once again, a group of women in their church prayed day and night, this time for Tony. God answered those prayers as well.

With great sadness and brokenness, Tony finally came home. "He realized how much he needed his family and how much we needed him," Ron said.

Gratefully, this story had a happy ending. But Travita said, "I still pray as intensely for my children. I don't want to get complacent, knowing that the enemy is always waiting."

Friend, the adage says, "Prayer changes things." I say, God changes things through prayer. The Kenolys are a perfect example.

HIS WORD

"In the morning, O LORD, you hear my voice; in the morning I lay my requests before you and wait in expectation" (Psalm 5:3).

MY PRAYER

God is a God of love and mercy. His love is perfect every moment of every day. It never changes. Like a father, He's waiting with all of that love for you to return to Him. All you have to do is call out to Him. Remember, God answers prayer. Tell Him your greatest need today. Talk with Him every day. And watch for His answers.

MY STUDY

Luke 15:11–31; Psalm 51:10–12

Trusting God

On the outside, Becky's father was the picture of health. But on the inside, he had a dangerous heart condition. He needed extensive heart surgery.

After a long day of flights, Becky arrived at her dad's hospital bedside. He looked good. He was talking and visiting with other family members. Then Becky asked to pray with him. They all bowed their heads while she asked God to watch over her father.

Early the next morning, they all met in his room. Again, Becky led them in prayer. Becky and her brother, Richard, walked alongside the gurney as he was wheeled through the hospital.

Richard said to Becky, "We may never see him again."

As their dad was wheeled away to an uncertain future, they watched until the closing doors blocked their view.

Seven long hours later, the word came that the operation was successful. But the doctor was having trouble getting him stabilized.

Soon it seemed alright, and they were allowed to see him. He was unconscious, cold, and had needles and tubes everywhere, but still they talked and encouraged him – and Becky prayed.

Suddenly, his blood pressure dropped dangerously low. Everyone was scared. Becky called family and friends all over the country and asked for prayer. As she paced the waiting room, she told God, "If you want to take Dad home, Lord, it's okay. But, truthfully, I'm not ready to lose him."

She gathered the family and led them in prayer again.

Later, the doctor said if things didn't improve in two hours, he'd have to go back to surgery. Tearfully, the family prayed again. And they waited.

The doctor returned after only one hour, this time with a good report. The bleeding had stopped. Several hours later, he was stable and on his way to a full recovery.

Dear friend, God hears and answers our prayers.

HIS WORD
"Then they cried to the Lord in their trouble, and he saved them from their distress" (Psalm 107:13).

MY PRAYER
I have no idea what's troubling your heart today. Whatever it is, God knows. And He'll help you through this distressful time. When you talk with God, you're telling Him you trust Him. Today, tell Him what's on your heart. Tell Him you need His help. Show Him you trust Him. You'll be amazed at what He will do.

MY STUDY
Philippians 4:6,7; Joshua 1:9

Stop Nagging, Start Praying

Lisa was growing in her relationship with Christ. But as fast as she grew, her husband's relationship with God went on a downhill run.

He became absorbed in his work. His job demanded many business trips. There were times that he wasn't home to attend church with her.

Lisa was very concerned – and frustrated.

Lisa's story is told in Stormie Omartian's book *The Power of a Praying Wife*. Sadly, I don't think Lisa's story is all that uncommon.

Lisa longed to grow together with her husband in the spiritual dimension. She wanted it to be a lifelong shared experience, but that's not what was happening.

She occasionally spoke with her husband about the problem, but he would become defensive and blame it on his work. It wasn't long before his work became a greater challenge, causing him a lot of stress. In her heart, Lisa knew that if he would turn back to God, he would find the strength he needed.

At this point, Lisa knew he wasn't going to listen to her about it any longer. So she began praying every day that God would develop a desire in his heart for God to be more a part of his life.

She prayed consistently and fervently for months, with no change. Then to her surprise, one morning he said, "I'm going to the office earlier today because I need time alone with the Lord before I do anything else."

God answered her faithful prayers. For the past few years, he's gone in early on a regular basis to spend time with God. Lisa's husband is a changed man in many ways.

Many of us want another person to change, but we are powerless to change others. God isn't. It's His business to change people. And He will. I will say this strongly: stop nagging and start praying.

HIS WORD

"Evening, morning and noon I cry out in distress, and he hears my voice" (Psalm 55:17).

MY PRAYER

Today, if there are changes you want to see in your husband's life, be careful. Ask God if there's a similar change He wants in your life. Invite God to make that change. Then, pray daily for the needs in your life and in your husband's life. God will change your heart and his.

MY STUDY

James 5:16; Proverbs 25:11

Good Gifts from God

T ed was a senior in high school. Like many teenagers, what he wanted most for graduation was a car.

In anticipation of this milestone in his young life, Ted and his father spent a lot of time looking at cars. In fact, after months of searching, they'd found the perfect one, the one Ted was sure would be his graduation present.

When Ted's graduation day arrived, he was excited. His youthful dream would soon come true. He'd have his own car, the one he wanted so badly.

That evening, Ted's dad handed him a package. It was gift-wrapped and about the size of a book. As Ted opened it, disappointment washed over his face. The gift was a Bible, and there were no car keys.

In a split second, Ted's disappointment turned to anger. He threw the Bible down and left the house in a rage. Tragically, the father and son never saw each other again.

Sometime later, Ted did go home, but it was after his father died. As he was going through some of his dad's things, Ted found the graduation Bible. He held it in his hands. Then he opened it.

There, tucked inside the pages, was a cashier's check. Yes, it was a check for a car. Dated the day of Ted's graduation, it was written for the exact amount of the "perfect car," the very one he and his father shopped for and found together.

This reminds me of the way people treat their heavenly Father. They pray for something. He answers differently than they expect. They're disappointed. Then they walk away from Him, even though God's answer always works out so much better. God promises to meet your needs. Maybe not in the way you expect, but He *will* do it. Trust Him.

HIS WORD

"If you, then, though you are evil, know how to give good gifts to your children, how much more will your Father in heaven give good gifts to those who ask him!" (Matthew 7:11).

MY PRAYER

Write down one thing you need and one thing that's a desire deep in your heart. Put today's date on it and tape it inside your Bible. Then talk with God. Every day thank Him for the answer. It may not come exactly as you expect, but the answer will be perfect because He is perfect.

MY STUDY

Romans 8:14–17; 2 Corinthians 6:18

When Bill and I celebrated our fiftieth wedding anniversary, it was a time of joy and reflecting. Fifty years equals 18,250 days. Life is lived one day at a time and each day is a gift from God.

Looking back always allows a person to think of the things she might have done differently. I am so thankful that I have very few regrets.

There are wonderful qualities I appreciate about my husband, powerful principles I've learned about marriage, words of wisdom I could pass on to others.

But there is one thing, *one solitary* thing that has made our marriage strong and enjoyable. It has enabled us not only to *stay married*, but also to *keep* delight and joy in our marriage and keep our love growing.

That "secret" is that both my husband and I have an unbending devotion to Jesus Christ. He is our focus! As we've focused on Him individually for fifty years, He's brought us closer and closer together. We're much happier today than even the day we married. Our Lord gets the glory. We praise Him!

Devotion is the key to any lasting relationship. The closer we walk with the Lord, the closer we feel to each other. Our devotion for Christ has deepened through the years as has our devotion to each other.

Our culture today is on a fast track to everything! But we can't develop devotion on a fast track. Devotion is developed one day at a time as we submit to the leading of the Holy Spirit and allow Him to work in and through us.

The seasons of our lives demand varying amounts of emotional and physical energy, but our need for devotion to Jesus Christ is consistent. When we keep Christ first, all the other things take on proper perspective. Then when we look back, we can rejoice at what God has done.

HIS WORD

"Blessed is the man who does not walk in the counsel of the wicked or stand in the way of sinners or sit in the seat of mockers. But his delight is in the law of the LORD, and on his law he meditates day and night. He is like a tree planted by streams of water, which yields its fruit in season and whose leaf does not wither. Whatever he does prospers" (Psalm 1:1–3).

MY PRAYER

"Lord Jesus, thank You for Your devotion to me. May Your Holy Spirit continue to guide me as I walk in the path of righteousness. I love You, Lord. Amen."

MY STUDY

Matthew 6:33; Deuteronomy 6:4–9

Heavenly Guidance

Whatever you do, work at it with all your heart,
as working for the Lord, not men.

COLOSSIANS 3:23

Most of the hours of our day are spent on "maintenance" requirements – doing things that must be done again the very next day. If we are not careful, we can spend the majority of our life maintaining and never pressing forward to expand our minds and broaden our scope of influence.

Women have a wonderful ability to balance many tasks and to patiently work toward the completion of long-term goals. That is the very essence of a life strategy. Paul described his life in Philippians 3:14: "I press on toward the goal to win the prize for which God has called me heavenward in Christ Jesus." I encourage you to prayerfully ask God to guide you as you develop a strategy for your life. Spend time in His Word, and after prayerful consideration, write out a strategy. You will find that it defines the purpose for your future activities. It will then be easy to determine how many activities in your day support or detract from your life strategy.

Having self-imposed goals without a strategy may bring you frustration and a sense of defeat, but having a life strategy allows for various detours and interruptions, providing a base of confidence that the goal is still in view.

Be certain to base your strategy on a Christ-centered lifestyle that will bring glory and honor to your heavenly Father.

Don't Give Up!

Florence Chadwick was a seasoned long-distance swimmer who, in 1952, set out to swim the channel between Catalina Island and the California coast. She had many obstacles to overcome that July day. The shark-infested water was incredibly cold. The fog was so thick she could barely see the boats alongside her.

After fifteen long, grueling hours, she felt as though she could swim no longer. Her muscles screamed with pain and she was totally exhausted.

Her coach, of course, pleaded with her to keep going. "It's just a little farther. You're almost there! Don't give up!"

But when Florence looked ahead, all she could see was a blanket of fog. Tired, cold, and totally discouraged, Florence quit. She quit! Florence had a goal, but her view was clouded. She couldn't see the shoreline.

Have you ever strived to reach a goal only to quit because your view became clouded with unimportant issues, difficulties, or sin? As Christians, our ultimate goal is to follow Christ. Hebrews 12:2 advises us, "Let us fix our eyes on Jesus, the author and perfecter of our faith."

If we fix our eyes on Him, we will reach His goal for our life.

What Florence didn't know when she quit was that the shoreline was a mere half-mile away.

Two months after her first attempt, Florence tried the swim again. This time, she not only made it, but also set a new speed record! What made the difference? The shoreline had not moved closer. The water was still very cold. But this time, the sky was blue, and Florence could see land!

Dear friend, like Florence, we can lose heart when we lose sight of our Guide, our end-marker. Fix your eyes on Jesus, and you will finish the race no matter what obstacles you encounter.

HIS WORD
"You need to persevere so that when you have done the will of God, you will receive what he has promised" (Hebrews 10:36).

MY PRAYER
"Lord Jesus, when the fog rolls into my life, help me to keep my eyes fixed on You. Your light is a beacon in the darkness, guiding me home. With You leading me, I will complete the race. In Your matchless name, amen."

MY STUDY
Psalm 141:8–10; Isaiah 2:5

How Do I Know?

"How do I know God's will?" You may have asked that very question. Here are a few guidelines for helping you to determine God's will.

First, God's will for your life will never run contrary to His Word. For instance, the Bible says you shouldn't lie. So if you find yourself with a job opportunity where you are asked to lie, that job isn't God's will. He'll never require you to do something that is in direct conflict with what is spelled out in Scripture.

Second, pray for God to show you His will. Be specific. God answers prayer, but first we have to ask Him. Then, listen for His response – perhaps not in an audible voice, but in the gentle leading of the Holy Spirit.

Third, let me encourage you to not sit idly by waiting for the clouds to roll back and God's voice to speak to you directly. An old saying goes, "It's easier to steer a moving vehicle." Take practical, logical steps to determine God's will: talk with friends; ask questions of those who know you; look for input from those who have been in a similar situation.

Then lastly, when seeking God's will, remember that His plan for you is not confusing, but crystal clear. Let me assure you, if the answer is not obvious, then you may be headed in the wrong direction.

The apostle Paul encourages us through his letter to the Corinthian church, "God is not a God of disorder, but of peace" (1 Corinthians 14:33).

If God hasn't given you peace or your decision is not absolutely clear, then *wait*!

Dear friend, God will always be faithful to show you His will. But it's important to remember: His timing is perfect. Although we may be thinking we need to know right now, His purpose might be fulfilled only after a delay. Trust Him!

HIS WORD

"Teach me to do your will, for you are my God; may your good Spirit lead me on level ground" (Psalm 143:10).

MY PRAYER

Are you struggling to determine God's will on a particular issue in your life? First pray, asking God for guidance. Then follow the steps laid out in today's devotion. God promises that if you seek Him, He will be found. God is faithful. You can trust Him to always keep His promises.

MY STUDY

1 Kings 22:5; John 12:26

His Perfect Timing

As a young girl, Sandra dreamed of studying English or psychology and pursuing a related career. But Sandra's graduation was placed on hold when she married Bob and gave birth to their first son.

Investing in her children gave her great satisfaction. Her family was her first priority, but Sandra never allowed her dream to die.

A few years later, Sandra and Bob became full-time missionaries with Campus Crusade for Christ. With their four young sons, they moved to Kenya, East Africa. In Kenya, Sandra was asked to teach a six-week class on parenting, providing practical information on building a healthy home. The participants enjoyed the class so much that she agreed to teach it three times a year.

This class gave Sandra a platform to cultivate her gifts and underscored her need for professional training. Her childhood dream of obtaining a degree in psychology was rekindled.

After eleven years in Kenya, Sandra and Bob felt God calling them back to the U.S. With her youngest son in high school, Sandra had the freedom to finish college and get her master's degree. Now Sandra works full-time in counseling missionaries, conducting team-building workshops, and interviewing prospective missionaries. She's living out her childhood dream!

Do you have any dreams on hold? You may be at home, investing in your family. Let me urge you to stay at this all-important task. At the same time, don't be tempted to believe your dream has died. Life is a journey, and often God takes us on the scenic route before we reach the "promised land."

Sandra says that by obeying God's calling, she has had a far more exciting and satisfying life than if she'd merely set out to accomplish her own goals.

My friend, God has some great adventures for you if you are willing to listen to His call, go wherever He leads, and wait for His perfect timing.

HIS WORD
"Wait for the LORD; be strong and take heart and wait for the LORD" (Psalm 27:14).

MY PRAYER
Whatever you're doing today — if you're in school, if you're a mother, if you're developing a career — make yourself available to the Lord. Follow His leading. He will use your interests and abilities, and in His timing, will take you places you never dreamed possible.

MY STUDY
Isaiah 30:18; Hebrews 6:13–15

Tell Your Story

Nancy was programmed to succeed. She'd been a nationally ranked swimmer, graduated *cum laude*, and become a company executive. She was co-authoring a book and dating a wonderful man. From the outside, her life was going extremely well. But inside, she was deeply dissatisfied.

She and her colleagues went out almost every night to drink and brag about their achievements. But back home in the stillness of the night, Nancy knew that she wasn't that wonderful. The "happy hours" didn't make her very "happy." She wondered if she'd ever find true contentment.

Sensing the problem had something to do with a spiritual void, she visited church occasionally, went to retreats, read lots of books, and prayed. But nothing seemed to work.

Then one Sunday, she attended a church where people shared stories of how the Lord had changed their lives. Strangely attracted to this group, she came back the next Sunday and the next. As Nancy listened week after week, she realized these people had truly found joy and fulfillment. She wanted *desperately* to be like them.

So Nancy took a class at the church on how to write a personal testimony. She thought that once she wrote out her story, she'd be able to see how God had changed her life, too.

The instructor read Nancy's detailed autobiography and said, "This is quite a confession. But when did you receive Jesus as your Savior and Lord?"

Nancy was floored by this question. It had never occurred to her that a Savior and Lord was available to her, but that very night, she received Christ. She was flooded with a sense of God's peace — what she'd been hungry for all her life. It felt like coming home.

My friend, no worldly accomplishment will satisfy the longing in your heart. Only experiencing God's love and forgiveness can fill that void. Walking daily with His Spirit will sustain your joy.

HIS WORD

"He says, 'In the time of my favor I heard you, and in the day of salvation I helped you.' I tell you, now is the time of God's favor, now is the day of salvation" (2 Corinthians 6:2).

MY PRAYER

When sharing Christ with others, don't judge whether or not they'll be ready to accept Him. Remember, it's God who prepares hearts so they're ready to receive Him. All you have to do is tell your story. Write your testimony and be prepared to share it when the occasion arises.

MY STUDY

Psalm 18:6; Isaiah 45:22

Joanne, an American college student, went on a short-term evangelistic mission trip to Kenya. When she arrived, Joanne was assigned to help a Kenyan family – not as an evangelist, but as a housekeeper.

At first Joanne accepted her chores – doing the laundry, cooking, and dishes – without complaining. She bided her time, waiting for the "real" ministry of evangelism to start.

By the second week, she began to get angry. As she did the laundry, she thought, *I didn't come all this way to get a degree in housekeeping! I'm better than this! They just want me to be their servant.*

Suddenly, she remembered Philippians 2:5,6: "Your attitude should be the same as that of Jesus Christ: Who ... did not consider equality with God something to be grasped, but made Himself nothing, taking the very nature of a servant."

Clearly, she saw that doing the family's laundry was being like Jesus. *That* was her mission.

The work around the house didn't change, but Joanne changed. She relaxed into the role God had given her, not to be an evangelist, but to serve the family as best she could.

A week after Joanne's return to America, she overheard some Kenyan students talking about their mission trip. They knew what had happened to Joanne. Her time as a housekeeper in their homeland had made quite an impression on them. Her attitude and willingness to serve made the Christian message even more attractive.

As a result, the following summer, Kenyan students joined with the American students for an evangelistic outreach. Hundreds came to Christ and the students worked together because of the unprecedented fact that an American girl had served as a housekeeper in a Kenyan home.

My friend, to be a person of real influence, we must learn to be a servant of all. We are called to imitate Jesus Christ – the ultimate Servant.

HIS WORD

"When pride comes, then comes disgrace, but with humility comes wisdom" (Proverbs 11:2).

MY PRAYER

"Lord Jesus, Your willingness to humble Yourself to become a servant of men is truly an example to me. You place great value on humility. Help me to be a humble servant to those around me. In Your holy name, amen."

MY STUDY

Zephaniah 2:3; Luke 1:46–49

Big Dreams

Do you ever lie awake at night and think about your greatest dream? The thing you'd like most to achieve?

Dreams and goals are wonderful. We all should have a few. I believe God gives each person talents, abilities, likes, and dislikes. God places on our hearts goals, aspirations, and ideas that drive us to attempt great achievements for Him.

I'm not promoting worldly success. But what I am encouraging you to do is to pursue your dreams. Dream big dreams. Ponder big thoughts for God. Believe Him for the goal, for the dream. Then take the steps needed to make your dream come true. Persevere. Keep on going. Don't give up.

At one time or another, all of us have had to face discouragement and rejection. It can feel like the end of the world. At those times, never forget that God cares deeply about you. And He promises to never leave your side. Joshua 1:9 says, "Be strong and courageous. Do not be terrified; do not be discouraged, for the LORD your God will be with you wherever you go."

Your dream may be to go to school to get an advanced degree. Perhaps you'd like to get your family out of debt and begin giving greater sums to charitable concerns. Maybe your dream is to share the gospel with one person each week.

Whatever it is, with God's strength you *can* do it. And whatever it is, you can use it to touch the lives of others.

Don't be surprised when you see your dream come true. God is a God of His Word. He will accomplish it through you and will allow your life to make a difference!

My friend, don't settle for little dreams. Fulfill the purpose God has planned for you! You will be able to accomplish great things through God's Spirit.

HIS WORD

"The LORD will fulfill his purpose for me; your love, O LORD, endures forever — do not abandon the works of your hands" (Psalm 138:8).

MY PRAYER

Choose to be strong and courageous today. Make time today to write a brief statement about your dream. Write out Joshua 1:9 at the very top of the paper. Then choose one thing you can do today to start fulfilling that dream.

MY STUDY

Job 17:9; Colossians 1:10–12

The Big Picture

Louie Giglio's dad was a gifted commercial artist. On one occasion, his father came home with a gigantic piece he called the "Abstract Magician." More than nine feet tall and almost four feet wide, it was a looming, gruesome figure with a bow tie, cape, and colored scarf.

Louie's mom hated it, and she wasn't thrilled when he hung it at the top of the staircase for all to see. Graciously, Louie's dad modified the "Abstract Magician" by lopping off a huge chunk from the bottom of the picture. He put this smaller and nicer rendition back on the wall.

A few years later, Louie's father was struck with a near-fatal brain virus, leaving him physically and mentally disabled. It kept him from doing any more artwork.

Many years later, Louie found the part of the painting that had been lopped off. He hung this discarded piece in his office.

Louie says he has people come into his office all the time who declare, "That's the ugliest thing I've ever seen!" His quick response is, "That's because you can't see the whole thing. When I look at it, I never see this small painting. I see the whole guy, all nine feet of him. And I think about my father, the artist."

Louie's point is that life is a series of snapshots, a series of paintings that are halfway finished, or a series of paintings that have been re-framed. Humans can't see the whole thing. But God always sees the entire canvas. It may not be until heaven that we finally say, "Now ... now it makes sense!"

Have you become so engrossed with a little corner of the canvas you've lost sight of the big picture?

God wants to use you. And He has a plan — a big, beautiful piece of art bearing your likeness. Take heart, dear friend! You can trust God with your snapshots. He *always* sees the big picture.

HIS WORD
"We are God's workmanship, created in Christ Jesus to do good works, which God prepared in advance for us to do" (Ephesians 2:10).

MY PRAYER
God has not given us the whole picture of our lives because He wants us to trust Him. Whatever you are facing today, know that the God who loves you sees the whole picture. In fact, He created the picture.

MY STUDY
Genesis 5:1,2; Psalm 22:9,10

The Partner

In 1903, with a little experience in dairy products, a young man moved to Chicago to start a business. If he could put his cheese-making theories to work, he knew he would turn a profit. To get started, he bought cheese from a manufacturer to sell.

He arrived in Chicago with $65 in his pocket. He bought a cart and rented a horse. He and Paddy, the horse, worked very hard.

By the end of the first year, however, he was $3,000 in debt. Soon he could no longer get credit to buy cheese. He kept trying and working harder, but still had no success. Then one day, determined to sell $100 worth, he loaded the cart full of cheese. At the end of the long, hard day, he counted his money: $12.65. That's all he'd made.

Can you imagine the disappointment he must have felt? He and Paddy walked sadly toward home. Dejectedly, he wondered aloud, "What's the matter with me anyhow?" Just then, he thought, *I'm working without God rather than with Him!* So right then and there, He made God his business partner.

I'm sure you're familiar with this man's business. He's J. L. Kraft, the founder of the Kraft Cheese Company! And I don't have to tell you how God blessed his business — *after* he made God his partner.

My friend, when you make God a partner in your life, He'll bless you more than you can imagine. It may not be in dollars, but it will be in personal satisfaction, meaning, and purpose.

No matter what your business is — whether you're an interior decorator, a stay-at-home mom, a lawyer, a sales clerk, or a teacher — God wants to be your partner.

Paul told the Philippians, "I can do everything through him who gives me strength" (4:13).

When you allow God to give direction to your life, you *can* do all things.

HIS WORD
"Blessed is the man who makes the LORD his trust, who does not look to the proud, to those who turn aside to false gods" (Psalm 40:4).

MY PRAYER
In your work, what do you want to accomplish? What are some of your goals? Write those down on paper. Put today's date on it. Then begin praying right now for God to show you what to do and how to do it. Then start doing it!

MY STUDY
Isaiah 26:4; 1 Timothy 6:20,21

Lasting Rewards

Steve was a wrestler on his high school varsity team. After school, he would put on two sweat suits for a strenuous work out. The students were required to do fifty pushups without stopping. If even one person faltered, the whole team had to start over. Even if they'd done forty-nine pushups, they had to start over.

Then the coach would make the wrestlers run up and down stairs twenty-five times. Finally, they would wrestle as though they were in a real match. To top it all off, after practice Steve would run home.

For dinner the night before a match, Steve drank skim milk and ate very lean meat. The next day, he'd head straight for the scales. If he were even an ounce over 119 pounds, he'd be required to suck on a lemon and spit all day in an effort to rid himself of that ounce.

Steve did all that for one reason—he wanted to earn a letter jacket. That jacket was Steve's reward!

First Corinthians 9:25 says, "Everyone who competes in the games goes into strict training. They do it to get a crown that will not last."

Today, I'm sure Steve has no attachment to that jacket.

The verse goes on to say, "But we [who follow Christ] do [our work] to get a crown that will last forever." This "imperishable" crown will never tarnish, fade, or lose its value.

Every day, you and I are motivated by rewards. Most of the rewards don't last. There's only one thing we can do that lasts, and it's tied to our relationship with Jesus Christ. We can trust and obey Him.

If that's your desire, dear friend, no matter what you do today, you'll be investing in eternity. And when you see Him face to face, you'll receive the greatest and most lasting of all rewards: His pleasure in you. You'll hear Him say to you, "Well done, My good and faithful servant."

HIS WORD
"The nations will see your righteousness, and all kings your glory; you will be called by a new name that the mouth of the LORD will bestow. You will be a crown of splendor in the LORD's hand, a royal diadem in the hand of your God" (Isaiah 62:2,3).

MY PRAYER
What do you need to do today? Care for a child? Meet a deadline at work? Share your faith? Pray, "Lord, You know that I need your help. You've promised in Your Word to work through me. Help me trust You and be obedient to all You've called me to do today."

MY STUDY
Psalm 19:9–11; James 1:12

No Regrets

William Borden was born into a family of great wealth and was heir to the family's fortune.

After graduating from high school, he traveled abroad. During this time, God impressed it upon his heart to give his life to missions.

While William was in college, his father died. His family asked him to take over the family business. But William was committed to following God's direction. He wrote on the flyleaf of his Bible, "No Reserve." And without reservation he continued preparing for the mission field.

Later, he finished seminary studies. His friends encouraged him to stay in America and to become a pastor. But no, God had called him to go. On the flyleaf of his Bible, he added this: "No Retreat." And with that he never looked back.

Soon he was on his way to Cairo, Egypt. Four months into his mission service, he became ill. William Borden died. His body, with his Bible resting on his chest, was shipped back to Chicago.

As his brokenhearted family looked through his Bible, they found one more inscription, written the day before William died. He wrote these words: "No Regrets."

William's story influenced thousands of young people to get involved in the Student Volunteer Movement. They gave their lives to taking the message of God's love to the world. There's never been anything quite like it since.

William Borden could have commanded a fortune. But it's unlikely his wealth could have influenced more people for the cause of Christ. It was his character, his commitment to God, and God's call on his life that touched so many lives. He set an example others could follow. And they did.

Friend, whatever God calls you to do, do it. Don't ever give up. Be one of the few like William Borden. Be committed. Write his words in the cover of your Bible: "No Reserve. No Retreat." You will have "No Regrets."

HIS WORD

"Jesus said to them, '… Everyone who has left houses or brothers or sisters or father or mother or children or fields for my sake will receive a hundred times as much and will inherit eternal life'" (Matthew 19:28,29).

MY PRAYER

"Faithful Lord Jesus, You have said that You will never leave me nor forsake me. Because of this constant assurance, I can follow You with my whole heart, mind, soul, and strength. You are worthy of my complete allegiance. In Your mighty name, amen."

MY STUDY

1 Samuel 3:7–10; Psalm 57:7

Thelma Wells had just graduated from high school and was ambitious about her future as a secretary. After calling the secretarial school for registration information, she excitedly put on her new blue dress and rode a bus to the school.

Enthusiastically, Thelma burst through the school door. Within minutes, she was on her way back out. When the admissions officer saw her face to face, he refused to let her enroll. She met all the qualifications for the school except for one detail. Thelma is black, and in the early sixties, this particular school was open only to white students.

Crushed and humiliated, Thelma went home. As she told her great-grandmother, she cried. Her great-grandmother was understanding and encouraging. "Oh, honey," she said, "don't worry. God will make a way."

Later, her grandmother, who worked as a housekeeper, mentioned the situation to her employer. The employer had compassion on Thelma. "Thelma," she said, "I want to pay your tuition and expenses for college. I require only two things. You must keep your grades above a C average, and you mustn't marry until you finish school."

So Thelma Wells, with her dream to attend a two-year secretarial school, became the recipient of a much greater gift – a four-year college education – and became the first in her family to earn a college degree. God made a way – and His way was much better.

Today, Thelma is an author and motivational/inspirational speaker. She tells her story all over the country, imparting hope and faith to those who struggle with disappointment. God knew the plans He had for Thelma Wells. His plan was even greater than she'd imagined.

Discrimination is sinful, and God hates sin. But He is not limited by it! How I rejoice that He sovereignly provided for Thelma in spite of sin. Dear friend, He will sovereignly provide for you. He has a plan.

HIS WORD

"In this hope we were saved. But hope that is seen is no hope at all. Who hopes for what he already has? But if we hope for what we do not yet have, we wait for it patiently" (Romans 8:24,25).

MY PRAYER

Does someone or something seem to be holding you back today? Are you discouraged because the disobedience or sin of another seems to be a barrier to the fulfillment of your dream? Don't be dismayed. God can work through any circumstance and most likely has a better plan.

MY STUDY

2 Samuel 7:9–11; Psalm 111:4–6

Undivided Devotion

Many Christians desire marriage, but God has called some to a life of singleness. Listen to what Crusade staff member Nancy Wilson says about being single.

People ask Nancy why she's not married. Her answer? It's not God's will. She has come to look at her singleness as a gift, and God's Word teaches that every good and perfect gift comes from Him. "Singleness may not be one of the spiritual gifts listed by the apostle Paul in his letters," Nancy says. "But he certainly treated his own singleness as a gift. In 1 Corinthians 7:8, he says: 'Now to the unmarried and the widows I say: It is good for them to stay unmarried, as I am.'"

Many years ago, Nancy thought she'd met her Prince Charming. After she told God all the reasons why this man was the one for her, she sensed God's reply: *But Nancy, how much more can you glorify Me if I teach you how to live with an unfulfilled desire?* Understandably, she didn't want to hear that. But through her tears she said, "Father, I want Your will more than mine. Take away anything that's not Your will for me." God took away not only that relationship, but others.

Singleness is a calling to a deeper love relationship with Jesus, to undivided devotion to Him. It is also a calling to love others as He loves us – unselfishly, generously, and universally.

Nancy says, "If you're single, take time to talk with God, to embrace His gift of singleness to you and offer it back to Him so He may sanctify it for His purposes."

We can be honest with God about anything, including emotions about singleness. Though Nancy has struggled at times, her perspective on her singleness is encouraging and godly.

Dear friends, single or married, if you focus on your relationship with Christ, you will live a life of contentment and will glorify God.

HIS WORD

"An unmarried woman or virgin is concerned about the Lord's affairs: Her aim is to be devoted to the Lord in both body and spirit" (1 Corinthians 7:34).

MY PRAYER

If you're single, talk with God about any struggle you have and seek to embrace your singleness as a perfect gift from Him. Only God knows tomorrow, but today, God has called you to be single. Say yes to the fullness God has for you.

MY STUDY

Psalm 63:2–4; Isaiah 26:9

Ten years ago, Amy began a lifelong friendship with God. She heard someone speak about Abraham being God's friend, and Amy decided she wanted to be God's friend, too. So she put her faith in Christ. Her commitment to God changed her earthly friendships forever.

Over the years, Amy has been taught a few truths about friendship, especially friendships with other believers. She learned that friends are also a wonderful source of love and encouragement. First Thessalonians 5:11 says, "Therefore encourage one another and build each other up." Here are a few other lessons she learned.

First, Christian friendships can be a safe place to be real and accepted. Friends refine us by keeping us accountable to each other. Proverbs 27:17 tells us, "As iron sharpens iron, so one man sharpens another." And in Proverbs 17:17, we read, "A friend loves at all times, and a brother is born for adversity."

Second, in friendships we learn about forgiveness. Colossians 3:13 tells us, "Bear with each other and forgive whatever grievances you may have against one another. Forgive as the Lord forgave you." God commands us to forgive one another. I have found that the more I forgive, the more I understand Christ's love and forgiveness of me.

Third, we learn to work through conflict. The Bible tells us that before we offer our gift at the altar, we must "first go and be reconciled to your brother; then come and offer your gift" (Matthew 5:24). God wants us to live in peace. It is a priority for Him. He knows that we will have conflict, but He wants us to practice the kind of humility with each other that will bring about reconciliation.

From her friendship with God, Amy has learned invaluable lessons about being the kind of friend He wants her to be. When you're a friend of God, He will help you be a better friend to others. Let Him be your guide.

HIS WORD

"Whatever you have learned or received or heard from me, or seen in me — put it into practice. And the God of peace will be with you" (Philippians 4:9).

MY PRAYER

"Lord, thank You for my friends. Help me to exhibit the Christlike qualities of a good friend that You have demonstrated to us. Help me to be loving, encouraging, accepting, forgiving, and humble. I need the strength of Your Spirit. In Your matchless name, amen."

MY STUDY

Ruth 1:16,17; Psalm 133:1

Gentleness

What would you like others to notice about you? Your eyes? Your smile? Perhaps your answer to this question would be the same as Sara's, a Campus Crusade for Christ staff member.

She looks to the qualities described in 1 Peter 3:4, which says that a gentle and quiet spirit is of "great worth in God's sight." A gentle and quiet spirit is characterized by peace. Being a peaceful person is the opposite of being an overwhelming, overpowering, and dominating person. It is the opposite of demanding your own way.

The world tells women of today that we need to be strong by taking charge of a situation and by not being dominated by anyone. The world views as weakness the gentleness and quietness described in the Bible. But God's Word tells us these qualities are precisely what we should strive to exhibit.

Philippians 4:5 says, "Let your gentleness be evident to all. The Lord is near." Gentleness is an exterior quality that will be seen clearly by others.

What does it mean to be gentle? *Baker's Evangelical Dictionary* defines "gentleness" this way: "Sensitivity of disposition and kindness of behavior, founded on strength and prompted by love."

Gentleness should not only be part of our personality or disposition, it should be an act of our will, a behavior. "Be completely humble and gentle; be patient, bearing with one another in love" (Ephesians 4:2).

Sara prays that nonbelievers will notice these imperishable qualities in her — and then be drawn to the Lord because of it. She says, "I want my life to radiate the sweetness and love of God."

My friend, we should all seek to radiate the sweetness and love of God. Pray for a gentle and quiet spirit and ask God to help you display these qualities before others. Then watch God weave them into your life.

HIS WORD
"The fruit of righteousness will be peace; the effect of righteousness will be quietness and confidence forever" (Isaiah 32:17).

MY PRAYER
In which situations do you find the most difficulty in exhibiting a gentle spirit? Seek ways to calm your spirit when you start to feel irritated or impatient. Ask God for assistance during these times. Let His Spirit fill you with gentleness and peace in dealing with difficult circumstances.

MY STUDY
Psalm 131:2; James 3:17,18

Rejoice!

Psychologist Neil Clark Warren asked a chronically discontent woman what would make her happy. She said, "A better job with better pay, a better boss, a better marriage – and a two-week vacation to Maui."

Dr. Warren believes many of us are also unfulfilled, empty, and discontent. He says: "Contentment has everything to do with what's going on inside [of us]. Show me a person who is happy because she is vacationing on Maui, and I'll show you a person who has only a few days to be happy. But show me a person who has learned to cultivate deep-down contentment, and I'll show you a consistently contented person."

Friend, contentment is cultivated in and through God and His Word. Paul speaks to us about contentment in Philippians 4:11,12: "I am not saying this because I am in need, for I have learned to be content whatever the circumstances. I know what it is to be in need, and I know what it is to have plenty. I have learned the secret of being content in any and every situation, whether well fed or hungry, whether living in plenty or in want."

Paul learned the secret of being content. What is this secret? We can look a few verses earlier for evidence of what the "secret" is. In verse 4 Paul tells us, "Rejoice in the Lord always. I will say it again: Rejoice!" Does this verse say we should rejoice only when things are going well? No. It says we should rejoice always, even when things aren't going well and we are experiencing pain.

Contentment doesn't happen automatically. It takes an act of the will to decide to respond to life in a godly manner. If we can learn to "rejoice in the Lord always," we will be cultivating a life of "deep-down contentment." We will be spreading God's secret to living abundantly.

HIS WORD

"May all who seek you rejoice and be glad in you; may those who love your salvation always say, 'The LORD be exalted!'" (Psalm 40:16).

MY PRAYER

In life, we all encounter situations or circumstances that are not what we would choose for ourselves, and we can end up feeling discontent. Make it a daily practice to cover any discontentment with rejoicing in the Lord. Then contentment will come.

MY STUDY

Deuteronomy 12:7; Acts 2:25–28

A Good Thing

Where do you work? Perhaps in an office, at a construction site, or at home with your children. No matter where we are, we all have work to do.

God created work all the way back in the beginning. In Genesis 2:15 we are told, "The LORD God took the man and put him in the Garden of Eden to work it and take care of it." So, work is a good thing. We were meant to labor and take care of what God has given us.

The *New Geneva Study Bible* explains the concept of work this way: "Man was to find fulfillment, not in idleness, but in a life of rewarding labor in obedience to God's command."

God mandated work to make our lives full and meaningful. Have you ever been sick at home, unable to do your normal activities? If you are like I am, you tend to feel restless, like there is more you should be doing. That drive to be productive with our time was put there by God. It is this drive that enables us to provide for our families, fulfill our dreams, and accomplish the tasks God sets before us.

God did not say that the work would be easy, but He did give us a guideline about how we should do whatever work we are doing. In Colossians, we're told this: "Whatever you do, work at it with all your heart, as working for the Lord, not for men" (3:23).

Dear friend, although we work to fulfill earthly needs, we should not work to please men. But we should work to bring honor and glory to God, who is the Creator of work. When we work this way, we will feel a deeper sense of fulfillment and purpose. As you look at your daily life from this perspective, my prayer is that it will renew your strength as you labor for the God who loves you.

HIS WORD

"Blessed are all who fear the LORD, who walk in his ways. You will eat the fruit of your labor; blessings and prosperity will be yours" (Psalm 128:1,2).

MY PRAYER

"Heavenly Father, thank You for providing me with a means to earn a living, but also a place to use the talents You have given me. Help me to make all that I do pleasing in Your sight and fruitful for Your kingdom. In Jesus' name, amen."

MY STUDY

Exodus 35:30–35; 1 Thessalonians 4:11

I like Thelma Wells' description of a bumblebee. She tells about the insect at the Outrageous Joy conferences, a conference for women held around the United States.

Thelma says that, aerodynamically speaking, bumblebees shouldn't be able to fly. Their bodies are too heavy for their narrow wing span. But the bumblebee doesn't know it can't fly. And it doesn't lie in bed asking, "Should I fly?" No, the bumblebee just flies, doing what God intended for it to do.

Unlike the bumblebee, we as humans often get blinded by our own inadequacies. Our finite minds get caught up in analyzing why we can't do something. We tell ourselves that we don't have a certain talent or ability. We tell God that He is asking the impossible of us. Then we never get around to doing what God has intended for us to do.

God does not assign tasks to us because of our strength. He assigns them based on *His* strength. The Bible gives us an encouraging word in Philippians 4:13: "I can do everything through him who gives me strength." God alone is our source of strength.

Where we are weak, He is strong. Paul tells us in 2 Corinthians 12:9, "He said to me, 'My grace is sufficient for you, for my power is made perfect in weakness.' Therefore I will boast all the more gladly about my weaknesses, so that Christ's power may rest on me." In fact, it is when we are weak and accomplish great things in His power that we bring the greatest glory to His name.

Dear friend, take it from the bumblebee: Don't spend your energy worrying about what you can and cannot do. God made you, so He knows where you are weak. Just follow where He leads and trust that whatever He asks you to do, He will give you the strength to do it. Then give the glory for your accomplishments to Him.

HIS WORD

"Proclaim the power of God, whose majesty is over Israel, whose power is in the skies. You are awesome, O God, in your sanctuary; the God of Israel gives power and strength to his people. Praise be to God!" (Psalm 68:34,35).

MY PRAYER

What is God asking you to do right now? Is it something you feel completely inadequate to do? That's good. God wants you to know that, apart from Him, you can do nothing. He is the Source of your strength. Ask Him to work through you each day.

MY STUDY

Judges 6:14–16; Colossians 1:10–12

Step by Step

We all have goals that we want to accomplish. God-given goals are not a bad thing. God wants us to have goals, targets to strive toward. But even if we have a goal or target, what God really wants from us is to allow Him to guide our steps, day by day.

When I have deadlines to meet on a large project, I'm tempted to procrastinate. The task before me can seem to be overwhelming, and at times, I have no idea where I should start.

One way to keep from procrastinating is to set daily and weekly goals for yourself. These step-by-step markers can keep you from becoming intimidated by a large task, which is often the reason we procrastinate. It is in these individual steps that God wishes to guide us.

Proverbs 16:9 tells us, "In his heart a man plans his course, but the LORD determines his steps." With God's help, we can plan the general direction of our lives, but God also wants to be with us each day leading and directing us with His Holy Spirit. In other words, He sets the course, then He enables us to get to the goal.

Having a schedule or a step-by-step guide is good in that it keeps us disciplined and focused, but I never want to be an inflexible slave to my schedule. I want to be open to the leading of the Holy Spirit so that I can accomplish all that God has called me to do and to be. If He changes my course, I want to fall right in line with His plan.

Friend, what has God called you to do and be today? Do you have a game plan for accomplishing that? Remember, God is with you each step of the way and wants to enable you to accomplish the challenging tasks He has assigned to you. Trust Him, today and every day.

HIS WORD
"I know, O LORD, that a man's life is not his own; it is not for man to direct his steps" (Jeremiah 10:23).

MY PRAYER
"Almighty God, thank You that You give me goals to strive toward. But thank You most of all that You do not expect me to get there by myself. You are with me every step of the way. In Your Son's faithful name, amen."

MY STUDY
Proverbs 12:5; John 16:12–14

The Body

Have you ever wondered how God really wants you to serve? First, you need a willing spirit.

Read Lynne's story. Fresh out of college, she eagerly told God, "Use me, Lord!" And He did – as a young wife.

Later, Lynne again prayed, "Use me, Lord!" He did – to change diapers and to serve her young family.

When the children were in school, she cried again, "Use me, Lord!" He did – to drive carpools and volunteer.

God did not use Lynne to blaze trails the way she had thought He would. But He used her as an effective servant: as a godly wife and loving mother. These are both very important and exalted roles.

In 1 Corinthians 12, we read about God's plan for us all to have different roles. "The body is a unit, though it is made up of many parts; and though all its parts are many, they form one body. So it is with Christ. For we were all baptized by one Spirit into one body ... God has arranged the parts in the body, every one of them, just as he wanted them to be. If they were all one part, where would the body be? As it is, there are many parts, but one body" (vv. 12,13,18–20).

We are all different parts of the Body of Christ, the worldwide church. Each of us has a valuable function. Some functions are more public than others. But whether you have a public function like a mouth or a hand, or you have a private function like a heart or an appendix, each part is important to the complete functioning of the body.

My friend, wherever you are in your life, pray Lynne's prayer, "Use me, Lord!" Then rest assured that He will use you in the function for which He designed you, and be content knowing that you are fulfilling the purpose He has for you.

HIS WORD

"Just as each of us has one body with many members, and these members do not all have the same function, so in Christ we who are many form one body, and each member belongs to all the others" (Romans 12:4,5).

MY PRAYER

What part of the body are you right now? Whatever part that is, rest assured that God has a unique purpose for you. No one else is just like you, so no one else can function in the body like you can. Thank God for His wisdom in placing you exactly where you need to be.

MY STUDY

Psalm 138:8; Isaiah 41:10

Follow Me

As a teen-age hemophiliac, Steve Sawyer contracted the AIDS virus through a blood transfusion. A few years later, while in college, Steve placed his trust in Christ.

"I know I've been given heaven. So what am I going to do about it?" he once said.

This is what he did: He dropped out of college and began traveling worldwide, speaking to more than 100,000 students about Jesus Christ. Some 10,000 accepted Christ as their Savior.

Steve died in 1999 at age 24. His short lifetime is an example to us of what it means to "take up our cross and follow Christ."

As a Christian, you, too, have been given heaven. But the one-time act of salvation does not mean that you go back to living for yourself. You are not your own anymore. You belong to Christ, and He expects complete devotion.

The phrase "follow me" is used throughout the Gospels in the New Testament. In Luke 9:23,24, Jesus said to His disciples: "If anyone would come after me, he must deny himself and take up his cross daily and follow me. For whoever wants to save his life will lose it, but whoever loses his life for me will save it."

To be a true follower of Christ, we must die to our own desires each day and follow the path that He lays out for us. The amazing, heavenly logic of God's plan is that when we lose our life in this way, we will actually be saving it.

Dear friend, perhaps you are not facing a life-or-death situation like Steve Sawyer was, but we can all learn from his example. Don't wait for tomorrow to begin living your life completely sold-out to God, dead to yourself. As Jesus said, "Whoever loses his life for me will save it."

HIS WORD
"I wait for your salvation, O LORD, and I follow your commands" (Psalm 119:166).

MY PRAYER
Are you completely dead to yourself? Do you submit your will to Christ daily? Begin each morning by asking God to use you and work through you. Give up your own rights that His will may be done. Throughout the day, remind yourself through prayer whose life you are living.

MY STUDY
Deuteronomy 13:4; Matthew 10:37–39

Dealing with uncertainty and the unexpected can be difficult. Most people like stability, and they like to see their plans work out.

Gary learned on an overseas mission trip not to expect his plans to work out. In a foreign country, too many variables left holes in his plans. But as each hole occurred, he watched God, in His sovereignty, fill in the gaps. And when God worked, He always exceeded Gary's expectations.

Gary looks at variables differently now. Whenever plans don't go as expected, Gary trusts God to work in a different way.

Gary said, "Rather than be discouraged or frustrated because my plans didn't happen, this trip helped me learn to trust God more. My plans don't have to work out for God's work to be accomplished."

We read in Proverbs 19:21, "Many are the plans in a man's heart, but it is the LORD's purpose that prevails." We can make plans. It's part of leading a disciplined, productive life. But we need to realize that God is in control. When our plans don't work as we want them to, we can trust that God's plans will be better for us and enable Him to receive the glory.

Friend, God is working for your good. The familiar verse in Romans reassures us of this: "We know that in all things God works for the good of those who love him, who have been called according to his purpose" (8:28). He is working in everything that happens in your life – good and bad, expected and unexpected – to teach you, to bless you, to stretch you, to lead you.

Exceed your own expectations. Seek God's will in your planning. Make Him the focus of your plans and the center of your dreams. Then know that even when life doesn't go as you intended or expected, you can trust that our all-knowing God has it all under control.

HIS WORD

"The foolishness of God is wiser than man's wisdom, and the weakness of God is stronger than man's strength"
(1 Corinthians 1:25).

MY PRAYER

"Almighty God, You want what is best for me. I will trust that Your sovereign power will work everything to my benefit. Help me to let go of trying to control the world around me, which only leads to worry and disappointment. I trust You, Lord. Amen."

MY STUDY
Job 37:14–16; Psalm 18:31–33

Ambition

Ambition is defined as "an eager or strong desire to achieve something." Although ambition can be a positive trait, the Bible gives us evidence that it can be considered a negative trait. Numerous times in the New Testament, believers are warned against "selfish ambition." This is ambition that seeks to satisfy one's own desires above those of God or even the best interests of the people around you.

In Philippians 2:3 we read, "Do nothing out of selfish ambition or vain conceit, but in humility consider others better than yourselves." Be watchful of your motives. It is always better to act with humility and concern for others.

Dr. Ted Engstrom, the leader of Youth for Christ and World Vision for almost four decades, believes ambition is a positive trait when it is done under the guidance of the Holy Spirit. Dr. Engstrom says, "I asked the Lord, in the midst of strong ambition, to make sure that I understood what His will was for my life. God said He'd guide me with His eye – I leaned heavily on that."

He was referring to Psalm 32:8, in which God says: "I will instruct you and teach you in the way you should go; I will counsel you and watch over you." Dr. Engstrom is talking about ambition that is in line with God's will.

Paul was himself ambitious, and in Romans 15:20, we are told the reason for his ambition: "It has always been my ambition to preach the gospel where Christ was not known." Paul's desire to spread the good news of Christ was a godly ambition.

Dear friend, God has given us ambition to keep us striving toward new goals. But this drive is subject to the leadership of Christ. Be ambitious for God. Seek Him first and ask Him to watch over you and guide you. Strive to let all you do bring Him glory. That's godly ambition!

HIS WORD

"'Therefore I will teach them — this time I will teach them my power and might. Then they will know that my name is the LORD'" (Jeremiah 16:21).

MY PRAYER

What are your ambitions? Is there a goal you would like to achieve? First, ask God and search the Scriptures to determine if this goal is godly. Then, allow the Holy Spirit to guide you as you move step by step toward your goal.

MY STUDY

Psalm 119:66; 1 Timothy 4:8–11

Facing a deadline, Ginger was tremendously burdened by the pressure to complete her task on time.

As she prayed, she remembered Psalm 138:8, which says, "The Lord will accomplish what concerns me" (NASB). The *New International Version* of the Bible translates the verse this way: "The Lord will fulfill his purpose for me."

In the midst of her preoccupation, Ginger prayed just the opposite. She prayed that she would accomplish what concerned God. She said, "It revealed the attitude of my heart. I was doing everything in my own strength."

Immediately, she confessed her self-sufficient attitude to God, and she asked Him to accomplish His purpose through her. As a result, she didn't feel so overwhelmed. She knew God was helping her to finish the project.

All of us feel overwhelmed at times. Perhaps it is a large project you are working on or maybe it's just the daily demands on your time and energy from family, friends, work, and church. When that happens, we need to stop and ask ourselves, "Am I working under my own strength or am I allowing God to work through me?" If you are feeling burdened, you are probably working on your own.

Jesus addressed this issue in Matthew 11 when He said, "Come to me, all you who are weary and burdened, and I will give you rest ... For my yoke is easy and my burden is light" (vv. 28,30). When we learn to rest in the Lord's strength, the burdens will lift and we will feel at rest.

Friend, don't try to live each day on your own or confine God to certain areas of your life. That is relying on your own self-sufficiency. Instead, in all that you do, allow God to work through you. He will give you the strength that you need to accomplish His purposes for you.

HIS WORD
"Blessed is she who has believed that what the Lord has said to her will be accomplished!"
(Luke 1:45).

MY PRAYER
"Lord Jesus, when I am overwhelmed, I only need to come to You, lay my burdens at Your feet, and rest assured that You are in control. By giving You control, I will receive peace. Please accomplish Your purposes through me. Amen."

MY STUDY
2 Kings 19:31; Psalm 81:6,7

Stand Firm

What does it mean to be faithful? *Webster's Dictionary* defines "faithful" this way: "Firm in adherence to promises or in observance of duty." God has demonstrated His faithfulness to us through His adherence to His promises. The Bible tells us in Deuteronomy 7:9, "Know therefore that the LORD your God is God; he is the faithful God, keeping his covenant of love to a thousand generations of those who love him and keep his commands."

Throughout history, Christians have demonstrated faithfulness to Christ and His Great Commission to bring others to a saving knowledge of Him. Their acts of faithfulness have been felt generations later.

In the 1800s, one obscure Sunday school teacher helped lead D. L. Moody to faith. In turn, Moody influenced thousands through his own ministry.

Joseph Stowell, president of Moody Bible Institute, wrote: "Even Billy Graham's conversion can be traced to a succession of converts that extends from D. L. Moody ... God has far more in mind for us than simple faithfulness for today. He uses our commitment to His cause to set the stage for things greater than we could dream of, far beyond the borders of our lives."

Faithfulness is the characteristic that produces a many-fold blessing. Jesus said in Luke 16:10, "Whoever can be trusted with very little can also be trusted with much, and whoever is dishonest with very little will also be dishonest with much." As we prove ourselves faithful in our daily duties, God will give us increasing amounts of challenges and responsibilities for His kingdom. But rest assured, we are only responsible for our faithfulness. The results are up to God.

Dear friend, always be faithful to the cause of Christ! Even during times of discouragement or pain, keep your focus on what you know God wants you to do. God will bless you and bring about wonderful results.

HIS WORD
"The LORD rewards every man for his righteousness and faithfulness"
(1 Samuel 26:23).

MY PRAYER
Are you having difficulty being diligent in the tasks before you? Perhaps you don't see the results of your labor, but believe that God is using your obedience. Ask God to help you stand firm in your faithfulness.

MY STUDY
Proverbs 3:3; Matthew 24:45–47

Worl-class consulting firms, Fortune 500 companies, family empires. These are the plans of Harvard Business School's best graduates.

Steve, a Christian, earned top honors at the Massachusetts Institute of Technology (MIT). But while working toward an MBA at Harvard University, he became keenly aware of the emptiness of worldly success.

As the last speaker at a banquet with his peers, Steve told of his plans after graduation. He said, "I'm joining the staff of Campus Crusade for Christ." Silence filled the room. Graduating from the mecca of capitalism only to work for a nonprofit organization was unheard of.

This gentleman is Steve Douglass. Today, he is the president of Campus Crusade for Christ (now called "Cru"). His ministry of more than thirty years has influenced thousands for Christ.

In Luke 16, Jesus says, "No servant can serve two masters. Either he will hate the one and love the other, or he will be devoted to the one and despise the other. You cannot serve both God and Money" (v. 13). Steve had a choice. He could let his life be led by the pursuit of material wealth, which he very likely would have gained, or he could let his life be led by His Master, which held no guarantee of material wealth but guaranteed peace and satisfaction. Steve chose the latter.

What choice have you made? What is your greatest priority? When we are making decisions in life, we often face two distinct paths. One is the path of worldly riches and accolades. The other is the path of heavenly riches and eternal life. One will provide temporary fulfillment and the other will bless with abundant life.

Oh, friend, reconsider the value of wealth and worldly success. In whatever you do, choose today to serve Christ. Someday you will hear Christ say, "Well done, good and faithful servant!"

HIS WORD

"His master replied, 'Well done, good and faithful servant! You have been faithful with a few things; I will put you in charge of many things. Come and share your master's happiness!'"
(Matthew 25:21).

MY PRAYER

"Almighty God, You are the Great Provider. You will sustain all my needs. Help me to choose the path of righteousness in all that I do. May Your Holy Spirit guide me and direct me. In Your Son's holy name, amen."

MY STUDY

Psalm 73:24; Isaiah 58:11

Her Mission

In high school, Tom told Diana he wanted to be a missionary. She thought it was a dream he would outgrow.

But in college, Tom continued to talk about missions. Diana began to recognize that God chose Tom for mission work. She also believed Tom was the man God would have her marry. So, she trusted God to work out the details.

At the end of seminary, Diana was asked about her call to missions. She answered honestly when she said, "I don't have a particular call to be a missionary. My call is being Tom's wife."

Diane has expressed a biblical view of marriage and the wife's role in it. Ephesians 5:23,24 says, "For the husband is the head of the wife as Christ is the head of the church, his body, of which he is the Savior. Now as the church submits to Christ, so also wives should submit to their husbands in everything."

Man is the head of the family as Christ is the head of the Church. God ordained that position. Although a wife may not have the same vision the husband does, God's role for her is to be a helper and supporter. If God is calling the husband to a certain area, rest assured that He is concerned about the entire family. If you will recognize God's leadership and submit to it, you'll find that He will change your heart to match that of your husband's. He will give you the heart to respond. He did that for me.

God wants a husband and wife to be unified, first in their devotion to Christ, next in their devotion to each other. Dear friend, put Christ first in your marriage, then you will see your family unit moving in the same direction – toward God's will. As you all move in the same direction, you will find that your differences and conflicts will be easier to resolve in God's power.

HIS WORD

"I want you to realize that the head of every man is Christ, and the head of the woman is man, and the head of Christ is God"
(1 Corinthians 11:3).

MY PRAYER

Is your family facing a tough decision, perhaps one in which you and your husband have differing opinions? Make sure your husband understands your opinion. But in any relationship, someone must make a final decision. God holds him responsible for that decision. And if the decision differs from your opinion, voluntarily submit, asking God to give you the heart to respond.

MY STUDY

Genesis 2:24; Proverbs 19:14

Brown Eyes

Have you ever desired to be physically different than you are? Is there some part of your body that you wish had been created differently? Before you answer these questions, read Amy's story.

Amy, a young Irish girl, desperately wanted blue eyes. One night she prayed for blue eyes, then confidently went to bed. When she awoke, she ran to the mirror. She was disappointed to still see her very brown eyes.

Years later, Amy Carmichael was a missionary to India. While there, she learned of young girls from poor families being sold as prostitutes. Courageously, she rescued them by staining her skin with coffee grounds and dressing in Indian garb.

What was the key reason this disguise worked? Amy had brown eyes! If her eyes had been blue, she couldn't have passed for an Indian woman. God gave her brown eyes so she could save hundreds of innocent girls!

Psalm 139:13–16 is a wonderful passage of Scripture telling about God's great care in creating each one of us and telling of His infinite knowledge of our lives. The passage says:

> You created my inmost being; you knit me together in my mother's womb. I praise you because I am fearfully and wonderfully made; your works are wonderful, I know that full well. My frame was not hidden from you when I was made in the secret place. When I was woven together in the depths of the earth, your eyes saw my unformed body. All the days ordained for me were written in your book before one of them came to be.

My friend, God "knit you together" the way He did for His very specific purpose. Your age, your size, the color of your skin and eyes. None of these attributes happened by chance. God was not only deliberate in His creation of your body, He is deliberate about the course of your life. Put Your trust in His care, each day.

HIS WORD

"The LORD God formed the man from the dust of the ground and breathed into his nostrils the breath of life, and the man became a living being" (Genesis 2:7).

MY PRAYER

"Great Creator God, thank You for Your thoughtfulness in creating every part of me. Help me to take good care of this vessel You have given me, but also help me to appreciate how I am different from others. You want to use me in a unique way. In Jesus' name, amen."

MY STUDY

Psalm 103:13,14; Matthew 10:29–31

Life of Humility

Maybe you've heard this saying: There is no limit to what God can do with a woman's life if she doesn't care who gets the credit. What quality does this saying describe? The biblical virtue of humility.

When we happen across a great idea or when we execute a plan with success, it's easy to become proud of our achievements. Perhaps we want affirmation or praise from others for who we are and what we have done. This is not an unusual human desire. But, as believers, God is in control of our lives. All the credit for successes or achievements should go to Him. He created us and He is in control of every circumstance in our lives. He gave us various talents, abilities, and strengths, and He provides the opportunities for us to use them. Therefore, humility, not pride, should mark our lives.

James 3:13 says, "Who is wise and understanding among you? Let him show it by his good life, by deeds done in the humility that comes from wisdom." Deeds done with humility show the presence of wisdom in a person.

In Proverbs we read about where wisdom comes from: "The fear of the LORD teaches a man wisdom, and humility comes before honor" (15:33).

So let's look at the progression. Fear (or reverence) for God teaches wisdom, and wisdom leads to humility. Then, in God's timing and for His purposes, honor will come your way. Perhaps it will be earthly honor, but rest assured there will be heavenly honor.

One thing is very clear: you can't find genuine humility on your own. God will provide it to a reverent heart, yielded to Him. And you will find, dear friend, there truly is no limit to what God can do with a woman's life if she doesn't care who gets the credit.

HIS WORD

"*Submit to one another out of reverence for Christ*" (Ephesians 5:21).

MY PRAYER

Practice reverence for God in the following ways: Seek His counsel through prayer on matters great and small. Under the power of the Holy Spirit, speak out against the sin around you. Give God the glory and praise for all the blessings He has given you.

MY STUDY

Proverbs 11:2; Daniel 6:26

Empty Arms

There are certain things money can't buy. Things like love, contentment, or a child.

As a young girl, Stephanie played with dolls, fantasizing about being a mom. When she and David married, it never occurred to her that they might have trouble becoming parents. But after several years, many medical tests, and numerous doctor visits, they were still unable to have a baby.

Stephanie says, "You would think that after many years I'd be used to a monthly disappointment, but the grief and pain never cease. I've read numerous books, all of which assure me that I'm not alone. Still, sometimes I feel like I *am* all alone in the struggle.

"At times I just want God to send me a telegram:

Dear Stephanie,

At this time I've decided not to give you children. You can quit bugging Me about it.

Love, God"

Stephanie knows that God doesn't work that way. So she continues to pray, wait, and hope. She says, "I have no guarantees that God will ever allow us to have children of our own, or that we'll ever be able to adopt. But this I know – He loves us. Our empty arms long to be filled with a child, but we must trust God to fill them with Himself instead."

Stephanie has learned that God can meet her need, and she's learned to wait on Him. In her relationship with Him, she's found contentment.

True satisfaction can come only from an intimate relationship with God. Times of need can help show us God's heart and help us trust Him more. There's no better place to begin learning than in His Word. Some have called it His love letter to His children.

I know the pain of disappointment. I know the frustration of waiting. And I know, too, the deep satisfaction that comes only from God. Let Him fill your empty arms today with His love.

HIS WORD

"I will make an everlasting covenant with them: I will never stop doing good to them, and I will inspire them to fear me, so that they will never turn away from me. I will rejoice in doing them good and will assuredly plant them in this land with all my heart and soul" (Jeremiah 32:40,41).

MY PRAYER

Are you experiencing disappointment? God is there to comfort you. Spend time with Him in prayer. Share your heart with Him and let His Words comfort you. Allow His Spirit to minister to you and your disappointment will begin to fade away.

MY STUDY

Proverbs 8:34,35; Philippians 2:1,2

Dream Big

Astronauts gain a perspective of earth very few people will have. As a little girl, Wendy Lawrence stared up at the stars and dreamed about being an astronaut and orbiting the earth.

From an early age, she was surrounded by people who dreamed big dreams. Her father was in the Navy and had come very close to joining the seven Mercury astronauts. John Glenn was a family friend.

Even though her friends insisted she was chasing a fantasy, Wendy went to work – excelling in high school and then joining the U.S. Navy.

Wendy pursued her master's degree at MIT. There she became involved with Campus Crusade for Christ, personally discipled by a Crusade staff member. She participated in Bible studies and attended several conferences. Her relationship with God was her number one priority – even during a hectic training schedule.

Finally, on March 2, 1995, she climbed aboard the space shuttle Endeavor with six other astronauts at the Kennedy Space Center. Her role was Mission Specialist One – Flight Engineer. The mission was a complete success, and it fulfilled a lifelong dream of someone who was told it couldn't be done.

As a young woman, Wendy committed her life to Christ and walked faithfully with Him. And she had a goal, a dream few women would dare to dream. She took her aspirations seriously and went to work. It required intense training – both physically and mentally.

As a result, a woman of Christian character represents our nation as an accomplished astronaut. When she's not on a space mission, she's accomplishing another mission – one she considers even more important: reaching others for Christ.

Someone asked Wendy about going into space and she responded, "While it's a wonderful adventure, there's no greater adventure than walking with God."

Having watched the earth spin in space from the shuttle – as few people have, or ever will – that's quite a statement. We serve a mighty God!

HIS WORD
"'I am the Alpha and the Omega,' says the Lord God, 'who is, and who was, and who is to come, the Almighty'" (Revelation 1:8).

MY PRAYER
Do you have a dream today? Are there mountains you'd like to climb? Goals to achieve? Has God placed a burden on your heart? Go for it! We desperately need women like Wendy who will take those heartfelt desires seriously. God may be waiting to use you, through your prayer and discipline, in a very special way.

MY STUDY
Exodus 15:11; Psalm 66:5

Sharon was hospitalized with severe depression. She had even lost the will to live.

One day she cried out to God in desperation. Then an unfamiliar woman came into Sharon's room. She took Sharon's face in her hands and said, "Jesus Christ can heal you."

Amazingly, Sharon never saw that woman again.

But after she was released from the hospital, Sharon started going to church and reading the Bible. She also sought counseling. Soon her heart was filled with joy and peace.

Through all of this, Sharon discovered a truth that is revealed in God's Word. Psalm 42:1 says, "As the deer pants for streams of water, so my soul pants for you, O God." As the life of a deer depends on water, so our lives depend on God.

Oh, precious friend, whatever you're facing today, your heavenly Father knows all about it. We can't rid our lives of those dark nights and difficult days. Even Jesus Christ experienced them while He was on earth.

You may be afraid, doubtful, or down at times, but you can be sure God loves you. That will never change. Not even when the storms of life are beating all around you. If your faith is in Christ, it may be shaken, but it will never be destroyed.

Claim this promise right where you are, in whatever circumstances you find yourself. And recognize God is using your situation to mature you, to prepare you to be a more effective servant for His kingdom.

Cry out to God in prayer. Fill your mind with Scripture and praise. This is the best prescription when you're feeling down.

HIS WORD

"Why are you downcast, O my soul? Why so disturbed within me? Put your hope in God, for I will yet praise him, my Savior and my God" (Psalm 42:5).

MY PRAYER

Friend, remember in times of distress that God is faithful to keep His promises. Put your hope in the Lord to get you through any dark nights or blue days you may have. He can truly restore joy and peace to your heart and soul.

MY STUDY

Psalm 34:1-3; John 14:27

Intimacy with God

I pray ... that all of them may be one, Father, just as you are in me and I am in you. May they also be in us so that the world may believe that you have sent me.

Some years ago at a party, a famous actor was asked by a pastor to recite the Twenty-third Psalm. The actor agreed on the condition that the pastor recite it also.

The actor went first. With great poise, he began, "The Lord is my shepherd, I shall not want." The words flowed eloquently, like lovely music. When he finished, the audience applauded enthusiastically and gave him a standing ovation.

Now it was the pastor's turn. In his eighties, he'd lived his life walking closely with God. From the depths of his soul, he recited the familiar words. He knew every word, believed every word, and loved every word.

The audience fell silent; there was no applause, only tear-filled eyes. The actor said, "I have reached your eyes and your ears; this man of God has reached your hearts."

Intimacy has been defined as a close, sustained familiarity with another's inner life. Knowing God intimately makes the very essence of our lives radiate His love. Intimacy can be achieved only by mutual consent. God desires intimacy with you, but until you respond and seek Him with your whole heart, you will not experience true intimacy with Him.

Make it your heart's desire to know God intimately. His Word will give you insight into His character and personality, and His presence will give you a sense of peace that will give others a desire to know Him as well.

My good friend, Becky Tirabassi, is a fun-loving, vivacious lady who draws people like a magnet. On fire for the Lord, she's always praying for opportunities to touch someone with His love.

Becky told me about sitting down for her first appointment with Vicki, her manicurist. Becky explained that she was a Christian writer and speaker who came into that line of work because of her checkered past.

As an insecure teenager, Becky used alcohol and drugs to be accepted. By age nineteen, she was an alcoholic. At twenty-one, she attempted to break the addiction on her own. Withdrawal proved much more traumatic than she imagined possible. Consequently, her habits continued.

Finally, on the brink of suicide, Becky found her release. She met a kind man, a janitor, who explained that Jesus loved her unconditionally, even in her current state. In desperation, she agreed to pray with him, confessing her sins and accepting Christ's offer to make her a new creation.

Becky's life was dramatically and immediately transformed. Not only did God take away her desire to drink, but He also filled her with such joy and peace that she began telling everyone she knew what God had done.

Becky's transparency paved the way for further discussions with Vicki. Every week, their conversation revolved around spiritual matters.

Becky continued to pray for Vicki. It wasn't long before Vicki placed her faith in Jesus. She also asked Becky to help her conquer *her* addiction to alcohol.

Dear friend, you don't need a dramatic story like Becky's to share Christ effectively. But when you share, be sure to let people know how God has freed you from the bondage of sin. People relate to pain and failure. Don't be afraid to reveal the dark side of your past. It is there that God's light will shine ever so brightly!

HIS WORD
"Indeed, in our hearts we felt the sentence of death. But this happened that we might not rely on ourselves but on God, who raises the dead. He has delivered us from such a deadly peril, and he will deliver us"
(2 Corinthians 1:9,10).

MY PRAYER
What secrets from your past do you have? Are you reluctant to share these things? Ask God to help you be more open with those in need. Ask Him to give you peace and boldness to share with others how God has revealed Himself through these circumstances.

MY STUDY
1 Samuel 17:34–37; Psalm 4:1

Intercession

Imagine trying to make an appointment with the President of the United States. He's quite busy!

Yet think about this. Any believer can bow his or her head right now and speak directly with the Creator of the Universe. In fact, we have the awesome privilege of coming boldly to the throne of God at any time. This is a privilege not to be taken for granted!

God has given us the privilege of *intercessory* prayer, a special form of prayer that allows us to "stand in the gap" for others, to ask God to act on their behalf. Paul admonished Timothy about this: "I urge, then, first of all, that requests, prayers, intercession and thanksgiving be made for everyone – for kings and all those in authority" (1 Timothy 2:1,2).

Why is this so important? Paul went on to say, "... that we may live peaceful and quiet lives in all godliness and holiness. This is good, and pleases God our Savior" (vv. 2,3). According to this instruction, prayer for world leaders is a primary responsibility of the praying Christian.

Men and women in public office carry great responsibility and exert far-reaching influence. Their decisions affect the church, the city, the nation, and sometimes the world.

In modern times, we see God's actions change the course of history. For example, the beginning of *glasnost*, which preceded the fall of communism in the Soviet Union, began in February 1987 – just one month after worldwide prayer for religious freedom for that country.

With God all things are possible. There is no need, no problem, no difficulty too great for God. He wants us to trust and believe Him so that we might plead with Him on behalf of others.

Let me urge you today, my friend, to call upon God's power. This is the time for all women to pray big prayers! Make intercession a regular part of your daily time with the Lord.

HIS WORD

"If my people, who are called by my name, will humble themselves and pray and seek my face and turn from their wicked ways, then will I hear from heaven and will forgive their sin and will heal their land" (2 Chronicles 7:14).

MY PRAYER

"Oh, God, you have promised to heal us when we humble ourselves in prayer. We want to turn from our wicked ways and pray that you will help us to continue to seek Your face so that our prayers and our lives can make a difference. In Jesus' name, amen."

MY STUDY

Psalm 141:1,2; Ephesians 6:18

Chuck Swindoll tells a story set in England during World War II. Enemy bombing raids had destroyed much of historic London. Hundreds of men, women, and children were forced into the streets.

Early one morning, while wandering through the rubble, an Allied soldier happened upon a young boy who had obviously been living off the meager scraps he could find. Longingly, the little guy had his nose pressed up against the window of a bakery.

Realizing the situation, the soldier slipped into the bakery to buy a few items. He went back outside and handed the boy a bag full of food.

The boy hesitated for a moment, then replied, "I don't have any money to pay for these."

The soldier lovingly answered, "I know. This is a gift."

The little boy looked at the bag, thought for a minute, and said, "Mister, are you God?"

Jesus said in John 14:9, "Anyone who has seen me has seen the Father." The life of Jesus reflected His Father's so closely that His behavior unmistakably represented God. All the qualities that are true of God are true of Jesus.

That's our mission, dear friend: to be a reflection of Jesus in the same way He's a reflection of the Father. Then, no matter what happens, others will see that there's Someone who loves them dearly and is there to meet them in their time of need.

That's a pretty tall order, and one that's absolutely impossible unless you've learned to trust Christ to live His life in and through you moment by moment. Through the power and control of the Holy Spirit, you can grow in your daily walk with Jesus Christ. You can become more like Him every day. Your life can reflect His beauty.

You might even catch yourself buying donuts for a small boy.

HIS WORD

"The Son of Man did not come to be served, but to serve, and to give his life as a ransom for many" (Matthew 20:28).

MY PRAYER

With God's help, determine to maintain a moment by moment relationship with the Holy Spirit to help you reflect Jesus to others. Once His Holy Spirit empowers you, people will say they know what God is like — because they've seen something of Him in you!

MY STUDY

Proverbs 19:17; Isaiah 52:7

Old Friends

Miriam and Ney were inseparable, childhood friends. But over the years, they lost touch.

Recently, Ney was making plans to go to her high school reunion. She called to make plans with her dear friend. Miriam's husband answered and told her something shocking: "Ney, Miriam is dead." A year earlier Miriam had committed suicide.

My heart goes out to Miriam's husband and family – and to Ney. It's so easy to assume all is well in the life of another. No one ever knew how difficult life was for Miriam. Her lifelong friend, Ney, would love to have known. She would have immediately gone to Miriam in her time of need.

Hearing this was very sobering and poignant for me. It made me want to be in touch with old friends I've known and loved. Someone from long ago may need to know that I still care.

Does someone come to your mind? Has the Lord put someone on your heart that might appreciate a visit or a phone call from you today?

Perhaps you more closely identify with Miriam. Your life has grown very difficult, almost impossible to manage. You may believe that no one on this earth understands how you feel. Your tendency is to keep all those thoughts and feelings to yourself. But, you know what? My guess is that there are those who care deeply about you. Let them know of your need. They can pray for you and be your friend.

God has put us in a body of believers to care for each other, pray for each other, and encourage one another. As the Bible says, "Let us consider how we may spur one another on toward love and good deeds … Let us encourage one another – and all the more as you see the Day approaching" (Hebrews 10:24,25).

No, you can't help *everyone*, but don't let that stop you from helping *someone*.

HIS WORD

"When they were ill, I put on sackcloth and humbled myself with fasting. When my prayers returned to me unanswered, I went about mourning as though for my friend or brother. I bowed my head in grief as though weeping for my mother" (Psalm 35:13,14).

MY PRAYER

Who needs to know you care deeply for her today? In the last few minutes, who has the Lord brought to your mind? Don't wait to be God's messenger. Pick up the phone. Give her a call today. You may be God's tool to reach the Miriam in your life.

MY STUDY

2 Samuel 9:1–7; Matthew 27:57–61

I once heard this story from Elizabeth Elliot.

It was Brenda's first rock-climbing trip. She was geared up and secured by a rope, ready for the climb.

She started up the rock with lots of enthusiasm, headed for the peak. Out of breath, she stopped and looked above. There, before her, was a very difficult ledge.

When Brenda tugged on the rope, it swung around taut and hit her in the eye. And her contact lens popped out!

Precariously, she hung there, searching for the tiny lens on the granite rock. It was nowhere to be found, so she kept climbing.

An hour later, sitting at the peak, Brenda reflected on her climb. Her vision was impaired – great on one side, fuzzy on the other. She thought about the verse that says, "The eyes of the Lord range throughout the earth" (2 Chronicles 16:9).

She was convinced God knew exactly where her contact lens had fallen. Still, she was resigned to never finding the contact again.

Dejected, Brenda headed down the path to the bottom where others were preparing to make the same climb. An hour passed.

Another girl, who had no idea of the missing contact, began to climb where Brenda had begun. Suddenly the girl let out an excited cry, "Hey, you guys! Did anyone lose a contact? There's an ant carrying a contact down the mountain!"

It was Brenda's contact!

Can you imagine that? God used a tiny ant to answer Brenda's prayer! There's nothing too small for Him to know. There's nothing too big for Him to handle. He will answer our prayers in ways we never imagined possible.

My friend, rest assured that God knows exactly where you dropped your lens. And it may be His sovereign plan to deliver it as you never expected! Special delivery. With love. From God.

HIS WORD

"When you did awesome things that we did not expect, you came down, and the mountains trembled before you" (Isaiah 64:3).

MY PRAYER

Do you need an answer to prayer today? Need a raven to visit you, like the one that came to Elijah? How about an ant, like the one that delivered Brenda's contact? God will provide an answer, but it may not come as you expected. Are you struggling with a problem today? Pray. Then, expect the unexpected!

MY STUDY

Psalm 5:3; Mark 11:24

His Best

No matter how long we have been Christians, we all need to know important elements of prayer. The Creator of the Universe has openly invited His children to approach Him with our concerns. Here are five elements of prayer that can refresh your prayer life, help you teach others to pray, or bring new life to a group prayer meeting. Try it!

First, thank God for something – anything. Thank Him for His love, for a beautiful cloudless sky, for health, for a sound mind. Expressing gratitude to God can transform your attitude.

Second, thank God for something *specific* that's happened in the last day. Perhaps, it's gratitude for a quiet evening at home with a friend or loved one or safety for your children.

The third step is to pray a "Please help me" prayer. Ask God for help for yourself or someone else.

Fourth, ask God for something specific. I'm convinced that many times we have not because we ask not. Jesus is still asking, "What would you like me to do for you?" He's waiting for our petition.

Finally, thank God for how He will *answer* your prayers. When Jesus prayed in the garden right before His crucifixion, He asked God to take away His suffering. But Jesus knew that God is good, that God is always in control, and that it would be better to suffer than to disobey God.

Jesus concluded His prayer by saying, "I want Your will, not Mine." That's what you're doing when you expectantly thank God for how He'll answer your prayer.

Remember, your heavenly Father doesn't promise to give indiscriminately whatever we ask. Just like any father, He'll give only what is best for us.

So, let me urge you to go to your heavenly Father in prayer. He wants to hear from you, and He wants to give you His best.

Now, who can pass up that invitation? Get ready – you'll be amazed at what God can do!

HIS WORD
"Everyone who asks receives; he who seeks finds; and to him who knocks, the door will be opened" (Luke 11:10).

MY PRAYER
"Lord Jesus, thank You for Your love and faithfulness. Thank You for the privilege of being able to come to You with my concerns. Thank You that You answer my prayers with every thought to my welfare. In Your holy name, amen."

MY STUDY
1 Kings 8:37–40; Psalm 66:16–20

When reading portions of the Old Testament, one man seems to stand out more than anyone else. His story is told with greater detail, his poetry is divinely inspired, and his example is continually held up for others to follow. That man's name is David.

What was David's secret? We know he wasn't perfect. He committed adultery; he compounded that sin by murder; and he suffered bouts of despair.

David's secret was his commitment and devotion to God – not just to the laws of God, though he valued them highly, but to God Himself. David and God had a dynamic, incredibly intimate relationship.

David sought the Lord every time he made a decision. He kept a tight rein on his emotions. And when he found something impure and displeasing to God, he repented. He loved the laws of God. When he broke those laws, his repentance was absolute.

Listen to David's total honesty and trust in God as he confessed his sin and made things right between himself and God:

> Surely you desire truth in the inner parts; you teach me wisdom in the inmost place ... Hide your face from my sins and blot out all my iniquity. Create in me a pure heart, O God, and renew a steadfast spirit within me. Do not cast me from your presence or take your Holy Spirit from me. Restore to me the joy of your salvation and grant me a willing spirit, to sustain me ... O Lord, open my lips, and my mouth will declare your praise (Psalm 51:6,9–12,15).

To David, even failure and horrible sin were opportunities to learn more about God. Through his weakness, David learned how dependent he was on God for having a pure heart and doing what is right. David loved the Lord wholeheartedly. His life was yielded to God with no reservations.

Dear friend, cultivate your relationship with God. Depend on Him and love Him wholeheartedly.

HIS WORD

"Jesus replied: 'Love the Lord your God with all your heart and with all your soul and with all your mind'" (Matthew 22:37).

MY PRAYER

Read through all of Psalm 51. What emotions do you think David was feeling when he wrote these words? Is there any evidence of how God responded to David? How can you apply these thoughts to your life?

MY STUDY

Psalm 40:7,8; Jeremiah 3:13

Refreshment

Belinda clenched her teeth, holding back the impatience threatening to spill out. Her two-year-old Hilary was whimpering and pulling on her leg, demanding attention. The toddler's wailing had started before the sun came up. Belinda hadn't enjoyed a moment to herself since then.

First, Hilary needed a diaper change. Then she needed to be fed. Then played with. Then comforted. Then changed again. Now Hilary wanted to play again.

"Lord," Belinda silently prayed, "I need some time with You. I don't have the strength to mother this precious child. How can I nurture her if I can't find the time to be nurtured by You?"

Even as Belinda cried in desperation, Hilary quit tugging at her leg. She toddled off to her room and began to play contentedly.

Bursting with gratitude, Belinda rushed to her own room and found her neglected Bible. She curled up in a chair to drink in the Word of God. Pouring out her heart to God and receiving His comfort, her soul was strengthened, her energy renewed.

Half an hour later, bright-eyed Hilary wandered into Belinda's room, announcing, "Mommy, I'm hungry!" This time Belinda responded to her child with love.

Isaiah 40:31 tells us exactly what to do when we're exhausted: "Those who wait for the Lord will gain new strength; they will mount up with wings like eagles, they will run and not get tired, they will walk and not become weary" (NASB). Waiting on the Lord requires listening to God and spending time reading His Word.

Belinda found that the only way she could be patient and loving with Hilary was to spend time with God.

But this principle is true in any circumstance. To endure the demands of life, it's essential to pray, read God's Word, and listen to His voice. My friend, let me encourage you to take time for this every day.

HIS WORD

"Repent, then, and turn to God, so that your sins may be wiped out, that times of refreshing may come from the Lord" (Acts 3:19).

MY PRAYER

What has you feeling desperate today? Whether you're a single woman with lots of responsibility, a mother whose children have all left the nest, or a mother of young children like Belinda, you can find hope and rest by spending time with God frequently.

MY STUDY

Exodus 33:14; Psalm 142:1–3

Take Heart!

When George Mathieson was a young man, he met and fell in love with a beautiful girl. They planned to be married after college graduation.

But George had a serious health condition that caused progressive blindness. As his blindness grew worse, his fiancé became scared. She couldn't imagine being married to a blind man, so she left him.

Can you imagine the devastation he felt? Losing his eyesight and the one he loved at the same time. Twenty years later, he was *still* feeling a sense of loss. It surfaced while attending his sister's wedding. He made a willful decision to enter into the joy of her big day while his own heart was aching.

That night he went home and wrote a song that has become one of the greatest hymns of the church. The hymn is called, "O Love That Will Not Let Me Go." Maybe you're familiar with the words:

> O love that will not let me go,
> I rest my weary soul in Thee,
> I give Thee back the life I owe,
> That in its ocean depth
> Its flow may richer, fuller, be.

George Mathieson learned his *greatest lesson* at the point of his *greatest pain.*

Friend, when things are the worst, that's when God's love and His presence are the most real and meaningful. So often we're surprised when these hard times come our way, but we shouldn't be. We've had good warning. Jesus said, "In this world you will have trouble." But then He added, "But take heart! I have overcome the world" (John 16:33).

I wonder, has there been a time when you've been disappointed, even devastated by what's happened to you? Remember, God's love is as deep as the ocean. And He wants to meet you at your point of need, to let you know you're not alone. He loves you like no other can.

HIS WORD

"Everyone born of God overcomes the world. This is the victory that has overcome the world, even our faith" (1 John 5:4).

MY PRAYER

"Loving heavenly Father, through the darkest of days I know You are always there to hold my hand, to guide me, and to comfort me. Thank You for Your never-ending love and care for me. I love You. Amen."

MY STUDY

1 Kings 8:56,57; Psalm 21:5–7

Shoelaces

Brenda was hurrying through the supermarket when she knocked over a display of shoelaces. Embarrassed, she threw one packet into her cart and paid for it.

She had stopped at the store to pick up a few things on her way to visit her friend, Donald, in the hospital. His arms and legs were paralyzed after he fell off a ladder.

"Brenda," Donald said when she arrived, "Sometimes I feel as though God just doesn't seem to care anymore."

All Brenda could say was, "You *know* He cares." As Brenda began to leave, Donald asked, "By the way, the nurse broke one of my shoestrings. Could you get me a new pair?"

Brenda opened her purse and pulled out the laces she had just bought and laced them into Donald's shoes.

They couldn't believe it! Even though Donald couldn't walk or tie his shoes, God had provided new laces just for him. Donald realized that if God cared about something as simple as his shoelaces, he certainly cared about his condition. The Lord does care about the details of life!

Jesus was in the boat with His disciples when a furious storm came up. Waves started breaking over the boat. The disciples looked for Jesus and found Him sleeping. Waking him, the disciples cried out, "'Lord, save us! We're going to drown!' He replied, 'You of little faith, why are you so afraid?' Then he got up and rebuked the winds and the waves, and it was completely calm" (Matthew 8:25,26).

Friend, God cared for Donald and for the disciples. But, just as important, He cares for *you*. He sees your needs, emotional or physical, down to the most minute detail.

So what's on *your* mind today? Are you riding the stormy sea? Or do you simply need a pair of shoelaces? God wants to provide for you. Open the door and, by faith, let Him in.

HIS WORD
"He is the Rock, his works are perfect, and all his ways are just. A faithful God who does no wrong, upright and just is he" (Deuteronomy 32:4).

MY PRAYER
Make a serious study of the Scriptures relating to God's provision (such as Matthew 8 and 10). Then, as a practical reminder, over the next several days and weeks, whenever you tie your shoes, remember that God loves you and that He cares for every detail of your life.

MY STUDY
Psalm 98:2,3; Matthew 21:21,22

Mary Ann was born with a cleft palate. As a student in Mrs. Leonard's second grade class, she felt very embarrassed when the other children asked her what happened to her lip.

One day Mrs. Leonard announced to the children that they'd be doing a whisper test to ensure that they had good hearing. She asked them to put one of their ears against the wall while she whispered into the other ear.

Usually Mrs. Leonard whispered something like "Your shoes are red," or "The sky is blue." But when it was Mary Ann's turn, Mrs. Leonard whispered seven unforgettable words.

She said in a hush, "I wish you were my little girl."

Oh, what a wonderful moment!

Sometimes we think our deficiencies make us unlovable. If anyone knew how bad we were, how ugly, how horrible, surely no one would claim us as their own, certainly not the Living God.

That must have been how the woman at the well felt in the Book of John, chapter four. She had at least three strikes against her the day she came to get water. She was a Samaritan, a cultural outcast according to Jewish tradition. She was a woman, an inferior member of her society. And she had a reputation for immorality. She had *every reason* to feel unworthy.

When Jesus began to speak with her, she was shocked. Why would this Jewish man talk to her? And with such *kindness*!

God loved this woman dearly. It frankly didn't matter what was wrong with her. He wanted to break through all the barriers that kept her from knowing Him. In essence, He whispered in her ear, "I wish you were my little girl."

And that is what He says to you right now. He loves you dearly!

He wants *you* to be His little girl. It's that simple. That, dear friend, is why they call it the Good News.

HIS WORD
"The LORD appeared to us in the past, saying: 'I have loved you with an everlasting love; I have drawn you with loving-kindness'" (Jeremiah 31:3).

MY PRAYER
What challenges are you facing right now, today, this week? Your heavenly Father wants to hear your expression of what you are going through. Talk to Him and share the burdens of your heart. Give those burdens to Him. Then let Him carry those burdens and love you as only He can.

MY STUDY
Psalm 138:2; Romans 8:38,39

A Gift

In April 1994, Sharon was rushing to a choral rehearsal. Amazingly, the quarter-mile walk to her car left her huffing and puffing like never before.

The next day the doctor withdrew two liters of amber-colored fluid from her lungs. By the end of the week, Sharon's worst fears were confirmed. Cancer.

The first chemotherapy treatment was devastating. For eight days, she lay in her hospital bed suspended between life and death. All she could think was, *God, I know You love me, and I know You're here.* While she was surprised by her condition, she knew God was not.

Sharon said candidly, "I decided at some point in my life that if God were with me, the valley wouldn't be so terrible. Well, He was with me and He is with me, but it was still the valley. At times I could only get by minute-by-minute. I say this not to be dramatic, but to be honest."

Sharon went through five chemo treatments, lost all of her hair, had a bone marrow transplant, and a complete hysterectomy.

Then her doctor discovered that Sharon had microscopic cancer. This disease can't be cured apart from a miracle.

Through all this, Sharon remained optimistic about the future. "Part of trusting God," she says, "is receiving each day as a gift and living it to the fullest." It means guarding your heart from despair or self-pity, retaining a good sense of humor, staying active and engaged in life.

Whether you're in a difficult situation right now or simply dealing with everyday life, remember, God meets you at the top of the mountain, and, surely, He meets you in the lowest valley.

To the end, Sharon lived each day to the fullest. She knew the character of God and understood that He loved her.

My friend, remember that life is a gift. Thank God for every day. Live life fully.

HIS WORD
"See how I love your precepts; preserve my life, O LORD, according to your love"
(Psalm 119:159).

MY PRAYER
"Lord Jesus, thank You for the privilege of life. I am but a breath, but You have seen fit to give me many days of life. Help me to live each day to the fullest through Your Spirit and for Your glory. In Your matchless name, amen."

MY STUDY
Nehemiah 9:5–7; 1 Timothy 6:11,12

Together

When Corinne moved to Bulgaria with her husband and four children, she expected the adjustment to be stressful. But she had no idea how bad it would become.

When they first arrived, they lived on the fifteenth floor of a dilapidated hotel with no elevator and no hot water. She was concerned about the safety of her children.

With almost no training in the language, Corinne was drained doing even basic activities. Corinne knew it would take at least two years to learn enough Bulgarian to share Christ with her first friend.

Initially, the stress caused Corinne to turn to the Lord for wisdom and strength. It was an adventure for the family, drawing them together.

Corinne admits she gradually began responding to the stress by withdrawing. Instead of trusting God, she tried to deal with everything alone. Instead of supporting her husband, Brooke, she tried to function independently.

She finally came to recognize her selfishness as sin. After discussion, Corinne and Brooke made an agreement. Whenever they felt the stress level rising, they would ask each other, "What is the one burden I can help you with?" With that question, they'd be willing to offer practical help.

We all know you don't have to go to Bulgaria to experience stress. No matter where you are, the principles Corinne learned are true for you, too.

Stress can be *good* when it produces growth in your relationship with God and your loved ones. Stress can be *bad* when it results in self-reliance and isolation from God and others. What makes the difference? Your attitude. You can either choose to trust God or to ignore Him and fend for yourself.

Let me urge you, friend, to aggressively make your relationships a priority during times of strain and struggle. Choosing to foster intimacy with God and your loved ones is the only way to survive the inevitable stress of life.

HIS WORD
"Rise up; this matter is in your hands. We will support you, so take courage and do it" (Ezra 10:4).

MY PRAYER
Are you having difficulty connecting with your loved ones? Build into your schedule time to communicate concerns. If possible, take walks together. My husband and I have found nothing more productive than quiet time to share and pray together. These actions will strengthen any relationship.

MY STUDY
Psalm 2:11; Ephesians 2:22

Free to Love

Diana was just five years old when her mother died. Her father, overwhelmed with the responsibility of rearing six children, disappeared after the funeral. Diana and her five siblings were divided among relatives.

Placed with a loving aunt and uncle, Diana felt that she had finally found security.

But her happiness was short-lived. Within two years, her uncle died. Shortly thereafter, her aunt became ill. As Diana knelt beside her aunt's bed, she pleaded, "I'll do anything you want ... just please don't die!" The thought of losing her precious aunt was unbearable.

The next morning, Diana learned that her aunt had died during the night. As she viewed the lifeless body, Diana told herself, *I'll never love anyone again. When I love someone, they die. I don't want people dying and leaving me anymore.* With that, Diana began to build an impenetrable fortress around her heart.

The years passed and Diana grew up. She eventually married a successful dentist and by age thirty-one, had four beautiful children. From the outside, Diana's life looked perfect. Inside, though, she was frightened – waiting for death to leave her abandoned once more.

One day, a friend invited Diana to a neighborhood Bible study. Much to her surprise, Diana found herself listening to the leader's every word. For the first time, she understood the message of God's love, that God gave His only Son to die for her so that she could know Him and have eternal life. Diana was impressed that Jesus promised to never leave her, to never abandon her. No one had been able to make that promise before!

In the security of God's love, the fortress around Diana's heart began to crumble. She asked Christ to come into her life. Diana felt truly free to love. The fear of being abandoned was gone and replaced with the love of a caring heavenly Father.

HIS WORD
"He who fears the LORD has a secure fortress, and for his children it will be a refuge" (Proverbs 14:26).

MY PRAYER
You may have had experiences in your life where someone you love has abandoned you or turned his or her back on you. You're not alone. Thank God that He will always love you and will always be there for you.

MY STUDY
Deuteronomy 33:12; Hebrews 6:16–20

Loneliness often strikes when you least expect it – in a crowd or by yourself. Loneliness can stem from the death of a loved one, a romantic breakup, a serious illness, or a long-distance move.

God uses these feelings to stretch us, strengthen us, refine us, and help us to relate to a world that doesn't know Him.

Bonnie's most profound experience of loneliness began with a phone call from her doctor who explained that she would never conceive a child. Over the next few years, she and her husband, Rick, felt a deep sense of loss and grief, and Bonnie experienced intense loneliness.

Certain activities were painful. Bonnie specifically remembers the time she saw a group of children and their parents en route to a parade. As she looked at the sweet faces of the youngsters, the same intense longing swept over her.

She went home sobbing before the Lord. She poured out her pain, yelled out her frustration, pleaded for mercy. Then Bonnie experienced His presence in a new way. She knew God cared.

As Bonnie stopped trying to fill the emptiness with meaningless activity, she and Rick researched adoption agencies and submitted themselves to God's will. Ultimately, they both felt adoption was the right choice. An attitude of submission helped Bonnie move from self-pity to peaceful acceptance.

Many biblical heroes went through times when they were all alone but experienced God's power and faithfulness – people like Joseph, Moses, Jonah, Jeremiah, and Paul. Our Savior Jesus experienced loneliness in a way no one else has. Jesus even cried out, "My God, my God, why have you forsaken me?"

As Christians, we know nothing separates us from the love of God, and that suffering won't last forever.

God deeply loves and cares for you. I encourage you to accept loneliness from God as a gift – a time of pursuing depth in your relationship with Him.

HIS WORD

"Therefore, my dear friends, as you have always obeyed — not only in my presence, but now much more in my absence — continue to work out your salvation with fear and trembling, for it is God who works in you to will and to act according to his good purpose" (Philippians 2:12,13).

MY PRAYER

In what ways are you lonely right now? Will you, by faith, thank God for this gift, this time to draw closer to Him? Then, as feelings of loneliness come over you, run into His loving arms. It is there that comfort awaits you.

MY STUDY

Genesis 39:19–23; Psalm 73:23,26

With You

Every day, Sharon held an informal discussion with her first-graders that she called "family talks." These few moments were often the high point of the day, a time for students to express their feelings and ask questions.

One morning, Sharon asked the class, "What do you enjoy most about the first grade?"

Little hands shot up immediately. Sharon thought their answers might be "recess" or "lunch time." Looking over her students, curly-haired Jeremy caught her attention. He was fidgeting and wildly waving his hand. Sharon asked, "What do you like best, Jeremy?"

His answer burst forth, "I like being with you!"

Sharon loved that. That simple declaration reminded her that it's not recess or lunch time that means the most to a child. It's the relationship that has the deepest influence.

On the way home, she pondered what had happened. She thought about her relationship with God. Sharon valued all she was learning about God. But most of all, she was growing in her appreciation of just being in the Lord's presence – just being with Him.

What about you? What do you enjoy most about God? Can you answer with the enthusiasm of Jeremy that it's the relationship you enjoy the most, just being with Him?

There's no formula to enjoying a deeper, more intimate relationship with God. Just like any relationship, it takes time. And that's where I find many women missing out. The demands of life become a huge distraction for one of the most enjoyable, fulfilling, and meaningful aspects of life in Christ.

Being a Christian isn't only what God does for us; it's the relationship *with Him* that gives meaning and purpose to our whole life.

Find time to be with God. As your relationship with Him grows, you'll discover how much pleasure and joy there is in knowing Him. His delight is in hearing us say, "I like being with you."

HIS WORD
"The man who loves God is known by God" (1 Corinthians 8:3).

MY PRAYER
Set aside time each day to spend with God. Perhaps early in the morning, or late at night. Maybe you could make your coffee break a time to read one of the psalms or a portion of a devotional book. You may also find time alone while in the car. In those brief moments, spend time with God.

MY STUDY
Nehemiah 1:11; Psalm 119:174–176

As a young Christian in college, Shirley joyfully spent hours reading God's Word. But the joy Shirley experienced eventually began to fade. She reached her first spiritual slump as a busy wife and mother. Receiving little encouragement, she began to withdraw from other Christians.

Shirley felt as though she had nothing to give. She had ritual instead of joyful communion.

Gradually, she found herself drawn back to God's Word. She set open Bibles on the kitchen counter, on the dining room table, and in the bedroom. As she worked around the house, Shirley would read the verses and meditate on them.

As she let God's Word soak into her heart, her attitude began to change. Once again that delight in God was part of her life.

Many years later, entering a new season of life, Shirley found herself in another spiritual slump. She didn't feel like doing much of anything and wanted a break. Unfortunately, she also took a break from regularly meeting with God.

Instead, she read other books, watched television, or played computer games. She distracted herself and lost her delight in God.

Facing another spiritual rut, this time Shirley knew how to return to her first love for God. She committed to focusing her attention on His Word.

This meant turning off the television and the computer and picking up her Bible. It meant carving out some special time to take a walk, to pray, and to read. It meant joining a Bible study to be around other Christians who could encourage and pray for her.

Oh, dear friend, life in Christ is a process, an ongoing adventure that never ends. So if you feel as Shirley did, a bit discouraged at times, don't give up! Continue to pursue the One you love. Allow Him to renew your spirit and to refresh your heart.

HIS WORD

*"Jesus answered,
'It is written: "Man does
not live on bread alone, but
on every word that comes
from the mouth of God"'"
(Matthew 4:4).*

MY PRAYER

*Can you relate to Shirley's story? You may be saying to yourself,
That's me. I feel like that! Well, friend, there's hope. Ask God
to give you strength as you let go of the things distracting you
from Him. Then be diligent, taking time to maintain a closeness
with Him.*

MY STUDY

Psalm 35:9; Jeremiah 15:16

He Understands

The ladies were taking their places around elegantly decorated tables, but Alice was standing alone in the middle of the room. There was no place for her to sit.

For a moment, she stood frozen, her mind racing backward in time. She was transported back forty-five years, right into Mrs. Isabel's first-grade classroom. It was her first day at the school. She was the "new kid" once again.

Because there weren't enough desks in the classroom, Alice was seated at a table next to the wall, well away from the other children. In that remote place, she was often overlooked when supplies were passed out. She *felt* left out.

Back in the present, those old feelings caused tears to well in her eyes as she watched the hostesses quickly preparing another table for the overflow crowd. Throughout the luncheon, Alice maintained her composure. But when she got in her car to leave, the floodgates opened. She cried and told God about the pain.

She was convinced that He was trying to teach her something by stirring up those old feelings. God reminded Alice that His Son, Jesus, endured intense times of rejection.

His earthly life was filled with rejection. The night before His arrest, rather than join Him in His anguish, the disciples slept. At His trial, His closest companions abandoned Him. On the cross, Jesus suffered great emotional agony when He was separated from God the Father.

As Alice began to think on these things, she was comforted in knowing that God understands. She thought, *He's been right where I've been.* In this truth, she found peace and comfort.

My friend, I don't know what you're going through, but God does, and He understands. Isaiah 53:3 says Jesus was "despised and rejected by men, a man of sorrows, and familiar with suffering."

Whatever you are feeling today, rest assured, my friend. God truly understands.

HIS WORD

"I tell you the truth, you will weep and mourn while the world rejoices. You will grieve, but your grief will turn to joy" (John 16:20).

MY PRAYER

"Lord, there are times when I feel rejected by others. I know that You understand how I feel. Thank You for Your comfort and peace during those times. Thank You for Your loving Spirit who draws me close to You. Amen."

MY STUDY

Psalm 10:14; Lamentations 3:31–33

A s a city girl, Jeanne often went to visit cousins in the country. Her cousin Tom was just a year older, but he was much wiser in the ways of country living. And he loved scaring Jeanne.

There was a swinging bridge stretching high above a rushing stream. Made of flexible steel cables and wooden slats, the bridge swayed with every step.

Whenever Jeanne went to visit, Tom always had something to show her – on the other side of the bridge! He would run across the bridge first. On the other end, he'd stand waiting. Yelling at Jeanne to hurry up, he'd grab the cables and shake them as hard as he could.

Not as sure-footed, Jeanne held on for dear life. Frozen with fright, she'd beg him to stop. The more she pleaded for him to stop, the harder he laughed and taunted her.

Finally, Jeanne had had enough. She begged her dad to make Tom stop. But Jeanne's wise father told her she was the only one who could do that.

He told Jeanne that when she was on the bridge she mustn't look down or yell, and she must keep walking. She should then focus her eyes on the great big tree trunk in front of her to which the bridge cable was attached and walk toward it.

It sounded like great advice. So when Tom wasn't around, Jeanne practiced. She learned to walk across that bridge with confidence!

That's a great illustration about walking with God. At times, it feels like someone's on the other side shaking the very cables of our lives. Sometimes we forget to Whom those cables are attached.

On those days – when the children are demanding, your husband isn't being very understanding, or your boss is really crabby – look up and keep your eyes on Jesus. Focus on Him and keep walking with confidence.

HIS WORD

"When Jesus spoke again to the people, he said, 'I am the light of the world. Whoever follows me will never walk in darkness, but will have the light of life'" (John 8:12).

MY PRAYER

To focus on Jesus is to take Him into account in every situation. As you race through those difficult days, stop for just a minute and call out to Him. Be specific. Ask Him to give you His peace. Then keep walking in faith.

MY STUDY

Psalm 23:4; Isaiah 55:6

Born Again

Thirty years ago, a young girl was raped by someone she trusted. She naively drank until she passed out. Then her boyfriend raped her. She became pregnant.

Horrified, she considered suicide. Her dad, a prominent politician, took her immediately to a city where he'd arranged an adoption. When she realized this, she protested. She wanted to keep the baby.

Her father then insisted she marry the baby's father. All trust and respect for this boy had been lost, but her father overruled, and they were married.

A baby boy was born, but the relationship was never restored. They were divorced.

This girl's life had been one disaster after another. She'd been brought up in church but kept God "on a shelf," to be used when she needed Him. She had no idea how He could help her now.

Her son, conceived in such unfortunate circumstances, grew up and entered Stanford University. While there, he became a Christian through the Campus Crusade for Christ ministry.

When he went home, he said to his mom, "I've been born again." She was stunned. "How could you be? I'm the one who gave you birth!" He tried to explain, but she didn't understand.

The night before her fortieth birthday, she decided to tell her son the circumstances of his birth. She also prayed that night to a God she'd never known. "Oh, God, I don't know how to be born again. But I promise you, I'll read this Bible every day of my life."

She kept that promise and came to know Jesus personally.

Dear friend, God can do anything. He's never limited by unfortunate circumstances or mistakes. God is never "on the shelf," and He has the most creative ways of resolving horrifying dilemmas. All we need is to trust Him. As Romans 8:28 says, "In all things God works for the good of those who love him."

HIS WORD
"'Do not let your hearts be troubled. Trust in God; trust also in me. In my Father's house are many rooms; if it were not so, I would have told you. I am going there to prepare a place for you'" (John 14:1,2).

MY PRAYER
"All-powerful God, because You control heaven and earth, I can trust You with my life. Because You love me infinitely, I can trust You with my heart. Thank You for watching over me, guiding me, and protecting me. In Your Son's holy name, amen."

MY STUDY
Psalm 20:6–8; Jeremiah 39:17,18

The Shepherd

Growing up in the Scottish countryside, Sheila Walsh was surrounded by sheep. She tells stories showing parallels between sheep and shepherds and her relationship with her Savior.

Sometimes in a herd of sheep, a headstrong lamb will refuse to submit to its master. Such rebellion is very dangerous for the little lamb. If it wanders off, it could get into serious trouble.

In such cases, the shepherd takes the misbehaving lamb and breaks its leg. While it seems cruel and painful, the shepherd knows that, in the long run, it's the loving thing to do. The shepherd then puts the lamb on his shoulders and carries it around until the leg heals.

During that process, the shepherd and the wayward sheep form a bond that's never broken. When the lamb heals, the shepherd sets him "free," but the lamb stays close by, never striking out in rebellious independence again.

Sheila says as a younger person, she was independent, self-sufficient, wanting to go her own way. Then she came to a place of brokenness. She realized that controlling her own life left her in big trouble. She turned to her loving heavenly Father and surrendered to His will.

She saw God's love in a way that she'd never known and her intimacy with Him became the core of her life. She never wandered away again.

"Interestingly," she says, "in my time of need, God didn't show me my bright future to help me get through the despair. He showed me Himself. Then I knew that no matter what the future held, He would hold me and I had nothing to fear."

Oh, dear friend, God is completely trustworthy. His faithfulness knows no bounds, and His love never ends.

Don't be like the lamb that only learns the lesson when its leg is broken. Learn it from God's own Word, "The Lord is *your* shepherd." And He takes good care of His sheep.

HIS WORD
"'I am the good shepherd. The good shepherd lays down his life for the sheep'" (John 10:11).

MY PRAYER
"Lord Jesus, You are the Great Shepherd. When I stray from Your care, You find me and return me to the fold. When I rebel from Your leadership, You lovingly do what's necessary to keep me out of harm's way. You always take good care of me. Thank You. Amen."

MY STUDY
Psalm 80:1,2; Ezekiel 34:11–13

Best Friends

Friends are a special gift from God. When Virelle's best friend moved two thousand miles away, Virelle felt utterly alone. She appreciated her friend's wit and godly advice. Her feeling of withdrawal from the daily conversations left her wondering if anyone would ever again understand her.

Then one morning, Virelle sensed God asking, "How about letting Me be your best friend?" Proverbs 18:24 says, "There is a friend who sticks closer than a brother." As she tried the idea, she discovered four truths about God's friendship that changed her life:

- God listens when no one else will. At any time of the day or night, you can call out to God and He will listen to your prayers.

- God knows you thoroughly and loves you anyway. God knew you before you were born. He knows your heart and every thought in your head – good and bad. But He still gave the life of His Son for you because He loves you.

- God acts powerfully on your behalf. He can do what earthly friends cannot. God has sovereign control of the universe. He is capable of doing anything for you, and He is faithful to do only what is best for you.

- God craves closeness with you. As your heavenly Father, God longs to hear from you, to help you with your problems, and to comfort and bless you.

My friend, the next time you feel lonely or feel there is no one to talk to, remember that God is one friend who will never move away and is always there to help. As it says in Jeremiah 33:3, "Call to me and I will answer you and tell you great and unsearchable things you do not know." God not only wants to be your friend, He wants to have an intimate relationship with you. What more could you ask from a friend?

HIS WORD

"Now may the Lord of peace himself give you peace at all times and in every way. The Lord be with all of you"
(2 Thessalonians 3:16).

MY PRAYER

Talk to God as you would your closest friend. Tell Him what's on your mind and what's on your heart. You might even try using a notebook as a journal to record your conversations and prayers. Set aside daily time and make it a priority in your life.

MY STUDY

Psalm 142:1,2; Isaiah 44:23

Cheryl loves students, and she has developed a dynamic ministry among them. But after ten years, she was burned out – life became routine and passionless. "Life seemed to be crumbling in around me," she wrote. "I wanted to drop out."

One night she cried out in desperation, "Jesus, I know You're supposed to be enough, but You do not feel like enough. Please help me."

Cheryl was honest with God. And He answered her desperate prayer by filling her heart with His presence.

God wants us to seek Him no matter what we are feeling, even if we are having doubts about Him working in our lives. The Bible tells us in 1 Chronicles 16:10,11, "Glory in his holy name; let the hearts of those who seek the LORD rejoice. Look to the Lord and his strength; seek his face always." This verse tells us several things.

First, we are to glory in His name. His name holds the power of the universe, so it is worthy of honor and praise.

Next, we are to seek the Lord. Seeking God is a conscious, willful act on our parts.

Then, as we are seeking the Lord, we should rejoice because we know that He hears our prayers and is faithful to answer them. He is the source of our strength.

Finally, it says we are to "seek his face always." No matter what we are going through or how we are feeling – happy, sad, apathetic – we should seek after Him, to see Him up close and personal, face-to-face.

If that isn't encouraging enough, look at Proverbs 8:17, which says, "I love those who love me, and those who seek me find me." What a wonderful promise!

Friend, don't drop out. Instead, seek Him diligently and desperately. Get to know Him. Be honest with God. Talk with Him. He is always there to be your strength.

HIS WORD
"If from there you seek the LORD your God, you will find him if you look for him with all your heart and with all your soul"
(Deuteronomy 4:29).

MY PRAYER
"Lord Jesus, You are worthy of all praise, honor, and glory. I earnestly seek You as the source of my comfort and strength. My heart rejoices in thankfulness of Your love for me and Your openness to me. May I always seek Your face. Amen."

MY STUDY
Psalm 27:4; Colossians 3:1

Covenant

Dr. Bruce Waltke is an Old Testament scholar. He recently stated, "We are never more like God than when we make unconditional vows of commitment to one another."

Dr. Waltke was speaking of the marriage relationship, the most important covenant relationship humans can have with each other. A covenant is an agreement or bond. When we make commitments to each other in the context of marriage, we have God's covenant with us to use as our model.

Covenants are very important to God. When God makes an agreement, it is permanently binding. Psalm 105:8 tells us, "[God] remembers his covenant forever, the word he commanded, for a thousand generations." What wonderful security it is to know that when God makes a covenant, it will stand true for eternity. This covenant demonstrates unyielding commitment.

In the New Testament, God established a new covenant with His people. "In the same way, after the supper he took the cup, saying, 'This cup is the new covenant in my blood, which is poured out for you'" (Luke 22:20). Christ gave His blood as a sacrifice for our sins.

Marriage is also a covenant that requires commitment and sacrifice. In the marriage relationship, it is assumed that both parties are committed to each other and are willing to sacrifice their own desires for the benefit of the union. In a biblical marriage, a man and a woman become one flesh – a unit joined by God to love each other, serve each other, and serve God.

Dear friend, don't let the modern attitudes of disposable marriages influence your own marriage. Honor the commitment before God that you made to your husband. Honor it in word, in thought, and in deed. This is contrary to what the world teaches. All around us we hear that we have a right to break up our marriage if we are not happy or fulfilled. But God will honor you for your faithfulness, and you will be blessed.

HIS WORD
"I will maintain my love to him forever, and my covenant with him will never fail"
(Psalm 89:28).

MY PRAYER
"Faithful God and Savior, thank You for Your commitment and sacrifice. Help me to show love toward my spouse in the same way You have shown love toward me. Help me to have a marriage of commitment, sacrifice, and love. In Your holy name, amen."

MY STUDY
Genesis 9:11–13; Galatians 3:14–16

As a single woman, Nancy used the television for noise and companionship, but through it she was becoming desensitized to what was spiritually important.

She said, "I knew my walk with God would be clearer, fresher, more fruitful, and whole if I'd just turn off the TV. Finally, I raised the white flag of surrender." She promised God she wouldn't watch television whenever she was alone.

The Bible tells us in Romans 12:2, "Do not conform any longer to the pattern of this world, but be transformed by the renewing of your mind. Then you will be able to test and approve what God's will is – his good, pleasing and perfect will."

As followers of Christ, we are to be constantly in the process of renewing our minds to contrast with the pattern of this world. As we do this, we will be better able to discern God's will for our life.

Our minds are constantly being bombarded with information. If we are putting the wrong information into our minds, we will find ourselves less peaceful and less able to resist the temptations of the flesh. That is why God listed in a very specific way the kinds of things we should spend our time thinking about.

Philippians 4:8 gives us a helpful list of items with which we are to fill our minds. We are told, "Finally, brothers, whatever is true, whatever is noble, whatever is right, whatever is pure, whatever is lovely, whatever is admirable – if anything is excellent or praiseworthy – think about such things."

Be careful, my friend, what you expose your mind to. If we think about evil things, we will exhibit evil actions. If we think about righteous things, we are more likely to exhibit righteous, Christlike actions. Let the things of Christ so permeate your thoughts and your life that there is no room for anything else.

HIS WORD
"The mind of sinful man is death, but the mind controlled by the Spirit is life and peace"
(Romans 8:6).

MY PRAYER
Monitor the kind of information to which you expose your mind. Study Philippians 4:8. Take each of the eight subjects mentioned and write down a few thoughts or events in your life applicable to each subject. Throughout the day, think about these things.

MY STUDY
Psalm 119:37; Isaiah 26:3

His Light

Some people believe becoming a Christian will solve all the problems they face. Unfortunately, it isn't that simple.

Lisa learned this lesson in her own life. Her temptations for alcohol and promiscuity didn't immediately go away after she came to know Christ. Even though she was determined to please God with her new discipline and purity, overcoming the temptations was a real struggle.

One night, in desperate frustration, Lisa realized she needed to surrender every part of her life to the power of the Holy Spirit. Since that night more than three years ago, Lisa has not had another drink and has remained sexually pure.

I wonder, is there a habit that plagues you? Something difficult to let go?

In Luke 9:23 Jesus tells us, "If anyone would come after me, he must deny himself and take up his cross daily and follow me." Each day we must make the conscious choice to deny ourselves, including the desires of the flesh, take up our cross, and follow Christ. Living the Christian life is a day-by-day walk.

But we do not walk alone. Christ is there with us to light our way. Jesus said, "I am the light of the world. Whoever follows me will never walk in darkness, but will have the light of life" (John 8:12).

We also have the power of His Spirit to help us withstand temptation. Romans 8 tells us, "If by the Spirit you put to death the misdeeds of the body, you will live, because those who are led by the Spirit of God are sons of God" (vv. 13,14).

As you walk through the Christian life, let Christ in you light your way. Depend on the power of the Holy Spirit to give you strength. Soon, the temptations won't be as tempting anymore. You will experience victory.

HIS WORD

"He gives strength to the weary and increases the power of the weak" (Isaiah 40:29).

MY PRAYER

"Lord Jesus, my Savior, You are the light in a dark world. You are the strength for a weak body. Thank You for living Your life in me to be my guide and my strength. Through your power, help me to stand against any temptations that come my way today or any day. In Your holy name, amen."

MY STUDY
Psalm 28:7; Matthew 26:41

Kay Arthur is a well-known and much-loved author and Bible teacher. But it wasn't always so.

Kay's life came crashing down when she divorced the man of her dreams. That started her search for love.

She led an immoral lifestyle for several years. At the end of her rope, she turned to Jesus. Kay prayed to God to take control of her life and give her peace. Her life was immediately transformed. She began a personal quest through the Scriptures.

Eventually, Kay met and fell in love with a single missionary named Jack Arthur. They have enjoyed many wonderful years of marriage together.

Her life is such a testimony of what God can do with imperfect people.

There was another imperfect person. A man named Saul, who became the apostle Paul, was a Jewish persecutor of Christians. He was zealous for his cause. But one day on the road to Damascus, the Lord visited Saul. He blinded him for three days. Saul's companions led him into Damascus. There, God restored Saul's sight through a man named Ananias, and Saul was dramatically transformed.

In Acts 9 we read about what Saul did after he was healed: "Saul spent several days with the disciples in Damascus. At once he began to preach in the synagogues that Jesus is the Son of God. All those who heard him were astonished and asked, 'Isn't he the man who raised havoc in Jerusalem among those who call on this name? And hasn't he come here to take them as prisoners to the chief priests?' Yet Saul grew more and more powerful and baffled the Jews living in Damascus by proving that Jesus is the Christ" (vv. 19–22).

God is not discouraged by your flaws. God takes you as you are and, through the power of His Spirit, transforms you into the person He wants you to be. Let God transform your life, moment by moment.

HIS WORD
"Summon your power, O God; show us your strength, O God, as you have done before"
(Psalm 68:28).

MY PRAYER
What temptations do you face each day? As you face them, remind yourself that God has given you His Spirit as a resource, to give you strength against temptations. Each morning, ask God to keep you from temptation, then rely on His strength.

MY STUDY
Joshua 4:23,24; 2 Corinthians 13:4

His Counsel

My friend's friend is a gifted, caring, attractive woman in her early fifties. She's a devoted mother and grandmother who's been a Christian all her adult life.

More than ten years ago, this woman left her husband of fifteen years. They were active in church, and her husband was a deacon. But he was disappointing to her. He was faithful and had many friends, but he couldn't keep a job.

He bored easily and hopped from job to job seeking a better position. He was charming, but irresponsible. This woman could hardly bear his lack of motivation, and she became disgusted with her own spirit, which had become nagging and negative. Convinced it was better to be on her own than to continue in this stagnant, frustrating atmosphere, she divorced him.

In the years since, she's lived in several cities, and has gone from job to job just to make ends meet. She struggles to sustain herself financially. Her children are now adults, so she lives alone in a small apartment.

Her husband remarried and has remained his social, jovial self.

My friend has asked this woman, "Do you ever regret your decision to leave your husband?" Sadly, she said, "Yes, I really do. And it's caused so much pain for my children and even my grandchildren. I had no idea it would be so hard on them. The scars are very deep."

I don't know all the circumstances of her life and marriage or the agony and fear she felt. I do know this. Sometimes, the easy way out, isn't.

Often, in our effort to rescue ourselves from a difficult place, we make poor choices. Sometimes we opt for a permanent solution to a temporary problem. Sometimes we think something is impossible when it isn't.

Dear friend, be very careful about the choices you make today. Seek God's counsel diligently. Let His Word and His Spirit guide you.

HIS WORD
"Since you are my rock and my fortress, for the sake of your name lead and guide me" (Psalm 31:3).

MY PRAYER
Is there something in your life right now that you feel you can't bear for one more day? Perhaps you're on the verge of making a very big decision, one you'll have to live with for the rest of your life. Let God meet you where you are. Let Him be your solution.

MY STUDY
Isaiah 57:18; Luke 12:30–32

At His Feet

In the first century, a woman's value was determined primarily by the social status of her husband and by the number of male children she bore. But Mary, the sister of Martha and Lazarus, pushed those boundaries.

Jesus and His disciples had been traveling near Bethany. As they passed through the village, Martha invited the whole group to stay in her home. No sooner had Martha extended the invitation than her sister Mary became fascinated with their houseguest. The Bible says she "sat at the Lord's feet listening to what he said."

Mary's position seated at Jesus' feet was traditionally reserved for males only. No woman could be taught by a rabbi in this way. According to the first-century norms, both Jesus and Mary were violating very explicit social and religious customs observed by all devout Jews.

Then Martha complained that she was left to do the kitchen work all on her own. Let me suggest there was something more behind Martha's frustration. She knew Mary was out of place by sitting at Jesus' feet, and she was concerned about protecting the reputation of her family. If anyone heard about what Mary had done, they'd be the laughingstock of the town.

That's when Jesus responded, with kindness, "Martha, Martha, you are worried and upset about many things, but only one thing is needed. Mary has chosen what is better, and it will not be taken away from her" (Luke 10:41,42).

Jesus was willing to break the social mores in order to have Mary at His feet. He honored her desire to learn from Him.

My dear friend, don't let *anyone* sell you the lie that Christianity suppresses or devalues women. Let's take our cues from Jesus. He invites all of us, men and women, to sit at His feet, to listen and to learn from Him.

HIS WORD

"A voice came from the cloud, saying, 'This is my Son, whom I have chosen; listen to him'" (Luke 9:35).

MY PRAYER

In your time with God today, try something a little different. Take your Bible and a pillow or blanket and sit on the floor. As you read God's Word, think of yourself sitting at Jesus' feet, listening to the words coming out of His mouth. Respond in prayer to what you have read.

MY STUDY

Psalm 73:28; Lamentations 3:56–58

Better Than One

Brielle and Kyrie Jackson are twin sisters. Born twelve weeks premature, their entrance into the world was dramatic. *Reader's Digest* told their tender story.

Kyrie was the big sister at two pounds, three ounces. She gained weight and slept calmly. Brielle, however, had a more difficult start. She had breathing and heart-rate problems. The oxygen level of her blood was low. She lagged *far* behind.

At about a month old, Brielle's condition suddenly worsened. She gasped for breath, turned bluish, and her heart rate increased rapidly.

The parents watched closely and were terribly afraid they'd lose her. The nurses tried everything medically possible. Still, Brielle showed no sign of improvement.

One of the nurses then asked the parents for permission to try a procedure she'd read about that was common practice in Europe. With their permission, the nurse put the babies in the same incubator! It wasn't a fancy medical procedure, but it wasn't the norm, either.

In an instant, the sick baby snuggled up to her sister. She calmed and her vital signs improved significantly. As she dozed, Kyrie wrapped her small arm around her tiny sister.

Soon little Brielle was gaining strength. Eventually, both girls became strong and healthy. What a miracle!

The Book of Ecclesiastes says, "Two are better than one, because they have a good return for their work: if one falls down, his friend can help him up" (4:9,10).

That's so true. God's design is for each person to be in relationship with others. Working together. Helping one another. It's true in daily life, in the work of ministry, and in prayer.

When you feel weak and inadequate, nothing helps like having a friend. One who is stronger, at least at the moment! There's great encouragement in someone hearing your heart and helping you carry a burden.

Two *are* better than one, my friend.

HIS WORD

"May the God who gives endurance and encouragement give you a spirit of unity among yourselves as you follow Christ Jesus, so that with one heart and mouth you may glorify the God and Father of our Lord Jesus Christ" (Romans 15:5,6).

MY PRAYER

"Father God, Thank You for the people that You have placed around me. Thank You for the times when I can support them and for the times when they can support me. Thank You most of all that You are the greatest friend of all. Amen."

MY STUDY

Psalm 133:1; Isaiah 41:13

It was late one evening when Don's phone rang. His sister-in-law's family had been in a terrible car accident. Craig, Susan, and three boys miraculously survived, but their oldest son, Jeremy, was killed.

Don felt compelled to write a song to comfort Craig and Susan. Based on a verse in Isaiah he wrote, "God will make a way, where there seems to be no way. He works in ways we cannot see."

The verse Don used is Isaiah 43:19, "See, I am doing a new thing! Now it springs up; do you not perceive it? I am making a way in the desert and streams in the wasteland."

When tragedy happens, life can seem like a harsh desert or a barren wasteland, devoid of life and never-ending. But one of God's amazing qualities is His power to turn tragedy into triumph.

After the funeral, Susan told Don, "We've seen the truth of that scripture. As a result of Jeremy's death, many of his friends have received Christ. God really did make a way for us."

Dear friend, have you stood at the graveside with a friend who has just buried a child? It's devastating. Words are never adequate in times like those. Only God's Word, carefully spoken and directed by the Holy Spirit, can even begin to help the grievers comprehend and experience God's love and grace.

With the Holy Spirit's leading, you can tell burdened people that they are loved by the God of all comfort. In fact, Jesus had a special word for people who were grieving in Matthew 5:4, "Blessed are those who mourn, for they will be comforted."

Ask God to help you be sensitive to the hurts of those around you ... to be ready to give comfort and share the good news of a loving heavenly Father. God *will* use you for His glory, and He will always make a way for streams in the wasteland of grief.

HIS WORD
"As the heavens are higher than the earth, so are my ways higher than your ways and my thoughts than your thoughts" (Isaiah 55:9).

MY PRAYER
"Lord, you never promised us a life free from tragedy, but You did promise to never leave us. Help me to always remember this truth and share it with others who need to hear it in their times of grief. Thank you for being the God of All Comfort. Amen."

MY STUDY
Job 2:11-13; 2 Corinthians 1:3-4

Growing with God

*Perseverance must finish its work so
that you may be mature and complete,
not lacking anything.*

JAMES 1:4

In our culture, achievement and success are applauded and rewarded. We use the power of affirmation even with those of a very young age. With cheers of joy and claps of applause, parents coax their baby to take those first brave steps. As the toddler wobbles into open arms, their smiles affirm the great accomplishment. Their encouragement helps the baby keep trying until he can successfully walk without assistance.

In our walk with Christ, we are not called to be successful, but we are called to be faithful. Even if our spiritual steps are unsteady at times, we must press on. Developing a life of faithfulness requires our careful attention to choices we make every day. In most cases, the seemingly insignificant little things may be pivotal to our desire to be faithful to God.

Every event in our lives presents an opportunity for us to grow. God wants us to mature and develop a faith that will sustain us through the difficult times in our lives. He rewards us when we persevere. God's faithfulness gives us the assurance and encouragement that we can grow in our expression of faithfulness to Him.

Every time you take a negative thought captive or share your faith with a friend, you are taking "baby steps" of faith and your heavenly Father is pleased with your growth. Each new step is an achievement. And heaven cheers!

Pride is an insidious enemy, creeping unsuspected into our hearts and minds. Left unattended, it will destroy us. Humility, on the other hand, is the source of life.

From our earliest days we are nurtured by secular philosophy, which says we've got to believe in ourselves, express ourselves, and have self-confidence; we must be independent, self-assured, and self-reliant. Our culture says these qualities make us successful. But without God, my friend, all of these are pride. Pure and simple.

Through the Beatitudes, given by Jesus, we see a compelling scale by which our pride should be measured. Jesus said, "Blessed are the poor in spirit, for theirs is the kingdom of heaven" (Matthew 5:3). What does this mean?

Being poor in spirit doesn't mean suppressing a vivacious personality. Nor does it mean becoming a doormat. Instead, it defines how we view ourselves and how we come face to face with God. To be poor in spirit is to realize our need for a Savior.

Let me share the insightful words of Max Lucado from his wonderful book, *The Applause of Heaven*:

> You don't impress the officials at NASA with a paper airplane. You don't boast about your crayon sketches in the presence of Picasso. You don't claim equality with Einstein because you can write $E=MC^2$. And you don't boast about your goodness in the presence of the Perfect.
>
> The jewel of joy is given to the impoverished spirits, not the affluent. God's delight is received upon surrender, not awarded upon conquest. The first step to joy is a plea for help, an acknowledgment of moral destitution. Those who taste God's presence have declared spiritual bankruptcy and are aware of their spiritual crisis. They don't brag. They beg.

Don't be deceived. God does not value selfish pride. Only when we realize our own inadequacy are we then able to experience the fullness of God's power and blessing in our lives.

HIS WORD

"Woe to those who are wise in their own eyes and clever in their own sight" (Isaiah 5:21).

MY PRAYER

Have you been deceived? Are you placing too much trust in your own ability to perform? Ponder your own helplessness to redeem your life and trust in Christ's righteousness to save and forgive. Have confidence, not in yourself, but in the God who loves you and gives you life.

MY STUDY

Proverbs 22:4; Matthew 5:3–10

Difficult?

The Christian life is not difficult. No, it's not difficult at all. It's impossible!

Have you really come to grips with that truth? Or do you continue to strive for perfection?

Almost every day I talk to Christian women who constantly feel frustrated and defeated in their lives. They say things like, "I try to do what I'm supposed to do, but I just can't."

Barbara is a dear friend who came to know Christ when she was about thirty. She went to church, taught Sunday school, and by all outward appearances, seemed like a model Christian woman. Yet inside, she was miserable.

She talked about *love* ... but deep down, she held hatred in her heart.

She talked about the *peace* of God ... but Barbara was prone to worry herself silly.

She spoke of *patience* ... but her family knew about her short fuse.

No matter how hard Barbara tried, nothing seemed to work.

Then one day, a friend told her how she could walk in the power and control of the Holy Spirit and explained that the Christian life was not difficult – it was impossible. Only through a complete surrendering to the Holy Spirit could Barbara ever be all she was created to be. Barbara realized the freedom of placing her life in God's hands and living by His power.

No one can live the perfect Christian life except Jesus Christ. He lived an absolutely sinless life. But what's amazing is that He wants to give us the power to live that kind of life, too. We can't achieve sinless perfection on this earth, but He wants to live His life in and through us right now.

Dear friend, like Barbara, you can depend on God moment by moment. He will give you the strength to make right choices and maintain proper attitudes.

HIS WORD

"If the Spirit of him who raised Jesus from the dead is living in you, he who raised Christ from the dead will also give life to your mortal bodies through his Spirit, who lives in you" (Romans 8:11).

MY PRAYER

Jesus promised, "I will give you a Helper to be with you and to abide in you." That Helper is the Holy Spirit, and He empowers us to follow Christ as we should. This life-changing power is the key to supernatural living. Ask God to transform your efforts into trusting in Him to meet your need.

MY STUDY

Psalm 31:5; Ezekiel 36:27

Today's woman is a busy woman. Her world is filled with responsibility and distractions. Whether single, married, working, or staying at home, her daily schedule includes a continual series of tasks, punctuated by little surprise detours along the way.

Can you relate to the woman I have described? Have you set aside just a few minutes to regain your bearings and restore your joy?

Too often the most important aspect of our lives gets squeezed out when the tyranny of the urgent encroaches. I'd like to challenge you and me to take a fresh look at what's really essential in our lives. If we're genuinely committed to the man in our life, the children who call us "Mom," or the grandchildren who call us "Grandma," then it's imperative to preserve and protect our personal time.

We can't possibly be strong for them if we're not healthy ourselves – physically, emotionally, and spiritually.

So set aside a few minutes each day just for you. If it means getting up before the rest of the family, do it. If it means locking yourself into the bathroom just to ward off the distracters, do it.

Sometimes the telephone, the newspaper, a television program, or a request from one of the kids interrupts your personal time. But don't allow the enemy to rob you of this time with God.

Avoid approaching this time with your own agenda. Create an open, quiet space in your heart for God to come in. Ask Him to show you through His Word exactly what you need.

The Bible is the only book where the Author joins you when you read it. And if you ask Him, the Author will explain its meaning and impact in your life. That's amazing!

Your devotional life can become one of the most valued and treasured parts of your day.

HIS WORD

"Acknowledge and take to heart this day that the LORD is God in heaven above and on the earth below. There is no other" (Deuteronomy 4:39).

MY PRAYER

Seek God, not just with a few minutes of your day, but with your whole heart all day long. He will satisfy and bless you more deeply than ever before. Walking daily with God's direction and control gives great security and satisfaction. You will find your life more productive than you could possibly imagine.

MY STUDY

Psalm 27:7,8; Luke 2:19,20

The Golden Rule

"Do unto others as you would have them do unto you." Remember that verse from Sunday school? Unfortunately that statement, the Golden Rule, has almost been forgotten.

You know how you feel when you go to a restaurant and receive rude treatment from the waiter. You know what it's like to get cut off in traffic or have someone behind the counter bark orders at you.

Who wouldn't want the world to be a kinder place? But how do we get there?

It sounds impossible until we remember that the Golden Rule was God's idea in the first place. And we know that, with Him, nothing is impossible. It is His will that we treat others as we would have them treat us. He is the One who can empower us, by His Holy Spirit, to live that out in our daily lives.

Let me challenge you to put Him to the test. Ask God to help you put others' needs before your own today and every day. Pay close attention to your behavior and how you respond to those you encounter. When you fall short, confess that to the Lord and ask Him once again to fill you with His Spirit and empower you to live by the Golden Rule.

When you find yourself being unusually kind and sensitive, be sure to give Him the credit. Thank God for what He is doing in you and through you.

Much emotional energy is wasted when we feel frustrated by someone who has violated us, and we can become discouraged by feelings of resentment or bitterness we may have toward someone. It sounds pretty inviting to replace those feelings with kind and gracious thoughts. It makes me know that when I do unto others as I would have them do unto me, it is not only good for them, God is at work in me.

HIS WORD

"In everything, do to others what you would have them do to you, for this sums up the Law and the Prophets" (Matthew 7:12).

MY PRAYER

"Lord Jesus, you know that I cannot put others before myself in my own power. It's impossible. But I want to do what you've asked me to do. Give me the ability today to put others' interest and needs before my own. In Your powerful name, amen."

MY STUDY

Leviticus 25:35–37; Proverbs 22:9

A few years ago, a friend of mine was riding the public transit system in the former Soviet Union. When Jo Anne reached her destination, she got off the train and almost tripped over a man lying on the walkway. At first glance, she thought he had passed out from a long night of drinking.

Then she took a closer look. His arms and legs were mangled. He was dead. It appeared he'd fallen stone drunk in front of the train.

Jo Anne did some heavy reflecting that morning. *What would his life have been like had he known Jesus? What would my life be like if I didn't know the Lord?*

She began to see this man from a much different perspective. Without God, she could have been on that sidewalk. *There, but for the grace of God, go I*, she thought. Without the hope of Jesus, Jo Anne knew she could have turned to alcohol and even suicide to relieve the pain of hopelessness.

Most Americans still want to believe that happiness is found in a bigger paycheck or living in a better neighborhood. Yet, hopelessness is running rampant in our country. Despair is not unique to the former Soviet Union. In our nation, it's the byproduct of abundance and godlessness.

Those of us who are privileged to know God's love and forgiveness must spread the word. So often, all it takes to introduce someone to Christ is to tell the story of what God has done for you. Sharing your faith takes only a little thought and preparation. You may be surprised how easy it is.

Men and women all around us are as desperate as that man on the street. If you know Jesus Christ, you have the answer. If you tell just one person today, God can use you to rescue one life from heartbreak.

HIS WORD
"The LORD gives sight to the blind, the LORD lifts up those who are bowed down, the LORD loves the righteous" (Psalm 146:8).

MY PRAYER
Take time before the end of the day to ask yourself the question, "What would my life be like if I didn't know the Lord?" Then pray that God will lead you to someone who needs to hear your answer. You'll be delighted to see what comes your way!

MY STUDY
Isaiah 38:17; 1 John 4:10

Throwing Stones

"Sticks and stones may break my bones, but words will never hurt me." Oh, really? Words can hurt. In fact cynical comments or derogatory remarks are tough to put out of your mind. Words can cause irreparable damage.

We've all been there, standing in a group of friends when the conversation, in just a matter of seconds, shifts to a person who's not there. The gossip and criticism begin. At that moment, we may try to change the subject, but often we put in our perspective or just stand back and listen.

Perhaps you're at a social gathering when you get cornered by someone you consider dull. Wanting to be with your friends instead, you feel stuck. As you're listening to this person, you're looking over her shoulder – eager to begin a conversation with someone else. Those are *thought stones*.

Perhaps you're walking down the street and bump into a neighbor who doesn't quite meet your standards. Without saying a word, your face tells the whole story; disapproval comes through loud and clear. Those are *action stones*.

Now, let's look at a familiar scene recorded in the New Testament. A group of self-righteous cynics had captured an adulterous woman and brought her before Jesus. These Pharisees are ready to throw sticks and stones, and they want Jesus to do the same!

Instead, He showed compassion and forgiveness. Quickly turning the focus back on her accusers, Jesus said, "If any one of you is without sin, let him be the first to throw a stone at her" (John 8:7). In the silent moments that followed, you could hear the rocks drop onto the dirt.

Wouldn't you say it's about time we drop the stones, too? Those stone-shaped *words* are irretrievable. Those stone-shaped *thoughts* are sinful. And those stone-shaped *actions* are shameful. Dear friend, because God desires us to edify one another, there's no doubt His Spirit will empower us to do so.

HIS WORD
*"You shall not give false testimony against your neighbor"
(Exodus 20:16).*

MY PRAYER
"Holy God, please forgive me for the stones I have tossed and for the damage they have caused. Help me to be more cautious and considerate toward others with my words, thoughts, and actions so I may be a blessing to others. Amen."

MY STUDY
Proverbs 10:19; Matthew 12:34–37

You may remember a novel a few years ago that caught the attention of many women.

The story was about an Iowa farm wife who falls madly in love with a traveling photographer. Their steamy love affair lasted only four days. But for both of them, the passion was more intense than anything they'd ever experienced.

After his four-day photo assignment was over, he begged her to run away with him. She decided not to. She sacrificed what she felt was true love for the sake of her family. Then she regretted her decision for the rest of her life, nursing the longing to run away with her passions and follow her heart.

This story, which captured the imagination of women all across America, begs these questions: What's so compelling about a story of betrayal and adultery? Is the monogamous life really that dull?

The theme of the book is nothing more than a modern woman's fantasy. An illusion. A daydream. By entering into this fictitious scene, a woman can momentarily escape her own real problems. For a few hours, she can pretend her life is different.

The problem with escape is that the reality of life doesn't change. After finishing a novel, your husband doesn't turn into a handsome, sensitive movie star, and the kids don't quit fighting. The roof still leaks, and the car won't start. Life continues.

Look carefully and honestly at life. There's nothing spectacular about a four-day illicit love affair. It will tear your home apart! No relationship sustains that kind of intensity over time. So don't be looking over your partner's shoulder, hoping someone more exciting will come along. And if you're single, don't believe you need to compromise your standards to find excitement in your life.

Dear friend, the life God will give you will be much more exciting than any romance novel. And it will be real!

HIS WORD

"His divine power has given us ... very great and precious promises, so that through them you may participate in the divine nature and escape the corruption in the world caused by evil desires" (2 Peter 1:3,4).

MY PRAYER

If you're looking for passion — and a love relationship that will endure — invest your life in the one you love. Give yourself completely to that person with whom you share a lifelong commitment. Let God build that relationship, and you will experience a love you never could have imagined.

MY STUDY

Genesis 2:21–25; Proverbs 17:1

Finding Happiness

Everyone in the world is looking for happiness. I'm convinced the reason so many people come up empty-handed in their search for happiness is that they've never discovered the joy of servanthood.

You see, so many people are self-centered that they fail to realize that real satisfaction comes from helping others – reaching out, instead of taking in. Jesus said, "It is more blessed to give than to receive" (Acts 20:35).

My friend Judy spent a summer in South America. While there, she discovered what made her truly content. Judy traveled throughout Argentina showing the *JESUS* film.

One evening she found herself standing on a dirt road. Children were playing all around her, watching the sun set over the mountains. She began to sing the chorus, "How lovely are the feet of those who bring good news." At that moment, Judy realized what truly satisfies her in the deepest places. That night she wrote these words in her journal:

> It's really strange. I am totally content and my spirit is happy but I don't have any of the conveniences of American life. All of the things that I thought made me happy are back home, but for some reason I am content. I am satisfied. Fulfilled. Right here in the middle of Argentina.

Judy learned that contentment comes not from external things, but from knowing she is in God's perfect will, doing what He wants her to do.

Where are you looking for contentment? God has given us some wonderful things to enjoy while we're on earth, but the deepest longings of our soul can be met only by Him. This can happen only when His Spirit reigns in our lives. Then we will be exactly where He wants us to be and doing exactly what He wants us to do.

In the center of His will, we will find peace and contentment.

HIS WORD

"Why spend money on what is not bread, and your labor on what does not satisfy? Listen, listen to me, and eat what is good, and your soul will delight in the richest of fare. Give ear and come to me; hear me, that your soul may live" (Isaiah 55:2,3).

MY PRAYER

Genuine happiness is found not in self-centeredness, but in walking daily in the Holy Spirit and giving of yourself to God and to others. As you apply these principles, you'll find yourself humming as Judy did, "How lovely are the feet of those who bring good news."

MY STUDY

Psalm 145:17–19; Hebrews 10:5–7

Several years ago, a new man started working in Jane's office. Even though she was married, she was very drawn to him both physically and emotionally. He would ask her questions and engage her in meaningful dialogue. He constantly affirmed her and began to meet many of her emotional needs.

Jane said, "I was having teenage feelings all over again. It was like a crush, an infatuation."

How can women have victory over temptation like this?

I think it's imperative to identify the source of the temptation. Jesus said, "The thief comes only to steal and kill and destroy; I have come that they may have life, and have it to the full" (John 10:10).

Jesus is not a killjoy. He wants us to have a full and meaningful life. On the other hand, it's clear that our enemy, the devil, has a diabolical plan.

The Scriptures say, "Test the spirits to see whether they are from God" (1 John 4:1). Jane knew the lustful attraction was not from God. So she embarked on what she called a "21-day experiment."

Every day when the temptations would arise, she'd admit, "Lord, I'm feeling lustful thoughts toward this man, but I refuse to allow lust to take over my life. I choose to be faithful in my marriage. You are the only One who can help me." But the pressure was immense. She said, "Sometimes I'd have to renew my mind fifty times a day."

On the nineteenth day, peace came. By the grace of God, she had won the battle.

Is Satan robbing you of an abundant life? Has he stolen the peace and freedom the Lord has promised? Do you harbor some overwhelming feeling that is displeasing to God?

Dear friend, let God help you. Tell Him your struggles. He is waiting and wanting to help you.

HIS WORD

"Watch and pray so that you will not fall into temptation. The spirit is willing, but the body is weak" (Mark 14:38).

MY PRAYER

Please try your own 21-day experiment to help you deal with a temptation, whether it's lust, a critical spirit, pride, or something else. Your prayer may be as brief as "Lord, help me!" Before you go down a destructive path, give God an opportunity to deliver you from temptation.

MY STUDY

2 Samuel 22:2; Proverbs 4:14,15

The Path

There's a wonderful legend in Uganda about believers in that country who had a great commitment to prayer. Each believer chose a favorite spot in the open air for extended times of prayer. No one else would use this quiet place.

When a person went regularly to pray, he inevitably would wear down the grass, making a path to that place. If he stopped going to his place, the grass would grow over the path. Therefore, everyone knew whether or not he was neglecting prayer!

Prayer is such a private matter. No one, except God, really knows the extent of your prayer life. But in Uganda, if someone's path became too overgrown, his friends would ask if there was a reason he wasn't praying more!

External motivation may be important for some, but let me assure you, there are many more reasons to pray. Let me give you four reasons to pray.

1. We're commanded to pray.
2. Prayer strengthens our most important relationship – our relationship with God.
3. Prayer relieves our hearts of anxious thoughts and worries.
4. God answers prayer.

Dear friend, being a Christian is *not* following a formula of religious beliefs. Being a Christian is *not* a list of do's and don'ts. Being a Christian is *not* a schedule of activities that wins us favor with a distant God.

Being a Christian is having a mutual, loving relationship with the holy, almighty God of the universe. It's knowing Him intimately and well. It's growing in our understanding of who He is and what He desires for our lives. It's knowing we're His creation, made to have fellowship with Him.

God is committed to you and desires a relationship with you. Once we realize that, we'll be racing to His side at every moment.

The grass would never grow over our path – the path that leads us to Him.

HIS WORD
"Seek the LORD and His strength; seek His face continually" (1 Chronicles 16:11, NASB).

MY PRAYER
"Heavenly Father, forgive me for not spending more time talking with You. Thank You for desiring to have fellowship with me. Thank You for Your patience with me and care for me. I will endeavor to spend more time with You each day. In Your Son's holy name, amen."

MY STUDY
Psalm 65:2; Mark 6:45,46

W hat began as the happiest moment in her life quickly became Catherine's deepest valley.

It wasn't supposed to be this way! Katie was the new baby that she'd always wanted. But within three days of the birth, this first-time mother fell into a deep depression. Normally very cheerful and upbeat, Catherine tried desperately to fight off the nagging feeling of sadness. She found herself crying spontaneously and uncontrollably.

To top it all off, she felt guilty. She thought, *Here I just had this beautiful baby girl and she's absolutely wonderful. And I'm feeling absolutely awful.*

While the doctor assured her that depression was common with childbirth and would pass, his words didn't take away the pain.

She was so weary, she couldn't focus on reading the Bible. So Catherine got creative and listened to the Scriptures on tape. She especially loved the psalms. It was her time with God that sustained Catherine. He became her refuge and her strength.

After six weeks in the valley, most of the depression lifted.

For Catherine, her struggle lasted for just a season. For others, it's a lifelong battle. Statistics show that, in this country, one in four women and one in nine men will suffer from a depressive disorder at some point in their lives.

If you find yourself dealing with depression, realize that you're not alone. Many others have experienced the same thing. You can rest assured in knowing two things. First, God promised to never leave you nor forsake you. He is always with you, to listen, to encourage, and to soothe. Second, many godly men and women find great joy in helping others deal with depression and other emotional issues.

Don't let guilt over your feelings keep you from getting the kind of help that you may need. God wants you to live a joyful life, and He will help you do that.

HIS WORD

"Therefore we do not lose heart. Though outwardly we are wasting away, yet inwardly we are being renewed day by day. For our light and momentary troubles are achieving for us an eternal glory that far outweighs them all" (2 Corinthians 4:16,17).

MY PRAYER

Whatever you're dealing with today, I urge you to find a refuge in God. He's not surprised by anything you're feeling or thinking. He knows right where you are, and He will meet you there. He will comfort you. He will give you strength. Just ask Him.

MY STUDY
Job 23:8–10; Psalm 73:21–26

Friendship

There are people everywhere! Yet, loneliness has reached epidemic proportions.

Having more people around does nothing to improve our sense of closeness or desire for friendship. In fact, when the neighbors get too close, we just construct a higher, thicker wall!

There's no greater cure for loneliness than friendship. And there's no more powerful tool for influencing others for Christ than building relationships.

Recently, I ran across some practical ideas for busy women.

First, make appointments with your friends. It's all too easy to say, "Let's get together for lunch sometime," and then "sometime" never comes. Instead, try setting appointments for a specific time and place.

Then, develop a few friendships that are more informal. Everyone needs someone with whom she can be spontaneous.

Also, take some time to jot a note or e-mail a friend, even if she lives in the same town. It takes less of your time than a phone call and can be read and enjoyed by your friend again and again.

Thoughtful little reminders of your friendship take almost no time, yet go a long way in saying, "I care about you." Mail a friend a newfound recipe for her collection. Or send a magazine clipping about a subject in which she's personally interested.

Set aside a specific time each week and use it to call your friends. Even if you have only thirty minutes, you can call two or three different friends each week and work through your entire circle fairly often.

Don't forget to be faithful with follow-up. When a friend has a problem, write yourself a reminder to call back to see how the situation turned out.

Finally, when you can't be with a friend who's hurting, take time to pray – a wonderful way to offer hope and encouragement.

As God has encouraged you, seek to encourage others and be a blessing.

HIS WORD
"I thank God every time I remember you. In all my prayers for all of you, I always pray with joy because of your partnership in the gospel from the first day until now, being confident of this, that he who began a good work in you will carry it on to completion until the day of Christ Jesus" (Philippians 1:3–6).

MY PRAYER
"Father, help me to invest my time wisely in friendships. Help me to be deliberate and thoughtful about nurturing friendships. Keep me from being passive about this essential aspect of the Christian life. Amen."

MY STUDY
Proverbs 17:17; Ecclesiastes 4:9,10

Guilty?

Some people are never happy. They gripe about everything from the weather to the government. Yet, if we're honest, we'd all have to admit there are times when we're guilty of complaining, too.

Maya Angelou, a poet and author, tells about being reared in Stamps, Arkansas, by her grandmother who owned the local market.

Her grandmother had a routine for whenever people who were known to be complainers entered her store. She'd call Maya to come inside and listen when Brother Thomas would begin complaining about the summer heat. Grandma would wink at Maya.

Then she'd listen to a farmer gripe about his blistered hands and his stubborn pack of mules. Again, Grandma would wink knowingly at little Maya.

When the customers left, she'd say to her granddaughter, "Maya, there are people who went to sleep last night all over the world, poor and rich and white and black, but they will never wake again. And those dead folks would do anything to have just five minutes of this weather or ten minutes of plowing. So, watch yourself about complaining, Maya. *What you're supposed to do when you don't like a thing is change it. If you can't change it, change the way you think about it.* Don't complain."

In the thirteenth psalm, David started with an open admission. He felt as though God had deserted him. There was no denial, no cover up. He was honest with his emotions.

But soon, after a time of focus on God's character, David's attitude began to shift. By the end of the psalm, he was full of praise for God's faithfulness.

What happened? David decided to trust in the goodness of God. His circumstances hadn't changed, but because he chose to think about God's character rather than his own problems, his whole attitude was transformed.

Dear friend, whether or not God changes your circumstances, you can change your attitude.

HIS WORD

"Do everything without complaining or arguing, so that you may become blameless and pure, children of God without fault in a crooked and depraved generation, in which you shine like stars in the universe" (Philippians 2:14,15).

MY PRAYER

Is something bothering you today? If you find yourself tempted to complain, don't. Take your feelings to God and express them to Him. Then, meditate on His character. He is absolutely trustworthy. No circumstances are beyond His control. He cares for you. Resolve to trust Him.

MY STUDY

Job 8:20,21; Psalm 13:1–6

Communicating

Karen had a knack for saying the right things in the wrong way. She had a gracious heart, but she could sometimes be abrasive.

Others would flinch whenever Karen would offer ideas. If she disagreed, her response would be, "That doesn't make sense at all!" or, "That will never work. Haven't you thought of this or that?"

Even though her observations were valid and her ideas were right, people didn't want to listen.

Karen's roommate, Sallie, saw this happen time and time again. She really wanted to help her friend be less abrasive. So she prayed about what to say and that Karen would be open.

One day, Karen walked in and unexpectedly said, "Sallie, something's wrong. I don't get it. What is it about me that causes people to react whenever I make a suggestion?" That was the golden opportunity for which Sallie had been praying. Karen was ready to listen.

She talked to her about the three M's of communication. First, the *message* – the content must be filled with truth. Second, the *motive* – our intent must be absolutely pure. Third, the *manner* – our style must be filled with grace.

There was no question about Karen's message. Usually, she had the right thing to say. And her motive was good. She wasn't self-promoting. The third one though – her manner – was the problem. Together, the roommates worked on that.

Think of the people in your life – your spouse, your children, your friends, your coworkers. Do they tend to bristle when you speak your mind? Does your input get rejected? At times, do you find your "pearls of wisdom" are ignored?

Practice the three M's of communication and let God's Spirit help you. You'll find your words will have a more godly impact on those around you. People will hear your words and recognize your motive when you say something with grace and love.

HIS WORD

"Let your conversation be always full of grace, seasoned with salt, so that you may know how to answer everyone" (Colossians 4:6).

MY PRAYER

How can we ensure that our speech is seasoned — flavored — with grace? The best way is to allow the Holy Spirit to control our lives. With His help, the fruit of the Spirit will come out: love, joy, peace, patience, kindness, goodness, faithfulness, gentleness, and self-control. These character traits will surface in our speech. Season everything you say with grace.

MY STUDY

Proverbs 22:11,12; Ecclesiastes 10:12

Mary and Martha, the sisters of Lazarus, were tired of waiting. Four days after they had sent a message for Jesus, He finally came to heal their brother. But by then, Lazarus was dead.

Jesus raised Lazarus from the dead, displaying His power not only for the sisters, but for all who were present. Mary and Martha found Him worth the wait.

Sometimes for us, the wait is so long that we begin to doubt God's goodness and His power. That's exactly how Earl and Sandy felt. Their two youngest children were away at college and they enjoyed a nice suburban lifestyle. Earl had a good job as a computer parts manager and his wife worked part-time.

Then, after twenty-eight years of faithful service, Earl was laid off. It was quite a blow to the family, but especially to Earl's self-esteem. He never pictured himself unemployed. Now he was jobless, and without a college degree. The stack of unpaid bills grew daily.

Résumés, interviews, phone calls – the process began and continued for months. Then the months became years. Earl was overqualified for most jobs. He was approaching age fifty-five and getting tired of people asking, "How's the job hunt going?" Finally, right before Christmas of year number three, God provided a job. The wait had ended!

Let me share some valuable lessons Earl learned through waiting. You can remember them with the acrostic WAIT.

W – *Worship*. When waiting, don't lose sight of God's character. His goodness and faithfulness never change.

A – *Attitude*. Guard your attitude. See the situation through God's eyes.

I – *Involvement*. While waiting, stay involved in God's work in the lives of others. This will keep you from withdrawing and wallowing in self-pity.

T – *Training*. Remember, consider this to be a time for training in godliness.

God uses waiting for our benefit. Make the most of these times and know that God is at work.

HIS WORD

"Those who hope in the LORD will renew their strength. They will soar on wings like eagles; they will run and not grow weary, they will walk and not be faint" (Isaiah 40:31).

MY PRAYER

"Almighty God, thank You for giving me times of waiting. I know that You intend them for my benefit, part of the step-by-step process of helping me to become more godly. I will wait patiently for You to bring me through each step. In Jesus' faithful name, amen."

MY STUDY

Psalm 27:14; 1 Corinthians 4:5

Cindy's Heart

Diane had just begun working at a school when the teachers went on strike, and she didn't feel she should participate. Along with a few other teachers, Diane crossed the picket line. The strike was resolved quickly, but the impact lingered.

The gym teacher, Cindy, was tough and loud. Because Diane had crossed the picket line, Cindy had it in for Diane and did everything to make her life miserable. Cindy would humiliate and degrade her in front of the other teachers. Naturally, Diane wanted to avoid Cindy, but she knew that was not what God wanted.

So Diane looked for ways to be kind. Cindy was surprised when Diane inquired about her health after an illness. Over time, Cindy's anger lessened, and little by little, she softened.

One day, Cindy asked Diane if they could talk. She began crying as she told Diane about several personal problems. Cindy said, "Diane, everybody thinks that I'm really tough because I put up this front. I'm not. I'm just like everyone else." Diane gave her a hug and told her that she would be praying for her.

After a few years, Diane resigned from the school to join the staff of Campus Crusade for Christ. While Diane learned to share her faith, Cindy kept coming back to mind. So Diane wrote to her and enclosed a booklet called the *Four Spiritual Laws*, which explains how someone can know God personally. Cindy wrote back right away, saying only that she'd read the booklet. But God was working on Cindy's heart.

Six months later, Cindy wrote to Diane again, saying, "Diane, I've been dating John. For Christmas, he gave me a Bible, sat me down, and shared the gospel with me. I accepted Christ!"

Diane had planted seeds in Cindy's life, and God used her faithfulness to work on Cindy's heart. My friends, be faithful to share Christ with others.

HIS WORD

"Then I heard the voice of the Lord saying, 'Whom shall I send? And who will go for us?' And I said, 'Here am I. Send me!'" (Isaiah 6:8).

MY PRAYER

Look for opportunities to demonstrate God's love and concern for someone who is not so easy to love. Share the good news with that person. Like Diane, you'll be amazed at how God can use you to influence your friend's life for Him.

MY STUDY

Psalm 96:2,3; Mark 5:18–20

Richard and Nancy were newlyweds and new believers. One night they had an argument. The longer it went on, the more Richard persuaded himself that he was right and Nancy was wrong.

As Richard walked into another room, a verse came to him: "Do not let the sun go down while you are still angry" (Ephesians 4:26). Richard thought, *Boy, am I glad it's already nighttime. I can be angry 'til tomorrow!*

That's what I call "accommodating theology"!

Scripture is clear that we're not to coddle and nurture feelings of anger. We're to work toward *resolution*, quickly and with love.

God knows that unresolved anger festers and turns into bitterness. Paul said that holding onto anger will "give the devil a foothold" (Ephesians 4:27).

Picture the enemy climbing an icy mountain. All the devil can do is slide down unless there's a notch to grab. Bitterness provides that place. And once he's latched on, he does not easily let go. As a result, individuals, marriages, churches, and even nations are destroyed by unresolved anger.

You have a choice in how you will respond to people and to problems. You can choose to respond with humility and love or you can choose to respond in anger.

Ultimately, you need to remember how Jesus Christ has loved and forgiven you. Each one of us has given God countless reasons to be angry. Yet He continually extends His mercy to us.

Are you struggling with unresolved anger today? Don't let it continue, giving the enemy a foothold! Humble yourself before God and before the person with whom you are angry. It won't be easy. But you can't accept the free gift of God's grace without recognizing your obligation to let go of your own anger.

When you deal righteously with your anger, you will be at peace with yourself, at peace with others, and at peace with God.

HIS WORD

"You used to walk in these ways, in the life you once lived. But now you must rid yourselves of all such things as these: anger, rage, malice, slander, and filthy language from your lips" (Colossians 3:7,8).

MY PRAYER

You cannot influence your world for Christ when you're angry. Be filled with grace and love. And the only way to truly demonstrate grace and love is to be filled with the Holy Spirit and to allow Him to work through you.

MY STUDY

Proverbs 29:22; Ecclesiastes 7:9

Seen, Known, Heard

From totally different backgrounds, Tara and Joy became friends during college.

Tara had been to church only a handful of times, whereas Joy had grown up memorizing Scripture and attending church three times a week. But as Joy grew older, she began to have doubts about Christianity.

College became a time of spiritual testing for Joy. She found it too difficult to talk about her faith to Tara. She had too many questions and too few answers. Even when they lived together, Joy read her Bible in private and was very vague about where she stood spiritually.

Two years after graduation, Tara visited Joy. Joy was a different person! For the first time Tara heard her talk openly about her relationship with God. She met Joy's parents and Christian friends and attended church with Joy.

At the end of their weekend together, Tara said that she was impressed. "I've seen a lot of hypocrites," she said. "But you guys actually do what you say."

Then Joy explained to Tara, "When I left college, I felt spiritually bankrupt. But I've come to a fresh understanding of God's love and forgiveness." Tara did not accept Christ from this experience, but she was able to see the difference a relationship with God made in Joy's life. Joy trusts that, in time, she'll be able to introduce Tara to Christ.

Someone has said that to share the gospel effectively, you need to be *seen*, be *known*, and be *heard*.

To be *seen* means that your life must look different because of your relationship with God.

To be *known* involves loving non-Christians – showing genuine interest in their activities and relationships; being transparent; honestly letting them see God working on your weaknesses.

To be *heard* means expressing openly your thanks to God for the gift of salvation.

My friend, let your life draw others to Christ as they see Him in you.

HIS WORD
"Sing to the LORD, for he has done glorious things; let this be known to all the world" (Isaiah 12:5).

MY PRAYER
"Gracious heavenly Father, the people in my life — friends, family, coworkers — are there by Your design. Give me boldness as I allow others to see You working in me. I desire to make a difference for eternity as I am seen, known, and heard. Amen."

MY STUDY
Psalm 67:1–3; Acts 1:8

Bonnie, a woman in her mid-thirties, felt stuck in a very difficult work environment. Her boss was a tyrant. Even so, Bonnie didn't feel she could quit her job.

In trying to cope, she began to eat. Over a six-month period, she went from size 8 to size 14. Bonnie became very depressed and felt terrible about herself. Then a friend gave her a weekend getaway at a hotel. While there, she tried the exercise machines and discovered that she really enjoyed working out.

So Bonnie began to exercise at home. After four months, Bonnie lost twenty pounds and felt terrific – both physically and emotionally. She gained the courage to quit her job and find a much better one.

Depression is something most people go through at some point in their lives. But while experiencing the blues is part of being a normal human being, we don't have to stay blue.

As Bonnie discovered, exercise can strengthen both the body and the spirit. And there are other simple but effective ways to get beyond mild depression.

First, don't avoid talking to God because you feel you're not worthy. Take everything to the Lord in prayer. He can handle it! Remember that God's love for you is limitless, and He has promised special help for the broken and weary.

Next, don't get stuck in guilt or bitterness about the past. As Paul says, "Forgetting what is behind and straining toward what is ahead, I press on toward the goal to win the prize" (Philippians 3:13,14).

You've heard the old hymn, "Count your blessings, name them one by one." Being grateful for what you have is an excellent remedy for pessimism and self-pity. Inventory all your personal assets and give thanks. Gratitude will always give you a fresh perspective on life.

Finally, help someone else. Caring for someone who is hurting will take your focus off your own pain.

HIS WORD
"The LORD is good to those whose hope is in him, to the one who seeks him"
(Lamentations 3:25).

MY PRAYER
The next time you are feeling blue, take your feelings to the Lord in prayer. Share your heart with Him. Don't focus on sins of the past, but look at how God has blessed you, in the past and in the present. Then, reach out and do something nice for someone around you.

MY STUDY
Psalm 42:11; 1 Peter 1:3

Quiet Times

You're in a hurry to get to an appointment, so you hop into the car, speed down the road, then realize, "Now, how do I get there?" You've forgotten your map.

That's the way it is in the Christian life, isn't it? We rush through each day without paying attention to the map, God's guidebook, the Bible. He's given us a compass to correct our direction. All we need to do is stop and look!

I know it can be a struggle to make time for daily devotions. But spending quality time with the Lord every day is absolutely essential if you expect to grow spiritually. For busy people, quiet times won't just happen. You have to plan them.

Most of us find early mornings work best. In fact, the Bible sets a precedent for that. It's recorded a number of times that Jesus rose early in the morning, went to a quiet place, and prayed to the Father.

Our Lord knows how difficult it can be to take time alone with Him. If you're a mother, perhaps your child's afternoon nap may be the best time, or maybe just before bedtime. The important thing is to *plan* the time. Make up your mind to do it and stick to it.

If you don't know what to read, start with a particular book of the Bible. (I suggest the Gospel of Mark or John.) Before you begin reading, pray for the Holy Spirit to teach you. Read a few verses or a chapter. Concentrate on those select lines. Then ask, "What does this passage teach me about God, about myself, about sins to confess or avoid, about commands to obey, about Christian love?"

Keep a notebook or a spiritual journal. Write down what you're learning from each passage. Incorporate what you've discovered into your day. Memorize the verses that are especially meaningful to you.

HIS WORD

"My soul yearns for you in the night; in the morning my spirit longs for you. When your judgments come upon the earth, the people of the world learn righteousness" (Isaiah 26:9).

MY PRAYER

As you take time to study God's Word — the road map of life — and as you enjoy His love and fellowship, your life, and the lives of those around you, will be revolutionized! Begin today to set aside time for Him. Getting to know God is the greatest essential of life.

MY STUDY

Psalm 119:1,2; 2 Timothy 3:14–17

After a year of trouble in her marriage, Terri went to a male coworker for advice. He responded with sympathy. His concern was innocent at first, but then his interest in her grew. He started complimenting her looks, not understanding how a man could reject her. Before long, his comments became very suggestive. It had been so long since a man had been attracted to her, the attention felt wonderful. She even considered it healing.

Eventually, she completely gave in to her feelings for this man. Predictably, her marriage ended – and so did her newfound relationship. Terri was devastated.

Consumed with bitterness and rage, Terri went to her pastor and his wife. Instead of blaming herself or the coworker, she said through clenched teeth, "I asked God for help, and He led me to this man. It's God's fault! He's to blame for what has happened!"

Our human tendency is to find someone else to blame when we've made a mess of things. At times, we place the blame on God. But Scripture says there's no one to blame but ourselves. James 1:14 tells us, "Each one is tempted when, by his own evil desire, he is dragged away and enticed."

Sin begins in the mind with an evil thought, often well-disguised as something respectable. That fantasy promises to bring pleasure, power, or success. It becomes sin when we dwell on the thought and allow it to result in wrong attitudes or actions.

My friend, we all face temptation every day, but we don't have to give in.

The first step to breaking its power is to *take responsibility* for your wrong actions or attitudes. Second, *confess to God* that you are to blame and no one else. Third, *thank Him* for the forgiveness you have through Christ. Finally, *flee from temptation*. Resisting the temptation won't get easier. You must get away from it.

God has the victory over sin, and through Him, we can too.

HIS WORD
"Submit yourselves, then, to God. Resist the devil, and he will flee from you" (James 4:7).

MY PRAYER
"Righteous Savior, thank You for providing me with the power to put to death my sinful desires and to choose what is right. When I follow Your law and obey Your Spirit, I will live a more fulfilled, peaceful, and joyful life. Protect me from yielding to temptation. In Your holy name, amen."

MY STUDY
Joshua 24:15; Proverbs 4:14,15

Sweet Aroma

Rick and Becky wanted to send their children to a Christian school, but there was a shortage of space in the kindergarten class. One of their twins, Heather, took the only opening. Her twin brother, Hart, ended up in public school. Becky prayed for him every day that God would allow him to be a "fragrant aroma of Christ" to the teachers and the children in his class.

Soon, Becky noticed that he hadn't eaten his dessert for several days, and one day Heather questioned him about it. Hart responded, "Well, you know, Heather, when you're trying to talk to God about something, and you give up certain foods so you can talk to God better? Well, that's what I've been doing!"

Becky was shocked that her little boy had been fasting! Later as she tucked him into bed, Hart told his mother he had been fasting so that he could tell Brook about Jesus. Brook was a boy in his class who was continually mean to him. He said, "Mommy, I told Brook Jesus loved him and died for him."

Becky was praying for her children to be a "fragrant aroma of Christ," and her prayers were being answered!

God delights in His children and in their lives. As we live in close relationship with Him and lovingly speak of Him to others, some will come to faith in Him. To them, we are a sweet fragrance of life, eternal life.

My heart was so touched that a little boy fasted and prayed for another child who seemed to be his enemy. Many times in our society, nonbelievers describe Christians as hateful and mean. Yet, Jesus was the most loving person the world has ever known. And He lives in us! He wants us to demonstrate love to those we encounter, to be a sweet aroma to them.

HIS WORD

"We are to God the aroma of Christ among those who are being saved and those who are perishing. To the one we are the smell of death; to the other, the fragrance of life" (2 Corinthians 2:15,16).

MY PRAYER

Pray today that you will be a sweet aroma to those around you. Consider fasting for a day, a week, or however long God leads. Through fasting and prayer, you will deepen your outreach to those who do not know Christ.

MY STUDY

Psalm 36:10; Ezekiel 20:41

A Right?

The angry customer refused to fill out the form. Pushing the paper over the desk to the clerk, he said, "Look, I've already filled this thing out three times. I'm sorry you people can't get it right, but this time, you do it."

The clerk jutted out her chin and pushed the form back. "It wasn't my mistake," she said. This battle of wills ended when a supervisor intervened.

Nancy witnessed this heated scenario and thought the customer had overreacted. Yet, all that clerk needed to do was apologize for the inconvenience and take care of the matter for him. Instead, she had to be right.

Those words brought a familiar convicting nudge to Nancy's conscience as though the Lord was saying to her, "What about the times in your marriage, your friendships, when you have to be right, instead of soothing a situation with a soft word?" The Lord brought Nancy face-to-face with one more stronghold in her life: the right to be right.

Christ sometimes calls us to lay down this right. Christ emptied Himself of all rights for our sake. Following Him means we must die to ourselves. Even though we love Christ and desire to be like Him, it is often hard to take on the qualities of meekness and humility.

Our goal is to obey Christ, not gain the upper hand in our relationships. Controlled by the Spirit and not self, we will be "kind and compassionate to one another, forgiving each other, just as in Christ God forgave you." That's how Ephesians 4:32 describes what our behavior and our attitude should be. It's not important that we're in control, but that we demonstrate His love.

Nancy knows it's hard to lay down our rights when we've been offended. We want to wound those who've wounded us. It may be normal and natural, but it is completely unworthy of Christ.

HIS WORD
"How is it to your credit if you receive a beating for doing wrong and endure it? But if you suffer for doing good and you endure it, this is commendable before God (1 Peter 2:20).

MY PRAYER
We are complete in Christ, made whole by His love. Therefore, we follow in His footsteps. He helps us be open and humble when we're hurt, misunderstood, or rejected. Laying down the right to be right makes us more like Christ. And when others see this, they see Him.

MY STUDY
Psalm 125:5,6; Isaiah 57:15

Eternity

After retiring from the United States Air Force, Colonel Glenn Jones joined forces with Campus Crusade for Christ. He was director of our Military Ministry for several years. Then my husband, Bill, recruited Glenn to work with him in his office.

As a military officer, Glenn was a gentleman in every respect. He was a quiet, humble, and honorable man. He loved God and was committed to helping take the gospel message throughout the world. Like my husband, Glenn shared his faith wherever he could.

Once when Glenn was on an airplane, he noticed the perfume a flight attendant was wearing. It was a pleasant fragrance. He thought it might be nice for his wife. So he said to the flight attendant, "May I ask what perfume you're wearing?"

She said, "It's Eternity by Calvin Klein."

Glenn, who was so attuned to God, saw this as an opportunity to share Christ. He asked the attendant, "Have you heard about eternity by Jesus Christ?"

In the moments that followed, Glenn shared with the flight attendant how she could know God personally. And right there, in the aisle of that airplane, at her own initiative, she got on her knees to pray. With Glenn leading her in prayer, she trusted Jesus Christ with her life.

That's how Glenn was. He seized any opportunity to open a conversation. Especially if it could lead to a discussion about the gospel.

Sometimes that's the hardest part of sharing our faith, isn't it? Just getting the conversation started. Sometimes, we can simply say, "Hello." Sometimes, we can ask a question. Sometimes, we begin by answering a question. The important part, however, is always being friendly. When you're friendly, others will be, too. When you reach out first, others will respond in like manner. Friendliness is the first step in reaching the hearts of others.

HIS WORD

"The fruit of the righteous is a tree of life, and he who wins souls is wise" (Proverbs 11:30).

MY PRAYER

Are you friendly to others? Do you talk with others at work, at school, or at church? Do you talk with the person standing next to you in line at the grocery store? At the post office? Your child's soccer game? Smile a lot. Initiate a conversation to make the other person feel valued. Seek an opportunity to share Christ.

MY STUDY

Isaiah 6:8; John 3:13–15

Mary Jane grew up in Birmingham, Alabama, with one objective in mind: to find a handsome husband, create a beautiful home, have adorable children, and accumulate enough money to enjoy life to the fullest.

She achieved her objective. Her husband was a successful businessman who provided generously for his family. They lived in a lovely home on a lake. They had four darling daughters. Life was very rewarding for them.

There was nothing wrong with her husband, her home, or her children. But there was something wrong with *her*.

In spite of all her blessings, she often felt short-tempered and frustrated. All too often she heard herself getting angry with the children. No matter how often she resolved to quit, her outbreaks of rage kept occurring.

Mary Jane felt increasingly worse about her actions. They were embarrassing to her, and she worried about what she was doing to her little girls.

Although she'd gone to church all her life, it was at a Bible study where she first heard that God wanted to help her. She was desperate for help. She put her faith in Christ and gradually her life began to transform. Her anger subsided.

She realizes now, many years later, that she'd become a new person. She stopped feeling so angry and screaming at her children. She became a better mother, wife, and person. Perhaps the most important change was relief from the anxiety over her own behavior. Today Mary Jane has close relationships with her daughters and their families.

Is there something in your life over which you seem to have no control and want to change? That, my friend, is what Jesus wants to do for you. He wants to change your life!

It sounds almost too good to be true, but it is true. God wants to do away with the old things in your life. He has the power to do it.

HIS WORD

"This is what the Sovereign LORD, the Holy One of Israel, says: 'In repentance and rest is your salvation, in quietness and trust is your strength" (Isaiah 30:15).

MY PRAYER

My friend, God loves you. His plan is for you to be free from hindrances that bind you and hold you back. No matter how hard you try to make yourself better, it never works. Confess your sin to Him. Receive His forgiveness. Invite Him to come into your life and to make you a new creature. He will change your life.

MY STUDY

Proverbs 16:32; Romans 6:6,7

The Internet

My friend Rebecca was on a mission trip in Russia where she and her team met with Russian teachers. They taught them about Jesus, the Bible, morals, and ethics.

Tanya, a Russian teacher of English, told Rebecca, "I knew we would be friends the first time I saw you." In a matter of hours, a wonderful friendship began.

Tanya grew up in communist Russia. Taught by the Orthodox priests in her family, she believed in the existence of God. But that's all.

Today, she knows and believes in His love and forgiveness in her life. Tanya and Rebecca live worlds apart, but computers have kept them connected.

Rebecca has continued helping Tanya grow in her faith through conversations.

In an early correspondence, Rebecca told Tanya about the biblical principles involved in building a trusting friendship. Tanya wrote back with these words, "In this letter you gave me an excellent lesson of friendship and Christianity. I've printed it and keep it in my purse. It helps me to overcome the difficulties of everyday life."

My friend, this really is a beautiful picture of how God works, isn't it?

God has a plan for Tanya's life. In that plan, He sent Rebecca to disciple and encourage Tanya in her faith. Tanya has been very involved in a vital ministry work in her city. She is devoted to sharing her faith. And Tanya's English lessons now have biblical themes. Her family, colleagues, and students are learning about God.

Rebecca's letters are a testimony to Tanya of God's unfailing love. Tanya has put her trust in God, and she's letting Him show her the way to reach others. That's what discipleship is all about. It's coming alongside another person to help her grow in her faith. It's building a relationship on more than external matters, but on the foundation of Christian love.

HIS WORD

"The things you have heard me say in the presence of many witnesses entrust to reliable men who will be qualified to teach others" (2 Timothy 2:2).

MY PRAYER

My friend, let God work in your life. Seize the opportunities He places before you. Use the phone, letters, or the computer to do whatever it takes to communicate God's love to others. You will meet someone today who needs to grow in her faith in Christ. Be ready to disciple her.

MY STUDY

Ezra 7:10; Psalm 89:1,2

On the south coast of China is the city of Macau. Established hundreds of years ago by Portuguese colonists, it's the gateway to China.

Many years ago, import-export businessman John Bowring visited the area. He brought with him a supply of goods from England and Europe.

In those days, there were no electronic communications, so Mr. Bowring and his crew didn't know a typhoon had devastated the island of Macau a few months earlier. They were shocked to see it in utter ruins. But there was one remaining structure: a huge stone Anglican cathedral. Its looming cross, glimmering in the sun, captured their attention.

Mr. Bowring was so moved by the sight of that cross that before he set foot on land, he wrote a hymn we often sing today. Imagine what he saw as he penned these compelling words: "In the cross of Christ I glory, Towering o'er the wrecks of time."

When Mr. Bowring went ashore, he got a closer look at the church! The heavy, hand-carved oak doors were still in place, and the cross was right where he'd seen it from the harbor. But, when he went inside, he found it totally empty. There was absolutely nothing!

Marauders had pillaged and burned the structure. Now, all that remained was the stone facade, just as it stands to this very day!

My friend, I wonder how many of us are like that remarkable structure?

People know we call ourselves "Christians." But if they were able to look *inside* our lives, what would they see? Would there be emptiness?

Like the facade of a movie set, things look real but they're just "pretend." They're fake. They're hollow!

Dear friend, Jesus had strong words for people like that. But He wants you to be genuine in your faith. Let Him change you on the inside and the outside will follow.

HIS WORD
"The lamp of the LORD searches the spirit of a man; it searches out his inmost being" (Proverbs 20:27).

MY PRAYER
Are you feeling "dead" spiritually? You don't have to stay that way. There are three things you can do right now. Pray — talk with God. Ask Him to make you alive. Read — study His Word daily. Spend quality time reading the Bible and allowing God to speak to your heart. Share — talk to another person about the things you're learning as you pray and read.

MY STUDY
Jeremiah 17:10; Romans 7:21–25

Are You Ready?

Annette felt there had to be more. If she could rate her sense of satisfaction, it was about fifty-fifty. Half of the time, things were manageable and even pleasant. But the other half, life was dull, even awful.

Annette was a career woman who liked her job. She was highly skilled and was often applauded for her efforts.

She'd been married for four years to her college sweetheart. Things started out great, but now the honeymoon was over. Reality had struck. She admitted that when he traveled, it was a relief. She'd begun to enjoy time to herself.

Annette thought there just had to be more to life than this. She began to seek spiritual answers. She read a few of Shirley Maclaine's books, read some articles about angels, and even joined a local Bible study. She was a seeker, but not yet a Christian.

One morning, while waiting in an airport, Annette looked around the terminal and thought to herself, *I wonder if anyone around me knows where to find the answer. And if so, I hope I can sit by them on this flight.*

Sure enough, my friend Sharon ended up in the seat next to Annette. Before long, they were reading through a booklet called *Would You Like to Know God Personally?*

As they reached the end of the flight, Annette understood how she could have a relationship with Christ. She said to Sharon, "I want to open my life to Christ. This is what I've been looking for."

Most of us assume that people don't want anything to do with hearing the gospel. Yet, dear friend, many times their minds are reeling, searching for the answers that will give them purpose, looking for ways to increase their fifty-fifty existence to one that is filled with meaning. They don't know the way. Lead them to the answer — Jesus Christ.

HIS WORD
"Be ready to speak up and tell anyone who asks why you're living the way you are, and always with the utmost courtesy" (1 Peter 3:15, The Message).

MY PRAYER
"Lord Jesus, I encounter people every day who are searching for answers to their problems. Help me to be sensitive to their needs and then be ready to give the answer: that You alone are the way, the truth, and the life. You are the answer. Amen."

MY STUDY
Psalm 40:9,10; Isaiah 43:10–12

Clean Slate

A friend told me about her pursuit of a "clean slate" in her life. It started when she heard a Christian speaker talk about having a blameless conscience before God and others. That meant dealing with sins of the past.

Battling against pride, she knew what God was calling her to do.

The first visit was with her insurance broker. She'd lied on an application for auto insurance, claiming she drove forty miles a week to work when it was actually 200 miles. She offered to pay him back. He declined the offer but thanked her for her honesty.

Next, she went to her banker. Six months earlier, she had borrowed some money and been untruthful about the purpose of the loan. She confessed and apologized. Amazingly, the banker was sympathetic and didn't take any action against her.

Then came the hardest part. In a college course, she'd cheated on a test by peeking at her Bible to jog her memory. Deep down she knew it was wrong. Even though seven years had passed, she went to the professor – someone she greatly admired – and confessed. It was so embarrassing for her, but the professor was grateful and forgiving.

Perhaps you're thinking, *What's the big deal? Is it really necessary to make things right with people who may not even care?*

Yes. It is. God wants us to reflect His character. In 1 Peter 1:16, God said, "Be holy, because I am holy."

Like my friend, there are times when we have to retrace our steps in order to have a blameless conscience. Believe me, I've been in that position!

Ask God to show you any unconfessed sins. Make a list as the Holy Spirit brings them to mind. Then, seek out those you've offended and ask for their forgiveness. Finally, ask God for His forgiveness. You will find your burden lifted – and few things are more liberating than forgiveness!

HIS WORD
"He who conceals his sins does not prosper, but whoever confesses and renounces them finds mercy"
(Proverbs 28:13).

MY PRAYER
Is there someone you've deceived? Perhaps you've been dishonest with your boss about a project on which you're working. Or perhaps you've told your children you would do something you never intended to do. Confess to them and to God. Unburden your heart.

MY STUDY
Job 33:26–28; Luke 5:31,32

Your Secret

Contentment is rare. *Webster's Dictionary* defines the word as "being satisfied with one's possessions, status, or situation." Let me ask you, how often do you feel content?

It seems we are dissatisfied more often than we are content. When you're single, it seems life would be better if you were married. When you're married, it seems life would be sweeter if you had children. And when children are small, it seems life would be simpler if the children were older. And on and on.

But if Paul, having gone through all that he did, could be content in all circumstances, can't we? If you're dissatisfied with your life, possessions, or position, try these three practical steps to contentment.

First, make a list of what troubles you today. Write down what you do not like about your life.

Second, thank God for each item on your list. Even if you don't necessarily feel thankful, thank God for your situation.

Third, ask God to do whatever is necessary for you to experience His contentment.

When you've taken these three steps, rest and watch Him work. As much as you want to be content, He wants it for you even more.

What's really interesting is this. People in Paul's culture were amazed at the quietness and peace in his soul. When they asked him, "What's your secret?" he talked genuinely about what God had done.

When you learn to be content, others will ask, "What is it about you that's so different?" And God will use the contentment He's given you to reach others with the good news of His salvation.

Choose contentment! Don't fall into the trap of always wanting something better or something different. Don't wait until your life has passed you by to realize that you never got what you really wanted all along – contentment.

HIS WORD
"The LORD will guide you always; he will satisfy your needs in a sun-scorched land and will strengthen your frame. You will be like a well-watered garden, like a spring whose waters never fail" (Isaiah 58:11).

MY PRAYER
"Loving Lord Jesus, forgive me for the times I have been dissatisfied with my life. I know that You are in control. Everything in my life comes from You alone. Help me to cultivate contentment through You. In Your holy name, amen."

MY STUDY
Proverbs 17:15; 1 Timothy 6:7,8

The Willing Heart

We must not be satisfied with exteriorly submitting to obedience and in things that are easy, but we must obey with whole heart and in things the most difficult. For the greater the difficulty, the greater also is the merit of obedience. Can we refuse to submit to man for God's sake when God, for love of us, submits to man, even to His very executioners?

Jesus Christ was willingly obedient during His whole life and even unto the death of the cross, and am I unwilling to spend my life in the exercise of obedience and to make it my cross and my merit?

THOMAS À KEMPIS
IMITATION OF CHRIST

I don't know if my husband originated the phrase, but we've stated it so many times that we feel ownership: "God is more interested in availability than ability."

Being available to God should come naturally to the woman who has placed her heart in His hands. Knowing that the hands holding our life securely will also guide our life safely gives us the confidence to take bold steps of faith and actively become a breath of fresh air to a world stifled by Satan.

I have seen young women timidly step out in faith and become available to serve. Many women around the world are making a positive impact on people and cultures simply because they made themselves available.

"Being available" doesn't mean we will be required to leave husband and home to accept some demanding task. Neither is it a passive attitude where we sit and wait for something to drop like autumn leaves into our lap. We need to seek opportunities to share our faith and demonstrate a biblical view of life.

As our willing heart actively pursues a deeper relationship with God, He will send opportunities beyond our imagination – but we must choose to accept them. When a heart directed by the Holy Spirit embraces with loving obedience the challenge at hand, great accomplishments for Christ are realized.

House of Hope

In 1985, Sara founded Orlando's House of Hope, a home for runaway teenage girls. It is a home where spiritual counseling and prayer were first priorities for the staff.

The House of Hope was established through a series of miracles – from raising the money to buying land, to hiring trained staff and volunteers. Once the doors of the house opened to the first residents, the miracles continued in the hearts and lives of troubled girls and their families.

The House of Hope provides twenty-five teenage girls – ages twelve to seventeen – with a Christ-centered refuge from a life of degradation and exploitation. The basic goals are to introduce each girl to Christ and to stimulate family reconciliation. This is done through education, Christian counseling, and spiritual guidance – administered in a loving, home-style environment. And, as one staff member emphatically added, a lot of prayer.

Sara told me that she saw more change in the lives of her girls in eight months than during her fifteen years in a government institution. She and her staff attribute the transformed lives to the life-changing work of Jesus Christ in the hearts of the girls and their families.

Sara explained the success of the program to me. At the time we spoke, more than 225 girls had gone through the program, and not one had graduated without asking Jesus Christ to come into her heart. Only two were lost back to the streets.

One woman. One dream. Hundreds of changed lives.

What about you? What's your dream? Have you ever considered that God could use you to make a difference right where you are? Is there a burden on your heart today, something you care deeply about – an issue or an area in life that you'd like to see changed?

God can use you. Together, one woman at a time, we can help to change the world.

HIS WORD

"Because of the service by which you have proved yourselves, men will praise God for the obedience that accompanies your confession of the gospel of Christ, and for your generosity in sharing with them and with everyone else" (2 Corinthians 9:13).

MY PRAYER

It doesn't take an army to change the world. Changing the world always begins with one person. It starts with you and me. Take the initiative today to follow the dream God has given you for helping people. Pray for God's guidance, then map out a plan of action.

MY STUDY

1 Samuel 12:24; Psalm 25:4–6

Do Something!

One day, Mary was watching TV and happened upon a special news commentary on Somalia. Depressed at the whole situation, she flipped to another channel.

Suddenly, she was rebuked about her reaction. She thought, *When God sees disaster, He doesn't turn the channel. He doesn't ignore the suffering in Somalia, and neither can I.*

So Mary flipped back to the channel, and there she saw something she'll never forget – the picture of an infant trying to nurse from the breast of his dead mother.

Mary recalled, "Suddenly, God had my attention. I began to weep for the mothers of Somalia. I imagined having to hunt for food and run in the streets to get it for my children."

Ten months later, she flew to Somalia herself and had the opportunity to share Christ with Muslim women there. Reaching out to women who didn't know about Jesus, she reveled in bringing Living Water to thirsty Somalians.

You know what I love about Mary? She responded to that stirring in her heart and did something. God used her because she was willing to go and do whatever He asked of her.

In Matthew 10:8, Jesus says to His disciples and to us, "Freely you have received, freely give." God has given us so many blessings at absolutely no cost to us, so we must do the same for others. This may include a simple gesture like giving up your seat for someone on a crowded bus, or traveling around the world to feed hungry people.

Let's be inspired by Mary's example today. The next time opportunity knocks at your door, whether you're in your living room, at the office, in the supermarket, or somewhere else, don't turn the channel. Don't look away. Do something!

If you do, you will become rich in a way you've never experienced before.

HIS WORD

"Command them to do good, to be rich in good deeds, and to be generous and willing to share" (1 Timothy 6:18).

MY PRAYER

"Loving Lord Jesus, please forgive me for turning away from the needy around me. Thank You for opening my eyes to the apathy I have had in my heart. I now commit myself to being more sensitive to Your leading and to helping others as I can. Amen."

MY STUDY

Deuteronomy 15:10,11; Proverbs 14:31

Lifeline of Help

Robin was a single mother providing for herself and two small girls on her meager income. After paying for rent and child-care, she had a small amount left over for food.

Because Robin didn't have money for the deposit, she and her girls were without electricity. No electricity meant no hot water, no refrigerator, no stove, no lights, no heat!

They lived one day at a time. Robin would buy just enough food for a single day and keep it in a cooler. Food was cooked on a small charcoal grill. They used a kerosene lamp to provide light.

During that time, Robin said, "I just wanted to give up; I felt like there was no hope. As a mother, I felt like a failure because I couldn't even provide the basics for my kids!"

Embarrassed, Robin kept her plight to herself. She didn't want to tell her family or coworkers. No one seemed to notice Robin's predicament.

But one astute, caring neighbor did! As Michelle made her way up the stairs to her own place each night, she noticed that there were no lights coming from Robin's apartment.

One day, Michelle and Robin bumped into each other and began to chat. Robin told her the whole story.

Michelle's resources were limited so she couldn't do much, but she could do something. She ran an extension cord from her apartment, over the balcony, into Robin's apartment. Now Robin and the girls could turn on a light or listen to the radio – things you and I take for granted.

Something like running an extension cord might seem quite trivial – even primitive. But in this time of great need, it was a lifeline of hope.

Dear friend, one small act could give the encouragement and hope someone needs to face another day. And it can also open the door to further ministry in that person's life.

HIS WORD
"Let no debt remain outstanding, except the continuing debt to love one another, for he who loves his fellowman has fulfilled the law" (Romans 13:8).

MY PRAYER
I encourage you to be a student of those around you. Get to know your neighbors and your coworkers. Notice things about them. Ask questions. And when you learn of a need, think creatively about at least one thing you can do to help.

MY STUDY
Psalm 147:10,11; Lamentations 3:19–24

Free from Bondage

K im couldn't bear the thought of revealing her secret struggle. She was wasting away inside with guilt about her compulsion.

Finally, she cried out to a friend, "I throw up my food!" She then described the classic patterns of anorexia and bulimia – obsessing with food and exercise, and eating, then purging. Even a glance at a vending machine would ignite her lust for food and trigger a binge.

Today, Kim is helping young people overcome this devastating compulsion, an epidemic among high school and college women. It's likely you know people who are trapped in the jaws of some compulsive disorder. How can you encourage and strengthen them?

Let me share several principles Kim passed along:

- First, be a non-threatening, gracious friend. You can't make people admit they need help (their first step toward healing), but you can be available to them.

- Be a source of acceptance as well as accountability. Lovingly listen and be supportive, but ask the tough questions when needed.

- Get into the Word with them. Consistent Bible reading was the key to Kim's recovery. God's Word became her food as she memorized Scripture. She was able to replace wrong, compulsive thinking with His righteous truth.

- Pray for them fervently!

- Most of us are not certified counselors. Recognize when your friends need more help than you are able to give, and refer them to someone who can help.

Jesus said, "Then you will know the truth, and the truth will set you free" (John 8:32). His truth set Kim free from the bondage of a compulsive eating disorder.

Be a willing model and messenger of truth, bringing freedom and hope to the captives around you.

HIS WORD
"Therefore each of you must put off falsehood and speak truthfully to his neighbor, for we are all members of one body" (Ephesians 4:25).

MY PRAYER
Do you know someone struggling with a compulsive disorder? Ask God to give you wisdom and courage to help your friend. Perhaps you can also discretely ask others to pray for this person as well. You can make a difference in someone's life.

MY STUDY
Psalm 20:1,2; Isaiah 58:9,10

Like Daniel

Daniel is one of my heroes. As a teenager held captive in Babylon, he was selected by the king's officials for a royal education. He quickly rose to become one of the king's most influential advisors and friends.

A student in the king's court, Daniel had access to all the luxuries of the palace – sumptuous food, rare wine, and scintillating discussions with the country's intellectual leaders.

Daniel took advantage of the great education. *But he refused to indulge in the king's food and wine.* Why? The food and wine were dedicated to the Babylonian gods before they were served, and Daniel didn't want to compromise his worship of the one true God.

He refused to turn away from his convictions, even if it meant offending the king. Daniel could have been killed for his refusal, but he dared to face that consequence.

God honored Daniel for his integrity, giving him exceptional knowledge and understanding. After three years, the king tested Daniel and the other young men to see who was best and brightest. Guess who won the contest! Daniel.

Daniel served the king for at least seventy years. Many times he reiterated his commitment to live by the Word of God regardless of the consequences.

But this life of faith might never have been possible if Daniel hadn't lived out his convictions at the first opportunity. By taking a public stand for God in the beginning, he laid a solid foundation for a life of consistent faith.

Daniel decided to please God regardless of the consequences. He declined to do anything displeasing to the Lord, and God blessed Daniel with great spiritual growth.

God wants your devotion and mine as well. Whether you're rearing children at home or working in the marketplace, integrity marks the life truly committed to God.

Dare to be a Daniel. God will bless you.

HIS WORD
"The LORD has dealt with me according to my righteousness; according to the cleanness of my hands He has rewarded me" (Psalm 18:20).

MY PRAYER
How committed are you to God as the Lord of your life? Do you stand up for God and His truth? Refresh your commitment to God and His principles. Then ask Him for the courage you need to live them daily.

MY STUDY
2 Samuel 22:21,22; Ephesians 6:5–8

Have you ever watched two pre-schoolers fight over a toy? Neither is willing to share, so they both end up miserable!

My friends Lin and Byron developed some creative and successful ways to teach their children to give cheerfully to others. They understand young children need to see the results of their gifts if they're to understand the joy of giving and sharing.

The Smith family began by adopting a needy family at Christmas time. Each year, the Smith children set aside part of their Christmas gift money to buy presents for the children of that family. It became a joyous annual tradition.

Their tradition led the family to make cheerful giving a daily occurrence. One evening, the family saw a World Vision special on television. The Smith children were touched when they saw youngsters their own age going hungry.

Together, the family decided to do something very creative. After much discussion, they planned to eat a refugee-type meal once a week. It would consist of a little rice or oatmeal. The money they saved by eating less they would send to World Vision for famine relief in Africa.

That weekly lesson taught the whole family to appreciate the abundance of food they usually took for granted.

My friend, it is very exciting to watch your children develop compassion for others and a willingness to share with those in need. You need to take the first step by setting an example.

As you model generosity and sacrificial giving, explain to your children why you're motivated to share. Teach them that when we give to those in need, we are obeying Jesus, who was very serious about the importance of giving.

Finally, explain that the reward of passing on our blessings is great. God has promised an eternal reward in heaven. But He has also promised the greatest earthly reward we could want – joy.

HIS WORD

"Give, and it will be given to you. A good measure, pressed down, shaken together and running over, will be poured into your lap. For with the measure you use, it will be measured to you" (Luke 6:38).

MY PRAYER

If you receive unexpected money, consider donating it to a friend in need. Make a practice of inviting people to your home for dinner after church. Open your home to your children's friends; let them know your home is a safe place to be. Delight in sharing the Lord's blessings.

MY STUDY

Deuteronomy 24:19–22; Psalm 112:9

Jump In

A woman was riding her bike along her favorite mountain trail, which she traversed every morning. The river sparkled beside her, the sun was shining brightly, and the warmth of the breeze felt good to her shoulders.

Then she heard screams coming from below. "Help me," someone said. "You've got to help me!"

Without hesitation, she jumped off her bike and slid down the embankment nearly a hundred yards to the river. She hopped into the water and waded out where she could put her arms underneath the drowning woman.

The current was stronger than she'd anticipated, and suddenly they were both moving rapidly downstream. She realized they were in trouble and began to call out for help.

As they came around a bend, they saw three people perched on a ledge, watching. Two of them were videotaping their plight!

She screamed, "Can't you see we're drowning? Shut the cameras off, jump in the water, and help us!"

The spectators dropped their cameras and ran down-river. The three of them waded out into the current and created a human chain. When the two desperate women arrived, they were able to use their collective strength to catch them and pull them safely to the shore.

What can we learn from this story?

Friend, we're watching the very nation we love begin to sink. We're in trouble. We have a moral dilemma of historic proportions on our hands. Sometimes it feels like we have spectators on the shore who are doing nothing more than documenting the tragedy on video!

What kind of contribution can you make?

Working together, we can make a difference, shaping a nation for future generations to enjoy and giving glory to God. God bless you as you look for ways to serve Him. You'll be glad you did.

HIS WORD
"Blessed is the nation whose God is the LORD, the people He chose for His inheritance" (Psalm 33:12).

MY PRAYER
Perhaps you see a need in your local school, or you're outraged by the anti-God politics in your community. Maybe you're concerned about the sanctity of human life, and you have yet to help your local crisis pregnancy center. Make a commitment to give more time and energy to these worthy causes. You will make a difference.

MY STUDY
Isaiah 60:10–12; Titus 3:1,2

True Heroism

During Adolf Hitler's reign of terror in World War II, there were glimpses of goodness and heroism in those who opposed him.

At the beginning of the war, twenty Nazi soldiers arrived in a village with two empty buses. They were there to take away the Jews who were in hiding.

The soldiers confronted one of the local pastors. At the risk of his life and the lives of his parishioners, the pastor quietly, but defiantly, refused to hand over a single Jew who had come to him for refuge.

Incredibly, the Nazis went away. But as the war dragged on, they came back again and again, searching for Jews.

Several villagers were arrested; some were killed. However, not a single one of their endangered Jewish friends was betrayed during the entire occupation. In fact, during those four years, the villagers actively rescued as many as 3,000 Jews – many of them children.

Here, in the midst of human cruelty and depravity of the *worst* kind, we find a story of heroism of the *best* kind.

I live in Orlando, Florida, and if I live here the rest of my life, I'll probably never have the opportunity to rescue 3,000 people from death. So what does it mean to be a hero in my world and yours?

All it requires is honoring God in the little things, as well as the big. That's it. It's simply being a woman of conviction. A woman who is willing to step out and speak for what is right, to become an activist rather than a spectator, to risk ridicule or embarrassment.

Is this easy? Certainly not! But that's why it's heroic.

Decide today that you're willing to be a hero. Like the citizens of that tiny village, it means doing what is right – not simply what is easy.

Dear friend, true heroism is an ordinary life lived well.

HIS WORD
"Whatever you do, work at it with all your heart, as working for the Lord, not for men" (Colossians 3:23).

MY PRAYER
Pray this wonderful prayer offered by the French philosopher Pascal: "Lord, help me do great things as though they were little, since I do them with Your powers; and help me to do little things as though they were great, because I do them in Your name."

MY STUDY
Esther 4:12–16; Psalm 84:10,11

Take a Stand

Shannon was a senior in high school. When she came home one evening, her mother told her about a school-board meeting that night. Student-led prayer at the graduation ceremony could get voted down.

Without hesitation, Shannon left for the meeting. She had no idea what she'd say to the school board. She could only think, *If I don't take a stand, who will?*

Shannon felt that Jesus was her best Friend, and true friends always stand up for each other. She wanted to end her twelve long years of school by thanking God in prayer.

That night, as Shannon spoke to the board members, she was nervous — but impassioned about what she knew was right.

As the meeting came to an end, it was time to vote. With one vote remaining, the count was a tie. The last board member said, "This young lady has really influenced me." Then he cast his vote in favor of prayer.

Shannon was relieved but unprepared for the flood of media attention that followed. During the late local news that night, a video clip of Shannon was telecast, showing her standing before the school board.

Unfortunately, the next day, a motion was filed to stop the school board's decision. A non-profit organization came to Shannon's legal aid. A temporary court injunction upheld the school-board decision, so the senior class representative prayed at the graduation ceremony.

Can one person really make a difference? Shannon did. Her act of courage made a huge difference.

My prayer is that each of us will be ready to stand up and be involved as representatives of the living God.

Shannon's story gives me courage. I hope it does you, too. Today's high school students are tomorrow's national leaders. By influencing their lives for Christ in this generation, we can expect to have more *good news* in the next!

HIS WORD

"With your help I can advance against a troop; with my God I can scale a wall" (Psalm 18:29).

MY PRAYER

Whether you're a student, a parent, a teacher, or just a concerned citizen, you can scale a wall wherever you are. You can join a prayer group, write a letter, attend a school-board meeting, or teach a Bible study. One stone thrown in a pond can ripple across the whole body of water.

MY STUDY

Micah 3:8; Hebrews 11:30

Charles Finney was one of the greatest preachers of all time. Thousands came to Christ as a result of his ministry.

But most of us have never heard the name of Lydia Andrews, the faithful woman who undergirded his ministry with prayer.

Lydia began praying for Charles long before he became a Christian. Finney, a lawyer by profession, was cynical about the church, but Lydia prayed for his salvation.

Several years after his conversion, they married. She continued to support his ministry with prayer. In fact, prayer was the hallmark of Finney's outreach. Lydia organized ten prayer groups who met every day in Rochester, New York, solely to pray for the hand of God in Finney's preaching ministry.

These prayer meetings were huge! Crowds of up to a thousand people would gather to pray. Those who couldn't get into the packed church building would kneel in the snow outside! It was a marvelous movement of prayer in the 1800s.

The result? Countless thousands came to know Christ, and generations have been impacted by the ministry of Charles Finney.

I fear, at times, that Christians appeal to prayer as a last resort, hoping to change God's mind at the last minute. But when you pray, you are not choosing the last resort! You are choosing the *only* resort, what should be the *first* resort!

My friend, I urge you to pray. Pray for big things: that God will reach nations with His Word, that walls would fall, and that truth will prevail. But as you pray for the nations, never fail to pray for individuals, for the hearts of men and women who need the Savior.

Wherever you are in developing your prayer life, I want to challenge you to take the next step *on your knees*. You may never be a great preacher like Charles Finney, but you can be a great pray-er like Lydia Andrews.

HIS WORD
"They all joined together constantly in prayer, along with the women and Mary the mother of Jesus, and with his brothers" (Acts 1:14).

MY PRAYER
"Holy Lord Jesus, thank You for the wonderful privilege of prayer. Forgive me for not making it the first resort whenever needs arise. I commit now to making prayer a vital part of my life and walk with You. In Your blessed name, amen."

MY STUDY
Psalm 122:6–9; Daniel 6:10–23

My Hands, His Heart

In his book *Fearfully and Wonderfully Made*, Dr. Paul Brand tells this story.

During the war, a cathedral in England was all but destroyed in a bombing raid. Following the war, German students rebuilt the bombed-out cathedral.

Work progressed on the building, but there was a large broken statue of Jesus. He was standing with arms outstretched, and on the statue were His words, "Come unto Me."

The German volunteers discussed at great length how the statue of Jesus could be restored. Careful patching could fix most of the statue, but Jesus' outstretched hands posed a much greater problem. Bomb fragments had destroyed them. Reshaping the hands would be a very delicate, tedious task. The workers decided it would be best to leave them as they were.

Today, this statue of Jesus has no hands, but the workers left another inscription: "Christ has no hands but ours."

Amazing! Out of destruction, God can raise up beautiful lessons of life!

Jesus dwelt among us for a short time. He had hands, and He used them – first as a carpenter and then as the loving Son of God. He embraced the leper, healed the lame, and tenderly held the children.

When He asked us to follow Him, He commissioned us to be His hands and carry on His ministry.

He told us to go and make disciples, to love our neighbors, to pray for one another, to feed His sheep. There are hundreds of other things. There are multitudes of ways you can be His hands and show His love.

Friend, find one thing you can do today to show the outstretched hands of Jesus and to reach out in His love. Watch how He confirms the work of *your* hands.

Remember, He has no hands but ours.

HIS WORD
"She opens her arms to the poor and extends her hands to the needy" (Proverbs 31:20).

MY PRAYER
Call a friend, perhaps one you don't see often. Tell her you want to pray especially for her this week. Ask about her special needs, and do what you can to help. Pray for her every day the rest of the week, then follow up to see how God has answered.

MY STUDY
Leviticus 25:35; James 2:15–17

When Jan was in sixth grade, she asked her mom, Tara, to lead a Bible study for her class.

Tara was reluctant because she didn't feel qualified to teach children. But she told Jan she'd pray about it. Soon, she found herself writing out invitations.

The first week, six of Jan's classmates came, and they came week after week. Every Wednesday afternoon, those children came to hear Tara share about God. She prepared a snack, a Bible story, and a simple activity.

The children learned about God creating the world, about Adam and Eve, about Noah and all the animals. They learned about Jesus, that He was the Son of God, that He gave His very life to pay the penalty for man's sin, and that God, in His magnificent power, raised Jesus from the dead.

At the end of the school year, Tara planned to break for the summer. But the first Wednesday afternoon of the summer, her little Bible study group arrived on her front porch. The children had voted and decided they wanted to meet through the summer.

So Tara made popcorn and popped in the *JESUS* video. Based solely on the Gospel of Luke, this movie clearly tells the story of Jesus' life.

For the next few weeks, Tara showed the children segments of the film. Then she'd lead a discussion about what they'd seen. By the end of summer, each one of those children had placed their trust in Jesus.

There are so many children who don't have anyone to teach them about God. They'd love to be in a Bible study like Tara's. You may not feel qualified to lead one, but if God has put it on your heart, you can do it!

Dear friend, teach the children about God's love. Some day they will thank you. And they'll spend an eternity with Jesus!

HIS WORD

"Jesus called the children to Him and said, 'Let the little children come to me, and do not hinder them, for the kingdom of God belongs to such as these'" (Luke 18:16).

MY PRAYER

Talk with your pastor or check with your local Christian bookstore for materials designed for children. Think of neighborhood children, your child's classmates, or fellow team members from soccer or softball. Invite several of those young people to your home for a Bible study. Your influence will be immeasurable and eternal.

MY STUDY

Proverbs 22:6; Isaiah 48:17

When You Pray

As a young woman, Becky Tirabassi committed herself to pray for at least one hour every day. Through the years, she's kept her commitment.

Becky is a well-known author and conference speaker. She tells this story in her book, *Wild Things Happen When I Pray*.

When Becky and her husband moved into a new neighborhood, she learned her neighbors' names right away. She wrote them in her prayer journal and prayed for each one every day. She prayed they'd learn of God's love and then trust Jesus Christ.

But Becky wasn't putting action to her prayers. She wasn't looking for opportunities to share the gospel message. In fact, she actually thought God would hear her prayers and then lead her neighbors to *other* Christians in their lives. And then *they'd* invite them to church and share their faith with them.

After more than three years of praying for her neighbors, name by name, something happened. One day, Becky was driving home from teaching an aerobics class. As was her habit, she was listening to Pastor Charles Stanley's radio program, *In Touch*.

One sentence in Dr. Stanley's message pierced Becky's heart. He said, "Don't pray about anything you wouldn't want God to do through you." Becky began to realize she just might be the very one God would want to use in the lives of her neighbors.

When Becky's neighbor Barbara knocked on the door a few days later, Becky began putting action to her prayers. First, she told Barbara how she prayed for her daily. Then, she invited her to church. As they became more acquainted, they talked often about church, God, and faith. Eventually, Barbara placed her faith in Christ.

Oh, dear friend, your neighbors need you to pray for them *and* tell them about God's love and forgiveness. Allow God to use you to tell others of His love. As you do, you'll develop friendships that will last through eternity.

HIS WORD
"The LORD detests the sacrifice of the wicked, but the prayer of the upright pleases him" (Proverbs 15:8).

MY PRAYER
Pray faithfully, name by name, for your neighbors, and ask God to give you opportunities to share your faith. Invite your next-door neighbor over for coffee. Have a barbecue for the family across the street. Take a crafts class with the woman down the block. Most importantly, take the time to share your faith in Christ and lead them to His love and grace.

MY STUDY
Job 42:10; Jude 20–23

Jay loves fishing. When he landed one of the biggest fish in a contest, he was awarded a nice cash prize. Jay considered the prize money a gift from God, so he wanted to use it wisely. He wondered whether he should save it, invest it, or spend it on family needs.

In the meantime, Jay's eight-year-old daughter, Brittany, expressed concern about a classmate. Brittany's friend Cassie was often teased by other children. Cassie wore old clothes and rarely smiled. Brittany wanted to help her friend, so she asked her dad if they could use some of his prize money to help Cassie.

He loved the idea and was delighted at his young daughter's desire to help someone. So Brittany and her mother, Rita, bought clothes, shoes, and toys for Cassie.

To remain anonymous, they asked a teacher to deliver their surprise. When Brittany next saw her, Cassie said with delight that a "secret angel" had sent the gifts. Brittany was thrilled. She said, "Mom, I didn't know Cassie could smile like that!"

Because Rita knew a small gift was just a bandage for Cassie's problem, she had included a note to Cassie's mom in Cassie's gift box. She told her that as Christians they'd like to help her. The two women developed a friendship, and Rita was able to share the gospel message of God's love with Cassie's mom. Rita, Jay, and Brittany continue to help with the family's needs.

Oh, dear friend, there are people right next door, down the street, or in the adjacent office who need your help. They need someone to reach out and care, someone to be a friend.

God wants us to show His love to others in tangible ways. Have a willing heart to help. And remember, whatever you do, always take time to share God's message of love. Like Cassie, you'll be God's secret angel!

HIS WORD

"If anyone has material possessions and sees his brother in need but has no pity on him, how can the love of God be in him? Dear children, let us not love with words or tongue but with actions and in truth" (1 John 3:17,18).

MY PRAYER

"Merciful God, please forgive me for not sharing out of the abundance of Your blessings. Because You have commanded us to love one another, I want to show my love in tangible ways. Help me to be sensitive to the needs of others and to have a giving spirit. Amen."

MY STUDY

Proverbs 22:2; Isaiah 61:1–3

Love in Action

First Corinthians 13:1 says, "If I speak in the tongues of men and of angels, but have not love, I am only a resounding gong or a clanging cymbal." Love, *real* love, is not just words. *God's* love is action!

Is your home a place where friends, neighbors, and visitors feel welcome? Or is your home a refuge for only you?

When it comes to expressing God's love, do you do more than talk about it? Do you demonstrate your love?

Chris and Karen demonstrate God's love through hospitality. They've helped many of us understand some of the practical ways of using our homes. They remind us that the amount of love in a home is far more important than the amount of space.

A ministry of hospitality can begin by inviting people over to dinner – international students, senior adults, new church members, neighbors, single moms, visiting missionaries.

Let me challenge you. Within the next month, invite someone to your home who's never been there. Ask God to show you who that would be – a neighbor, a coworker, the family of your child's friend. Ask God to give you an idea of what to do for the evening.

Ask God to make the time meaningful and what He wants it to be. Remember, as a Christian you are God's ambassador; you represent Him. Our goal should be to minister to people, not just to entertain.

Author Karen Mains wrote, "True hospitality comes before pride. It has nothing to do with impressing people, but everything to do with making them feel welcome and wanted."

We have a great opportunity to help others know and experience the love of Jesus for themselves. Invite them in! With each visitor comes a chance to touch that person for eternity, to love that person, and to point him or her to the Lord.

HIS WORD
"In the same way, faith by itself, if it is not accompanied by action, is dead" (James 2:17).

MY PRAYER
"Loving Lord Jesus, as You gave Your life willingly and freely, so I want to give of myself to others. I commit myself and my home to You. Help me to use them for Your glory. Amen."

MY STUDY
Joshua 24:15; Proverbs 11:24

The Bible says, "In his heart a man plans his course, but the LORD determines his steps" (Proverbs 16:9).

That's what Emma Morris found out a few years ago. The corporation she worked for offered her a promotion, but the new position would require traveling and time away from her husband.

"At the same time," she said, "I felt a strong call to go into full-time ministry."

To make a wise and informed choice, Emma sought guidance through prayer and God's Word. Then she spoke to her husband and several dear friends. She examined her gifts and talents and how they might be used in a ministry. As she carefully considered all her options, the tug on her heart to go into ministry only increased. So she turned down the promotion and left the company.

While investigating ministry opportunities, she began working as a consultant. Her meetings took her into the offices of CEOs of various companies. What happened surprised her. She said, "In every case, I was able to share my faith with the person who most influenced the rest of the organization."

Months later, she realized she was, indeed, a full-time missionary. She said, "My mission field was the business world and, specifically, its leaders!"

Emma knew in her heart that she needed to reach out to others with God's love. As she did, God showed her that her mission field was right where she was.

Friend, if you're not sharing God's love in your neighborhood and community, you won't do it in the mission field either. The best training ground in the world for evangelism is right where you are.

Begin talking about Jesus Christ wherever you go because, at this moment, that's your mission field.

HIS WORD

"We proclaim him, admonishing and teaching everyone with all wisdom, so that we may present everyone perfect in Christ. To this end I labor, struggling with all his energy, which so powerfully works in me" (Colossians 1:28,29).

MY PRAYER

Friend, you can make a difference for Christ right where you are. There are people who need a Savior just outside your front door, down the street, and in your workplace. Ask God for boldness as you seek to share His life-giving Gift with others.

MY STUDY
Psalm 28:8,9; Habakkuk 3:2

His Passion

After graduating from college in Boston, Julie and a roommate moved to New York City to pursue careers in journalism. Unfortunately, the competition was overwhelming, so Julie was forced to take a temporary job as a waitress.

It didn't take long for Julie to feel disillusioned. Getting a job was tougher than she thought. While waitressing, Julie saw the seedy side of New York and began to wonder if she'd ever have a legitimate career.

Finally, she got an interview for a page position at NBC.

About that time, Julie's sister, who lived in Miami, trusted Christ. As a result, she urged Julie to attend a worship service in New York.

It was at church that Julie met a woman who worked for ABC. When she told this seasoned professional about her upcoming interview, she told Julie she'd pray for her. Julie was impressed!

The interview was grueling. Several network directors and seven other applicants sat around a table as each candidate was grilled. It was a tough experience, but Julie got the position.

She was convinced prayer was the primary reason for success, so Julie took the woman who had prayed for her to lunch. The woman, in turn, invited her to a Bible study.

To Julie's surprise, at the Bible study she found authentic people who really wanted to know God – women who were not afraid to share their struggles and fears, fulfilled women who had purpose in their lives.

Through this group of women, Julie became a believer. She also began working in full-time ministry to reach professional women. Her passion for reaching women has exceeded her passion for journalism.

God has a way of turning His passion into your passion. If you will only follow Him wherever He leads, He will give you the desires of your heart. A heart devoted to Him will be blessed indeed.

HIS WORD
"In your unfailing love you will lead the people you have redeemed. In your strength you will guide them to your holy dwelling" (Exodus 15:13).

MY PRAYER
Make it your goal this week to reach out to a person like Julie. Go out for coffee. Talk to her about the direction of her life. Show your concern and interest. Then, commit yourself to pray for her. Become a friend. In a loving way, teach her what God has taught you in your own life.

MY STUDY
Psalm 5:11,12; John 10:3,4

As a missionary to Brazil, Karen helped to found the House of Hope, a Southern Baptist hospice to AIDS patients — prostitutes, homosexuals, and young mothers who've contracted AIDS.

Karen prays with the patients. Her ten-year-old daughter, Katie, visits with patients as well. One day, Katie's attention was drawn to a young Brazilian mother whose once healthy body was now emaciated.

Katie's innocence allowed her to see beyond the sickness to the woman's clear, green eyes, framed by long dark lashes to a face that maintained striking beauty. "Look, Mommy," Katie called out, "what a pretty girl!"

That's when Karen realized how far she was from her quiet Alabama hometown. All because one day, her pastor encouraged the congregation to love and comfort the sick and dying, despite their spiritual condition. Right then and there, she unmistakably felt God telling her to go.

For so long, she'd pointed a finger of judgment at those with AIDS. Today, she shares God's love. She said, "I was born and reared and lived my life in a comfort zone. Stepping out of that has been a real learning and growing experience."

Dear friend, you don't have to go to Brazil to help others and show God's love. But have you been willing to step out of your comfort zone? To reach beyond those borders to touch someone with the love of Jesus? Can you reach out in love and acceptance instead of pointing a finger of guilt and shame?

Jesus taught that we need to forgive one another and help each other recover from a sinful lifestyle. There are hurting people right outside your front door. They need someone like you to encourage them with God's message of love. Reach out to them today.

Step out of your comfort zone so that you too can look beyond appearances and say, "Look! What a pretty girl!"

HIS WORD
"When he saw the crowds, he had compassion on them, because they were harassed and helpless, like sheep without a shepherd. Then he said to his disciples, 'The harvest is plentiful but the workers are few. Ask the Lord of the harvest, therefore, to send out workers into his harvest field'"
(Matthew 9:36–38).

MY PRAYER
"Lord Jesus, forgive me for pointing fingers of blame instead of reaching out in love. I want to follow Your example of forgiveness and love, to give hope to those who have none. In Your name, amen."

MY STUDY
1 Chronicles 28:9,10; Psalm 51:12

Love Your Neighbor

It was a dark day when Ann's neighbor discovered that she'd been abandoned by her husband. They'd been married forty-two years. Ann's neighbor was a Christian, and the breakup of her marriage was devastating.

Ann began to reach out to her neighbor, and a deep friendship grew. They studied the Bible together, memorized Scripture, and sought God's direction. Ann stepped right in and became an encouragement to her new friend. Before long, God's love began to take over, creating something very beautiful out of a broken life.

To the right and left of your home, up and down the street, are households filled with opportunities for ministry. In many of those homes, men and women are enduring tremendous personal pain and suffering, much of it completely unnoticed by those nearby.

Do you know the names of those who live in your apartment complex or your neighborhood? Do you have any idea what they're going through – good or bad?

Today, Ann's neighbor is in ministry overseas. She trusted God, by faith, to open this door of opportunity, which He did. She's in Ecuador, using her skills to help spread the gospel in South America.

My friend, be looking for those opportunities to reach out to women in need, women who live next door or down the street. As we reach out right where we live, we will eventually reach the world.

It's easier than you think. Jesus put it very simply in Matthew 5:43: "Love your neighbor."

Here's what I think He meant: Do for others what you'd want someone to do for you. If you were in need, what would you appreciate? How would you want someone to respond when you face a crisis? What would you want her to say and do for you? Then love your neighbor with the love of Jesus, and find a way to show that love.

HIS WORD

"Do not forsake your friend and the friend of your father, and do not go to your brother's house when disaster strikes you — better a neighbor nearby than a brother far away" (Proverbs 27:10).

MY PRAYER

How well do you know your neighbors? You can get to know them by planning opportunities to socialize, such as block parties, barbecues, and dinners. Take the initiative and help to organize the events. That is the first step in being able to share God's love with them.

MY STUDY

Leviticus 25:35; Romans 13:9,10

It was a cold, wintry day. Sleet pelted the streets, making it a slushy walk to New York's Grand Central Station. People walked briskly with their heads huddled inside their coat collars, hardly noticing one another in their fight against the weather.

One young man struggled with two large, heavy suitcases. Slipping and sliding, he rushed to catch a train. Suddenly, another man reached out his hand and grabbed one of the suitcases. In a pleasant voice, he said, "Let me have that, Brother. In this bad weather, it's hard to carry so much!"

At first, the young man was apprehensive about the man's help. But as he looked up, the friendly smile put him at ease. As they walked together, they struck up a conversation like two long-lost friends.

Several years later, the young man, the great educator Booker T. Washington, said, "That kindly deed was my introduction to Theodore Roosevelt."

Friend, reach out to help someone with a heavy load. A simple act of kindness could be the key to winning someone's heart to faith in Christ.

God tells us several times in Scripture to be kind to each other:

- "Therefore, as God's chosen people, holy and dearly loved, clothe yourselves with compassion, kindness, humility, gentleness and patience" (Colossians 3:12).
- "Be kind and compassionate to one another" (Ephesians 4:32).
- "The Lord's servant ... must be kind to everyone" (2 Timothy 2:24).

Kindness is attractive. People appreciate kindness. The grocery store clerk needs a smile and a courteous "thank you." The taxi driver dodging traffic for hours could use a bigger-than-usual tip. The faithful babysitter would enjoy a movie ticket for herself and a friend.

I'm sure you can think of many more acts of kindness. By demonstrating kindness, you are obeying God's command and showing His love to others.

HIS WORD

"Finally, all of you, live in harmony with one another; be sympathetic, love as brothers, be compassionate and humble" (1 Peter 3:8).

MY PRAYER

Today, make a list of at least five specific acts of kindness that you can do in the next week to show God's love to those you encounter each day. After you complete each action listed, note the person's response and your own feelings about the interaction.

MY STUDY

Ruth 2:20; Proverbs 14:21

A Lifetime of Influence

Jonathan was a lonely little boy who seemed to have a knack for getting into trouble. One day while playing with matches, he started the grass on fire in the yard of an elderly woman who lived next door to Norma Jean.

"He's no good," the elderly neighbor complained to Norma Jean. "He'll never amount to anything. I don't understand why you even waste your time with him." After the fire, Norma Jean wondered, too.

But Norma Jean, the mother of two toddlers, cared for this little child who hungered for love and attention. He'd come to her home for cookies and to play with her children. She'd tell him stories about Jesus. Sometimes, Jonathan would go to church with her family.

Unfortunately, Norma Jean was pressured by the elderly neighbor not to invite Jonathan over anymore. After that, Jonathan's mom, a working single mother, wanted him to stop going to church with them. Norma Jean's opportunity for influencing this child diminished.

Norma Jean's family eventually moved away. Whenever Jonathan popped into her mind, she prayed for him.

Several years later, as she put her son on a bus to a Christian youth event, a voice called out, "Hey, I know you." It was Jonathan.

Norma Jean was anxious to know if he'd placed his trust in Christ. She was thrilled to hear his answer. "Yes!" he said. "I was saved two years ago." Their conversation was brief. But as Jonathan turned to leave, he called back to Norma Jean, "Thanks for all the cookies."

A busy young woman took time to be a friend to a lonely little boy, and God used her influence to help lead him to faith.

Ask God to show you the child who needs love and attention. Open your heart to him or her. Your influence will last a lifetime. One day you'll hear, "Thanks for all the cookies." It will melt your heart!

HIS WORD
"May the Lord make your love increase and overflow for each other and for everyone else, just as ours does for you" (1 Thessalonians 3:12).

MY PRAYER
"Lord Jesus, You love the little children. Please help me to love them as You do. I desire to be sensitive to their needs and hurts so I can let Your love show through me. In Your wonderful name, amen."

MY STUDY
Psalm 78:5–8; Isaiah 40:11

Contagious Faith

Nancy Wilson has been a Crusade staff member for many years. Although she's small, she's a fireball of energy with a contagious love for God. She easily shares God's message of love and forgiveness wherever she goes.

Once, Nancy and I were both at a conference with leaders in our ministry. It was a typical conference with many meetings, and we had a few very informal buffet-style meals in a large conference room.

During those mealtimes, lots of conversations were going on among the ministry leaders. The waiters and waitresses mingled quietly and courteously among us. No one really noticed them. Except Nancy. She noticed Earl. Earl was standing back, keeping an eye out for empty plates and glasses. So with her big, warm smile, Nancy approached Earl. She began talking with him.

Nancy carries little "blessing cards." As she pulled one out, she said, "Earl, I want to give you a blessing today." Then she handed him the card, which told of God's great love.

As he looked at the card, Nancy asked, "Earl, do you know God's love?" Earl read the card, but he didn't directly answer Nancy's question. He said, "I'll give it to my wife."

In Nancy's sweet way, she said, "No, Earl, God told me to give it to you!"

Then they began to talk about God. Nancy shared the gospel message with Earl. Right there, in the hustle and bustle of lunch, Earl trusted Jesus Christ as his Savior and Lord. That's "lifestyle evangelism." It's simply talking with those in our midst about God's great love.

Take note of five people you see every week whom no one really notices. Pray for those on your list to be open to God's love. Ask Him for opportunities to share your faith.

Delight in telling others about God's love wherever you go. Like Nancy, your love for God will become contagious.

HIS WORD
"'Everyone who calls on the name of the Lord will be saved.' How, then, can they call on the one they have not believed in? And how can they believe in the one of whom they have not heard? And how can they hear without someone preaching to them?" (Romans 10:13,14).

MY PRAYER
"Wonderful Lord Jesus, I confess that I have not taken advantage of opportunities to share Your love and forgiveness. I want to be prepared to tell others about You and to take the initiative in opportunities I encounter. In Your holy name, amen."

MY STUDY
Psalm 105:1; Joel 2:32

Not in Vain

The annual National Day of Prayer (the first Thursday of May) was approaching. This day has been set aside for people of America to pray for leaders of our nation, our communities, our homes, and each other.

Wendi looked forward to this day with great anticipation. She hoped one of her coworkers would arrange a prayer time. Nobody did. Finally, Wendi determined that maybe she should be the person to organize this meaningful time. So with faith that her labor would not be in vain, Wendi posted on the employee time clock a sign that read: "Today is the National Day of Prayer. If you're interested in praying for our country, contact Wendi."

Then she waited for people to respond. No one contacted her, but when she called some of her coworkers with a personal invitation, five joined her to pray. The time was meaningful, but what really made an impression on Wendi was what happened afterward. One of Wendi's coworkers asked Wendi to pray for her father.

Wendi didn't realize that a day of prayer for the nation would lead to her praying for a personal need of which she was previously unaware. Wendi said, "Now I'm more sensitive to others' needs. I'm consistently given the burden to pray for people. The Lord used my small, uncertain leap of faith to open doors to minister through prayer."

The apostle Paul wrote, "Therefore, my dear brothers, stand firm. Let nothing move you. Always give yourselves fully to the work of the Lord, because you know that your labor in the Lord is not in vain" (1 Corinthians 15:58).

It can be scary taking that first step of faith, but Wendi took the initiative in declaring her faith to her coworkers. Now she has a ministry of prayer.

Willingly give your efforts to God. He will guide you into joyful service to Him. The results will be more than you ever imagined.

HIS WORD
"I will instruct you and teach you in the way you should go; I will counsel you and watch over you" (Psalm 32:8).

MY PRAYER
My friend, don't wait for someone else to initiate something God has placed on your heart to do. If He has told you of a need, then He will provide you with the strength and resources to do it. Most importantly, He will bless your efforts.

MY STUDY
Isaiah 30:21; John 16:13

Cheryl and Susan were college roommates. One Sunday, Cheryl came home from church to find something unusual going on – Susan was serving lunch to an elderly man. Having no family, he lived in a small, trash-filled motel room. Susan had befriended him and was helping to take care of some of his needs.

Cheryl was surprised to learn that Susan had been helping this man for months. She had not known anything about these acts of kindness. Susan hadn't told anyone because she wanted to do something for Christ that no one knew about. She wanted to keep her motivation pure and untainted by pride.

Matthew 6 gives us clear direction about being cautious with our motivation when we perform acts of kindness. "Be careful not to do your 'acts of righteousness' before men, to be seen by them. If you do, you will have no reward from your Father in heaven. So when you give to the needy, do not announce it with trumpets, as the hypocrites do in the synagogues and on the streets, to be honored by men. I tell you the truth, they have received their reward in full. But when you give to the needy, do not let your left hand know what your right hand is doing, so that your giving may be in secret. Then your Father, who sees what is done in secret, will reward you" (verses 1–4).

When God puts you in a position to help someone, do it with little or no fanfare. Your work "in secret" will help prevent unwholesome attitudes such as pride from distorting what you are doing. There is no need for recognition from others because God knows what you did. His is the only opinion that matters in the light of eternity.

How much greater will be our joy when we hear God's compliment, "Well done," rather than the temporal praise of those around us.

HIS WORD
"Blessed are the pure in heart, for they will see God" (Matthew 5:8).

MY PRAYER
Friend, you can experience a blessing today. Ask God to show you how you can help a person with a special need. Don't expect recognition or even a thank you. Do it for God, because it's the right thing to do, and because He wants you to.

MY STUDY
Proverbs 16:2; Isaiah 66:2

Step of Faith

Marilyn sensed God leading her to teach a Bible study for women. She was hesitant because she felt inadequate and embarrassed by her inexperience. The other women were older and more sophisticated.

God persisted in His leading. Finally, she thought, *All I have to do is invite them. They'll say, "No, thank you," then we'll move on.*

Marilyn invited thirteen women. Guess what? They all came! Wonderfully, one by one, they each trusted Christ. Marilyn humbly states, "That says a lot more about God than it does about me!"

What Marilyn didn't understand at first was that all God requires of us is a step of faith. He will take care of the rest. His Word tells of His faithfulness. In 2 Thessalonians 3:3 we read, "The LORD is faithful, and he will strengthen and protect you from the evil one." Deuteronomy 31:8 says, "The LORD himself goes before you and will be with you; he will never leave you nor forsake you. Do not be afraid; do not be discouraged."

God is the source of our strength and He provides protection. He will never leave us. Therefore, we should not be afraid or discouraged. Even when we are afraid, we do not need to let that stop us from ministering in the Lord's name. Sometimes the activities that we fear most become the greatest blessing to us and to others as we rely on God's strength and wisdom.

Let's look at Marilyn again. With little faith and less courage, she took the first step of obedience in faith. And look what God did! He blessed far beyond her highest expectations.

Where is God leading you? What is He telling you to do? Dear friend, will you take a step of faith? God will be with you. Trust me, and trust Him.

HIS WORD

"Have I not commanded you? Be strong and courageous. Do not be terrified; do not be discouraged, for the LORD your God will be with you wherever you go" (Joshua 1:9).

MY PRAYER

"Faithful Lord Jesus, I confess that sometimes I am afraid to respond to challenges. Please help me to step out in faith and trust You. Thank You for being the ultimate source of courage and strength. In Your name, amen."

MY STUDY

Psalm 31:23,24; Hebrews 3:6

Age doesn't limit what love can do. That's the lesson Gwen's father-in-law taught her family one long winter. Gwen and her family lived in South Dakota, and her husband was on an overseas assignment.

So much snow fell that winter that Gwen didn't know where to pile it. Sensing things were tough for Gwen and her family, her 79-year-old father-in-law drove 350 miles from Colorado to help. He not only assisted with the monumental job of removing snow, he stepped in as a "man of the house" as well. He helped his grandson build a small wooden car. He even attended a Valentine's banquet as Gwen's date so she could get out of the house and wouldn't be alone. His time there encouraged the whole family.

The Bible tells us in 1 Peter 1:22 to "have sincere love for your brothers, love one another deeply, from the heart." Gwen's father-in-law exhibited this kind of deep, sacrificial love. He also showed that age has no bearing on the principle applied to this command.

Whether you are young or old, God's Word is the same for us all. We are responsible for reflecting God's love to others. Perhaps you can't do the same kinds of things that you used to – things that require more physical strength – but you can always do something. You can be a prayer warrior, a willing confidante, a gracious encourager, a faithful friend. You could volunteer at a homeless shelter, or call a mother of a toddler to give her some encouragement. Send a note to your pastor thanking him for his servant's heart.

Dear friend, don't let your age – whatever it is – keep you from being a blessing to others. God wants to use you at every stage in your life. God will give you what you need to bless others, and then He will bless you.

HIS WORD
"Is not wisdom found among the aged? Does not long life bring understanding?"
(Job 12:12).

MY PRAYER
"Eternal Father, time means nothing to You. You are the same yesterday, today, and forever. Help me to not dwell on my age but to dwell on You who can strengthen me at any age. I want to serve and glorify You for as long as I am on the earth. Amen."

MY STUDY
Ecclesiastes 8:5; Hebrews 13:8

Bold as a Lion

When the Germans invaded France, Pastor Donald Caskie fled for his life. On foot and on bicycle, he made his way to southern France.

In his new home, he had an opportunity to aid in the war effort. Night after night, he helped escaped prisoners of war find safe passage across the mountains into Spain. As it became increasingly dangerous even in southern France, his friends tried to persuade him to escape as well. He simply answered, "I am needed here."

Oh, I love his spirit. Even when it was difficult, Pastor Caskie stood firm. Proverbs 28:1 says, "The wicked man flees though no one pursues, but the righteous are as bold as a lion." Pastor Caskie was "bold as a lion." When everyone else was fleeing, he understood God's call on his life, and he fulfilled it.

Pastor Caskie was a wonderful example of the kind of determination Paul spoke of in Acts 20:24: "I consider my life worth nothing to me, if only I may finish the race and complete the task the Lord Jesus has given me — the task of testifying to the gospel of God's grace." All around him was chaos and destruction, and he was encouraged to leave. Yet he did not retreat from the task God had given him — seeing others to safety.

Friend, we all have tasks. We all are needed. Whether it's rearing children with integrity, helping at a crisis pregnancy center in your community, or sharing God's love on a foreign mission field, stand firm in doing God's work. Many times, you may feel discouraged or even afraid, but call on God for your strength and courage. Keep your eyes focused on Him rather than on your situation. Be "bold as a lion" and "complete the task the Lord Jesus has given [you]."

HIS WORD
"When I called,
you answered me;
you made me bold
and stouthearted"
(Psalm 138:3).

MY PRAYER
"Lord Jesus, I want to be as bold as a lion as I minister in Your name. As I work on the tasks You set before me, help me to be diligent and to persevere to complete these humble deeds. In Your holy name, amen."

MY STUDY
2 Samuel 22:33,34; 2 Timothy 4:6–8

It was a rainy night during the racially turbulent '60s. An older black woman was stranded with car trouble on an Alabama highway. When she bravely flagged down a car, a young white man stopped to help her. After he had finished repairing her car, she thanked him and wrote down his address.

A week later, a gift arrived at his home. The note attached to it read: "Thank you so much for assisting me ... Because of you, I was able to make it to my dying husband's bedside just before he passed away. God bless you for helping me." Signed, "Mrs. Nat King Cole."

In the parable of the Good Samaritan (Luke 10:25–37), someone asked Jesus, "Who is my neighbor?" In response, Jesus told him a story. A man traveling from Jerusalem to Jericho was attacked by robbers and left for dead. At least two people, a priest and a Levite, passed by the wounded man without offering assistance. Then a Samaritan came by. He selflessly tended to the man's wounds, used his donkey to take the man to an inn, and paid for the man's lodgings while he recovered.

At the end of the story, Jesus gave this command: "Go and do likewise."

There are people all around us who have been wounded – physically, emotionally, or spiritually. In the parable, Jesus shows us that we must not only help those close to us, we are to help *anyone* we encounter who is in need. If God has placed us in a circumstance to know of a need in someone's life, it is God's will that we assist them as we are able.

Dear friend, the next time you become aware of someone in need and you have the means to help that person, it isn't necessary to ask what God's will is. You already know it: "Go and do likewise."

HIS WORD

"Praise be to the God and Father of our Lord Jesus Christ, the Father of compassion and the God of all comfort, who comforts us in all our troubles, so that we can comfort those in any trouble with the comfort we ourselves have received from God" (2 Corinthians 1:3,4).

MY PRAYER

Someone around you is in trouble. Perhaps a spouse has left or a child is rebelling. Maybe this person is depressed or has an eating disorder. Don't pass them by, friend. Tend to their wounds and help them to safety. It's what Jesus would want you to do.

MY STUDY Psalm 119:76; Isaiah 61:1,2

Big Dreams

William Wilberforce was twenty-one when he began his celebrated political career. When he became a member of Parliament in 1780, his closest friend and confidant was the young Prime Minister William Pitt. Wilberforce was well-positioned to succeed him as prime minister.

By age 25, with little reverence for political correctness, his heart was on fire for an unpopular mission. Even the temptation to become prime minister would not deter him.

He recorded this life-calling in his personal diary, simply saying, "God Almighty has set before me two great objects. The suppression of the slave trade and the reformation of manners."

England in the early nineteenth century was fueled by the economic benefits derived from slave trading. This heinous practice generated millions of pounds sterling and reached to the fashionable country homes of the aristocracy. Imagine the audacity of this young member of Parliament! To think that he could alter the economic base of England and transform the civil and moral climate of his times by "the reformation of manners."

Forty-six years later and only three days before his death on July 26, 1833, the bill for the abolition of slavery passed its second reading in the House of Commons. One historian stated, "In the process, Wilberforce went from being one of the most vilified men in Europe to one of the most loved and revered in the world." One person can make a difference! We must not escape into a private world of defeat or apathy.

Let me challenge you to find inspiration in William Wilberforce. Dream big dreams. Fight tirelessly for what is right and true. Pray for our nation. Find ways to become involved in your neighborhood, community, state, and nation.

Let's not be known as a generation of peope who stayed silent, but rather, a generation of courageous people, willing to speak their convictions and make a difference.

HIS WORD
"As for you, brothers, never tire of doing what is right" (2 Thessalonians 3:13).

MY PRAYER
Dear friend, there are issues for the glory of God that you care about, causes close to your heart. Find out how you can join with others to make a difference for Christ in these areas. Then purpose to devote time and resources in a meaningful way.

MY STUDY
Deuteronomy 6:18; Psalm 33:4,5

Are You Willing?

A man walking on a boat dock tripped over a rope and fell into the cold, deep water. He came up sputtering and crying for help, then he sank again. The man couldn't swim. He was in trouble.

His friends were too far away to help. But only a few yards away, on another dock, a young man was sunbathing.

While the desperate man begged for help, the young man – an excellent swimmer – did nothing. He actually watched the man drown.

The drowned man's family was so hurt by the callous indifference of the sunbather that they sued him. They lost.

In this 1928 precedent-setting case, the Massachusetts court ruled that the man on the dock had no legal responsibility in the accident and had every legal right to mind his own business.

As Christians, are we to mind our own business when someone is in need? The answer is no. When we have Jesus in our lives and we live according to His teaching, we can't be indifferent to the needs of others.

By His example and His words, He taught us to be involved in the lives of others, to help those in need. To be like Christ, that is our only option.

You may not have the opportunity today to save a drowning man, but there are many ways to be intentionally involved in the lives of others. It's not our responsibility to take over or to meet all of someone else's needs. However, it is our responsibility to live unselfishly, to consider the needs of others, and to do what we can.

Remember Jesus' words in Matthew 25:40: "Whatever you did for one of the least of these brothers of mine, you did for me."

Dear friend, a heart held in God's hands is one that is willing to help others in their time of need. Are you willing?

HIS WORD

"Be imitators of God, therefore, as dearly loved children" (Ephesians 5:1).

MY PRAYER

Here are a few suggested ways you can help others: Provide a safe after-school place for a child in your neighborhood. Be a friend to single parents in your church. Drive an elderly person to the grocery store. Give a few dollars or provide food to a family in financial difficulty.

MY STUDY

2 Samuel 9:1–13; Psalm 82:3,4

Seize the Moment

Dan was flying to Denver on Monday, September 10, 2001. During the flight, he noticed one of the flight attendants breaking ice with a wine bottle. "Isn't there a safer way you can do that?" he asked.

The flight attendant was moved by Dan's concern. After some conversation, he gave her a gospel tract.

She said, "This is the sixth one I've been given recently. What does God want from me?"

Dan answered, "Your life."

A few minutes later, she prayed to receive Jesus Christ into her heart.

Later, Dan read the names of those who had died on the two flights that were hijacked and forced to crash into the World Trade Center. The flight attendant he'd talked to was on the list.

Oh friend, have you talked with anyone about Jesus Christ during the past week? During the past month? In the past year? Since you became a Christian?

I'm not asking this just to lay a guilt trip on you. In fact, I'm sure you're not alone if you haven't witnessed as much as you'd like. But you know what? When you fail to share your faith, you miss out on one of God's greatest blessings.

I can't tell you the number of times on an airplane, in a department store, or with one of my children that God used the moment to give me just the right words to share Jesus and His wisdom.

Today, take advantage of one of the opportunities God will give you. You'll experience incredible joy in sharing Christ.

Like Dan's story, it may begin with a very simple comment and lead in to a full-blown conversation about God's love and salvation through Jesus.

Share God's truth with someone today. We never know how long people have to choose Jesus Christ.

HIS WORD

"We are therefore Christ's ambassadors, as though God were making his appeal through us. We implore you on Christ's behalf: Be reconciled to God" (2 Corinthians 5:20).

MY PRAYER

Ask the Lord to open your eyes to the people you encounter each day. How can you show God's love to them? How can you share the life-changing truth that God loves them, too, and wants to spend eternity with them? Now, let His Spirit lead you as you walk as Christ's ambassador.

MY STUDY

1 Corinthians 2:1-5; Colossians 1:28-29

Simplicity

*I tell you the truth, unless a kernel of wheat falls to the
ground and dies, it remains only a single seed. But if it
dies, it produces many seeds. The man who loves his life
will lose it, while the man who hates his life in this world
will keep it for eternal life. Whoever serves me must follow
me; and where I am, my servant also will be. My Father
will honor the one who serves me.*

JOHN 12:24-26

As I write to you about simplicity as a virtue, I find myself
in the task of creating a pictorial inventory of all our
possessions. Bill and I have received many beautiful treasures
from family and friends, and most of our possessions belong to
Campus Crusade. When Bill and I signed a contract to become
slaves of Jesus Christ, we committed to not accumulate
possessions. Our contract was not an attempt to simplify our
lives, but a covenant with God to prioritize serving Him.

Simplicity is not the absence of "things" or activities. A simple
heart can embrace activities with a deliberate attitude of
accomplishment, knowing that the priorities have been guided by
the Holy Spirit.

Simplicity is also not a matter of style but rather an attitude of
the heart. A heart surrendered to Christ has a priority that impacts
every thought and activity. Compassion flows from our hearts and
prompts us to provide for the needs of others. Simplicity of
emotions will purify our actions. Words will be spoken more
deliberately and anger will be replaced with patience.

The mystery of creation that we see in the season of autumn
reminds us that out of death comes life. A falling leaf enriches the
soil for the new sprout of spring. Dying to self and living with
Christ as our priority eternally enriches our lives. It is the ultimate
answer to all life's questions. And it is the foundation for simplicity.

Slow Down

Arch Hart, a popular author and speaker, tells a story of one harried week when the pressures of life had consumed him. Stress was running high.

Going home late one evening after a long meeting, Arch decided to treat his family to a quart of ice cream. It was after eleven o'clock when he dashed into the local grocery store. He was feeling impatient; his tolerance was low.

After he selected his ice cream, he rushed to the front of the store and saw the express line. Then he thought, *This is really crazy. I need to force myself to slow down.* So, instead of stepping into the express line, he chose the next register.

There he stood holding one quart of ice cream in his bare hands – with three people in front of him pushing carts spilling over with groceries.

The lady at the express counter looked at him oddly and said, "I can help you here!" Dr. Hart shook his head. He was determined to break the pace.

The woman with the cart in front of him looked exhausted. Their eyes met, and he asked sincerely, "How are you doing?" They began chatting, and just before she left, she turned around and tearfully said, "Thank you for speaking to me tonight. My life is falling apart. I'm trying to hold the family together, but I'm so tired. I'm so lonely. You may never know how much I appreciate someone looking me in the eye and talking to me." With that, she turned around and walked out.

Arch stood stunned and a bit rebuked, but at the same time very grateful that God had taught him a valuable lesson.

How about you? Are you feeling stressed out?

My friend, slow down. We live in a world of hurting people. Don't let the busyness of life keep you from being a blessing to others.

HIS WORD
"Therefore, as God's chosen people, holy and dearly loved, clothe yourselves with compassion, kindness, humility, gentleness and patience" (Colossians 3:12).

MY PRAYER
The next time you find yourself stressed out by the pressures of life, take a break. Go for a leisurely walk. Put on some soft praise music. Or take a bubble bath. When you are refreshed and clear-headed, you are better able to meet the needs of those around you.

MY STUDY
Exodus 33:19; Psalm 16:9

Most of us struggle with worry, yet the Scripture tells us, "Don't worry about anything." Corrie ten Boom, a model of trust in God, told a story that I absolutely love:

When I was in the German concentration camp at Ravensbruck, one bitter winter morning I woke up with a bad cold. My nose was running. I could not stand it.

"Well, why don't you pray for a hankie?" my sister asked. I started to laugh. There we were, with the world falling apart around us. We were locked in a camp where thousands of people were being executed each week, being beaten to death, or put through unbearable suffering – and Betsie suggests that I pray for a hankie! If I were to pray for anything, it would be for something big, not something little, like that.

But before I could object, Betsie began to pray. "Father, in the name of Jesus, I pray for a hankie for Corrie, because she has a bad cold."

I shook my head and walked away. Very shortly after, I was standing by the window when I heard someone call my name. I looked out and spotted a friend of mine, another prisoner, who worked in the hospital.

"Here you are," she said in a matter-of-fact tone.

I opened the little parcel, and inside was a handkerchief! I could hardly believe my eyes. "How did you know? Did Betsie tell you? Did you know I had a cold?"

She shrugged. "I know nothing. I was busy sewing handkerchiefs out of an old piece of sheet, and there was a voice in my heart saying, 'Take a hankie to Corrie ten Boom.' And so, there is your gift. From God."

Dear friend, use your worries, needs, and anxieties as a springboard to pray. Worry will immobilize you. Trusting in God – for *everything* – will set you free.

HIS WORD
"Who of you by worrying can add a single hour to his life?" (Matthew 6:27).

MY PRAYER
Today, you may be facing one of the greatest needs of your life or maybe you only need a hankie. Make a list of what you're worried about. One by one, confess your worries as sin, receive His forgiveness, and by faith acknowledge that the God who loves you can meet your every need.

MY STUDY
Psalm 9:10; Isaiah 50:10

Unusual Vows

Ann and Richard made an unusual vow as young newlyweds. Whoever survived longer, they decided, would dedicate his or her life completely to God.

In the meantime, they lived a life of prosperous luxury. Ann's vivacious personality attracted a wonderful circle of friends. She bore and reared ten children. She frequented the opera, traveled the world, and gracefully raised money for her favorite charities.

But their fruitful life together ended in 1984 when Richard died of cancer. So, true to their agreement, Ann began to make good on the vow that they had made many years before.

Over the course of three years, she sold everything they owned and dispersed the inheritance to their children. Then, she threw a party.

Eight hundred of her friends gathered to celebrate her sixty-first birthday. She told them, "The first two-thirds of my life were devoted to the world. The last one-third will be devoted to my soul."

The next morning, Ann entered the Carmelite Monastery in Chicago as a devoted nun.

While Ann may have expressed her devotion in other ways, I'm tremendously impressed with her willingness to let go of everything that she and Richard had acquired. I respect her sincere desire to please God.

Ann relinquished what most would hoard – wealth, fame, and a self-indulgent lifestyle – to give priority to the spiritual dimension of life.

I'm not suggesting that surrendering to God means entering a convent or living a Spartan existence. Obedience to God, wherever He might lead, brings the greatest satisfaction. In fact, the paradox is that when we hold onto possessions with a tight grip, we lose our happiness, but as we let go, the Lord fills our hearts with supernatural joy.

Let's learn a lesson from Ann. Let go of those things that you started out owning, but now find that they own you.

HIS WORD

"My prayer is not that you take them out of the world but that you protect them from the evil one. They are not of the world, even as I am not of it. Sanctify them by the truth; your word is truth" (John 17:15–17).

MY PRAYER

"Lord Jesus, You are the source of infinite joy, love, and satisfaction. Forgive me for placing too much importance on the things of this world. Help me to always remember that a life focused on You is the only life I need. In Your holy name, amen."

MY STUDY

Psalm 86:2; Isaiah 26:3

Do you ever get tired of cleaning? The house starts out spotless in the morning, but by afternoon it looks like a bomb exploded!

Our lives are sometimes like that. We get up in the morning, spend some devotional time with the Lord, get spiritually cleaned-up, but by midday, we're a total wreck.

How can we keep the trash from piling up in our lives? I believe the best way is regular maintenance rather than holding out for "spring cleaning." Moment by moment, we need to tidy up our hearts.

I have learned to confess my sin as soon as I'm aware of it. When I know I've thought or done something that does not honor God, I immediately "breathe spiritually." First, I exhale – confess my sin and agree with God that what I've done is wrong. Then, I inhale – take in the truth of God's Word that I'm forgiven and clean before Him.

When I first started applying this principle, I had two young sons, a very busy husband, and a telephone that never stopped ringing. Interruptions plagued me, no matter how cleverly I planned the day.

One time the phone rang at an inconvenient time, and I answered with a cheery – "Hello!" The voice on the other end said, "Oh, Vonette, it's always so wonderful to hear your voice. You're always so pleasant." My heart sank. I felt hypocritical. I wanted to appear spiritual, but my heart was far from it.

That day I learned it's better to trust God in the interruptions than to constantly be frustrated during them. I confessed my attitude to God and asked Him to enable me to use interruptions to honor Him. Exhale. Inhale.

Whatever has a tendency to dirty up your house, get rid of it! Sweep it out quickly! Inhale and exhale throughout your day. As you do, you'll know peace and joy as never before!

HIS WORD
"Cleanse me with hyssop, and I will be clean; wash me, and I will be whiter than snow" (Psalm 51:7).

MY PRAYER
Spiritual breathing will help you keep a short account with God. The more you practice it, the more it will become a routine part of your life. Try it for the next week, and see what a difference it makes in your life and your spirit.

MY STUDY
Isaiah 32:17; Hebrews 10:22

True Beauty

My friend Liz was packing for a weekend camping trip in California with other singles. She included her make-up kit just in case she needed it.

When she discovered there were no lights in the bathroom at the campground, Liz realized she'd be roughing it a little. So the next morning as she stood before the mirror, she had a decision to make. Make-up or no make-up?

She debated with herself for about five minutes. Finally Liz said to herself, *Hey, I'm camping! What does it matter?*

So, putting insecurity behind her, Liz walked out with no make-up on. She felt somewhat exposed. Would anyone notice?

Well, someone did notice. One of the single men took her aside and said, "Hey, Liz, you look good without make-up!" What a compliment! What an affirmation!

She learned she didn't have to hide behind foundation, lip gloss, and mascara. Liz could be herself and others would accept her.

In Scripture, Jesus had several encounters with women. He accepted each of them no matter what her background, race, status, or appearance.

The New Testament tells us, "Your beauty should not come from outward adornment, such as braided hair and the wearing of gold jewelry and fine clothes. Instead, it should be that of your inner self, the unfading beauty of a gentle and quiet spirit, which is of great worth in God's sight" (1 Peter 3:3). I'm not suggesting you throw away your make-up or wardrobe. But I do want you to examine your tendency to rely on your appearance *alone* for security and identity.

My friend, we are most attractive when we reflect the Lord's beauty. He is our mirror. He will show you who you really are because you are made in His image. You are His child, the object of His love. Concentrate on those things – in yourself and in others.

HIS WORD
"The Lord said to Samuel, 'Do not consider his appearance or his height, for I have rejected him. The LORD does not look at the things man looks at. Man looks at the outward appearance, but the Lord looks at the heart'"
(1 Samuel 16:7).

MY PRAYER
Do the women you know seem insecure about their appearance, afraid to be seen without make-up? Make it a habit to be an encouragement to them. Compliment the positive qualities you see in them, especially those that are not physical. Tell them how valuable they are.

MY STUDY
Job 29:14; Revelation 3:18

In the 1800s, John Paton was a missionary in the southwestern Pacific islands. To reach the islanders for Christ, he began to translate the Scripture.

Before long, he ran into a major hurdle. They had no word equivalent to our word "believe." Nothing even came close. For several weeks, John struggled to find a word or phrase to help these people know what it means to believe.

One day, a worker came into John's office, worn out from a hard day. He collapsed into a nearby chair. Then he stretched and put his legs up on another chair. As he breathed a contented sigh of relief, he told John it felt good to lean his whole weight on those chairs.

That was it! "Lean my whole weight on." He'd finally found the right words to explain the concept "to believe."

To "lean my whole weight on" brings to mind something I can totally rest in and depend upon. The fact that I can lean my whole weight upon something has nothing to do with the strength of my belief. It has everything to do with the *object* in which I'm putting my belief.

Believing in God has nothing to do with the strength or size of our belief, but it has everything to do with the One in whom we believe.

Friend, when you tell others about Christ, be very clear about what you're communicating. Don't take for granted that people will understand what it means to believe.

Tell them what Scripture says about the object of our belief: He is the Creator of the universe, all-knowing and all-powerful, the Holy One, faithful and true, the Great Shepherd, love.

Lean the whole weight of your world upon Him – your cares, your concerns, your heartaches. That is the essence of the gospel. That is what you need to communicate to your friends.

HIS WORD
"Trust in the LORD with all your heart and lean not on your own understanding" (Proverbs 3:5).

MY PRAYER
Do you lean the weight of your world upon Christ? You can do this by keeping an open line of communication with Him. Whatever you face throughout the day, give it to Him. Let Him take care of you.

MY STUDY
Jeremiah 17:7; Romans 10:10

A Gold Star

During World War II, banners were hung in the windows of homes all across America. They were a symbol that a soldier had gone out from that home.

A blue star was displayed in the window when a son was sent into battle, and a gold one was hung if he wasn't coming home.

One evening, a young boy was walking down the street with his father. The stars and the banners captured his attention.

Before long, he began counting, "One star in that window. And two in that one!" He clapped his little hands innocently and shouted, "Oh look, Daddy! There are three stars at that house!"

Then the boy asked, "What are those blue and gold stars for, Daddy?"

As they kept walking, the father tried to explain as best he could. His son listened carefully.

As Dad finished talking, they came to a vacant lot. There were no houses – no windows in which to hang service banners. But in the distance was a stretch of sky where one evening star brightly glowed.

"Oh, look!" the little boy exclaimed. "There's one star in *God's* window. That means God gave a Son, too." Noticing the gold color, he added, "And Daddy, God's Son died."

Out of the mouths of babes! Such a profound observation for a five-year-old.

He was right! The same way Americans posted gold stars in their windows, God the Father also gave a Son – His only Son. His death paid the penalty of sin, rescuing mankind from the sentence of death and reconciling to God all who repent.

But Jesus' death was only part of the process. For He not only died, He rose from the dead as well, claiming victory over sin.

Jesus, the shining Star, changed the world forever. A simple truth communicated in a powerful way by a five-year-old boy and a gold star.

HIS WORD
"Thanks be to God! He gives us the victory through our Lord Jesus Christ"
(1 Corinthians 15:57).

MY PRAYER
Jesus' death and resurrection were for you. All you need to do is accept His sacrificial gift and invite Him to enter your heart. You can do this by turning to "Beginning Your Journey of Joy" at the back of this book. This material will guide you.

MY STUDY
Psalm 25:5; Jeremiah 24:7

When communists took over Bulgaria, Margaret was fourteen. Soldiers stormed through the city, confiscating all the Bibles from churches, libraries, shops, and even homes. Miraculously, one older lady hid her beloved Bible under her skirt!

Not having God's Word was horrible for Margaret. When she was lonely, struggled with life, or needed strength, she had no record of God's faithfulness.

The lady who'd kept her Bible hidden began to feel guilty about not sharing it with others. So one day, she took the Bible to church. She carefully cut it apart, giving each person two pages.

The pages Margaret received contained Genesis 16 and 17 where God tells the story of Abraham and Sarah. In this story, Margaret saw how God provided for His people in miraculous ways. Every day she read her pages and prayed, "Oh, Lord, please provide Your Word for me." It was her deepest desire and prayer for almost twenty-five years.

After she became a world-class violinist, she escaped to America at age 37. She got out with her dearest possessions – her violin and the two Bible pages.

When Margaret first arrived in Los Angeles, where she played in the Philharmonic Orchestra, friends wanted to buy her a gift. There was only one thing she wanted: a Bible.

"You must understand," she said. "I didn't know this was not a difficult gift for my American friends to give me."

They took her to a Bible bookstore. When she walked in, she looked around to see shelves filled with Bibles. In awe, she fell to her knees. She began to sob. "Oh, God," she cried, "any minute now, I will have your Word."

Since then, Margaret has translated the Scriptures into Bulgarian and taken thousands of Bibles into her beloved homeland.

She's never forgotten what it was like to be without God's Word. She keeps those two precious Bible pages framed as a reminder of how precious God's Word is to us.

HIS WORD
"Oh, how I love your law! I meditate on it all day long" (Psalm 119:97).

MY PRAYER
"Heavenly Father, thank You for Your Word. How precious it is to me. The Scriptures are a constant source of comfort and help. The love You have poured into Your Word is made new each time I read it. May Your Word always be available to any who seek it. Amen."

MY STUDY
Deuteronomy 8:1–3; Colossians 3:16

The Report Card

A "C." That's what Rebecca's report card said for high-school typing. It wasn't exactly Rebecca's toughest class as a sophomore, but she didn't like it. She emphatically told God, "I'll never want a job that requires me to type!"

Ironically, a few years later, Rebecca enrolled in journalism school. Talk about typing! Being a journalist required typing under the intense pressure of tough deadlines. But the thrill of chasing the story won her over. Undoubtedly, this was where God wanted her.

Rebecca began her newspaper-reporting career in the days before computers. Time and again, she cranked a new sheet of paper into place, and off she'd go writing her story. Inevitably, she'd dislike the lead paragraph or would make a mistake.

First, she'd try to erase the error or use correction fluid, but they left smudge marks and were hard to use on whole paragraphs. Finally, she'd reach up, rip the paper out, wad it up, and toss it in the trash. Then, the process would repeat itself.

At her second newspaper job, the introduction of the computer was her saving grace.

Now, I don't know much about computers and they seem a bit complicated to me, but Rebecca assures me they've made her life incredibly easier. Now when Rebecca makes a typing mistake, she just hits the Delete key. It immediately erases her error.

As simplistic as this may sound, I am reminded of what God does with our sin. When Jesus Christ, the Son of God, died on the cross, He gave His life to forgive our sin. When we go to God and confess our sin, it's like God hits the Delete key. He immediately erases the sin – forever.

Dear friend, when you choose to put your trust in Jesus Christ, you're accepting His forgiveness for all your sin – past, present, and future. They're forgiven, "deleted" forever!

HIS WORD
"I will forgive their wickedness and will remember their sins no more" (Jeremiah 31:34).

MY PRAYER
"Merciful Lord, thank You for Your atoning sacrifice that made it possible for me to be forgiven of my sins. Thank You for taking them away forever, remembering them no more. Help me share this marvelous truth with others that they too may receive Your forgiveness. Amen."

MY STUDY
Psalm 130:3–5; Hebrews 10:17

Friends of mine, who were traveling in England, found that driving their rental car presented a real challenge. In England, unlike the United States, you drive on the opposite side of the road while sitting on the opposite side of the car and shift gears with the opposite hand!

Just a few miles down the road, the pressure of driving was intense. Mary said she had a knot in her stomach, a pain in her neck, tightness in her chest, *and* a headache. She was not having fun!

The quaint English countryside was beautiful, but Mary couldn't enjoy it. Fear kept her from taking her eyes off the road for even a second. She prayed that God would get them safely to their destination.

What Mary really needed was reassurance, and she found it on the side of the road. A small, obscure sign read "Jesus Cares."

Mary said to her friend, "Isn't that dear? The Lord put that little sign there just for me!"

As she got closer to the sign, she discovered it did *not* say "Jesus Cares." It said "Jersey Cream"! A farmer was selling dairy products to passers-by!

We've laughed and laughed about that story. But it was just the encouragement Mary needed. She learned a long time ago that Jesus cares about her. He isn't limited in His ability to assure her of His care.

Jesus is a personal God. He cares about you. He's intensely interested in who you are, what you experience in life, and what concerns you.

Friend, Jesus is moved with compassion about *your* need – no matter how great or small. If it matters to you, it matters to Him. When you come to Him with your need, He feels compassion. And He will meet you there.

Tell Him your need today. Be very specific. Trust Him to do what is best for you.

HIS WORD
"The LORD is good to all; he has compassion on all he has made" (Psalm 145:9).

MY PRAYER
What are your needs today? Consider keeping a prayer journal. Each day record the needs you have, and as God answers, record that next to the request. A prayer journal is a wonderful way to see and record God's faithfulness. Then you can rest assured that God hears your prayers and cares about you.

MY STUDY
Isaiah 63:7; Matthew 9:35,36

Middle C

Have you ever noticed that our personalities can differ, from day to day and even hour to hour? One day, someone's happy and cooperative. An hour later, he or she may be angry and defensive.

Thankfully, God is not like that. He's an emotional God, but He isn't moody. Every day He cares for you and loves you. His love never wanes or changes. It never vacillates from one day to another.

Here's a story to illustrate this concept:

While going to college, Lloyd C. Douglas, the author of *The Robe*, lived in a boarding house. Downstairs lived a retired music teacher who was ill and unable to leave his home. Everyday, Mr. Douglas would pop into the man's room. "Well, what's the good news?" he'd joyfully ask.

The music teacher would pick up his tuning fork. Then he'd tap it on the side of his wheelchair. As he held it up, the man would say, "This is middle C! It was middle C yesterday; it will be middle C tomorrow; it will be middle C a thousand years from now."

It's so easy to assume Jesus loves us only when we do good and right things, that God's love is as imperfect as ours is. Nothing could be further from the truth. All we have to do is go to the Bible to know the real Truth.

In Malachi 3:6, God says, "I the Lord do not change." And Hebrews 13:8 says, "Jesus Christ is the same yesterday and today and forever."

Take it from the Word of God. Like middle C, God never changes. So great is His love for you that He gave His one and only Son to pay the debt of sin for you. Show Him you're thankful for His selfless act by *believing* in the unchanging truth that He loves you. He always has; He always will.

HIS WORD
"I am the Alpha and the Omega, the First and the Last, the Beginning and the End"
(Revelation 22:13).

MY PRAYER
"Heavenly Father, Your unchanging nature is a constant source of security for me. Amid the ever-changing nature of life, You alone are the rock to which I can cling. Because You never change, my future is secure and eternal. I love you. Amen."

MY STUDY
Psalm 102:25–27; Malachi 3:6

Saying Grace

There's one thing many Americans will do once a year that they won't do at any other time. As families gather at Thanksgiving, for an awkward moment they will bow their heads to give thanks to God. The prayer will then give way to food, football, and family frolic.

Few people pause to truly give heartfelt thanks. But it wasn't too many years ago that saying grace – returning thanks – was as routine as the meal itself. Families ate together, and no one started eating before grace was said. Today, we're often surprised when we see someone in a restaurant pause to give thanks, although it's only a simple acknowledgment of God's provision.

Everyone experiences happy times and sad times, good times and bad, joy and sorrow. That's the way life is. Maybe Thanksgiving Day is nothing more than a painful reminder of how difficult your life is right now. So perhaps you don't feel like there's much to be thankful for. Even saying thanks for a meal is too much.

In 1 Thessalonians 5:18, God tells us to "give thanks in all circumstances, for this is God's will for you in Christ Jesus."

Dear friend, God knows all about your life. He knows what you're going through. As strange as it may seem, God wants you to express thanks for those desperate times. When you do, you're saying to Him, "I trust You." There's nothing more pleasing to Him than when we choose to trust Him for *everything*.

Express your trust in Him by saying "thank you." Begin with simple things like grace at mealtime. When you begin giving thanks in the little things, you'll find it easier to be thankful for *everything*.

When you bow your head at the Thanksgiving table, ask God to remind you daily to pause and give thanks for your meals. As you do, you'll see *His grace* in your life.

HIS WORD

"Then he took the seven loaves and the fish, and when he had given thanks, he broke them and gave them to the disciples, and they in turn to the people" (Matthew 15:36).

MY PRAYER

This morning when you reached down to slip on your shoes, did you remember that He provided those for you? What about the snack you fixed to tide you over until dinner? God provided that, too. As you go through your day, notice the little blessings, and pause to thank God for each one.

MY STUDY

1 Chronicles 16:8; Psalm 7:17

A Cup of Tea

It was four o'clock in the morning when nine soldiers with machine guns burst into the home of my friends serving Christ in their native Middle Eastern country. The soldiers ransacked every room looking for evidence of Christian ministry.

Unbelievably, the terrified woman offered to serve the soldiers tea.

They took her husband into custody and ordered him to stop his ministry work. With God's strength and grace, he told the soldiers, "No." He would never stop telling others about Jesus Christ.

The soldiers then showed him graphic pictures of the torture they'd inflict to force him into compliance. Again they asked if he'd stop. He answered, "No. And even if you take me to jail, I'll tell people *there* about Christ. If you let me go, *on the outside* I'll tell people about Christ."

The soldiers were perplexed about what to do. After some thought, one finally said, "We noticed your wife is pregnant, so we'll let you go." This soldier was one to whom the wife had served tea. His heart had been softened.

However, the family was put under strict surveillance for the next six months. Everyone who came to their home was interrogated, so eventually people stopped coming. Although alone and isolated, the family kept their faith and consistently demonstrated the love of Christ.

One day, one of the most brutal interrogators came to their home asking for prayer. The soldier's pregnant wife had fallen down, causing her to lose the baby. Also, his young son had developed a potentially fatal skin disease.

Part of this soldier's job was to read confiscated materials. As a result of reading one of the books, he placed his faith in Jesus Christ. Today, he's become one of this family's best friends.

God began with a godly woman simply serving a cup of tea and ended with another soul for the kingdom.

HIS WORD
"If your enemy is hungry, give him food to eat; if he is thirsty, give him water to drink" (Proverbs 25:21).

MY PRAYER
The amazing thing about kindness is that it never comes back void. The blessings from your kind act can come when you least expect them. Even if the act is not reciprocated, the joy you receive from blessing someone else is immeasurable.

MY STUDY
2 Samuel 24:14; Matthew 5:42–44

In the 1950s, Jim Elliot was martyred in Ecuador by primitive Auca Indians as he took the message of Christ to them. He was a young man whose life was completely committed to God. As a student at Wheaton College, the dean asked Jim to write a letter to his fellow students about what it means to "live Christ" during his vacation.

Although Jim's letter was written 65 years ago, it's amazingly relevant to us today.

He pinpoints two concerns about having time away from our routine: activity and inactivity. About activity, he says we have to be careful that parties and socializing, even doing good things, don't take the place of our quiet time with the Lord.

He wrote, "For the disciples it was the crowd that set up a barrier to quiet recuperation. This is what I mean by activity – the very need of those we are to contact becomes a snare that gives us occasion to neglect the sacred, secret [times] with Christ, which alone can fit us to fill that need."

Here is what Jim says about *inactivity*: "The let-down of an unscheduled period where no bells ring, no assignments come due ... tends to make us yawn-happy and will often keep us in bed, yielding to undisciplined sloth ... Consider the main gripe against spending time in prayer and Bible study: 'I just haven't got time.' No, but when vacation comes, we suddenly forget that we actually have time and use it to catch up on our sleep rather than on our Bible study."

What an exhortation to us! Dear friend, spend time with God. You will be changed by even a few minutes of prayer and reading His Word each day. Have you spent time with Him today? Do it now before other distractions crowd out that all-important meeting.

HIS WORD

"When you pray, go into your room, close the door and pray to your Father, who is unseen. Then your Father, who sees what is done in secret, will reward you" (Matthew 6:6).

MY PRAYER

The next time you have a vacation, take action to incorporate into your schedule quiet times with God. If you are away from home, perhaps you could find a beautiful spot outside, a quiet place of refuge for meeting with God.

MY STUDY

1 Samuel 1:26–28; Psalm 88:13

Little Evangelist

A friend of mine hosted two 16-year-old Japanese girls. They came to Orlando to learn to speak conversational English.

My friend's daughter, Meagan, was seven. They'd never hosted exchange students before, although they'd opened their home to many guests. This time their guests were nonbelievers. My friend explained to Meagan that most of the people in Japan do not know Jesus.

The girls went to church with their host family. The family helped them follow the format for worship and turn to readings in their Japanese/English New Testaments. In the car following the worship service, Reiko said she was surprised to see the word "ghost" in the Bible. My friend shot a puzzled look in her husband's direction as if to say, "How do you explain that one?"

Meagan, wedged between Reiko and Yoko in the back seat, took the challenge and started talking about God being three persons in one: "God the Father, God the Son, and God the Holy Spirit. You have to believe in Jesus and know Him so you'll go to heaven. If you don't believe in Jesus, you'll go to hell."

That was more blunt than my friend would've said it. She squirmed uncomfortably in her seat. But her husband winked and said to his wife, "Let her talk. She's a little evangelist." Coming from a child in her sweet voice, the gospel was presented non-offensively.

God gave Meagan a compassion for the lost. My friend is hoping her adult thoughts and ways never hinder her daughter's natural boldness in proclaiming the truth and praying for those who don't know God.

Children have a natural capacity to learn spiritual truth. I'm so grateful we opened our home to many guests when our sons were small. We talked about God and His love. Now our sons do this with their children. The gospel passes from generation to generation, just as God intended.

HIS WORD

"Send forth your light and your truth, let them guide me; let them bring me to your holy mountain, to the place where you dwell. Then will I go to the altar of God, to God, my joy and my delight. I will praise you with the harp, O God, my God" (Psalm 43:3,4).

MY PRAYER

Do you talk about God freely with your children? Do you explain how important it is to spread His good news to others? If children learn that God is concerned about people and their eternal destiny, they will likely speak openly about their faith.

MY STUDY *Isaiah 60:20; Acts 15:7*

With her Bible before her, Carolyn bent over a table in a bookstore. She was engrossed in the prayer she was writing in her journal. Then she heard a barely audible voice. She glanced up to see a very old man standing over her. She noticed that his wrinkled clothes didn't match.

"I see we serve the same Lord," the man said, smiling. Soon he was sitting at Carolyn's table, making polite conversation. Then he leaned forward and asked, "Do you know what I do every Monday, Wednesday, and Friday? I go to the hospital and pass out tracts. Then I go to McDonalds and pass out more tracts."

His smile never faded as he continued, "I can tell you the gospel in 30 seconds. Want to hear it?" Carolyn had warmed up to the man. "We had a debt we could not pay," he began, "that debt was hell. But Jesus paid our debt, and now we can spend eternity in heaven with Him."

This man was in love with Jesus Christ. No one was telling him he needed to spend time reading his Bible or sharing his faith. He told Carolyn that he's making the most of the time he has left on earth.

Before he left the bookstore, the old man returned to encourage Carolyn once more. "Two things I want to leave with you," he said. "Jesus tells us in John 15 to abide in Him, and we will bear fruit and to follow Him and He will make us fishers of men. Two things, abide in Him and follow Him." Then he walked away. Carolyn believes God sent that old man to encourage her.

Friend, as you abide in Jesus, you will be compelled to follow Him and tell others about Him. In so doing, you will glorify God and will accomplish His work for you while you are here on earth.

HIS WORD

[Jesus says,] *"Remain in me, and I will remain in you. No branch can bear fruit by itself; it must remain in the vine. Neither can you bear fruit unless you remain in me" (John 15:4).*

MY PRAYER

When people see you, do they see Jesus? Do your mannerisms, words, and actions, however small, glorify God? I encourage you today to reflect on what it means to abide in Christ. Look for someone you can encourage. Be a messenger sent by God to minister to another today.

MY STUDY

Psalm 63:3,4; Daniel 4:36,37

Peaceful Living

Smart phones, WiFi, tablets, gigabytes, streaming video. They're all buzzwords today. Only a few years ago, we hadn't the slightest idea what they meant!

We have small phones stuffed into our purses. We have digital step counters on our wrists. We have laptops to retrieve and sen. Overnight mail. Voice mail. Electronic airline tickets.

The convenience factor is wonderful, but sometimes I wonder: Have these things made life easier or more complicated?

Maybe you can identify with this writer, who eloquently composed this editorial for a major national magazine: "The world is too big for us. Too much is going on. Too much crime, too much violence and excitement. Try as you will, you get behind in the race in spite of yourself. It's an incessant strain to keep pace, and you still lose ground. Science empties its discoveries on you so fast you stagger beneath them in hopeless bewilderment ... Everything is high pressure. Human nature can't endure much more."

Guess when those words were written. This was an editorial in the *Atlantic Journal* on June 16, 1833. Two centuries ago, that writer was feeling what I sometimes feel!

When I start feeling overwhelmed and want to return to more serene times, it's important for me to remember, I don't find peace in the daily circumstances of life, in technology, or in convenience. Creature comforts are nice, but they don't bring peace. Peace comes from God.

Could it be that your family has fallen prey to a life so fast, so pressured, so given to technology that you've begun to place your confidence in hardware? Have you lost the wonder of silence? Simplicity? Surrender?

God alone delivers peace. Ephesians 2:14 says, "He himself is our peace." It's a timeless message.

In the maddening pace of modern days, place your confidence in God, and draw your peace from Him alone.

HIS WORD
"Since, then, you have been raised with Christ, set your hearts on things above, where Christ is seated at the right hand of God. Set your minds on things above, not on earthly things" (Colossians 3:1,2).

MY PRAYER
Consider starting a family tradition of one day a month (such as a Sunday) without media distractions — no television, no radio, no Internet. Make a commitment to communicate with each other and with God. The Holy Spirit will refresh you in the peace and quiet.

MY STUDY
Psalm 119:37; Exodus 12:13

Give Thanks

Do you get frustrated by life's little irritants – such as heavy traffic, waiting in line, or mundane tasks? Here are three ways God instructs us to look at even the smallest events in our lives.

First, we are to be thankful. God wants us to give thanks for even the smallest blessing or persistent irritant. First Thessalonians 5:18 says, "Give thanks in all circumstances, for this is God's will for you in Christ Jesus." When God says *all* circumstances, He includes the good and the bad, the big and the small, the important and the not-so-important.

Second, we are to glorify God. In 1 Corinthians 10:31 we are told, "Whatever you do, do it all for the glory of God." He wants us to live to glorify Him in whatever we are doing, whether we are making a major life decision or merely sitting in our cars maneuvering through traffic.

Third, we are to let God fill our hearts with gladness. In Ecclesiastes 5:19,20 we read, "When God gives any man wealth and possessions, and enables him to enjoy them, to accept his lot and be happy in his work – this is a gift of God. He seldom reflects on the days of his life, because God keeps him occupied with gladness of heart." God not only gives us the wealth, possessions, and everything – big and small – that we have, He also gives us the very gladness to enjoy them. The irritation we feel in life will fade away when we allow God to fill our hearts with gladness.

Dear friends, God is at work, even among life's little irritations. The next time you feel impatient, give thanks to God, seek to glorify Him, and delight in the gladness you feel. Focus on Him rather than on your problems.

HIS WORD

"Whatever you do, whether in word or deed, do it all in the name of the Lord Jesus, giving thanks to God the Father through him" (Colossians 3:17).

MY PRAYER

"Lord Jesus, enable me to realize that there really is no such thing as irritants, only opportunities to glorify and give thanks to You. Help me to look forward to these opportunities and accept them with gladness of heart, which also comes from You. In Your righteous name, amen."

MY STUDY

Psalm 9:1,2; Ecclesiastes 9:7,8

"This I Know"

"Jesus loves me, this I know." It's a simple children's song, yet more profound words have never been spoken.

My friend struggled for years to grasp God's love for her. Her father left home when she was very young, so she did not have a good earthly model to even begin to understand God's love for her. Because of her father's lack of love toward her, she couldn't grasp the depths of her heavenly Father's love.

For many years, my friend spent time learning how to truly know God. She experienced His faithfulness and blessing many times throughout her life. One day, she was finally able to say with certainty, "Jesus loves me, this I know."

How do we know that God loves us? John 3:16 tells us, "God so loved the world that he gave his one and only Son, that whoever believes in him shall not perish but have eternal life." God loved us enough to send His Son to earth to die so that we could spend eternity in heaven.

Romans 5:5 says, "God has poured out his love into our hearts by the Holy Spirit, whom he has given us." God fills our hearts with His love so that we may experience life to the fullest. What marvelous love He must feel for us!

Today my friend asks her children, "Who loves you?" Her three-year-old says brightly, "God and Jesus." Then she proceeds down the list of others in her life who love her: "Nana, Papa, Mama, Daddy." This simple phrase is used to pass on biblical truth to children.

"Jesus loves me, this I know ..." How? "For the Bible tells me so." The Bible is God's love letter to us. Friend, spend time in God's Word each day and find out for yourself how much God loves you.

HIS WORD
"So we know and rely on the love God has for us. God is love. Whoever lives in love lives in God, and God in him" (1 John 4:16).

MY PRAYER
When you spend time with your children or children that you know, find simple, yet creative ways to make God a part of the conversation. Explain that God loves each of us. Point out God's hand in the creation. Tell how God shows us, through objects and events all around us, how much He loves us.

MY STUDY
Deuteronomy 6:6–9; Psalm 102:18–21

A re you tired and weary of life's struggles? Of the mundane routine? Of your responsibilities? Of persevering through your Christian journey?

Life can be difficult. Sometimes the pressures of the day can seem overwhelming. Sometimes we think, *How can I possibly have the strength to get through all that is before me?*

I have good news for you, friend. Although we tire very easily, we can rest assured that God never gets weary!

Read these marvelous words in Isaiah 40:28–31: "Do you not know? Have you not heard? The LORD is the everlasting God, the Creator of the ends of the earth. He will not grow tired or weary, and his understanding no one can fathom. He gives strength to the weary and increases the power of the weak. Even youths grow tired and weary, and young men stumble and fall; but those who hope in the LORD will renew their strength. They will soar on wings like eagles; they will run and not grow weary, they will walk and not be faint."

Are there times when you feel that life is too complicated, too stressful, too exhausting? Do you sometimes think there is no way you can get everything under control? To combat these feelings and thoughts, remember this passage from Isaiah. God alone gives us the strength and power to face the challenges of each day. Memorize this phrase from that passage: "Those who hope in the LORD will renew their strength."

Oh, weary one, God is our hope and our strength. Because God is all powerful, He can help me with anything. He does not expect us to handle our problems alone. He is our eternal Father. Not only will He renew our strength, He will enable us to fly higher, run faster, and walk longer than we ever thought possible.

The One who never tires will refresh you. That is His promise to us, His children.

HIS WORD
"I pray that out of his glorious riches he may strengthen you with power through his Spirit in your inner being, so that Christ may dwell in your hearts through faith"
(Ephesians 3:16,17).

MY PRAYER
"Everlasting God, You alone can provide the strength I need to make it through the fast-paced, stressful days of my life. I know that if I put my hope in You, You will renew my strength. What a wonderful promise! In Jesus' matchless name, amen."

MY STUDY
Exodus 15:13; Psalm 18:1,2

In His Presence

Do you find yourself busy with family? Work? Church? Social activities? Does this busyness leave you longing for a moment to catch your breath? Perhaps you don't even realize how busy you are and how much you need rest. Perhaps your life is like Vickey's.

Vickey was in graduate school finishing a Master's degree in counseling. She was also working and seeing clients. She led a full and active life. Very suddenly, her busy life came to a screeching halt.

Doctors discovered Vickey had a rare blood disorder. She spent thirteen days in the hospital and had several plasma transfusions. But during this period of uncertainty, she leaned on God. As a result, she experienced His presence and joy in new ways.

When she was finally able to return home, she was a rested and renewed woman.

Sometimes we get so busy in life that we forget how to stop and enjoy God's presence. Unfortunately, it can take a tragic event or illness to slow us down. It is then that we are able to reevaluate our lives and reconnect with God.

When you are so busy that you don't know where to find rest, look to the Psalms. They tell us where to find our source of rest:

- "My soul finds rest in God alone; my salvation comes from him" (Psalm 62:1).
- "Find rest, O my soul, in God alone; my hope comes from him" (Psalm 62:5).
- "He who dwells in the shelter of the Most High will rest in the shadow of the Almighty" (Psalm 91:1).

Do these verses comfort you as much as they do me? I encourage you to use your Bible concordance to find other passages on the "rest" that comes from God.

Dear one, only in God will you find true rest. Rest in His presence. Tell Him your every concern. He will take care of you!

HIS WORD
"Very early in the morning, while it was still dark, Jesus got up, left the house and went off to a solitary place, where he prayed" (Mark 1:35).

MY PRAYER
When Christ ascended, the Holy Spirit was given to us as a comfort and guide. No matter how busy you find yourself, God is always with you. You can always find rest when you allow the presence of the Holy Spirit to fill you.

MY STUDY
2 Chronicles 6:18–20; Psalm 89:15

Each year for six years, I have fasted for forty days with my husband. Each occasion is a time of great spiritual and emotional intimacy.

The greatest benefit I have received during these fasts is the personal connection with God. Throughout the forty days, I focus on God and read His Word. Through His Holy Spirit, I am able to process the issues I am facing at the time.

One year, I was facing some age-related physical problems. It was hard for me to accept the fact that I could not do as much as in the past. But God helped me to honestly face my limitations.

Our human bodies are limited in their abilities, and over time, they will deteriorate. Even the most athletic people among us cannot maintain the same level of performance throughout their entire lives. Weakness is a part of life.

The apostle Paul had a lot of things to say about weakness:

- "The body that is sown ... in weakness, it is raised in power" (1 Corinthians 15:42,43).
- "If I must boast, I will boast of the things that show my weakness" (2 Corinthians 11:30).
- "The foolishness of God is wiser than man's wisdom, and the weakness of God is stronger than man's strength" (1 Corinthians 1:25).
- "But he said to me, 'My grace is sufficient for you, for my power is made perfect in weakness.' ... For when I am weak, then I am strong" (2 Corinthians 12:9,10).
- "[Christ] was crucified in weakness, yet he lives by God's power. Likewise, we are weak in him, yet by God's power we will live with him to serve you" (2 Corinthians 13:4).

Dear friend, our weakness is a blessing. It allows the power of God to work to the fullest. Don't hide your weaknesses; allow God to work through them.

HIS WORD
"God chose the foolish things of the world to shame the wise; God chose the weak things of the world to shame the strong"
(1 Corinthians 1:27).

MY PRAYER
"All-powerful God, I know my human weaknesses, but I also know You are a God of mighty strength. I ask Your Holy Spirit to control my life and to demonstrate Your strength in my weakness. You gave me access to this power when I became Your child. All I need is to submit to You and trust You. I do, Lord. Amen."

MY STUDY
2 Chronicles 32:7,8; Psalm 68:32–35

Contented Life

Oseola had one old Bible that lasted her entire lifetime. She lived a simple life in a simple house. She had no husband and no children. She didn't even have a car. But she had enough.

For eighty years, she worked faithfully, washing the clothes of the wealthier people in her community. When she retired at age eighty-seven, she astonished the world by giving $150,000 to a Mississippi university.

With her gift, she said, "I have everything I could want ... I had more money than I could possibly spend."

First Timothy 6:6,7 says, "Godliness with contentment is great gain. For we brought nothing into the world, and we can take nothing out of it."

Oseola is a wonderful example of living a life of contentment. She did not get caught up in the material trappings of this world. She provided for her own basic needs and wanted nothing more. The money she saved, she generously gave to benefit others.

I don't believe being content necessarily means living at the sparse level that Oseola did. Contentment is about the heart. Contentment is being satisfied, whatever your circumstances and whatever your possessions.

Hebrews 13:5 tells us, "Let your character or moral disposition be free from love of money – [including greed, avarice, lust and craving for earthly possessions] – and be satisfied with your present [circumstances and with what you have]; for He [God] Himself has said, I will not in any way fail you nor give you up nor leave you without support. [I will] not, [I will] not, [I will] not in any degree leave you helpless nor forsake nor let [you] down, (relax My hold on you), [Assuredly not!]" (Amplified).

Contentment has nothing to do with our possessions or our position in society; it comes from our security in the Lord. He will always be by our side. Everything else should only be enjoyed as a bonus, a blessing from a God who delights in making us happy. Friend, be thankful for all you have. Choose contentment. When you do, God will fill your heart with bountiful joy.

HIS WORD

"Jesus answered, 'If you want to be perfect, go, sell your possessions and give to the poor, and you will have treasure in heaven. Then come, follow me'" (Matthew 19:21).

MY PRAYER

"Heavenly Father, You have provided all I need and more than I deserve. Forgive me for placing too much importance on the things of this world. I choose now to be content in You and to be satisfied with whatever blessings You give me. Amen."

MY STUDY

Psalm 73:25,26; Isaiah 58:10

In 1999, death came to Cassie Bernall like a thief in the night. Twelve others also died at Columbine High School in Colorado on that tragic day.

Pointing a gun at Cassie's head, her killer asked, "Do you believe in God?"

Her response to his question carried a high price – her life. She said, "Yes, I believe in God."

Seventeen-year-old Cassie had been a Christian for only two years, and she died professing her faith in Christ. Her last words made headlines around the world.

The Bible says in 1 Peter 3:15, "Always be prepared to give an answer to everyone who asks you to give the reason for the hope that you have." As followers of Christ, we are to be ready at any time to respond to someone who asks the reason for our faith.

The Bible also tells us that Christ will bless us for our obedience. Matthew 10:32,33 says, "Whoever acknowledges me before men, I will also acknowledge him before my Father in heaven. But whoever disowns me before men, I will disown him before my Father in heaven." Cassie was presented with this challenge in a way that very few of us ever will be. Staring death in the face, she boldly acknowledged her faith before men. Although she lost her life on this earth, she gained eternity with the Lord in heaven.

In Philippians 1:21, Paul proclaims, "For to me, to live is Christ and to die is gain." When we are in Christ, live or die, we can't lose. Cassie didn't lose, and neither will we.

Dear friend, remember Cassie. Do not be afraid to confess your Lord before others! Boldly proclaim to all your belief in the risen Christ, and tell them how they can know Him, too.

HIS WORD
"We have seen and testify that the Father has sent his Son to be Savior of the world" (1 John 4:14).

MY PRAYER
Have you been faced with questions about your faith? How did you respond? Being prepared for these questions will make them easier to handle. Write down the five most common questions you or other Christians face. As you share the good news of the gospel in the power of His Spirit, you demonstrate the authenticity of the Christian life.

MY STUDY
Exodus 4:11,12; Psalm 51:15

Day by Day

Stress. It's the leading cause of many physical and emotional problems in these busy modern times. Even for Christians.

Eric suffers from stress periodically. When he is feeling overwhelmed by the pressures of life, his observant wife can read the signs in his demeanor and actions. To help relieve his stress, she first hugs him. Then, she gently suggests he spend some time with God.

Often, his first response to her suggestion is to list all the things he needs to do and to tell her that he doesn't have time. Fortunately, hearing these words from his own mouth is usually enough to help him regain perspective. He realizes that when he is too busy to spend time with God, he needs to reevaluate his priorities. He is living life in his own strength without dependence on God.

Eric's wife has the right idea. When we are stressed, we need to go to God. Jesus wants to live His life in and through us. He is the cure for stress. He says in Matthew 6:31–34: "Do not worry, saying, 'What shall we eat?' or 'What shall we drink?' or 'What shall we wear?' For the pagans run after all these things, and your heavenly Father knows that you need them. But seek first his kingdom and his righteousness, and all these things will be given to you as well. Therefore do not worry about tomorrow, for tomorrow will worry about itself. Each day has enough trouble of its own."

God knows our needs – all our needs. All we need to do is to submit to Him. That is a sure way to alleviate the stress and worry we feel. As our eyes turn to Him, they will turn away from the stress.

Dear friend, give God daily priority in your life. He doesn't want to be your helper. He wants to live His life in and through you. Let Him control your life as you tell Him about the tasks before you, and let Him set your priorities.

HIS WORD

"Ask and it will be given to you; seek and you will find; knock and the door will be opened to you. For everyone who asks receives; he who seeks finds; and to him who knocks, the door will be opened" (Matthew 7:7,8).

MY PRAYER

We all face stress. Take preemptive measures to prevent stress from becoming overwhelming. Seek God first for every need — social, physical, emotional, and spiritual. Then rest in the security that He is in control of it all. If stress does creep in, go to God with your concerns. He will help you.

MY STUDY *Deuteronomy 4:29; Psalm 20:4,5*

The Leaman family was taking a long road trip. To help keep harmony, one of the days was declared "kindness day."

After drawing names, family members were to be especially kind to that person all day, *without telling anyone* who it was. This ingenuous plan was a great success! Kindness and harmony ruled the day.

The next day, son Durelle suggested another "kindness day." Again, the names were put into a hat and each family member drew a name. As the day went on, it wasn't long until they noticed everyone was being kind to Durelle. The ingenious young man had put his name on every slip of paper in the hat!

That story is not only charming, it illustrates an important spiritual virtue – kindness.

Friend, the Bible tells us that kindness is evidence of the Holy Spirit's control in our lives. Galatians 5:22 says, "The fruit of the Spirit is love, joy, peace, patience, kindness, goodness, faithfulness, gentleness and self-control." The Holy Spirit living within is shown to others through the fruit of the Spirit. Kindness should be a part of our very nature as believers in Christ.

We can also see our responsibility to be kind in Colossians 3:12, which says, "As God's chosen people, holy and dearly loved, clothe yourselves with compassion, kindness, humility, gentleness and patience." We are to wear kindness like clothing, which is worn every day, for all to see.

Kindness benefits the recipient by meeting a need and allowing Christ's love to be expressed through us. Kindness also promotes harmony, where perhaps there would be none.

Dear friend, make every day "kindness day." Give an encouraging word. Lend a helping hand. Provide a shoulder to cry on. Forgive when you are wronged. As you allow the Holy Spirit's kindness to be expressed through you each day, you will be surprised at the wonderful effects – on others and yourself.

HIS WORD

"Perfume and incense bring joy to the heart, and the pleasantness of one's friend springs from his earnest counsel" (Proverbs 27:9).

MY PRAYER

"Father, allow Your spirit of kindness to be expressed through me this day and every day. Show me how to best minister to others, perhaps making someone's day special today. In Your Son's loving name, amen."

MY STUDY

Genesis 50:15–21; Romans 12:15–17

One Good Deed

Pastor Donald Caskie was a German prisoner during World War II. The day before his scheduled execution, he asked to take communion.

A German chaplain in the camp met with him. He even remembered Caskie's name from years earlier.

Ironically, the two men – now on opposite sides of this monumental human conflict – had crossed paths before the war. Pastor Caskie had graciously allowed this German chaplain's congregation to use his church building for worship.

On this day in the prison camp, the chaplain served communion to Pastor Caskie. Then he promised to do everything possible to save the pastor's life. With God's help, that is exactly what he did. The death sentence was commuted.

One good deed done years earlier meant the difference between life and death for Pastor Caskie. The German chaplain remembered the kindness shown to his congregation by granting the use of Pastor Caskie's church building. Despite the fact that they were enemies in this earthly war, the chaplain only saw the grace shown him and felt the need to reciprocate.

The Bible tells us in Galatians 6:9, "Let us not become weary in doing good, for at the proper time we will reap a harvest if we do not give up."

Pastor Caskie most likely did not realize years earlier exactly what his good deed would mean. His generosity was simply an outgrowth of a life led in service to Christ and His principles. When he needed it most, he reaped a reward of his very own life.

Friend, make it a lifestyle to do good to others. With whatever God has entrusted to you, be generous, gracious, and giving to others. You never know just how important one good deed will be.

And even if your good deeds go unrecognized for the moment, keep on working as unto the Lord. God knows! And He will reward your faithfulness.

HIS WORD
"Tell the righteous it will be well with them, for they will enjoy the fruit of their deeds" (Isaiah 3:10).

MY PRAYER
Kindness is a fruit of the Spirit. To live a life of generosity and graciousness, we must rely on the enabling of the Holy Spirit within us. Our natural tendency is to preserve our self interests. Let God, the Holy Spirit, empower you each day to put others before yourself. Then kindness toward others will flow from your heart.

MY STUDY
Psalm 141:3,4; Hebrews 10:24,25

Rebecca Manly Pippert, in her book *Out of the Salt Shaker*, tells the story of Bill. He became a Christian in college, and he loved the Lord. But Bill had the odd habit of always going barefoot – rain, sleet, or snow!

One Sunday, he decided to attend worship at a church near campus that was composed of well-dressed, middle-class members. When Bill, barefoot and in jeans, entered the church, he walked down to the front to look for a seat. Finding none, he simply sat on the floor.

With all eyes on the impending situation, an elderly man walked down the aisle toward the boy. This promised to be an interesting confrontation!

When the man reached Bill, he leaned over. Guess what he did next? He sat down next to Bill! They worshiped together on the floor! I love that.

Can you imagine what Jesus would have done in this situation? In His day, people complained that He hung around with "the wrong crowd." But He loved them as much as He loved "the right crowd." I believe Jesus would have sat on the floor alongside Bill and his new elderly friend!

God does not want us to discriminate against those who look different or act different. God wants us to look inside a person – at the heart. No matter what the person looks like, he or she is loved by God. We are commanded to love as Christ loved. Christ looks at the heart of a person; so must we.

What is it about people that puts you off? Out-of-fashion clothing? Uncultured speech? Unkempt appearance?

Next time you're inclined to judge someone who looks different from you and your friends, remember to look at them with God's eyes and with God's heart. Love others as He does.

HIS WORD

"If you show special attention to the man wearing fine clothes and say, 'Here's a good seat for you,' but say to the poor man, 'You stand there' or 'Sit on the floor by my feet,' have you not discriminated among yourselves and become judges with evil thoughts?" (James 2:3,4)

MY PRAYER

"Lord Jesus, forgive me for looking at others with eyes of judgment. Your love surpasses all our human differences. Help me to see people as You see them, and to love them with Your love. In Your wonderful name, amen."

MY STUDY

Deuteronomy 10:17,18; Psalm 84:9,10

The Simple Truth

Have you ever stopped to consider how simple the gospel message really is? Think about the death of Christ. The fact is, on that cross at Calvary, Jesus shed His blood for us to forgive our sin and give us eternal life.

The simplicity of the message was made real to me one day when my grandchildren were coloring. Keller, who was four-and-a-half years old, colored his page red. Then he matter-of-factly said, "This is Jesus' blood." Noel, who was only three years old, chimed in innocently, "And He shed His blood for our sins."

Over their coloring books, these children unwittingly exhorted a simple, yet powerful, truth! Christ died on the cross for us. He was the perfect sacrifice required to redeem us from our sins. Romans 3:24,25 says, "[All] are justified freely by [God's] grace through the redemption that came by Christ Jesus. God presented him as a sacrifice of atonement, through faith in his blood."

Simple doesn't mean cheap. Christ gave it all for us; He paid everything. Yet the only requirement for us to receive Christ's atonement for our sin is that we accept His freely given sacrifice and receive Him as our Savior. Jesus did the hard part more than two thousand years ago.

Oftentimes, I find that we try to make things more complicated than they are. Perhaps you have even heard someone say, "There must be more to it. Nothing is ever free. There's always a catch."

Dear friend, a gift has been offered to us. There are no strings attached. All we have to do is receive it. It's as simple as that.

There is no "catch" – only the unfathomable love of a righteous God trying to reach out to His creation. There is no need to question this gift; just praise God for it and tell others about the ease of receiving it.

HIS WORD

"I pray that you may be active in sharing your faith, so that you will have a full understanding of every good thing we have in Christ"
(Philemon 1:6).

MY PRAYER

To make sharing Christ easier, the truth of the gospel message has been presented in "Beginning Your Journey of Joy" at the back of this book. Use it to help you learn how to present God's plan of salvation. Ask God for opportunities to share the gospel with others.

MY STUDY

Psalm 13:5,6; Zechariah 9:9

An eight-year-old boy had a younger sister with leukemia. Without a blood transfusion, she would surely die.

His parents explained to the boy that if his blood was compatible with hers, he might be able to supply the transfusion. He agreed to have his blood tested, and it was a good match.

They told him that giving his sister a pint of his blood could be her only chance for living. He said he'd have to think about that overnight.

The next day, he said he was willing to donate the blood. So his parents took him to the hospital where he was put on a gurney beside his six-year-old sister. Both of them were hooked up to IVs.

As a pint of blood was withdrawn from the boy, it was immediately run into the girl's IV. The boy lay silently on his gurney.

When the doctor came over to see how he was doing, the boy opened his eyes and, in all sincerity, said, "Doctor, how soon until I start to die?"

The little boy had not understood that he was only giving a little of his blood to his sister. He thought he had to give it all. He was prepared to give his life.

What a wonderful story of love! This little boy was given the gift of life, and he was willing to give it away so that his little sister would live.

Friend, I'm convinced that many of us are falling short. We have received the most precious gift of all – life through Jesus Christ. Yet we're reticent to share that gift by telling others.

We may be giving money, but like the little boy, we need to give blood – to share straight from our heart. We need to tell others how Jesus changes lives through His personal touch – and about our eternal future through His blood.

Changing lives requires active, sacrificial love – a transfusion. We all have something to give.

HIS WORD
"In fact, the law requires that nearly everything be cleansed with blood, and without the shedding of blood there is no forgiveness" (Hebrews 9:22).

MY PRAYER
Perhaps you give money to your church or charities, but what do you give of your time, talents, or heart? Money is important, but a life invested is eternally significant. The next time you hear about someone who doesn't know our Lord, invest yourself in her life by giving out Jesus' words of life.

MY STUDY
Exodus 12:13; Psalm 51:14

Joy in Your Heart

*I have set the LORD always before me. Because he is at
my right hand, I will not be shaken. You have made known
to me the path of life; you will fill me with joy in your
presence, with eternal pleasures at your right hand.*

PSALM 16:8,11

If happiness could be packaged, I would have no trouble
finding investors. Advertisers can claim that a product will
provide happiness for an individual, but in reality, only the
individual can truly contribute to happiness. Sports events,
concerts, movies, and novels can create moments of pleasure.
Cheering for the home team or laughing at an author's
well-crafted humor is a fleeting experience.

Escaping from the reality and demands of life may offer a brief
interlude with a happy feeling, but all too soon the reality of life
reemerges and the deep attitudes of the heart impact our actions.

It is difficult to think of celebrating without a sense of joy
motivating the occasion. The planning and preparations required
to create a festive environment for birthday and anniversary
celebrations may become expected rituals without the heartfelt
joy of the giver.

But what a beautiful gift is given to the woman who has
accepted Jesus Christ as her Savior. A deep, sustained sense of
joy can fill her heart with the realization that every little blessing
in life is a treasure from her Creator. The joyful heart cannot be
erased by tragedy, stressful circumstances, or everyday routine.
Instead, this joy that God gives not only outlasts these problems,
it provides a foundation of strength.

How Do You Know?

When our oldest son was in high school, occasionally he would come home from school and say, "Mother, how do you really know the Christian position is right?" As I would answer his arguments, one point made a lasting impression when others seemed to fail. I would encourage him to look at the lifestyle of the true follower of Christ and consider how attractive it is. Then I would ask him to consider the non-Christian and the appealing qualities in that lifestyle. He would then come to his own conclusion that imitating the life of Christ was the most appealing way to live.

Every true believer in Christ desires to follow the instructions from God's Word; however, practicing those truths is often neglected because Christians do not know what the Word of God says. Without a knowledge and understanding of the Bible, we can let the philosophies of men cloud the purity and wisdom of God's Word. Without the Bible as the measure of righteousness, we can compromise our position or let others influence our thinking and, in turn, our lifestyle.

Christianity is a living relationship with the person Jesus Christ. However, as in any meaningful relationship, we must work at it. Just as we are available to talk to, listen to, and do things for those we love, so we must spend time in the same manner getting to know Jesus Christ.

The angels proclaimed peace on earth and good will toward men at the birth of Jesus, and as we get to know Him and become more like Him, we can understand what peace really means. The "good will toward men" is the greatest witness of the Christian life to an unbeliever. The heart full of God's joy is undeniable proof.

HIS WORD
"Let the peace of Christ rule in your hearts, since as members of one body you were called to peace ... Let the word of Christ dwell in you richly as you teach and admonish one another with all wisdom, and as you sing psalms, hymns and spiritual songs with gratitude in your hearts to God" (Colossians 3:15,16).

MY PRAYER
The peace of Christ is an added gift that comes when we accept His gift of eternal life. It is important that we show people a life transformed by the Holy Spirit. That is how others will know to Whom we belong.

MY STUDY
1 Samuel 20:42; Psalm 85:10,11

Fifty Years of Prayer

For seventy-five years, communism held a stifling grip on Russia. In this atheistic period, mothers could not tell their children about God and His great love without facing severe consequences. But while God did not have a place in the hearts of the new generations, He was not entirely forgotten.

After communism's fall, Campus Crusade for Christ held a four-day teachers' conference in Samara, Russia. More than 300 teachers learned how to teach a biblically-based morals and ethics curriculum.

In one of the main conference sessions, Nancy, a Campus Crusade staff member, listened with earphones to the translation of a Russian speaker. Her attention was drawn to a nearby aisle. An elderly woman slowly made her way into the auditorium and sat down.

The Russian speaker finished. Then an American speaker began. Nancy realized this elderly woman couldn't understand his message. She took her earphones and placed them on the woman so she could hear the Russian translation.

Immediately, the woman began to weep and thank Nancy profusely. Tears streamed down her cheeks as she listened to the message. Nancy asked the woman, Anastasia, why she was so moved to tears. Anastasia replied, "This is the answer to my fifty years of prayer."

My heart is so moved by a woman of God who never gave up, who prayed for half a century for her country to hear the message of God's love. I am so thankful God allowed her to see His answer to her prayers.

The Russian officials didn't want us to have a conference in Samara, a once-closed military city. But the prayers of one woman moved the hand of God, who in turn moved in the hearts of city officials to invite the conference to Samara. Today, many of the teachers are teaching hundreds of students about the God of the Bible.

HIS WORD

"Yet give attention to your servant's prayer and his plea for mercy, O LORD my God. Hear the cry and the prayer that your servant is praying in your presence this day" (1 Kings 8:28).

MY PRAYER

God is the One who answers prayer. Remember, the faithful, though silent, prayers of Russia's mothers and grandmothers would not let God be entirely forgotten. Today, don't let God be forgotten where you are. Pray every day for your community, your neighborhood, your coworkers. God will hear! And He will change lives.

MY STUDY *Psalm 17:5,6; Mark 11:23,24*

Holiday times require me to adjust my schedule, and reading the daily paper is one activity I put on hold. I catch enough news to know what is going on in the world, but I stack the papers for another day.

Following one of these beautiful holiday times with family and friends, I sat down to sort through the stack of papers accumulated near my desk. Many of the headlines reported violence and perversion that made my heart ache. But as I reached the papers dated closest to Christmas, I began to see various articles commenting on the holiday. One national newspaper reporter asked five people to respond to the question, "What does Christmas mean to you?" Four out of the five referred to celebrating the birth of Christ as central to their holiday.

One syndicated columnist stated quite boldly that "the true spirit of Christmas is found in imitating the life of Christ." What a refreshing experience. Secular media may not always be fair or balanced in the presentation of the facts of our sacred holidays, but I am reminded that not everyone paid attention to the Holy Night when God came to earth in the flesh as a baby, either. Jesus was born into a world busy with buying and selling. Certainly, the innkeeper had more on his mind than one weary pregnant woman. Even the reports of angels announcing His arrival to shepherds did not impact some folks.

You may not see your life as headline news, but to people who do not know Christ personally, you may be the boldest print they will ever read.

God has chosen us mere mortals as His delivery system of the great news of the gospel. What a privilege we have to make certain that our celebrations are Christ-centered and reflect His love.

HIS WORD

"As it is written, 'How beautiful are the feet of those who bring good news!'" (Romans 10:15).

MY PRAYER

"Heavenly Father, thank You for allowing me to hear the news of Jesus' birth. Help me to make every day a celebration of His life, but especially during the Christmas season when people are more likely to think about Jesus and who He is. Please give me boldness to share my faith with people who do not know the good news of the gospel. In Your Son's holy name, amen."

MY STUDY Psalm 132:16; Isaiah 7:14

Creative Gift Giving

Carrie is a single mother of two very active teens. Working full-time to provide for her family, Carrie was frustrated. She really wanted to reach out to her neighbors and to her community, but she never seemed to have enough time.

In December, her daughter and her friends were looking for a way to share the real meaning of Christmas with their neighbors. Carrie had an idea, so she showed the girls the *JESUS* video – a movie based on the life of Christ.

Carrie and the girls raised money to buy enough *JESUS* videotapes to distribute to each house on their street. Even their church donated money to help with their project.

A few weeks before Christmas, they wrapped the videocassettes in festive paper. Then they delivered the gifts in grand style – Christmas caroling at every house.

When Carrie told me about the project, I was almost as excited as she was! Here was a busy working mother who managed to creatively get the gospel message into many of the homes in her neighborhood. Not only that, but she helped her teenage daughter and her friends experience the challenge and joy of sharing Christ with others.

The quality of the video production was so excellent that several of the neighbors expressed their appreciation for the special gift.

Friend, teenagers may be willing to share their faith but may just need some creative input. Special memories of those times will be discussed for many years to come.

It may not have been possible for Carrie or the girls to share Christ with all their neighbors on a one-to-one basis, but the clear message in the video was sure to plant seeds of thought for days after the holidays. Many months after the holiday season has ended, these seeds will still be growing.

HIS WORD
"A gift opens the way for the giver and ushers him into the presence of the great" (Proverbs 18:16).

MY PRAYER
Encourage your family members to share with each other how God has used their words to reach someone's heart. Enjoy the sweetness of these spiritual moments with your family.

MY STUDY
Isaiah 40:9; John 4:10

Remember Your Journey

I encourage people to record in writing their prayer requests and then record God's answers. I've done so myself for years. It's exciting to see how God guided the circumstances and events of life. Susie, a Crusade staff member, records her prayers and thoughts to God in a journal. I think her explanation of why it is important might be helpful for you.

Sometimes when Susie feels discouraged, she pulls out one of her journals from the bookcase and takes a trip into the past. She might read about the summer she worked as a maid and had no money. She had asked God to send her five dollars for lunch, and He did. She was so young in her faith then; she hoped she'd prayed correctly. Through a tip left in a room she cleaned just before lunch, God actually provided more than the five dollars she needed for lunch. She remembers being astounded that God heard her prayers and answered them so specifically.

Or she might read the journal entry recounting a recent trip to Switzerland. Traveling there had been a dream of hers, and God fulfilled it. It was a business trip, but one day during some free time she stood in the Alps looking at a snow-covered wooden cross, amazed that God had blessed her with this trip.

Seeing the proof of God's love on her journal pages encourages her. It gives her hope when she's feeling dry in her spiritual life.

There's another book she turns to when she's wondering if God is still working in her life: the Bible. Sometimes when she reads God's Word, she feels like she's reading His journal. Time after time, God urges His people not to forget Him. "Remember Me," His pages plead, "and remember I love you." His words are a personal message to our hearts.

HIS WORD
*"Remember the wonders he has done, his miracles, and the judgments he pronounced"
(1 Chronicles 16:12).*

MY PRAYER
Today, pick up a pen and grab a notebook. Record God's work in your life, both past and present. Take a fresh look at the monuments of His love. Whether you're in a painful place or a "promised land," remember God has led you safely thus far, and He's with you now.

MY STUDY
Psalm 17:6; Mark 11:24

A Heart of Thanks

Just two words: thank you. It's one of the first things we teach our children to say because it's something they'll express throughout their lifetime.

We love to hear children spontaneously say, "Thank you." It is refreshing to be around people who demonstrate an attitude of gratefulness.

The opposite is true, as well. It's difficult to be around someone who is ungrateful. It is a rude person who takes advantage of another's generosity.

It is difficult to comprehend how anyone could be ungrateful for the touch of Jesus. In Luke 17, Jesus was on His way to Galilee when He passed through a village. Ten men had leprosy and knew of His reputation to heal, so they began to cry out, "Jesus, Master, have pity on us!" (verse 13).

These men were being devastated by one of the most unbearable, incurable diseases. No one dared to come near a leper.

Jesus took compassion on these men, and they were instantly healed. Completely renewed! No process! No waiting period! No performance necessary. No payment. Just complete restoration! They were 100 percent healed.

Then the passage describes how all the men left, but only one returned to thank Jesus. This man fell on his face at our Lord's feet – glorifying God and giving thanks.

This is what Jesus said at that moment, "Were not all ten cleansed? Where are the other nine?" (verse 17).

Dear friend, if you're like I am, you feel a bit embarrassed for those men. We can't believe they had the audacity to flee the scene without a simple word of gratitude.

Then I realize that I often make the same mistake. I don't always go running back to glorify the Lord and give Him thanks for His blessings. But we can change that. Give glory and thanks to God for *all* that He does for you and all that He is.

HIS WORD
"Now, our God, we give you thanks, and praise your glorious name" (1 Chronicles 29:13).

MY PRAYER
Before I knew the Lord personally, my life and future held no more hope than those ten lepers' lives did. My sin-sick heart looked just like theirs. Each time I read this passage, I'm reminded of how important it is to be grateful. Pray with me, "Thank You, Lord, for all You've done for me."

MY STUDY
Psalm 75:1; 2 Corinthians 2:14

So many lives are filled with broken relationships and emotional dysfunction. People are looking for happiness, but so few know how to find it. What is the secret to capturing joy, that enduring kind of happiness that gets us through the toughest of times?

The apostle Paul writes, "Rejoice in the Lord always. I will say it again: Rejoice!" (Philippians 4:4).

Joy is a command, but it is also a choice.

We have been sold a false bill of goods. We are led to believe that joy comes from personal gain. Happiness is winning the lottery. It's finding that a relative has left us lots of money. It's two new cars in the driveway. But is that really joy?

Paul did not just tell us to be joyful, but he gave us a profound example from his own life. "I've learned by now to be quite content whatever my circumstances. I'm just as happy with little as with much, with much as with little. I've found the recipe for being happy whether full or hungry, hands full or hands empty. Whatever I have, wherever I am, I can make it through anything in the One who makes me who I am" (Philippians 4, *The Message*).

That's the secret. Joy is not found in having; it's found only in the source of joy. That source, of course, is Jesus. He is the One who plants His joy in our hearts. His joy produces contentment and happiness.

Knowing Christ means knowing the source of all wisdom, power, beauty, and joy. Every good thing comes from His hand, and He freely gives to God's children. So, my friend, when you're having one of those days when everything seems to be going wrong and your first inclination is to complain or be depressed, rejoice in Christ for who He is and what He's done for you.

HIS WORD

"On that day they offered great sacrifices, rejoicing because God had given them great joy. The women and children also rejoiced. The sound of rejoicing in Jerusalem could be heard far away" (Nehemiah 12:43).

MY PRAYER

Happiness is the pursuit of all people, yet most people look for it in the wrong places. Don't keep this secret to yourself! Speak out! Share your source of joy with everyone who will listen. Every day, ask the Holy Spirit to teach you what it means to say with gratitude, "The joy of the Lord is my strength."

MY STUDY *Psalm 16:11; 2 Corinthians 8:1,2*

God's Grace

Have you ever thought about the words to the song *Amazing Grace*?

> Amazing grace, how sweet the sound, that saved a wretch like me.
>
> I once was lost, but now am found. Was blind, but now I see.

God's grace truly is amazing.

Grace is a gift given freely to one who has neither earned it nor deserves it. The gift of salvation was the ultimate work of grace. But God's grace was not a one-time act. God's grace can be seen in the constant love and care that He shows for us, even though we are undeserving of it.

Read what a few of our spiritual leaders have said about God and His grace.

Oswald Chambers: "God is more tender [toward us] than we can conceive."

Matthew Henry: "[God] will wait to be gracious … wait till you return to Him and seek His face. He will wait that He may do it in the best and fittest time, when it will be most for His glory, when it will come to you with the most pleasing surprise. He will … not let slip any opportunity to be gracious to you."

John Piper: "God is gracious. He is not limited by anyone's wickedness. His grace may break out anywhere He pleases."

John 1:16 tells us where our blessings come from. "From the fullness of [Christ's] grace we have all received one blessing after another." The blessings we receive come by the grace of God, from the depths of His love.

Dear friend, this priceless gift is yours. Sing out today with renewed hope, thankfulness, and joy. As you do so, think about the last verse of this wonderful song about grace. "'Twas grace that brought me safe thus far, and grace will lead me home."

HIS WORD

"The law was given through Moses; grace and truth came through Jesus Christ" (John 1:17).

MY PRAYER

"Gracious heavenly Father, You gave Your Son as the ultimate sacrifice as an atonement for our sin so that we could receive the gift of salvation. Your infinite grace sustains us each day. I thank You that this same grace will carry me through until I see You face to face in heaven. In Your Son's mighty name, amen."

MY STUDY

Psalm 94:17–19; Jeremiah 31:31–34

Boomerang Joy

Barbara Johnson, noted Christian author and speaker, has a "boomerang" theory about joy. She flings joy beyond her neighbor's fence, across town, and into the universe. Then it curves right back to her.

Proverbs 11:25 says, "He who refreshes others will himself be refreshed." Barbara refreshes others by flinging her joy far and wide at Women of Faith conferences. She's grateful that God allowed her broken life to become a fountain of joy for others.

When you pour out God's love on others, it boomerangs back to you. You don't have to be a conference speaker and author to refresh others with joy. Choose joy in your circumstances. When you are standing in a long line at the grocery store and dinner needs to be ready soon, or when you call someone and get put on hold for what seems like forever, decide to respond with a smile or cheerful comment. You may be surprised how the response itself, knowing that you controlled your reaction, will create a joyful feeling in your heart. Ask God to restore your joy. Joy will be yours, and as you send it out to others, it will return to you — just like a boomerang!

The key to spreading joy is that you must possess a measure of true joy before you can give it away. Your source of joy cannot be based on circumstances or the attitudes of others.

Knowing Christ brings a true joy that comes from a heart made clean and whole. He is a source of strength far beyond any human emotion, and He controls our very existence.

When you know and believe these things in your heart, joy will flow so abundantly that you won't be able to contain it. It will go out to everyone you meet, spreading the love of the Savior.

HIS WORD
"The LORD has done great things for us, and we are filled with joy" (Psalm 126:3).

MY PRAYER
"Holy Lord, Your mercy and love are never-ending. The joy You have given me is beyond description. Help me to show this joy to others that they may know Your love and joy as well. All the glory, praise, and honor go to You alone. In Your wonderful name, amen."

MY STUDY
Jeremiah 31:12–14; 1 Peter 1:7–9

Can't Judge a Book

It was a crowded flight, and I ended up next to a delightful, young executive. She wore the signs of success – meticulously dressed, carrying an expensive briefcase.

Before long, Sandy began to tell me her story. She left her husband because she was frustrated with his lack of motivation. She wanted him to join her on the fast track of success, but he didn't share her drive.

She began dating other men and met someone she thought was more promising. As she became intimately involved with this man, she discovered he was involved in some illegal activities. When she confronted him, he denied it. Then he promptly dumped her.

Sandy owns a very productive advertising agency. But as we began to talk, she admitted, "I've made such bad choices. I've been depressed for two weeks. I've hit rock bottom. I'm successful, but unhappy. My life is a mess."

After hearing her story, she asked me what I did. I told her about Campus Crusade for Christ and Women Today. She could hardly believe it! She said, "This is unbelievable! I knew when you sat next to me on this plane that something significant was going to happen."

I shared *The Four Spiritual Laws* with her. It turns out that Sandy was already a believer, but was living a defeated Christian life. So I talked with her about the Holy Spirit and living an abundant, powerful, and victorious life.

Sandy was very responsive. The whole situation had caused her to question the value system she had created for herself. She admitted that she was ignoring what was really important in life. Our conversation proved to be timely. God completely revolutionized and enriched her life.

What a wonderful opportunity for me. And what a great reminder that you can't judge a book by its cover.

HIS WORD

"Do not judge, and you will not be judged. Do not condemn, and you will not be condemned. Forgive, and you will be forgiven" (Luke 6:37).

MY PRAYER

Friend, take time to speak with those around you — people like Sandy who may appear very successful, but whose hearts are hurting, and who crave what you have to offer. You will find that God's message of love will break through any differences you may have with someone.

MY STUDY

Leviticus 19:15; Proverbs 16:21

Shortly before Thanksgiving in 1985, Jay had just finished a dinner meeting in Laredo, Texas, when he was paged for a phone call. It was his pastor from Florida. He said, "Jay, you need to come home. Jeff was hit by a car as he ran after a ball. He's in heaven with the Lord."

The grief Jay felt at the loss of his 10-year-old son was overwhelming. He remembered the passage in Philippians 3 where Paul says he wants to understand the fellowship of Christ's suffering. Jay asked God to help him understand as well.

When Jay arrived home, he found a house full of people. Suddenly, he remembered a piece of paper he and his wife, Debbie, had discovered earlier. Of all things, Jeff had written a little will a few months ago. They thought it was so cute that they decided to save it and give it to him when he was older.

Read what Jeff wrote. Just ten-years old, he said, "When I die, I am 100 percent sure I will go to heaven. I was saved on July 6, 1980. It wasn't that hard to understand, except the part that He loves us all. When I die, I want everybody me or my family knows to come to my funeral. Especially all my best friends. I will miss you all."

Amazingly, more than 600 people attended the funeral, and several accepted Christ as Savior during the service. Since then, nearly one hundred more have met the Savior as a direct result of Jeff's death and his written will.

Jay says that through his suffering, he learned that the depth of God's love is the greatest lesson of all. God cares when you suffer, and He longs to comfort you. No matter why you are suffering, you can find solace in His loving hands. He will restore your joy.

HIS WORD

"Shout for joy, O heavens; rejoice, O earth; burst into song, O mountains! For the LORD comforts his people and will have compassion on his afflicted ones" (Isaiah 49:13).

MY PRAYER

"God of All Comfort, You see every tear I cry and every sorrow I bear. You have a wonderful plan for my life, and I rest secure in the knowledge that You are in control of everything. You are the Source of all my comfort and peace. In Your Son's mighty name, amen."

MY STUDY

Psalm 119:49,50; 2 Corinthians 1:5,6

Party for Agnes

A few years ago, a pastor friend was in Hawaii on business. Because of the time change, he was wide awake in the middle of the night and decided to wander out from his hotel in search of some fresh air and a cup of coffee.

While my friend made small talk with Harry, the guy behind the café counter, the door opened and several young women entered. It was about three a.m. and the women were obviously prostitutes. Apparently, they were regular customers.

One of them, whose name was Agnes, mentioned that the next day would be her birthday. No one seemed to care.

Quietly my friend said, "Hey, Harry. Tomorrow, let's give Agnes a birthday party!"

The next morning at three a.m., he arrived at the cafe carrying balloons and streamers. Harry had baked a big cake. In walked Agnes and her friends.

My friend and Harry sang Happy Birthday, and everyone joined in. When Agnes saw the cake, she began to cry.

Harry got a knife to cut the cake, but Agnes stopped him. "Please wait," she said, "I've never had a birthday cake before, and I'd like to take it home to show my mother. I'd like to keep it for a few days before we cut it."

Dear friend, we may not look like Agnes or act like her, but from God's viewpoint, we're much the same. We've all sinned and fallen short of God's standard. We don't deserve anything from Him, any more than Agnes deserved a birthday party and cake from my friend and Harry.

But God celebrated each of our lives when He gave us the most cherished gift He had – His Son. "For God so loved the world that he gave his One and only Son, that whoever believes in him shall not perish but have eternal life" (John 3:16). Cherish this gift and pass it on to others.

HIS WORD

"Above all, love each other deeply, because love covers a multitude of sins" (1 Peter 4:8).

MY PRAYER

When you and I grasp what God has done for us — as undeserving as we are — it changes our lives. There are countless thousands of women out there like Agnes, who need someone like you to throw a party for them! Let's make it our life's ambition to celebrate the worth of people in God's eyes.

MY STUDY

Psalm 86:15; Isaiah 42:5–7

Horatio Spafford was no stranger to suffering. You may not know him by name, but you will recognize his testimony.

Tragically, Horatio and his wife lost a beloved son. Not long afterward, the family suffered a huge financial loss in a devastating fire.

Then, a year later, his wife and four daughters were sailing to Europe. Their ship was struck by another vessel and sank within twelve minutes. Hundreds lost their lives.

After reaching safety, Mrs. Spafford cabled a message of two words to her husband: "Saved alone." All four girls had died.

While on the journey to reach his wife, Horatio took his sorrow and pain, his doubts and fears to Jesus. He is the only One who could give peace and hope. On the sea, near where his daughters drowned, he wrote these familiar words:

> When peace like a river attendeth my way, When sorrows like sea billows roll; Whatever my lot, Thou hast taught me to say, It is well, it is well with my soul.

No bitterness. No blaming God for the tremendous losses he had suffered. He said that, whatever his lot, he had learned to say, "It is well with my soul."

Is there a secret to dealing with tragedy? Absolutely!

I believe what brings peace and assurance in any situation is a deep heart-knowledge of God. Not just knowing in our minds, but knowing to the very core of our soul.

Paul writes, "I have lost all things. I consider them rubbish, that I may gain Christ and be found in him" (Philippians 3:8,9).

Not only can we know Christ, but He is right here with us every step of the way, now and for all eternity. Whatever we are feeling, He knows and is waiting to comfort and help us. That gave Horatio Spafford hope, and it gives us hope, too!

HIS WORD
"Those who suffer he delivers in their suffering; he speaks to them in their affliction" (Job 36:15).

MY PRAYER
"Loving, powerful Savior, life can bring pain, heartache, and sorrow. But because I know that it is well with my soul, I know You will give peace and hope in the midst of any storm in my life. You meet the deepest needs of my heart."

MY STUDY
Psalm 119:106–108; Romans 5:1–5

The Spiritual Lifeline

Humans can live without food for forty days, without water for eight days, without air for four minutes. But how long can we live without hope?

A friend once told me about his lovely English grandmother, Grandma Dorothy.

Grandma Dorothy lived a full and beautiful life, giving her heart to Christ in her early twenties. She reared two sons, who gave her ten grandchildren and twenty-two great-grandchildren. She died at age 93.

Because she and her beloved husband brought Christianity into the family tree, generations will serve Him and find their hope in him. But one of her sons, now in his seventies, has yet to place his trust and faith in Jesus Christ. So the day of Grandma Dorothy's funeral, the family noticed a stark contrast in reactions.

For the unbelieving son, it was a day of deep mourning and tragedy. His tears fell from a heart without hope. He'd lived a life in denial of Jesus, placing his hope in success and wealth. When his mother died, the loss was more than he could bear.

For the believing son, however, the day was quite different. It was a time of sadness, but also a time of celebration, knowing that his mother was home with Jesus. He shared her hope, which far outweighed his sense of grief.

Friend, we can believe with conviction that when our hope is placed in Jesus, we won't be disappointed. We can have every confidence in Him.

I like Eugene Peterson's paraphrase of Hebrews 6: "We who have run for our very lives to God have every reason to grab the promised hope with both hands and never let go. It's an unbreakable spiritual lifeline" (*The Message*).

Don't place your faith in anything other than Jesus – the giver of every good and perfect gift! As you learn to put your hope in Him, you'll influence generations to come.

HIS WORD

"Blessed is he … whose hope is in the LORD his God, the Maker of heaven and earth" (Psalm 146:5,6).

MY PRAYER

What will the generations after you say about you when you are gone? Will they be able to say, "She trusted in Christ, and that gives us hope"? By your faithful example, it's never too late to instill hope in the generations that follow. Live your faith.

MY STUDY

Joel 3:16; Romans 8:23–25

One of the most memorable events of the 1984 Olympic Games in Los Angeles was the 20K walk. The race included several laps in the Coliseum, distance around the city streets, then a final lap in the Coliseum.

Soon after the start of the race, an unknown competitor from El Salvador fell significantly behind. Nonetheless, he kept walking as fast as he could. Eventually, the others caught up to him and passed him.

All the other walkers completed their Coliseum laps and headed out to the city streets, but the guy from El Salvador still had two laps to go. As this lone walker circled the track two more times, 100,000 pairs of eyes watched him.

He kept on walking. The crowd began to cheer. There was a sense of shared joy – pride even – that this one person, in the midst of a massive crowd, would stay in the race.

At first, spectators had cheered for their own countrymen. Now they were united for this lone walker. They cheered, clapped, waved flags, even chanted, "El Salvador! El Salvador! El Salvador!"

The cheering faded as he disappeared from the Coliseum into the city streets to try to catch up with his competition. Later, the walkers returned for their final lap, and the gold medal was won.

Much later, a figure appeared in the Coliseum tunnel. It was the El Salvadoran walker. Four hours after the race had begun, he finished his final lap.

The entire crowd stood to their feet. They cheered. They chanted.

He crossed the finish line! Then he collapsed. An ambulance came along and picked him up. Instead of discretely slipping out of the Coliseum, the ambulance circled in a victory lap. In unison, the crowd cheered.

Dear friend, God has given the victory at the end of your race. Persevere in your faith. The battle is won!

HIS WORD

"Therefore, since we are surrounded by such a great cloud of witnesses, let us throw off everything that hinders and the sin that so easily entangles, and let us run with perseverance the race marked out for us" (Hebrews 12:1).

MY PRAYER

My friend, you may not feel you have the perseverance of an Olympic athlete, but when your eyes are fixed on Jesus, you can finish the race. Keep moving one step at a time. Look to God for guidance, power, and support. He will provide it.

MY STUDY

Ecclesiastes 9:11; Isaiah 40:31

The Neighborly Gospel

My friends, Norm and Becky, lived in their first home for three years.

As friendly people, they visited with their neighbors over the backyard fence, in the front yard, and at block parties. During those visits, they told stories about their lives. However, they began to realize that they never once talked about God.

As Christians, Norm and Becky knew God wanted them to share with others about His love and grace, but they didn't know how.

One day, after having an argument over this very issue, Norm and Becky prayed. They asked God to forgive them and to show them what to do. Just a few days later, a friend invited them to a seminar to learn how to share their faith. That weekend changed their lives.

They learned to use *The Four Spiritual Laws*. It's a short booklet my husband wrote many years ago, which simply tells of God's love and how a person can know God in a personal way.

Norm and Becky began using their home as a place to share their faith with others. They started talking about God in casual conversations and planned outreach events. The first of those events was a Christmas party for twenty-five of their neighbors.

The evening began with the guests sharing Christmas memories. Then Norm told the story of how he came to trust Christ.

As Norm and Becky continued sharing their faith, many of their neighbors placed their trust in Christ. Now, more than twenty years later, the children and grandchildren of these neighbors are trusting Christ as well.

That is so exciting! When Norm and Becky asked God to show them what to do, He did. And because they were "neighborly" with the gospel, many others are now living for Christ.

You, too, can share God's love through hospitality. All it takes is a joyful heart that is open to sharing with others.

HIS WORD

"Each of us should please his neighbor for his good, to build him up" (Romans 15:2).

MY PRAYER

Ask God to show you how to reach out to your neighbors. Then pray for each one. Invite a few of them over for pizza, dessert, or a picnic. Plan a time of conversation. Tell briefly how you trusted Christ. Then share the gospel message using a simple evangelistic tool like The Four Spiritual Laws, *and encourage them to pray aloud with you the prayer at the end.*

MY STUDY *Deuteronomy 31:12; Psalm 143:7,8*

Many years ago, my friend Mary was timid about sharing God's love with others. She said, "I wanted to be a 'mysterious witness' for Christ. I only wanted to tell people about Him if they asked."

Then Mary met Joyce, a staff member with Campus Crusade for Christ. Mary admired Joyce and her knowledge of God. Together, they studied Bible verses about the character of Jesus. Deep in Mary's heart, she longed to tell others about Jesus Christ. But still, she was hesitant.

Joyce was at the early stages of developing a concept called Christmas Gatherings – an outreach ministry to friends and neighbors. These gatherings are coffees, teas, or dessert parties designed to tell others about Jesus Christ. During the Christmas season, a person invites several friends and neighbors into her home. After spending some time getting to know one another over coffee and cookies, there's a short Christmas program. Then a designated speaker tells how knowing Jesus Christ has made a difference in her life, briefly explaining the gospel message of God's love and including an opportunity for each one to trust Christ.

Joyce was scheduled to speak at a gathering, so she asked Mary to attend with her and to pray for her as she spoke. It was there that Mary understood how simple it can be to tell others about Christ.

During the next fifteen years, Mary became a Christmas Gatherings enthusiast. When her husband's job transferred the family to Hong Kong, she introduced this wonderful outreach concept to those in her church. Many Chinese nationals learned to reach out to their friends and colleagues using these parties. They're still having Christmas Gatherings today.

There is no greater news to share with others than the forgiveness available through Jesus Christ. And there's no easier time than during the Christmas season as we celebrate the birth of the King of kings and Lord of lords.

HIS WORD

"Therefore the Lord himself will give you a sign: The virgin will be with child and will give birth to a son, and will call him Immanuel" (Isaiah 7:14).

MY PRAYER

On the night Jesus Christ was born, angels went to the shepherds in the fields to tell them "Christ the Savior is born." Hosting a tea or luncheon in your home is a wonderful way to tell others this same news. Will you consider doing this for the people you know?

MY STUDY

Proverbs 15:30; Luke 2:8–20

High-Button Shoes

The barrel of goods arrived for Margaret's family. They were missionaries and that's how their supplies arrived. There was excitement as they opened it.

Margaret was only ten years old, and she learned a valuable lesson from her mother that day. Margaret's father unpacked the barrel. When he got to the bottom, he happily called out, "Look, Margaret. God answered our prayers. We have shoes!" Then he held up two pairs of old-fashioned, high-button shoes.

Margaret scoffed at the shoes. She wanted in-style oxfords, not the out-of-style high-button shoes. She cried out, "Oh, Papa, they are too big," hoping she wouldn't have to wear them. But Papa assured her that they could stuff cotton in the toes, and they'd last a long time.

Her loving mother quietly said, "Margaret, we prayed for shoes, and now we have shoes. Wear your shoes with a thankful and a humble heart, for it's not so important what you have on your feet, but it's very important where the feet go."

Margaret realized that she'd have to wear the shoes. But she'd have a choice in how she'd wear them: either with deep rebellion or with a thankful heart.

God knows you. He knows your every need. The Bible says that He even knows the number of hairs on your head, and that His thoughts about you are more than the grains of sand in the ocean. That's a God who cares. A God who wants what is absolutely best for you. A God who will provide for your every need.

Dear friend, trust God's provision and be thankful. Even if what you receive is not what you expected, thank God anyway. In time, you may understand more clearly God's provision for you. And a thankful heart will make all the difference in the joy you experience in life. God is worthy of your praise.

HIS WORD

"Everything God created is good, and nothing is to be rejected if it is received with thanksgiving, because it is consecrated by the word of God and prayer" (1 Timothy 4:4).

MY PRAYER

Today, make a list of your greatest needs. At the top of the page write the words: "Always be thankful." As you pray for these needs every day, thank God in advance for how and when He'll provide. Then rest in the assurance that He is faithful.

MY STUDY

Deuteronomy 8:10; Psalm 95:1–3

When birthdays come or Christmas approaches, what do you buy for the person who has everything? If you're like I am, it can take days, even weeks to find the perfect present for someone you love.

Through the years, however, I've been helped by some wonderful friends who have learned to break free from the traditional mold of gift giving – creative people who prepare thoughtful presentations that don't always require large sums of money.

One woman's husband had grown quite jaded about Christmas. The commercialism of the whole season had bothered him to the point where he couldn't enjoy giving or receiving presents. His wife knew he loved coaching the local high school wrestling team, and they needed new uniforms.

So she secretly donated new uniforms for the entire wrestling team. On Christmas morning, he opened an envelope that revealed her secret. She gave this team what they needed in his honor. It was their family secret. He was so pleased, and it ignited his passion for Christmastime. Every Christmas since, they've continued to give creative gifts.

Recently, a friend of mine celebrated her forty-first birthday. For nearly thirty of those years, she'd been a zealous witness for Jesus Christ.

Kim trusted Christ after Debbie shared the gospel with her in high school. Now Kim is married and has four small boys. To help Debbie celebrate her birthday, Kim sent a video of her sons chanting, "Happy birthday, Debbie. And thank you for leading our mommy to Jesus!" Debbie cried. It was the perfect gift of encouragement.

Giving gifts is not about how much money you spend. God gave us the most wonderful gift of all, and no amount of money could compare with it. Remember this the next time you need to get a gift for someone. Give creatively from the heart.

HIS WORD

"How priceless is your unfailing love! Both high and low among men find refuge in the shadow of your wings. They feast on the abundance of your house; you give them drink from your river of delights" (Psalm 36:7,8).

MY PRAYER

There are so many ways to express our love and appreciation for one another. Think of a way to give a gift without ever going to the mall. Plan ahead for birthdays, Christmas, or other occasions. The more time you have, the more creative you can be.

MY STUDY

Ruth 2:8–18; Matthew 6:1–4

The Savior

This was Michelle's first Christmas as a Christian. As a Jewish teenager, she'd placed her faith in Jesus Christ. Now, she longed to celebrate the birth of her Savior.

Michelle's parents were adamantly against her newfound faith. Although they didn't practice the rituals of their Jewish faith, they held it closely to their hearts.

They didn't let their daughter attend church with her Christian friends, but Michelle found other ways to grow in her faith. She read Christian books, met with other believers at school, and listened to Christian radio.

Michelle wanted to go to a Christmas Eve service, but her parents would not give permission.

On Christmas Eve, she went to her bedroom. She turned on the radio to listen to Christmas carols. Michelle said, "I heard them as if for the first time. They were like breathtaking praise." While the music played, Michelle spent the evening alone reading God's Word.

On Christmas morning, there was no laughter in her home, and there were no presents. But Michelle awakened with a sense of awe. Her joy overflowed as she realized she had the greatest gift of all – God's gift of His Son, Jesus Christ.

Michelle's first Christmas set the tone for many others to come. She seldom lets the hustle and bustle of the season rob her of the joy of celebrating the birth of Jesus Christ. She says, "Those years of celebrating alone in my room stripped the holiday of all but the Baby King resting in a manger."

Michelle has learned a truth many of us need to learn: The only thing that matters at Christmas is the fact that the King of kings was born in a manger. He was God's gift to us in human form. What a good reason to celebrate – at Christmas and throughout the year!

HIS WORD

"[Christ Jesus,] who, being in very nature God, did not consider equality with God something to be grasped, but made himself nothing, taking the very nature of a servant, being made in human likeness" (Philippians 2:6,7).

MY PRAYER

God became a human in the Person of Jesus Christ. Our relationship with Jesus gives meaning to our Christmas celebrations, public and private. This Christmas, focus on Jesus Christ — His birth, His life, His ministry, His death, His forgiveness, His deity, His resurrection, and His eternal love.

MY STUDY *Psalm 130:7,8; Isaiah 42:10–12*

The birth of Jesus is the most celebrated of stories, but it is sometimes told very modestly by excited schoolchildren for very proud parents.

Thirty years ago, *Guideposts* magazine told the story of nine-year-old Wally. Wally was a bit slower than others his age, but he was kind, helpful, and happy. Because he was bigger than his classmates, his teacher cast him as the formidable innkeeper.

The angels appeared in coat-hanger halos, and shepherds carried walking-cane staffs. It was magical. Mesmerized, Wally could hardly wait to make his entrance.

Soon Mary and Joseph wandered across the stage. Joseph knocked on the door of the inn. This was Wally's moment. "What do you want?" he asked. "We seek lodging," Joseph answered. "Seek it elsewhere. The inn is filled," the innkeeper said sternly.

Joseph kept pleading. The innkeeper kept refusing. "Please, good innkeeper, this is my wife, Mary. She is heavy with child and needs a place to rest. Surely you must have some small corner for her. She is so tired."

The innkeeper paused.

A voice prompted him from the wings. "No. Be gone," he repeated.

As the disappointed couple walked off, the innkeeper watched. Concern replaced his stern gaze. Tears filled his eyes. The tough innkeeper transformed into Wally, the kind-hearted boy.

"Don't go, Joseph," he called out. "Bring Mary back." Smiling brightly, he said, "You can have *my* room."

Wally's tender innocence magnifies how easy it is to allow our hearts to be desensitized to the meaning of Christmas. We may have accepted Christ as Savior, but life's activities and demands have crowded Him out. Making room in our hearts for Jesus should be a daily decision. Giving Him priority in our lives is the greatest way to demonstrate our thankfulness for His gift of eternal life.

HIS WORD

"Sing to him, sing praise to him; tell of all his wonderful acts. Glory in his holy name; let the hearts of those who seek the LORD rejoice" (Psalm 105:2,3).

MY PRAYER

"Dear Father, I want to always have room in my heart for Your Son. Thank You for the many blessings of the holiday season. I ask You to help me have a childlike wonder as I share the holidays with family and friends, and help me remember Your gift throughout the year. Amen."

MY STUDY

2 Samuel 22:26,27; Matthew 8:20

Trusting Relationships

It was a nice suburb where everyone minded his own business and went about day-to-day living. But for Joanne, the neighborhood had become a point of concern. She was deeply burdened for the women who lived in the well-maintained homes. The neighborhood was more than dwellings and yards and shade trees. These women were people with souls, and Joanne had reason to believe that most of them did not know Christ personally.

Joanne decided to work her way up and down the street – establishing friendships with those near her home. At first, her neighbors were suspicious of her motives. But with persistence – going back a second and third time and bringing baked goodies on occasion – the walls began to break down.

At Christmas time, she invited several people to her home for a party. To her delight, quite a few showed up.

Finally, after three years in the neighborhood, Joanne had comfortable and trusting relationships with five women near her house. She had even shared the gospel with them a number of times.

Although none of them had accepted Christ yet, they were quite interested in spiritual things and wanted to begin a Bible study together. None of this would have happened had Joanne not been persistent and patient in her pursuit of their friendship.

One of the greatest misconceptions among Christians is that people do not want to know God. In fact, just the opposite is true! People today are turning to God, hoping to find spiritual solutions to their problems.

There are men and women in your neighborhood who want answers to life's big questions. Dear friend, establish friendships with those around you. Let them see the love of the Savior in you. Then, maybe they too will come to know Christ – the One who can fulfill them and give them peace.

HIS WORD
"Whoever is wise, let him heed these things and consider the great love of the LORD"
(Psalm 107:43).

MY PRAYER
Do you know the people in your neighborhood? Take the initiative to meet them. Invite them over for coffee, dinner, or a family barbecue. Above all, be available to them as a model of Christ, demonstrating His love in all that you do. Ask God to help you and let Him work through you. He will.

MY STUDY
Jeremiah 33:3; Romans 5:6–8

Celebrate the temporary
Don't wait until tomorrow
Live Today
Celebrate the simple things

Enjoy the butterfly
Embrace the snow
Run with the ocean
Delight in the trees

Or a single lonely flower

Go barefoot in the wet grass

Don't wait
Until all the problems are solved
Or all the bills are paid

You will wait forever
Eternity will come and go
And you
Will still be waiting

Live in the now
With all its problems and its agonies
With its joy
And its pain

Celebrate your pain
Your despair
Your anger
It means you're alive
Look closer
Breath deeper
Stand taller
Stop grieving the past

There is joy and beauty
Today

It is temporary
Here now and gone
So celebrate it
While you can
Celebrate the Temporary!

By Clyde Reid

HIS WORD
"Therefore do not worry about tomorrow, for tomorrow will worry about itself. Each day has enough trouble of its own" (Matthew 6:34).

MY PRAYER
Each day is a gift from God. Take time today to refresh your spirit by reading God's Word. Spend time talking to Him. Enjoy His presence, sit quietly, and listen for His words to you. Allow the Holy Spirit full control of your life. Trust Him.

MY STUDY
1 Samuel 2:1; Psalm 33:21,22

The Blessings Book

Doreen and her husband moved to Orlando to attend seminary. Leaving family and friends was difficult, but when they arrived in Florida and stepped out of the rented moving truck, they felt they had entered a wasteland. The stifling heat was not how they had pictured Florida.

Doreen knew they had obeyed God's leading to attend seminary, and she made a decision to be very alert to every way that God blessed them in their decision. Doreen and her husband had trusted God to provide in the past, but this major move brought unique challenges for them financially.

Soon after settling into life as seminary students, they received $100 in the mail. No specific request had been made for the money, but God knew their need.

Doreen decided to create a "Blessings Book" to keep an account of the many ways God was honoring their obedience to His call. She wrote down every detail of God's provision for them that first year in seminary. Sometimes the entry was as simple as the blessing of "peace of mind" or "confidence for exams." The blessings of God recorded in the book created a beautiful journal for reflection and praise to the Giver of every good gift. If loneliness or frustration brought anxiety, Doreen could always read her journal and be reminded of the goodness of God and His faithfulness.

Long after the seminary days, the "Blessings Book" serves as a reminder to her of how many times God provided for the physical, emotional, and spiritual needs of a couple who stepped out in obedience to His call.

Dear one, God is blessing you every day. He has saved us from condemnation; He provides for our needs on this earth; and He is preparing us for eternity with Him. Give thanks to God for the things – big and small – that He does for you. Let your heart delight in His ever-present love.

HIS WORD

"Every good and perfect gift is from above, coming down from the Father of the heavenly lights, who does not change like shifting shadows" (James 1:17).

MY PRAYER

Choose to accept the blessing of God's presence in your life. I know He is willing and able to provide for all your needs. Start your own "Blessings Book," recording each blessing as you receive it. You may be surprised at how generous God can be.

MY STUDY

Psalm 77:11–15; Jeremiah 32:18–20

The Pursuit of Happiness

Life, liberty, and the pursuit of happiness. Isn't that guaranteed by the Constitution of the United States? Of course, we all know the key word is "pursuit." The manner in which we obtain happiness is very personal. The inward desires of our heart determine how actively we will pursue any goal.

Experts today have created elaborate prescriptions for finding true happiness, yet we know that many people are sad, lonely, and dejected. Talk shows offer solutions to many situations that might infringe on our happiness. In reality, we know that making the pursuit of happiness our life's goal can bring frustration and futility.

When Jesus taught the crowds in Galilee, He gave us the most accurate prescription for happiness. Interestingly, it doesn't include much of what our society would use as measurement. Allow these words of our Savior to mold your thinking about true happiness.

> Blessed are the poor in spirit, for theirs is the kingdom of heaven.
>
> Blessed are those who mourn, for they will be comforted.
>
> Blessed are the meek, for they will inherit the earth.
>
> Blessed are those who hunger and thirst for righteousness, for they will be filled.
>
> Blessed are the merciful, for they will be shown mercy.
>
> Blessed are the pure in heart, for they will see God.
>
> Blessed are the peacemakers, for they will be called sons of God.
>
> Blessed are those who are persecuted because of righteousness, for theirs is the kingdom of heaven.
>
> Blessed are you when people insult you, persecute you and falsely say all kinds of evil against you because of me. Rejoice and be glad, because great is your reward in heaven, for in the same way they persecuted the prophets who were before you (Matthew 5:3–12).

When we surrender our heart and life to Jesus Christ, we gain new perspectives on what brings happiness.

HIS WORD
"I rejoice at Your word as one who finds great treasure" (Psalm 119:162, NKJ).

MY PRAYER
"Blessed Lord Jesus, I recognize that true happiness comes from You, not from people or possessions. You want us to give when others take, to love when others hate, and to help when others abuse. In doing this, we gain and others lose. Use Your Word and Your Spirit to mold me into the person You want me to be. Amen."

MY STUDY
Isaiah 55:1–3; Romans 14:16–18

Just Enough Time

It is impossible to get through the holiday season without scanning at least one magazine that has the ultimate answer on how to organize your time and be "super-woman" for your family, friends, and coworkers. We all know it is not possible to do "everything," and yet we try and try again.

For the woman who has a time management plan throughout the year, the holiday season does not bring stress but an opportunity to demonstrate that a plan can work. Basically, time management is thinking ahead, planning what you are going to do before you do it. It encompasses stewardship of your time, talent, and treasure – of all that God has given to you. Time management involves determining what you really want to accomplish and then putting those goals into your plans for a week, a year, and a lifetime.

Many times people feel that a schedule is limiting. They don't want to be organized because they like to do what they want, when they want. Of course, some consider this liberating. However, I have found that nothing has liberated me more than planning ahead after seeking God's wisdom.

Time management is not designed to confine, but to give you freedom to organize yourself to accomplish the things you feel are important and worthwhile, and that contribute to making you the person you want to be. Remember to build time into your schedule to take care of yourself.

Time management is a part of God's plan. Remember, among the fruit of the Spirit is "self-control" or management of yourself. When you take the time to plan ahead, you are also consciously setting priorities in your life. The things that are important to you are then given due attention in your schedule.

Be a good steward of your time. God will multiply your effort.

HIS WORD
"The plans of the diligent lead to profit as surely as haste leads to poverty" (Proverbs 21:5).

MY PRAYER
"Father, thank You for a world of order. Your creation is glorious, and I marvel at Your handiwork. Please give me a heart to establish order in my life. I want to glorify You in the activities of my days and share Your joy with a searching world. In Jesus' matchless name, amen."

MY STUDY
Isaiah 32:7,8; James 4:13–15

Abba Father

Three little words contain the most profound statement of fact ever made: "God loves you!" But it wouldn't surprise me if there are times when you forget the *truth* in those words.

In his book *Abba's Child*, Brennan Manning tells this story:

Edward Farrell, a priest in Detroit, went on vacation to Ireland. He stayed with his only living uncle, who was about to celebrate a milestone birthday.

On the day of his uncle's eightieth birthday, the two men got up before dawn. Silently, they dressed for the day. Then they went on a quiet walk along the shores of Lake Killarney. They stopped to watch the sunrise. Still in reverent silence, they watched the splendor and majesty of God's creative handiwork.

Suddenly, Edward's uncle turned and left. When Edward looked up to see him, he was skipping down the road.

Edward called out to him, "Uncle Seamus, you really look happy."

"I am, lad," the uncle replied.

Edward was curious. He asked, "Want to tell me why?"

"Yes," Uncle Seamus began in his thick Irish brogue. "You see, me Abba [God] is very fond of me."

Do you know in your heart of hearts that your Abba – God the Father – is fond of you? That He likes you?

Brennan Manning asks this similar question: "Do you honestly believe God likes you, not just loves you because theologically God has to love you?"

God does like you. He created you. Yes, you do things that displease God. I do, too. But that doesn't discount the *reality* of God's very deep affection and abiding love for you! In fact, it *proves* He loves you.

Remember, John 3:16 says, "For God so loved the world that he gave his one and only Son ..." He didn't do it because He had to. He gave His Son, Jesus, because of His great love for each one of us.

HIS WORD

"Both the one who makes men holy and those who are made holy are of the same family. So Jesus is not ashamed to call them brothers" (Hebrews 2:11).

MY PRAYER

Turn to the Word of the God who loves you. Read five chapters in Psalms every day, and you'll finish the book in one month. As you do, write down every verse about God's love. Then, whenever you begin to feel unloved, or that God doesn't care, read through your list. You'll be reminded of the truth.

MY STUDY

Genesis 1:26–31; Psalm 149:4,5

Neighborhood Lighthouse

A few years ago, some friends in Orlando hosted a Christmas Gathering. They invited every woman in their neighborhood. Many came. They had an enjoyable time getting to know one another, sharing Christmas traditions, and hearing someone share the real meaning of Christmas.

The girl next door was unmarried but lived with her boyfriend. At first, she said she wanted to come to the neighborhood gathering, but later declined.

About two months later, very late one night, there was a knock at the door of my friend's house. The young woman was in the middle of a fight with her boyfriend and needed to talk. For a few hours, she poured out her heart to my friend.

She wondered if God was punishing her, if He loved her, if she was in trouble with Him. My friend talked to her about the love and forgiveness available in Jesus Christ.

Isn't it interesting? That person didn't even attend the Christmas dessert, but just by being invited, she knew my friend was safe if she needed help.

My friend's home is a lighthouse in that neighborhood. Jesus said, "Let your light shine before men, that they may see your good deeds and praise your Father in heaven" (Matthew 5:16).

Think for a minute about the street where you live. If someone on your street needed prayer or wanted to talk with someone, where would she go? If she wanted to know Jesus Christ, who could tell her how? Will you be the ambassador for Christ on your street?

Think of ways to open your home. Ask a woman over for coffee, or a few friends in for dessert. Have a couple over for dinner. Then turn these times of casual encounters into life-changing moments to talk about your relationship with Christ.

Celebrate Jesus in your neighborhood so that all may see Him.

HIS WORD
"I, the LORD, have called you in righteousness; I will take hold of your hand. I will keep you and will make you to be a covenant for the people and a light for the Gentiles" (Isaiah 42:6).

MY PRAYER
Ask God to help you be more aware of your neighbors and to be friendly when you see them. Learn their names. Pray for them individually. If you don't know what to pray, find Bible verses (such as Ephesians 1:18,19) to pray back to God.

MY STUDY
Psalm 119:105; Matthew 5:13–16

The date, time, and place had been set. The team arrived just a few minutes early. They waited and waited, but their Chinese contact never showed up.

Chris and his team were missionaries in China. They were carrying Bibles to a specific Chinese contact. But now what would they do? Afraid they were being watched, they walked all the way to the edge of town.

The team stopped in a park to rest, get a drink of water, and pray. They noticed three very dirty, ragged men under a nearby tree. Chris sensed God leading him to offer them some water. As he gave it to them, one man uttered, in clear English, the password – the very password their Chinese contact would have used at the "appointed" meeting place.

Chris's team was thrilled. They were awestruck as they listened to the men's story. They'd been walking for two-and-a-half months from north China. They had crossed snowy mountains, a desert, and several rivers. They didn't know the country and didn't have a map. They walked by faith in God.

The men could only explain that it was God who had shown them where to go. He told them when to be at this park and to expect a team to have Bibles.

When the travel-weary men saw the Bibles, they wept. Then they gave pure, genuine praise to their sovereign God.

Chris and his team then went the extra mile. They exchanged the clothes off their backs and even their shoes with the three men. Chris said it was an honor to wear those dirty rags.

My heart is touched by the deep, resolute commitment to God by both of these teams. When I hear stories like this, my faith seems so shallow.

My friend, how far would you walk by faith? Our God is faithful to walk beside us.

HIS WORD

"Commit your way to the LORD; trust in him and he will do this: He will make your righteousness shine like the dawn, the justice of your cause like the noonday sun" (Psalm 37:5,6).

MY PRAYER

"Lord Jesus, You are more than worthy of our praise. I am so humbled to hear of these men walking so far, not by sight, but by faith in You alone. Help me to walk by faith in my life. I want to trust You with every step I take. You are worthy, Lord Jesus. Amen."

MY STUDY

Matthew 17:20; 2 Chronicles 20:20,21

Enlarging Your Heart

It was almost Christmas, and Lauren was feeling desperately lonely. She'd just ended a romance and had no close friends. Lauren, an attorney in Miami, had achieved much success in her career, but her personal life felt empty.

An invitation she received in the mail from someone she'd known in law school intrigued her. It was an invitation to a Christmas Gathering. The invitation explained that there'd be dessert and they'd share Christmas traditions. Then someone would talk about the "real" meaning of Christmas.

Lauren decided to attend. At her friend's house, she heard the gospel. The speaker talked about God's forgiveness. Lauren said she was absolutely amazed to hear that God even forgave *her* sins – those of the past, present, and future. Lauren knew if there was anything she needed, it was forgiveness.

So that day in her friend's home over coffee and dessert, she trusted Christ. She received His complete forgiveness. She knew immediately that this truth was the most wonderful news she'd ever heard. As she looked around the room at the other women, she wondered, *Are you taking this in? Are you hearing what she's saying? This is incredible!*

When Lauren left that day, she sat outside in her car and cried for a long time. Tears of joy flowed as she realized that she really was forgiven for her sins. As she sat in her car, everything seemed bigger, the sky seemed bluer, the grass greener. "My own heart," she said, "had grown about ten sizes!"

Lauren now spends time telling others about this wonderful news of forgiveness through Jesus Christ and how they, too, can know Jesus as their personal Savior.

One believer shared with someone in need. That person then became a believer, grew in the faith, and shared with others. What a wonderful cycle of faith! God will use you, too, in this cycle if you will let Him.

HIS WORD
"The things you have heard me say in the presence of many witnesses entrust to reliable men who will also be qualified to teach others" (2 Timothy 2:2).

MY PRAYER
"Lord Jesus, my Savior, thank You for Your redeeming sacrifice on the cross. I know that there are people all around me who are hurting. Please use me to show these people Your love and to point them to Your salvation. In Your righteous name, amen."

MY STUDY
2 Chronicles 6:24–27; Psalm 25:8

Iremember the day a doctor walked into the room where I was waiting. He looked at me and said, "Mrs. Bright, your husband is a very ill man."

From the moment we were told Bill had contracted pulmonary fibrosis, our lives changed dramatically. His diagnosis was not what I expected, but I know God was not surprised.

Throughout my husband's illness, there were times of encouragement and times of concern. We experienced a mixture of pain, disappointment, frustration, joy, and great blessing.

No matter what, we enjoyed every day together and refused to complain. Our secret?

We lived by the verse found in Philippians 4:4, which says, "Rejoice in the Lord always. I will say it again: Rejoice!"

Bill and I lived a lifestyle of rejoicing. We rejoiced in the Lord *always* — even when things weren't perfect or pleasant.

Philippians also says to pray: "Do not be anxious about anything, but in everything, by prayer and petition, with thanksgiving, present your requests to God. And the peace of God, which transcends all understanding, will guard your hearts and your minds in Christ Jesus." (4:6-7).

So, according to His Word, we prayed. And we knew of many others who were praying for us, which uplifted us greatly.

Through it all, God was so good, and we saw tremendous answers to prayer. No matter the circumstances, God is always wonderful and faithful to give what is needed at that moment.

What are you facing today? Is it illness? Financial problems? Relationship struggles? No matter what the challenge is, I would encourage you to rejoice in the Lord always and give thanks to Him for His faithfulness. Then you can rest in the peace that only He can give.

HIS WORD
"Have mercy on me, O God, have mercy on me, for in you my soul takes refuge. I will take refuge in the shadow of your wings until the disaster has passed. I cry out to God Most High, to God, who fulfills [his purpose] for me" (Psalm 57:1-2).

MY PRAYER
"Dear Lord, I rejoice in You today. Thank you for your faithfulness. Your goodness, love, and mercy never end. I know you are always working, even when I can't see it. I will rest in You because I know You have everything under Your control, and I trust You. In Your matchless name I pray, amen."

MY STUDY *Philippians 4:4-9; Psalm 32:11*

Beginning Your Journey of Joy

These four principles are essential in beginning a journey of joy.

One – *God loves you and created you to know Him personally.*

GOD'S LOVE

"God so loved the world that He gave His one and only Son, that whoever believes in Him shall not perish but have eternal life" (John 3:16).

GOD'S PLAN

"Now this is eternal life: that they may know you, the only true God, and Jesus Christ, whom you have sent" (John 17:3).

What prevents us from knowing God personally?

Two – *People are sinful and separated from God, so we cannot know Him personally or experience His love.*

PEOPLE ARE SINFUL

"All have sinned and fall short of the glory of God" (Romans 3:23).

People were created to have fellowship with God; but, because of our own stubborn self-will, we chose to go our own independent way and fellowship with God was broken. This self-will, characterized by an attitude of active rebellion or passive indifference, is an evidence of what the Bible calls sin.

PEOPLE ARE SEPARATED

"The wages of sin is death" [spiritual separation from God] (Romans 6:23).

This diagram illustrates that God is holy and people are sinful. A great gulf separates the two. The arrows illustrate that people are continually trying to reach God and establish a personal relationship with Him through our own efforts, such as a good life, philosophy, or religion—but we inevitably fail.

The third principle explains the only way to bridge this gulf ...

Three – *Jesus Christ is God's only provision for our sin. Through Him alone we can know God personally and experience His love.*

HE DIED IN OUR PLACE

"God demonstrates His own love toward us, in that while we were yet sinners, Christ died for us" (Romans 5:8).

HE ROSE FROM THE DEAD

"Christ died for our sins ... He was buried ... He was raised on the third day according to the Scriptures ... He appeared to Peter, then to the twelve. After that He appeared to more than five hundred ..." (1 Corinthians 15:3–6).

HE IS THE ONLY WAY TO GOD

"Jesus said to him, 'I am the way, and the truth, and the life; no one comes to the Father but through Me'" (John 14:6).

This diagram illustrates that God has bridged the gulf that separates us from Him by sending His Son, Jesus Christ, to die on the cross in our place to pay the penalty for our sins.

It is not enough just to know these three truths ...

Four – *We must individually receive Jesus Christ as Savior and Lord; then we can know God personally and experience His love.*

WE MUST RECEIVE CHRIST

"As many as received Him, to them He gave the right to become children of God, even to those who believe in His name" (John 1:12).

WE RECEIVE CHRIST THROUGH FAITH

"By grace you have been saved through faith; and that not of yourselves, it is the gift of God; not as a result of works that no one should boast" (Ephesians 2:8,9).

WHEN WE RECEIVE CHRIST, WE EXPERIENCE A NEW BIRTH

(Read John 3:1–8.)

WE RECEIVE CHRIST BY PERSONAL INVITATION

[Christ speaking] "Behold, I stand at the door and knock; if anyone hears My voice and opens the door, I will come in to him" (Revelation 3:20).

Receiving Christ involves turning to God from self (repentance) and trusting Christ to come into our lives to forgive us of our sins and to make us what He wants us to be. Just to agree intellectually that Jesus Christ is the Son of God and that He died on the cross for our sins is not enough. Nor is it enough to have an emotional experience. We receive Jesus Christ by faith, as an act of our will.

Self-Directed Life
S – Self is on the throne
† – Christ is outside the life
● – Interests are directed by self, often resulting in discord and frustration

Christ-Directed Life
† – Christ is in the life and on the throne
S – Self is yielding to Christ
● – Interests are directed by Christ, resulting in harmony with God's plan

These two circles represent two kinds of lives:

Which circle best represents your life?

Which circle would you like to have represent your life?

The following explains how you can receive Christ:

YOU CAN RECEIVE CHRIST RIGHT NOW BY FAITH THROUGH PRAYER (Prayer is talking with God)

God knows your heart and is not so concerned with your words as He is with the attitude of your heart. The following is a suggested prayer:

> Lord Jesus, I want to know You personally. Thank You for dying on the cross for my sins. I open the door of my life and receive You as my Savior and Lord. Thank You for forgiving my sins and giving me eternal life. Take control of the throne of my life. Make me the kind of person You want me to be.

Does this prayer express the desire of your heart?

If it does, I invite you to pray this prayer right now, and Christ will come into your life, as He promised.

HOW TO KNOW THAT CHRIST IS IN YOUR LIFE

Did you receive Christ into your life? According to His promise in Revelation 3:20, where is Christ right now in relation to you? Christ said that He would come into your life. Would He mislead you? On what authority do you know that God has answered your prayer? (The trustworthiness of God Himself and His Word.)

THE BIBLE PROMISES ETERNAL LIFE TO ALL WHO RECEIVE CHRIST

"The witness is this, that God has given us eternal life, and this life is in His Son. He who has the Son has the life; he who does not have the Son of God does not have the life. These things I have written to you who believe in the name of the Son of God, in order that you may know that you have eternal life" (1 John 5:11–13).

Thank God often that Christ is in your life and that He will never leave you (Hebrews 13:5). You can know on the basis of His promise that Christ lives in you and that you have eternal life from the very moment you invite Him in. He will not deceive you.

An important reminder …

FEELINGS CAN BE UNRELIABLE

You might have expectations about how you should feel after placing your trust in Christ. While feelings are important, they are unreliable indicators of your sincerity or the trustworthiness of God's promise. Our feelings change easily, but God's Word and His character remain constant. This illustration shows the relationship among *fact* (God and His Word), *faith* (our trust in God and His Word), and our *feelings*.

FAITH
FEELING

Fact: The chair is strong enough to support you.

Faith: You believe this chair will support you, so you sit in it.

Feeling: You may or may not feel comfortable in this chair, but it continues to support you.

The promise of God's Word, the Bible – not our feelings – is our authority. The Christian lives by faith (trust) in the trustworthiness of God Himself and His Word.

NOW THAT YOU HAVE ENTERED INTO A PERSONAL RELATIONSHIP WITH CHRIST

The moment you received Christ by faith, as an act of your will, many things happened, including the following:

- Christ came into your life (Revelation 3:20; Colossians 1:27).
- Your sins were forgiven (Colossians 1:14).
- You became a child of God (John 1:12).
- You received eternal life (John 5:24).
- You began the great adventure for which God created you (John 10:10; 2 Corinthians 5:17; 1 Thessalonians 5:18).

Can you think of anything more wonderful that could happen to you than entering into a personal relationship with Jesus Christ? Would you like to thank God in prayer right now for what He has done for you? By thanking God, you demonstrate your faith.

To enjoy your new relationship with God ...

SUGGESTIONS FOR CHRISTIAN GROWTH

Spiritual growth results from trusting Jesus Christ. "The righteous man shall live by faith" (Galatians 3:11). A life of faith will enable you to trust God increasingly with every detail of your life, and to practice the following:

G *Go* to God in prayer daily (John 15:7).

R *Read* God's Word daily (Acts 17:11); begin with the Gospel of John.

O *Obey* God moment by moment (John 14:21).

W *Witness* for Christ by your life and words (Matthew 4:19; John 15:8).

T *Trust* God for every detail of your life (1 Peter 5:7).

H *Holy Spirit* – allow Him to control and empower your daily life and witness (Galatians 5:16,17; Acts 1:8; Ephesians 5:18).

FELLOWSHIP IN A GOOD CHURCH

God's Word admonishes us not to forsake "the assembling of ourselves together" (Hebrews 10:25). Several logs burn brightly together, but put one aside on the cold hearth and the fire goes out. So it is with your relationship with other Christians. If you do not belong to a church, do not wait to be invited. Take the initiative; call the pastor of a nearby church where Christ is honored and His Word is preached. Start this week, and make plans to attend regularly.